# THE CONSOLA TIONS OF WRITING

# THE CONSOLATIONS OF TIONS OF WRITING

LITERARY STRATEGIES
OF RESISTANCE FROM
BOETHIUS TO PRIMO LEVI

## RIVKAH ZIM

PRINCETON UNIVERSITY PRESS  PRINCETON AND OXFORD

Library of Congress Cataloging-in-Publication Data
Zim, Rivkah.
The consolations of writing : literary strategies of resistance from Boethius to
Primo Levi / Rivkah Zim.
pages cm
Includes bibliographical references and index.
ISBN 978-0-691-16180-8 (hardcover : alk. paper) 1. Politics and literature. 2. Underground
literature—History and criticism. 3. Protest literature—History and criticism. 4. Prisoners'
writings—History and criticism. 5. Autobiography. 6. Politics in literature. 7. Psychic trauma in
literature. I. Title.
PN51.Z485 2014
809'.93353—dc23       2013039659

British Library Cataloging-in-Publication Data is available
This book has been composed in Garamond Pro and Ideal Sans
Printed on acid-free paper ∞
Printed in the United States of America

FOR BENJAMIN AND TAMAR

JONATHAN AND DANIELLA

DANIEL AND ABIGAIL

AND

IN MEMORY OF MALCOLM PARKES

La nuit trouve enfin la clarté

—*Théophile de Viau*

# CONTENTS

# ACKNOWLEDGMENTS

This book has been growing, slowly, first at Pembroke College, Cambridge, and, since 1991, at King's College London, from seeds that germinated in chapter 3 of my first book, on sixteenth-century English metrical psalms. It is a great pleasure to acknowledge the many debts of gratitude to friends, colleagues, and postgraduate students that I have gladly incurred there, as elsewhere. Generous friendships that nurture the life of the mind have been most inspiring; among these I have been especially blessed by the encouragement, patient wisdom, and support of Christine Rees and David Ricks at King's, Jonathan Steinberg in Cambridge (long ago), and (always) the late Malcolm Parkes of Keble College, Oxford. As my work neared completion, Pamela Robinson, Alastair Minnis, Michael Questier, and John Stokes heroically, and most generously, gave me their scholarly advice and support by reading drafts of part or all of this book, which has been invaluable. I thank them all most warmly. The late Stephen Wall and the late Paul Korshin each made contributions to the development of my ideas in the mid-1990s, and since 2003 different cohorts of MA students at King's and colleagues at the Institute of Historical Research have helped me to clarify my ideas about writing in captivity. Students and colleagues at Victoria College of the University of Toronto, Boston College, the University of Minnesota, St. Scolastica's College, St. Olaf's College, the University of Pennsylvania, and Ohio-Wesleyan University kindly invited me to share early versions of some chapters as papers in progress during the 1990s and provided a warm reception in all weathers. I am also indebted to Norma Rinsler, Harry Guest, and Philip Kuhn for providing access to translations of Cassou's sonnets. I greatly appreciate all their efforts and contributions and hope that they may now take some pleasure from the completed work.

The dedication is jointly to my nephews and nieces with my love and great hopes for the future, and to the memory of Malcolm Parkes who died shortly after this book was completed but without whom it would never have been attempted or finished. Malcolm's friendship, generosity, outstanding scholarly example, and unfailing personal support over nearly forty years mean more than I can say.

# THE CONSOLA TIONS OF WRITING

# Introduction

You become a dissident when you first cross the line from doublethink and fear, and begin to say openly what you believe. The transition from hiding your thoughts to speaking them is a moment of tremendous relief and liberation. For the first time you achieve an inner freedom in which there is no discord between what you think, say and do.... As the pressure from the regime grows, you come to understand how terrified it is of your independence and how desperate it is to recapture the space you have conquered from it—your own mind.... In prison however, you realize most clearly a basic truth of life: that people do not want any life by any means, but rather a life of freedom, even if it is obtained at great personal cost. This is true of individuals, societies and nations. Paradoxically, it is in prison, behind bars and concrete walls, that one gains a level of moral clarity and simplicity that is impossible to achieve in almost any other situation.

—*Natan Sharansky*, The Times, *Friday, 10 December 2010, p. 37*

For centuries the experiences of European intellectuals in prisons of various kinds stimulated them to reconsider aspects of the human condition in their responses to personal crises, and Europe's turbulent history of wars, persecution, and revolution. While these writers' circumstances and contemporary attitudes to prisoners have varied greatly, similar forms, themes, and functions tend to recur in their prison writing. The structure of this book, juxtaposing different pairs of writers across national and period boundaries, from late antiquity to the late twentieth century, gives form to this aspect of its argument. Yet, while individuals have reacted to pain, loneliness, fear, and violence in similar ways, the external history of penal practice and state-organized mass persecution has changed the ethics, politics, and reception of prison writing. This is particularly owing to the unprecedented industrial scale of murder and slave labor in twentieth-century prison camps, the impact of totalitarianism, mass communication, and a wider appreciation of human rights based on religious ethics and ideals of justice and equity. These changes require and receive full historical contextualization for each case study offered here, including those from earlier periods, and explain the slight bias toward writers in history's new "age of hatred. "[1]

Even though the experience of different centuries and regimes varies greatly and there is no single category of space implied—all the subjects of this book suffered involuntary confinement in different conditions—being a prisoner or captive in any period means being cut off and kept apart from the continuities of normal life, however that was defined. As this book demonstrates, dialogue of various kinds becomes an essential tactic. The need for contact with normality and the outside world is so strong because it enables one to continue to recognize oneself. Introspection and lyric forms of writing associated with subjectivity, and self-impression as textual representation of an idea of selfhood, also predominate. Prisoners of state or political dissidents, prisoners of conscience, and confined victims of intolerance and hatred often feel a special need to maintain and defend their integrity and that core of convictions for which they have been imprisoned. Resistance may sometimes enhance chances of survival, but this is seldom sufficient; for personal and political reasons, the persecuted captive may decide one must survive morally or spiritually intact, which is why some prisoners regard suicide as a paradoxical means of self-preservation; similarly, martyrdom.[2] Such prisoners have always used various means to preserve and defend themselves against the corrosion of fear, uncertainty, and disinformation. Writing is one of the most important and durable of these methods. In captivity writing is often a continuation of the authors' ordinary vocations, but confinement and repression also prompt dissidents to speak out, either in self-defense or for their cause. Many prisoners wrote personal accounts that interpret their past, record present interrogations or suffering, and preserve memorial images of themselves and others as historic testimony. The Irish academic Brian Keenan indicated that he wrote about his experiences as a prisoner of Beirut militiamen, after his release, "to imprison" his own "psychic terror on paper."[3] Traumatic memories seem especially long lasting; yet writing with hindsight, after release, is always a different proposition from writing in extremis.

---

[1] See further Niall Ferguson, *The War of the World: History's Age of Hatred* (London: Penguin Books, 2007).

[2] There is considerable overlap in the themes and forms of writing by imprisoned political dissidents and religious martyrs. The combination of outer narrative of human fear and the violence attendant on imprisonment as well as the recourse to dialogue and dream visions in relating these outer and inner worlds of self-awareness and realization may be observed in several of the writers in this book who did not see themselves as martyrs for religion, and in the experiences of Christian martyrs throughout history. However, martyrology and testimony by dying is not my focus.

[3] *An Evil Cradling* (London: Random House, 1993), p. xiv.

Most of the works considered here are by writers, politicians, spiritual leaders, or other professional intellectuals whom most readers would now regard as men and women of conviction rather than criminal convicts. They were all writers used to expressing themselves in language inflected by their literary experience as readers as well as their personal experience of the world. They may have broken laws in defense of higher values than unjust laws, but their ethical concerns were recognized as important for their own time and place. (The exception appears to be Anne Frank, yet her posthumous standing as a thoughtful historic witness belies this apparent anomaly: she was an exceptional writer.) My aim was to sift out texts that might illuminate a literary phenomenon among European dissidents and prisoners of conscience, representing a range of periods, language cultures, and literary forms that could be conveniently made accessible to English-speaking readers. I hoped thereby to define a politics of prison writing. Many of these prisoners remain well known—Boethius, Thomas More, John Bunyan, Marie-Jeanne Roland, Oscar Wilde, Antonio Gramsci, Dietrich Bonhoeffer, Anne Frank, and Primo Levi—and have been discussed independently, in specialist studies. (For others, especially the poets Jean Cassou and Irina Ratushinskaya, there is very little secondary literature.) Yet their different kinds of writing in captivity have never been read alongside each other so closely and extensively as specific responses to their various kinds of imprisonment. In addition, whereas existing studies of the works of such well-known intellectuals as Gramsci or Bonhoeffer tend to concentrate on their ideas, the literary tactics that give these ideas their vitality and impact are seldom addressed.

Each section of this book therefore offers close readings of these disparate texts related by their pragmatic functions as strategies of resistance to their authors' conditions of imprisonment, confinement, and persecution. Overall, it juxtaposes a wide range of component subjects, including fiction, memoirs, letters, theology, poetry, and political philosophy, in pairing authors to propose hitherto unexplored similarities between their works, their ethical motives, intellectual lives, and responses to captivity and persecution. The rationale for their selection here implies not only their differences from each other as writers from several different periods and language cultures but also a comparative significance in their sites of textual production and recurrent themes.[4] Most of the Latin, French, Italian, and German texts have been read in more than one English translation with a close eye on the

---

[4] With the exception of Ratushinskaya's Russian poetry, which has been studied only in English translations that are nevertheless germane to the argument adduced from them—they saved her life—the linguistic range of texts has been limited by my variable competence and reading knowledge of primary and secondary sources.

original, especially for poetry. I believe that the same arguments could be adduced from different material; indeed, this project has been refined and distilled from a much larger range of subjects purely on practical grounds.

The structure of this book is unprecedented. It gives form to my argument for a series of overlapping, pragmatic strategies commonly used by writers in resisting enforced captivity: defense of ideas and values; self-defense and preservation; and testimony for mankind. Within each chapter close readings draw out the specificities of the individual texts yet also suggest the wider resources, including literary conventions, that would have helped the prison writer reconfigure strange or traumatic experiences for expression more easily or effectively. Each half chapter has a synchronic approach to writing produced within specific historical contexts; but the larger argument for identifying these works as part of an intellectual "tradition" of prison writing, based on the recognition of a special relationship between life and literature, derives from the arrangement of diachronic pairings of texts that illuminate recurrent features in prison writing across periods, language cultures, and genres. This approach can therefore offer new insights and opportunities for reassessment of well-known texts not usually considered for their historic literary qualities, as well as poetry that is rarely discussed in English, on the basis of their functions in acknowledged contexts. The authority of the writer's experience of imprisonment is granted by readers but was frequently assumed by writers to be an important part of the appeal of their work. One of the most celebrated and widely read prison authors of the nineteenth century, Silvio Pellico, described his writing program in his forward to *Le mie prigione* (1832):[5]

> I wanted . . . to help console some unhappy creature by this account of the evils that I suffered and of the consolations that, as I know from my own experience, a man can find amid the greatest misfortunes; to bear witness that in the course of my own long sufferings I did not find humanity so wicked, so unworthy of forgiveness, so devoid of excellent souls as it is usually made out to be; to inspire the noble-minded with a warm love for one another, to hate no one, but have an irreconcilable hatred only for vulgar pretension, mean-spiritedness, treachery, and all moral degradation; and finally to reassert a truth already well known but often forgotten: that Religion, no less than Philosophy, calls for energy of

---

[5] *My Prisons*, tr. I. G. Capaldi, S.J. (London: Oxford University Press, 1963), p. xxiv; Pellico's prison memoirs, written after his release, described his spiritual awakening in prison, which shocked and disappointed many of his former associates among radical Italian nationalist writers and thinkers; the text was widely circulated, in an average of six editions a year in Italy (see further p. xxiii), and translated into most European languages within ten years.

will and tranquillity of judgement, and that without these two together
there can be neither justice nor dignity nor sure and stable principles.

These aims to console and to testify to broad human concerns on the authority of personal experience (however partial) reflect the declared aims of
many other prisoners writing since antiquity.

Dialogic forms were frequently selected by prisoners as opportune in different practical and cultural situations. As traditional vehicles for philosophical argument, dialogue and dialectic were used to organize logical arguments adduced by Boethius in early sixth-century Italy, by Thomas More
in Tudor England, and by Antonio Gramsci in Mussolini's fascist Italy.
More, Gramsci, and Bonhoeffer, with many other prison writers in different
periods, also used the implied dialogue of letters (correspondence), ex-
changed with their families, relying on others to complete their meanings
by filling in the gaps between different centers of consciousness. Boethius
and Bonhoeffer, Cassou and Ratushinskaya also used the subjective monologue forms that are the generic basis of lyric, but even these forms imply an
intertextual dialogue with received literary traditions and engage readers'
expectations of these genres. It would be oversimplifying to argue that the
emotional intensity associated with lyric verse counterbalances the cerebral
concentration demanded by the theological and philosophical discourses of
Boethius or Bonhoeffer. Yet contrast and difference are rhetorically marked
or coded by a choice of different forms. Bonhoeffer had continued to nourish his spiritual life alone in his cell by singing psalms and hymns; his description of how surprised he was to find that in the midst of his scholarly
work he also started to compose lyric verse in prison suggests that this genre
had special value for a writer in prison. The Anglican priest Terry Waite reflected upon his own tactics for surviving four years of brutal captivity in
Beirut: "Good language, like good music," he wrote, "has the capacity to
breathe a certain harmony into the soul." Waite was already professionally
aware of the life of the spirit and realized at the time that if he were to endure long periods of solitary confinement and uncertainty, he would need
to develop a strong inner life. He persuaded himself that captivity presented
"a unique opportunity to take an inner journey" since he was unable to
travel to seek self-affirmation and stimulus externally, and later considered
that this strategy succeeded because he had been an avid reader in the past;
in childhood he had also been encouraged to learn poetry by heart, which
he was able to draw upon for comfort and consolation when he had no
books or contact with the outside world.[6]

---

[6] See Terry Waite, Opinion column, *The Times*, 13 March, 2010, p. 20.

Recurrent themes that permeate the functional diachronic pairings may be drawn out of these prisoners' texts. Madame Roland and Bonhoeffer each wrote about how they organized their cells and daily routine to maintain the self-discipline that they recognized was mentally liberating. This was a conscious strategy of resistance in exigent conditions to the shock of arrest, change, confinement, and isolation from friends and family. Writing distracted them, thus alleviating (to some measure) the contingent pressures of time and place; this was briefly consoling. These texts embody their specific, temporal resistance as prisoners and represent it for the consolation of other readers. Reordering the actual furniture created space for reordering thoughts and expectations: the furniture of their minds. Many of these imprisoned writers show themselves already aware of such functions for writing and used tropes of imprisonment and escape from confinement as they reassessed their responses to life, learning, and past literature in their new situations and works. No one writes in a vacuum, or without purpose, as even the density of prisoners' graffiti in the Tower of London can demonstrate; simple statements of faith and personal identity provoked others in the same space at different times to respond in similar ways. One inscription begat another.[7]

The literary experience of each writer in captivity also provided common themes and associative links. These include the power and freedom of the mind and the redemptive, consoling fruits of mental discipline and imagination; recognition of the importance of family relationships, especially the agency of a supportive feminine "other"; and a series of paradoxes (such as light in darkness) that reconcile conceptual oppositions in constructive modes and create gain by loss. Recurrent biblical tropes include: references to the struggles of Jonah, St. Peter, and Jesus; other figures of liberation or escape by flight, memory, dream, and death; prison tropes that stand for the world, the body, or obsessive thoughts; and the prisoner's consciousness of support from cultural traditions that expressed admiration for the ethical imperatives of conscientious struggle, dissent, endurance, and written testimony that define the politics of prison literature. Thomas More and Oscar Wilde as prisoners each meditated on transcendent meanings for the suffering of Jesus; More also identified himself with St. Peter and quoted from Boethius's great work of prison literature; Boethius had read and remembered Plato's dialogues commemorating the teaching of the condemned philosopher Socrates. Dietrich Bonhoeffer read and reflected on Dos-

---

[7] Cf. Ruth Ahnert, "Writing in the Tower of London during the Reformation, ca. 1530–1558," in *Prison Writings in Early Modern England*, ed. William H. Sherman and William J. Sheils, *Huntington Library Quarterly*, 72 (2009), 172–78 and references cited.

toyevsky's novel, *Notes from the House of the Dead*, that reworked aspects of the author's personal experience of imprisonment. Bonhoeffer also identified himself with biblical figures such as Moses, and Jonah, confined within the belly of the whale for disobeying God's commands when he failed to fulfill his ministry. Wilde and Primo Levi correlated the horrors of their respective situations with those of characters in Dante's *Inferno*, without appropriating Dante's theology. Roland and Anne Frank inscribed images of themselves within historical writing projects that have ensured their survival after death as literary voices on the page. Juxtaposing prisoners' texts from different periods and language cultures makes it easier to appreciate how often they converge in subtle and distinct ways, and how their similarities reflect the empirical reality of their authors' confined circumstances and, simultaneously, rise above them in uplifting responses that can move and inspire others. In short, these texts and authors have often been regarded as instrumental in helping others to live their lives. Brian Keenan's account of his four-year imprisonment described it as "a strange reality far removed from normal human experience, yet one in which, paradoxically, so much more of what we are as human beings was revealed" (p. xiii).

The focus of this book is the importance of the life of the mind as it is manifested in new writing produced from situations of captivity, confinement, and persecution rather than the cultural, political, or sociological significance of the "prison" as a site of mechanized brutality or social conditioning (as Michel Foucault has taught us).[8] It is written for specialist and non-specialist academic colleagues and graduate students with interests in comparative literature, cross-cultural history, religion, ethics, and politics, as well as for general readers who may be curious to explore evidence of the writing life and the resilience of extraordinary human beings. Among the questions explored are, What kinds of themes and forms recur in this writing, and why? How is this prison writing paradigmatic yet particular, constrained by conventions yet also rising above them? What gives a writer authority in the eyes of readers; and why does the carceral experience, and literary self-impression, of those acknowledged to be at the border of life and death seem important to others living comfortable lives faraway and in different periods? As it defines writers' literary strategies of resistance in response to their situations, this book is also concerned with their formal and rhetorical methods and retains an ethical concern for applications of writing and readers' responses to writing produced in several varied yet comparable kinds of captivity. In this way it differs from earlier studies of French or

---

[8] Michel Foucault, *Surveiller et punir: naissance de la prison* (Paris: Editions Gallimard, 1975); tr. Alan Sheridan as *Discipline and Punish: The Birth of the Prison* (London: Allen Lane, 1977).

North American prison writing, feminist approaches, and specialist period or author-centered studies of these works.

While there are effectively no precedents for this cross-cultural approach to the topic, studies of French literature have led the way in demonstrating the centrality of prison writing to various concepts of an established literary canon. In 1989 Jean-Marc Varaut briefly described the situations of fifteen poets in a chronological sequence.[9] Yet, as a lawyer and social scientist, he naturally concentrated on writers' experiences rather than their expressiveness, and he neither linked subjects thematically nor provided an overview of their relationships to other literary contexts, except to hint at the meditative and subjective qualities of carceral poetry. (I am grateful to Varaut for an introduction to Jean Cassou's sonnets.) By contrast, Elissa Gelfand's *Imagination in Confinement* (1983) had discussed five Frenchwomen's prison writings, from the late eighteenth to the twentieth century, within social and literary contexts (specifically, "the forces that shaped their lives" as women), to explore how their works might offer insights into "our own imprisonment in cultural prejudices" (p. 10) of the gendered "monstrous": antifeminism.[10] The large-scale recovery and publication of women's writing indicates the historic significance of Gelfand's pioneering study but also, inevitably, its limitations in terms of more recent historical studies of women's writing and its circulation. Her discrete subjects (including Marie-Jeanne Phlipon, better known as Madame Roland) are assumed to reveal universal preoccupations and attitudes: "establishing the threads that connect women's texts through time" (p. 23). Gelfand's book indicates that it was at least in part a reaction to the exclusion of women writers from Françoise d'Eaubonne's *Les Ecrivains en cage* (1970), which had ranged beyond French literature to include texts by St. John of the Cross, Silvio Pellico, and Dostoyevsky, yet explicitly omitted the writings of more obviously politically engaged prison writers. These she regarded as essentially "non-literary" agents of action that contested "la société elle-même" rather than the representative forms given to society in works of art (p. 222). D'Eaubonne antedated Foucault and read the *vie intime* of the writer in his text in the light of psychoanalytical theories from the 1960s.[11] By contrast, I write of the consolations of writing for all and do not presume equivalence between the writing self and the writer's literary self-impression however closely they

---

[9] *Poètes en prison. De Charles d'Orléans à Jean Genet* (Paris: Librairie Académique Perrin, 1989).

[10] (Ithaca: Cornell University Press). Gelfand's chapters are subtitled "The Biological Monster"; "The Social Monster"; and "The Intellectual Monster."

[11] *Les Ecrivains en cage: essai* (Paris: Editions André Balland). See also Nicole Thatcher and Ethel Tolansky, eds., *Six Authors in Captivity: Literary Responses to the Occupation of France during World War II* (Oxford: Peter Lang, 2006), for a collection of papers by different hands on a synchronic, localized topic.

may be related.[12] Active political engagement is no bar to the production of literature.

Following Foucault, and looking well beyond the French tradition, Ioan Davies did more to explain—as a professor of sociology—how prison writing relates to our everyday concerns and how "some issues in prison writing, which involve the telling of a particular kind of story," have become part of Western literature. His concern with "how prisoners, through writing, try to rescue themselves and us" (p. 7), lacks Gelfand's historical awareness but shared her commitment to contemporary social criticism.[13] His subjects are chiefly from the twentieth century; nevertheless, the range of reference extends (ahistorically) to Boethius, in order "to establish a sense of the themes that pervade prison literature." Davies covered vast historic and topographical fields, but his approach did not require him to locate his subjects in their own synchronic contexts; he used extracts from his selected texts as if they were all written by his contemporaries in order to illuminate late twentieth-century theoretical and political arguments. His range and resolute command of theory is impressive, yet his premises that, for example, the humanities in the postmodern world are "complicit in barbarism" and reduced to "absolute relativism" can seem reductive and strained. The cultural politics of Gelfand's and Davies's arguments epitomize a North American approach to prison writing pioneered by H. Bruce Franklin's *The Victim as Criminal and Artist: Literature from the American Prison.*[14] Franklin's thesis—also propounded in the wake of Foucault's *Discipline and Punish*—that understanding society and culture in the United States requires an understanding of "the role of the American prison" throughout its history, and the struggles of oppressed "minorities," was originally perceived as radical and iconoclastic. Hitherto marginalized, black writers were reassessed in the light of literary and oral traditions descended from cultural conditions in an early slave economy. By 1989 Franklin's revisionist agenda had succeeded so well that its author was able to affirm that "literature by American prisoners became recognized as a crucial part of our culture soon after the first edition" (p. xii).[15] I argue that following the medieval reception of Boethius's *Conso-*

---

[12] See further on this topic in late nineteenth- and early twentieth-century literature, Max Saunders, *Self Impression: Life-Writing, Autobiografiction, and the Forms of Modern Literature* (Oxford: Oxford University Press, 2010).

[13] *Writers in Prison* (Oxford: Blackwell, 1990).

[14] (New York: Oxford University Press, 1978). Expanded and revised, with a new introduction, as *Prison Literature in America* (1989).

[15] Cf. Doran Larson, "Toward a Prison Poetics," *College Literature*, 37 (2010), 143–66; the author is described as an associate professor of English in the United States and leader of a writing workshop "inside Attica Correctional Facility." Some of the best studies from North America on prison writing maintain the arguments initiated by Franklin and developed by Davies: e.g., Jason Haslam's focus, in *Fitting Sentences* (Toronto: University of Toronto Press, 2005), on late nineteenth- and twentieth-century texts in their related political and historical contexts illustrates three

*lation of Philosophy* (ca. 524–25) this was always the case in Europe, and since I am not concerned here with the history of social developments, penal policy, or contemporary popular culture, which often valorizes the delinquent, I refer to the prison or idea of captivity only where it is discussed in the prisoners' writing.[16]

Prison writing is not one genre, as some have argued, or even a hybrid (there is no standard typology of form).[17] Whereas lyric poetry and letter writing often predominate as short forms compatible with the arduous conditions of many writers' captivity, other kinds of episodic and fragmentary texts may be seen as pragmatic consequences of confinement, danger, and secrecy. However, these generic kinds are commonly used in many different writing contexts (including war, travel, or illness); and some specialized kinds of petition and witness statements by writers in prison also (exceptionally) take stylized literary forms, including verse.[18] In assessing how

themes: "Carceral Society," "Writing Wrongs," and "Prisons, Privilege, and Complicity"; it concludes with an impassioned argument for prison and sentencing policy reform in a contemporary North American context. Among other synchronic studies, Barbara Harlow's *Barred: Women, Writing, and Political Detention* (Hanover: Wesleyan University Press, 1992) highlights the role of women in exposing human rights abuses throughout the world in the late twentieth century. (I have learned from Harlow and Gelfand to pay due attention to the transmission and editing of prison writing texts and the special problems these matters of production and reception sometimes raise in respect of women authors.) Although Joanna Summers in *Late-Medieval Prison Writing and the Politics of Autobiography* (Oxford: Clarendon Press, 2004) also offered a synchronic approach to her fifteenth-century subjects, like Harlow, she did not consider form or genre in assessing their political role. Nevertheless, Summers elucidated important general aspects of prison writing that "attempts to overturn the impotency of the author's imprisonment" (pp. 3–4) and demonstrated how "writing as victim is an effective and persuasive textual strategy in attaining credibility and sympathy, and an empowering one in terms of propaganda value" (p. 133).

[16] E.g., by Bonhoeffer, Wilde, and Frank. See *The Oxford History of the Prison: The Practice of Punishment in Western Society*, ed. Norval Morris and David J. Rothman (Oxford: Oxford University Press, 1995). I have also found the following very helpful: Christopher Harding, Bill Hines, Richard Ireland, and Philip Rawlings, *Imprisonment in England and Wales: A Concise History* (London: Croom Helm, 1985); Michael Ignatieff, *A Just Measure of Pain: The Penitentiary in the Industrial Revolution, 1750–1850* (1978; London: Penguin Books, 1989); Clifford Dobb, "London's Prisons," in *Shakespeare in His Own Age*, ed. Allardyce Nicoll (Cambridge: Cambridge University Press, 1965), pp. 87–100.

[17] Larson's reductive approach reads the writing of contemporary prisoners as a "genre" dealing with "a common subject" that is directly linked "to the strategies of power exercised within prisons in general"; Larson, "Toward a Prison Poetics," 143. I am grateful to Rosalind Oates for this reference.

[18] This tendency must not be over emphasized. In the early modern period, for example, Cervantes' *Don Quixote*, and Bunyan's *Pilgrim's Progress* are traditionally ascribed to their authors' enforced leisure in prison without being recognizably distinct from other, more fortunate writers' prose fictions. Cellini wrote his autobiography as a prisoner, but it's not clear that this situation made him write differently from Thomas Whythorne, for example, who wasn't a prisoner. However, Walter Ralegh and John Selden used their long imprisonments to undertake extensive study; Ralegh wrote a history of the world which ended, after five volumes, having progressed only to the second Macedonian War, indicating that "it is enough for me (being in that state I am) to write of the eldest times"; *The History of the World*, ed. C. A. Patrides (London: Macmillan, 1971), p. 80 (preface). Selden borrowed Westminster Abbey's copy of the Babylonian Talmud (amounting to nearly 6,000 folio pages) to keep himself occupied in prison; see J. P. Rosenblatt, *Renaissance England's Chief*

writers' experiences of confinement and persecution, and their political, philosophical, or ethical incentives (either declared or implied) shaped the forms and substance of their texts to maximize their appeal for their first readers, it is important to consider the evidence for dynamic relationships between writers and their first readers in synchronic approaches to individual texts. Most of the writers discussed here realized that their lives were at stake, and many did not survive their captivity, which had repercussions for the transmission and reception of their texts.

The two most influential prisoners—Socrates and Jesus—wrote nothing that survives. Yet their exemplary lives and the ideas attributed to them, especially those associated with their deaths by execution, are pervasive in Western history, philosophy, religion, and literature. The representation of their intellectual and personal identities, defined and transmitted by others, became authoritative paradigms for prison writers, especially victims of ideological conflicts, and their readers. Plato created the record of the wisdom of Socrates in a series of dialogues that expound the philosophy of his teacher. Plato's Socrates became an iconic figure largely through the representation of his last days as a prisoner. His arguments for the immortality of the soul carry more weight for readers who are convinced (by their own emotional reactions) that these arguments sustained the prisoner's calm confidence in facing death, and rejecting opportunities to escape his sentence by compromising his teaching. St. Paul disseminated the ideas of Jesus, together with commentary on the evangelists' testimony of how these ideas were lived by Jesus, in a series of letters to new Christian communities throughout the Greek-speaking world. Paul's pastoral letters spoke for him, in his absence, including that enforced by his own situation as a prisoner in Rome. The advice and instructions in these captivity epistles in which it was thought that the apostle's experience of persecution tempered and thereby strengthened his message, helped to establish the church by reifying the spoken words and exemplary life, and death, of his master. The Christian theology of a prisoner's sacrificial death by execution that redeemed the sins of the faithful also imbued other prisoners' suffering and deaths with meaning. In classical and biblical texts, in later saints' lives, and chronicles or other histories of political worthies, different kinds of writers represent prisoners

---

*Rabbi: John Selden* (Oxford: Oxford University Press, 2006), pp. 2–3. For an extensive sequence of verse epistles petitioning individuals and groups for relief and justice, see the book of poems by Théophile de Viau (1623–25) printed while he remained a prisoner in the Conciergerie in Paris. These instrumental works survived him and were widely read in the eighty-eight editions published by 1696. Cf. Charles d'Orléans's campaign for aid toward his release in verse epistles petitioning the Duc du Bourgogne who replied in the same form (1439). See further my "La nuit trouve enfin la clarté: Captivity and Life Writing in the Poetry of Charles d'Orléans and Théophile de Viau," *European Journal of Life Writing*, 2 (2013), 79–109, http://ejlw.eu.

as superior or especially insightful beings. Aeschylus's Prometheus and the biblical prophet Jeremiah, for example, also suffered imprisonment for their teaching.

Many of the recurrent ideas and tactics of European prison writing can be found in Boethius's *Of the Consolation of Philosophy* (ca. 524–25), which must be regarded as a foundation text for both its strategic intellectual content and its tactical generic paradigms. Boethius, the poet, theologian, and philosopher in prison, quoted, or alluded to a wide range of ancient wisdom literature including works by his philosopher heroes (Plato and Seneca), Greek tragedy, and Cicero's Latin oratory. By means of this intertextual dialogue with literary and philosophical resources Boethius was able to project an image of his well-stocked mind that is more personal than the references either to his family and career or to the nebulous circumstances surrounding his imprisonment. The church made Boethius acceptable to medieval Christians several centuries after his death, but it is important to note the cross-cultural inclusiveness of his text that promotes a view of the world dominated by a providential power that is not specifically Christian. The dramatized fiction, within the text, of the condemned prisoner's mental and emotional recovery from self-pity, and his proof that thoughts are free, has inspired many generations of readers. Their reception of this work not only granted Boethius the immortality of his literary self-impression as a noble philosopher and learned poet but also stimulated readers to console themselves and overcome adversity in their own lives as they admired the resistance to persecution that is enacted in its formal structures. "The only way one man can exercise power over another is over his body and what is inferior to that, his possessions. You cannot impose anything on a free mind, and you cannot move from its state of inner tranquillity a mind at peace with itself and firmly founded on reason" (book 2, prose 6). This work had a profound impact. After Boethius, the writer in prison becomes a type, a hero who can be victorious in defeat, establishing another consoling feature of prison writing: the paradox of gain by loss. Thoughts are free, yet prescribed literary forms and tropes liberate creativity; and a literary afterlife enables the literary personality to live on after the writer's death: "Der springt noch auf." The Hungarian poet Miklós Radnóti's poetry notebook was recovered from his pocket when his body was disinterred from a mass grave after World War II. In one poem, "Letter to my Wife," he promised "I'll come back; / I'll stick as fast as bark upon an oak!" In one of his last poems, "Picture Postcards IV" (31 October 1944), the speaker described falling over the corpse of a comrade who had been shot in the neck. He whispered to himself, "that's how you'll end too / . . . Lie still; no moving. / Now patience flowers in death." As the poet disturbs the body, a German soldier quips, "Der springt noch auf," as if the dead man might rise again and escape. This prophetic epigram is a sign of the resistance that figuratively enabled the doomed poet's voice to live on in his verse after it was literally sprung from his grave.[19]

While humane empathy with prisoners' suffering and shared literary traditions help to make their writing accessible, the opportunities and sometimes the decisions to invite readers to share representations of the prisoners' ideas, experiences, and feelings were often made by others after the writer's death. The editorial roles and processes of these intermediaries also imply creative acts, developing the original authors' works for the benefit of new readers in new contexts. Such efforts remind readers (sometimes formally, in prefaces or notes) of the displacements of actuality in any writing. The essential "otherness" of the past—even one's own past—always requires the creative efforts of interpretation: imagination, experience, humility, a healthy skepticism, and a willingness to construct significance in the responsible sifting of responses. All readings are interpretations. Paradoxically, the most enduring works are always being revised and made new. All writers are, first, readers. In Auschwitz Levi attempted to teach another prisoner some Italian and resorted to his memory of Dante's Ulysses canto (from the *Inferno* in which Ulysses drowns) that he had studied at school; in the process of expounding Dante's malleable metaphors, he thought he grasped a fleeting insight into their unfathomable situation. The literary analogy they had grasped incompletely in the concentration camp became the foundation of a figurative bridge that Levi built to help others grapple with the unprecedented reality he later described, analyzed, and commemorated in new writing. Literary traditions become meeting places for different generations because they are shared and memorable even in the absence of reading materials, as Cassou, Levi, and Ratushinskaya all demonstrated. When the prison writers selected existing texts as resources and models for their new writing, they also translated and refreshed those earlier works' potent political or spiritual resonances in subtle, creative ways. I have assumed that the transmission and reception of these new works provide indications of their authors' eloquence and rhetorical persuasiveness for different readers. But fine words alone are not sufficient.

The impression of some common ground in human experience enables the urgency and clarity of many prisoners' expressions in extremis to register their resonance and interest for readers. Readers also invest texts with authority based on the experience they recognize, or believe they recognize, in

---

[19] *Foamy Sky: The Major Poems of Miklós Radnóti: A Bilingual Edition*, ed. and tr. Zsuzsanna Ozsváth and Frederick Turner (Budapest: Corvina Books, 2000), pp. 193–95, 213, and 217n.

writing produced in specific situations.[20] Our sympathies follow our interest, and many writers, or their editors, recognized the political value of writing that projects ideas and images of suffering humanity in contexts calculated to authorize that experience and generate new insights and sympathies in their readers. Most readers enjoy opportunities to forget themselves in reaching out to meet and engage with the constructs of other minds and times (as far as this may be possible); curious, thoughtful readers may enrich and develop their lives in response to the literary strategies and imagination of writers who had designs on readers' responses and thoughts, as well as reports on experiences to communicate.

Adversity was useful. Readers value experience. In early periods there may be very little supporting archival evidence for the prisoner's situation depicted in the text. In other cases external evidence (rather than the report) of textual transmission often provides opportunities to test the provenance and thus the authority of the experience represented. It is difficult to define and assess prison writing solely from internal evidence, not least because it is necessary to express and communicate the extraordinary by means of the familiar, and writers in prison use the same literary forms and tropes as their contemporaries may do in other situations; others may also appropriate the image of the prisoner for their own purposes.[21] The concept of the cell, the mental anguish of the prisoner, and readers' recognition of various ways in which these features metonymically configure aspects of the human condition imply wider applications for prison writing in many periods as well as the success of literary representations of imprisonment often unconnected with actual cases.

In the literature of the West, material prisons are frequently made into figures for existential states. The mortal body was commonly seen as a prison for the eternal soul, which may be freed only at death. In popular seventeenth-century English emblem books, based on Flemish models, graphic explication of this Platonic dualism is attached to biblical texts.[22] By an extension of this Platonic dualism of the spirit trapped by the body, it was

[20] Rivkah Zim, "Writing behind Bars: Literary Contexts and the Authority of Carceral Experience," *HLQ*, 72 (2009), 291–311.

[21] Cf. Victor Brombert, *The Romantic Prison: The French Tradition* (Princeton: Princeton University Press, 1979); Albert Camus, *The Rebel*, tr. Anthony Bower (Harmondsworth: Penguin Books, 1971).

[22] See Francis Quarles's emblems for Ps. 142:7, "*Bring my soule out of Prison that I may praise thy Name*," reprinted in my "The Reformation: The Trial of God's Word," in *Reading the Text: Biblical Criticism and Literary Theory*, ed. Stephen Prickett (Oxford: Blackwell, 1991), p. 102, showing a human figure (*Anima*) crouching within a bird cage and appealing to an angelic representation of Divine Love outside the cage; and Rom. 7:24, "*O wretched man that I am: who shall deliver me from the body of this Death*," showing Anima, the human soul, shaking the bars of her prison formed by the ribcage of a human skeleton, reprinted in my "Writing behind Bars," 293.

also traditional to represent the irrationality of sexual attraction and the power of human love as forms of imprisonment or slavery that can either degrade or ennoble human subjects endowed with free will. (This had a playful poignancy in the frustrated love poetry of Charles d'Orléans written during his twenty-five years of exile and imprisonment.) According to Christian theology, the soul is shackled by sin, and suffering was rationalized as God's chastisement; an actual prisoner was therefore doubly bound; and concern for prisoners was a religious duty. From the sixteenth century onward, popular images of prisoners, and contemporary applications for imprisonment themes, often reinforced the associations induced by these older traditions, which created a circle of influence. This includes religious traditions of charity toward prisoners, inspired by affective and ethical responses to biblical prisoners, especially to the iconic image of Jesus as a prisoner. Shakespeare's noble historic prisoners, including King Lear and Richard II, consistently reflect the idea that prisoners are heroic representatives of humanity who gain philosophical and ethical enlightenment from their misfortunes, and even redeem themselves through various kinds of resistance as prisoners, and become capable of articulating important truths for others. W. B. Carnochan's thoughtful, eclectic essay on "the literature of confinement" proceeds from an epigraph by Theodor Adorno: "There is no material content, no formal category of an artistic creation... which did not originate in the empirical reality from which it breaks free."[23] That liberation trope, Carnochan argued, "evokes the prison theme, that, broadly defined, has played a large part in a culture that understands artistic creation as an act, forever being repeated, of release from constraints" (p. 427).

All the works discussed here transcend generic expectations in several ways. Boethius's *Consolation of Philosophy* is biographical, philosophical, political, and dialogic in form as well as poetic: a work of art, patently mixing fact and fiction yet persuasively truthful in a historic sense and its feeling for life. More's *Dialogue of Comfort* is historical, political, and theological as well as fiction that engages complex literary codes. Wilde's letter *De Profundis* is part autobiography, part confessional conversion narrative, and also, in part, radical social and cultural criticism. Cassou's poetry, like Ratushinskaya's, is formal lyric, subjective, and essentially private, yet also (in part) intensely political and therefore public. Levi's narrative testimony, poetry, and essays mix biographical, historical, philosophical, and political elements in works that match the intellectual rigor and aesthetic complexity of Boe-

---

[23] "The Literature of Confinement," in *Oxford History of the Prison*, pp. 427–55 at p. 427; Carnochan gives the source as *Commitment* (1962). Cf. Adorno, *Aesthetics and Politics*, ed. and tr. Ronald Taylor (London: New Left Books, 1977), pp. 177–95 at p. 190.

thius's achievement and historic cultural standing, in defining and defending a more humane concept of civilization. These inspirational figures are my bookends.

From antiquity to the present, the rhetorical modes of prison writing have been subsumed within, and indivisible from, the authors' declared (or apparent) purposes in writing. Understanding how a prisoner's voice is constructed in any work—a letter, poem, journal entry, philosophical treatise, or personal confession—is a necessary preliminary to interpretation of these broadly comparable strategies of resistance, which are seldom mutually exclusive. These are first, to defend ideas or values, and either promote them in their authors' absence or warn readers to prevent future suffering (such testimonies can also give voices to those unable to testify for themselves). Secondly, to bear witness in an individual case and argue it before a wider tribunal, which may include an appeal to posterity, or a claim to fame and a reformed reputation. Thirdly, to sustain, comfort, or reconcile the writer and finally, to provide evidence of those responses in terms that convince the prisoners' associates and first readers. Authorial strategies may misfire in some situations, and they may be ignored by some generations of readers. Nevertheless, in demonstrating and analyzing one or other of these pragmatic functions in each section of this book, I have sought to define a politics of prison writing and highlight the principal characteristics of a literary phenomenon that transcends distinctions of genre, period, and language culture.

Part I considers writing as a means for intellectuals in prison to defend their ideas and cultural values against a dominant persecuting power. It pairs Boethius and Bonhoeffer as disciplined and dignified rational theologians to illustrate the cultural continuity of values identified with classical humanism, and Judeo-Christian ethics based on biblical traditions. It also exemplifies the basis of their ethical philosophies in human empathy and imagination through their intermittent recourse (as writers facing death) to lyric poetry. Thomas More's various prison writings are literal and figurative (intertextual) dialogues with classical and biblical traditions, literary forms, and exemplary models. Like Bonhoeffer he was concerned with the problems of Christian discipleship in the contemporary world. Yet, as a humanist lawyer, his mental habits, like those of the Marxist political philosopher Antonio Gramsci, were characterized by the formal challenges inherent in dialectic that were both ingrained by education and acknowledged natural predilections. The greater their sense of persecution, the stronger these predilections appear in each; and the more personal their problems as prisoners appear, the more public or political their significance. More's defense of the church was matched by Gramsci's concern for the state. Juxtaposing their works reveals "family" resemblances that modify our views of each and emphasizes their strategic political ambitions in using personal experience to interpret literary and philosophical models for the instruction of others. In these four prisoners' works, it is also striking how actual and imaginative reliance on a sympathetic feminine "other" emerges as a dominant shared trope.

Part II assesses attempts by several different types of prison writer, either to defend and preserve themselves, by pursuing consolatory tactics based on imagination, dreams, and personal memories, or to construct images of self-identities as memorials, to represent the writer after his or her death, using a variety of literary forms. Any autobiographical work reinvents the past in reframing selected incidents that are construed as the past by memory or imagination which, as St. Augustine had recognized, are contingent and non-essential.[24] The ancient world had developed many methods for committing complex matters to memory, including associations between known places and elements of the material to be remembered: in the first "place," in the second "place" were not dead metaphors in predominantly oral cultures. Consequently it became common to associate locations and matters of importance. The prison denoted a place of extreme suffering that forced attention on vital matters worthy of remembrance and careful consideration. The arts of memory may also be fixed and rendered distinct by the action of writing. Memory thereby also becomes shareable. John Bunyan and Oscar Wilde each wrote variants on the traditional pastoral letter in which they sought to justify previous actions that had led to trial and imprisonment. They used their introspection to promote lessons for others by drawing on their experiences of imprisonment to reconstruct images of themselves that challenged and resisted those of the judiciary. Yet, in the process, each writer addressed and reconfirmed his society's views of the nature and functions of imprisonment by also describing his exemplary spiritual conversion experience. Madame Roland and Anne Frank each wrote memorial narratives to preserve details of her life and times, believing not only that these were inherently valuable because they represented her ideas, feelings, and experiences in wider historic contexts but also that the activity of writing would help to sustain and comfort her in confinement. These four prisoners' works preserve variations on a form of dialogue with self and other in prose. Jean Cassou and Irina Ratushinskaya also constructed an alternative life of the

---

[24] *Confessions*, 10.15. Cf. "The wide plains of my memory and its innumerable caverns and hollows are full beyond compute.... My mind has the freedom of them all.... I can probe deep into them and never find the end of them. This is the power of memory! This is the great force of life in living man, mortal though he is!" Ibid., 10.17; tr. R. S. Pine-Coffin (Harmondsworth: Penguin Books, 1975), pp. 222, 224.

mind in prison, applying the arts of poetry and memory to sustain themselves, and to forge mental links between past and present that helped them to resist oppression. Their lyrics celebrate freedom in imagination and dreams, harnessed to a dissident humanism and the purposeful vigor of a political consciousness that rejected either fascist or Soviet oppression. Reading their poems in tandem demonstrates how far their resistance was personally rather than ideologically motivated in response to their circumstances: the French communist and the Ukrainian Christian endured and resisted totalitarianism by drawing on subjective and cultural memories in lyrics that then inspired others who were similarly oppressed. The mental discipline and imagination intrinsic to their poetry defended individual human beings and exemplified human rights to freedom of thought; these same strategies, albeit historically nuanced, were identified in the prison writing of Boethius. The art of memory and the memory of art sustained and consoled them all.

Part III examines the ethical commitment of one exceptionally conscientious and prolific writer, who, having survived imprisonment during which he was unable to read or write, began a series of historic, personal testimonies soon after his release. Primo Levi wrote in a variety of genres, both on behalf of fellow prisoners and, explicitly, to warn or teach his readers about the moral, social, and political dangers in what he had seen, and endured. His prose and poetry have the finished qualities of calm yet penetrating analysis, perfected over time (and with the ironic "benefits" of hindsight and haunting traumatic memories) in response to old and new problems in the life of his times. He has become widely recognized as one of the most important, and hence influential, moral philosophers and public thinkers of the late twentieth century, yet he wrote of human frailties, extreme cruelty, hatred, and moral apathy, and for the future. His reputation, founded on the authority of his experience as a prisoner and eyewitness who refused to judge, but never forgot or forgave his oppressors, places him in a direct line of prison literature traditionally derived from Boethius.

From Boethius to Primo Levi, the consolations of writing created order from chaos to focus willpower and resistance, to testify for posterity, and to maintain, for the writers' present, and future generations, some means to control the depredations of uncertainty, fear of moral failure, or the desolation that comes from a sense of waste and loss in conditions of deprivation. The completion of these strategies of resistance takes effect in the minds of readers who find in these works compelling insights into the dignity of humankind and evidence of the liberating imagination and cultural memories that protect and nourish the free mind. It is impossible to remain human and be unmoved by what we read.

# PART I

## In Defense of Civilization

CHAPTER 1

# The Disciplines of Reason and Lyric Poetry

## Anicius Boethius, *Of the Consolation of Philosophy* (ca. 524–25): The Foundations of Resistance in Dialogue and Lyric

Power politics, court intrigue, forged letters, and no opportunity to mount a defense against lying informers led Boethius, by his own account, to a death sentence in a "lonely place of banishment." He complained that he had inspired hatred for "freely follow[ing] his conscience" to "resist evil" and "defend justice."[1] The condemned man's suffering is always an intrinsic part of the message of *The Consolation of Philosophy,* which offers readers a defense of Boethius's ideas of Roman culture and civilization: self-sufficiency, religious devotion, book learning, imitation of ancient Greek ideals, and a strong tradition of public service. Boethius echoed and transmitted classical traditions and cultural premises that were to become the dominant intellectual heritage of Western Europe in the centuries after his death. The *Consolation* represents the values and forms in which that heritage was transmitted. But the authority of experience that readers throughout the Middle Ages perceived in his final work rests on the author's fictional representation, in affective lyric verses and in dramatic prose dialogue, of his feelings, ideas, and existential problems as a prisoner condemned to death by a corrupt political regime. In this case the particular is paradigmatic: it relates to his situation and establishes a typical pattern and model for others. Boethius's politics, philosophy, and influence on medieval literary culture are well documented. The *Consolation* was read by grammar school pupils and in some universities; it also circulated among lay readers at courts in various parts of Europe. It mediated complex ideas through affective imagery and the dialogue form that mirrored a process of education enacted within the text; it engaged its readers' interests and sympathies while stimulating their imaginations and intellectual curiosity. It was also adapted and imitated by some of the greatest vernacular poets of the Middle Ages, including Jean de Meun, Dante, and Chaucer.

---

[1] *The Consolation of Philosophy*, tr. V. E. Watts (Harmondsworth: Penguin Books, 1969, rpt. 1986), book 1, prose 4, p. 41.

This chapter seeks to demonstrate how Boethius's text established many of the themes and forms that spoke to and for later writers in prison. These include: consolation from the expressive power of ordered lyric meters set against the disorder of injustice and suffering in the real world; the importance of a well-stocked mind and imagination in maintaining resistance to oppression (memories of literature, learning, and life sustain the prisoner; images of nature mirror the order of creation and bring the beauty of the external, visible world into the confines of the prison); the expressive potential of paradox in reconciling apparent contraries and celebrating the creativity that may arise under situations of adversity (a process of gain by loss). The text also promoted the subtle simplicity of dialectic and patterns of opposing binaries used to resolve impossible tensions in apparently progressive forms of logical argument and related forms of dialogic exchange between different points of view represented in argument, correspondence, and intertextual allusiveness. Finally, it demonstrated the urgent need often experienced in the condemned cell to set the record straight (to name names) or to construct a memorial image of the authorial self (however defined) and, more objectively, to testify for humankind by offering insights derived from the prisoner's experience. The value of reason and intellectual argument as a bulwark against chaos or tyranny, which Boethius substantiated in this work, became a recurrent theme that mitigated the experience of many later prison writers. This was largely owing to the aesthetic and intellectual coherence of his text, its explicit but subtle associations with his own situation, and his enduring reputation as a persecuted writer and scholar.

## THE PRISONER

Anicius Manlius Severinus Boethius (ca. 480–ca. 525) was an intellectual allied by birth, upbringing, and marriage with the last patrician families of ancient Rome. This background set him apart from many contemporaries among the ruling class, most of whom had come to power with the Ostrogoths—a barbarian nation—during Boethius's lifetime. His learning and scholarship were rooted in veneration for a golden age long past. He claimed it was his ambition to revive contemporary Latin learning, and his models were ancient Greek commentaries on the works of Plato and Aristotle. Philosophy was the queen of sciences, and Boethius's persona in the *Consolation* also addresses her as the mistress (*O magistra*) of all virtues. His own surviving scholarly works include translations and commentaries on Aristotle's works, and treatises on arithmetic, music, and Christian theology.[2]

[2] See especially Henry Chadwick, *Boethius: The Consolations of Music, Logic, Theology and Philosophy* (Oxford: Clarendon Press, 1981) for authoritative chapters on Boethius's works; and for

His other intellectual masters were Seneca, Cicero, and St. Augustine. However this idealization of Greek culture and ancient Roman institutions came to carry political implications that eventually cost him his life.[3] By 522 he was Master of the Offices—a position comparable to head of the civil service—and the most powerful Roman in Theodoric's administration of the western Roman Empire. But such good fortune was short-lived. Since Theodoric ruled Italy under the nominal, but increasingly tenuous, control of Constantinople, loyalty to the old Roman imperial culture (by this time vested in the Greek-speaking eastern empire), might be construed as political disloyalty to the new order. Boethius claimed that his unspecified actions in defense of the Senate—a bastion of patrician Roman interests—at a time of crisis in relations between the eastern and western parts of the empire, had laid him open to a charge of treason (ca. 523–24). This charge led to his disgrace, exile, and execution at Pavia. Details of the conspiracy charges and, similarly, of the actual conditions under which he was held in Pavia are uncertain. Yet he appears to have had opportunities to write one last work, *The Consolation of Philosophy*, in which he drew on earlier cultural memories, personal experience, and scholarship.

The authorial persona constructed within the *Consolation*—a poet and former student of philosophy—is a condemned prisoner whose experience and family background overlap with that of Boethius, the historic individual known from other sources. In the earliest manuscript of the text, his words are indicated by the letter B in the margin.[4] This Prisoner's situation reflects the unjust persecution of a righteous individual who says he went into politics because he thought that he could make a difference in public life by applying philosophical principles. He had tried to benefit others but found himself "inevitably opposing the plans of selfish and unprincipled men."[5] The *Consolation* begins with a poem—a lyric complaint by the Pris-

background and bibliography *The Cambridge Companion to Boethius*, ed. John Marenbon (Cambridge: Cambridge University Press, 2009); see also Seth Lerer, *Boethius and Dialogue: Literary Method in* The Consolation of Philosophy (Princeton: Princeton University Press, 1985), pp. 23–24 (via Jonathan Barnes, "Boethius and the Study of Logic," in *Boethius: His Life, Thought and Influence*, ed. Margaret Gibson [Oxford: Blackwell, 1981], p. 73) for Cassiodorus (*Variae*, I. 45) on Boethius's achievements.

[3] See J. Moorhead, *Theodoric in Italy* (Oxford: Oxford University Press, 1992); for later opinions on the political background, see Marenbon, *Cambridge Companion*.

[4] For the layout of the text in Vatican, Biblioteca Apostolica, MS Vat. lat. 3363 (ninth century), see facsimile in M. B. Parkes, *Scribes, Scripts & Readers* (London: Hambledon Press, 1991), pl. 51 at p. 260.

[5] Anicius Manlius Severinus Boethius, *The Consolation of Philosophy*, tr. David R. Slavitt (Cambridge, MA: Harvard University Press, 2008), p. 11 (book 1, prose 4). I have acknowledged a variety of different translations, and selected among them according to fidelity to the Latin text and stylistic felicity. All quotations from the Latin text are from Boethius, *The Theological Tractates* and *The Consolation of Philosophy*, Loeb Classical Library, rev. ed., ed. and tr. H. F. Stewart, E. K. Rand, and S. J. Tester (Cambridge, MA: Harvard University Press, 1973, rpt. 1990).

oner who is emotionally overwhelmed by the crisis of his fall from office. The Prisoner goes on to lament that "in the effort to keep [his] conscience clear and do what was lawful and right, [he] offended a lot of people who were more powerful than [he was]." It is a familiar story with perennial resonance in politics. He insisted that he had taken his stand on the principles of Socrates in proclaiming that it is wrong "to assent to a lie or to obscure the truth." The Prisoner further indicated that he had made a written record of his side of the case adduced against him, "even though it was extremely distasteful to have to discuss these absurd forgeries" in which he had been accused of trying "to protect Roman liberties" (p. 14). He also complained that he had not been able to examine the prosecution's case and had been condemned to death, and all his property confiscated, without the right to speak in his own defense: "Whatever I may have done, I did not deserve to be treated in this way for a charge such as this. My accusers know that this is all nonsense, and they dress up their accusations with the further slander that I committed some kind of sacrilege in campaigning for high office" (p. 16). The Prisoner's energetic self-defense becomes a rant and after a few more pages in this vein it may well seem to a neutral reader that his indignation undermines his reputation as a philosopher. His complaints imply his need to redirect his mind and mental energies in order to benefit from any philosophical consolation. In the early chapters this miserable and over-agitated prisoner is a sympathetic figure, but his self-pity makes him seem unreliable.

The narrative setting for the entire work—as frequently illustrated—is the Prisoner's bedside in his cell. However, the main impact of the opening sections arises from Boethius's creation of his second persona—a surreal, feminine personification of his life's vocation, the love of wisdom: Philosophia. As a heavenly figure she seems a manifestation of the divine intervention required to restore the Prisoner to his senses, but she is not a goddess. She has piercing eyes and varies from human size to a height that enables her (symbolically) to penetrate the heavens. She appears to be of great age and her dress is tattered and dusty, though of a finely woven, imperishable fabric that she had made herself with "meticulous workmanship" (bk. 1, pr. 1, p. 3). The sign of theta, embroidered on the top hem, signifies contemplative philosophy, including theology and metaphysics. (As Henry Chadwick points out, theta also denoted a condemned prisoner.)[6] On the lower hem of her dress, the sign of pi signifies practical philosophy, including ethics. Philosophia suddenly appears by the bedside of the distraught Prisoner from nowhere (while he is venting his woes) to diagnose his mental confu-

---

[6] Chadwick, *Boethius* (1981), pp. 225–26.

sion (the dis-ease evident in the opening lyric complaint), as indicative of his urgent need for the moral medication of *consolatio*: "It is time for healing, not lamenting."[7] He is lost, she decides, because he has forgotten who he is. Yet the Prisoner soon recognizes this stern but kindly authority figure as his former nurse. She sits on his bed, wipes the tears from his eyes, and identifies him as the man "brought up on the milk of my learning": a philosopher. The Prisoner is struck dumb with amazement, and we, as readers, are also intrigued and enchanted as she attempts to clear the "blinding cloud of worldly concern" from his eyes. She is a commanding yet compassionate presence, and the initial impact she has on the Prisoner (and Boethius's readers) retains its force throughout the work. She towers over him (as his intellectual superior), and after a while he recognizes the lady Philosophy, his first and last teacher.

> "My poor boy (*alumne*)," she replied, "why should I desert you now? Should I not help you with that burden you bear in no small measure because of my teachings and the hatred of my name? Do you suppose I would be frightened by unmerited accusations? Will Philosophy abandon an innocent man and not be a companion to him on his journey? Should I be distressed by false accusations? I am horrified at such a thought! I am accustomed to being attacked and was a veteran of such battles even before the time of my servant Plato. In Plato's own time was I not with his teacher, Socrates, who was put to death unjustly—a death that turned out in the end to be a . . . triumph (*victoriam mortis*)?" (bk. 1, pr. 3, Slavitt, pp. 7–8)

Dealing with persecution is part of the philosopher's job description. Her role is to instruct as well as comfort the Prisoner, who thereby rediscovers the philosophical basis of his life's work, and his composure. During the course of their dialogue, as the substance of the text unfolds over five acts or books, Philosophia brings the Prisoner back to himself literally and figuratively. She promises to give his "mind wings on which to lift itself," and she fulfills her promise (bk. 4, pr. 1, Watts, p. 117). Her teaching is restorative and therapeutic; its literary process enacts its function which may be repeated at every reading by any reader who engages with the text's different levels of operation and appeal.

Many early exchanges between them are so lively it must have been easy for naive readers to forget that both personae are fictions created by the actual prison writer, Boethius. Philosophia as logician tempers her reliance on dialectic to her pupil and patient's capacity to understand. He learns fast,

---

[7] Bk. 1, pr. 2, Watts, p. 38.

regaining his composure and intellectual grasp, as her arguments develop. By the end of the *Consolation of Philosophy*—the reenactment of Philosophia's therapy—he catches up with her command of metaphysics, and the distinction between the two voices diminishes. Subdivisions of the text into prose dialogue for argument and thirty-nine poems interspersed regularly in different meters, for (as stated) lyric distraction, imaginative refreshment, and reinforcement of the argument, enable the Prisoner to transcend the material reality of his imprisonment.[8] The text ends in a universal ethical and moral imperative, voiced by Philosophia addressing the Prisoner (and all Boethius's readers).

> Avoid vice . . . and cultivate virtue; lift up your mind to the right kind of hope, and put forth humble prayers on high. A great necessity is laid upon you (*vobis*), if you will be honest with yourself, a great necessity to be good, since you live in the sight of a judge who sees all things. (bk. 5, pr. 6, Watts p. 169; Loeb, p. 434)

While the text opens with detailed reference to the life of the Prisoner in a prefatory frame of personal memoir, which is important in engaging the interest of Boethius's reader, this framework of personal narrative, running through books 1 and 2,[9] is not closed off. The text's open ending broadens its message to include anyone who empathizes with the Prisoner. Yet it is important to register that the representation of the Prisoner's attitude always arises from a retrospective view of an uncompleted narrative action. After the first lyric complaint by the Prisoner, this retrospective implies that his struggle to compose himself philosophically, within the action of the text, was resolved before he first picked up his pen. Even though it was produced in adversity, the *Consolation* is a polished literary work that meshes closely with Boethius's earlier writing; it is not a prisoner's diary. (This is an important distinction in all prison writing.)

While Boethius's story gives the Prisoner a personal history, it also places the authorial persona in a recognizable cultural context, which I shall argue is part of his wider political purpose in the *Consolation*: to define and defend his values through the intellectual and artistic coherence of the work. The autobiographical passages also fill out the portrait of the Prisoner, making him more credible and thus able to address and represent others in different kinds of adversity. Boethius's choice of literary forms and use of two voices aids these purposes. Yet it is also clear from the earliest copies of the

---

[8] Cf. bk. 4, pr. 6, Slavitt, p. 139: "You are tired. What you need is some relief in the charms of poetry. I offer you a refreshing drink so that you will be able to concentrate when we continue our reasoning."

[9] Cf. also bk. 4, pr. 5.

text that readers of the *Consolation* have always associated the author with the Prisoner.[10] At the end of book 3 Philosophia explains that on the authority of Plato "we must use language akin to the subject matter of our discourse" (bk. 3, pr. 12, Watts, p. 113). The Socratic method used literary forms of dialogue and dialectic as performative representations of teleological argument. (These arguments proceed in a series of binary oppositions to conclusions preordained by their premises.) This dramatic present-tense form enabled a teacher to demonstrate a process of argument progressively, stopping to clarify queries as necessary, and creating opportunities for attractive examples along the way. Boethius's dialectic and dialogue are modeled on Greek philosophical teaching texts; this method was heuristic, conventional, and also in accordance with his life's work and known intellectual loyalties.

## THE PRISONER AND HIS IDEAS

The problems addressed in the *Consolation of Philosophy* are paradoxically universal and specific to Boethius's time, place, and culture. Universal problems include the suffering of the good, how a righteous man may protect his moral integrity, and the nature and consequences of evil. Boethius made subtle distinctions between the operation of fate and divine providence in an imperfect world and concluded with an argument—largely founded upon the principles of Aristotelian logic—for the necessity of human free will. He also emphasized the functions of memory and reason as the supreme characteristics of humanity and demonstrated how important they were to individuals facing loss, misery, danger, fear, and death. The situation of his Prisoner persona made consideration of these concerns by the philosopher Boethius seem especially authoritative and valuable, yet his ideas transmitted ancient cultural values attached to reason by Aristotelian logicians and to memory by Platonists and neo-Platonists, who had described the ascent of the soul to its heavenly home. This scholarly background explains the nature of Boethius's responses to his situation. The Prisoner has placed his trust in reason and natural religion—an ethical, humanist creed, which is neither specifically Christian nor pagan. His trust in these unifies the various and different intellectual resources deployed without his having to repudiate the values implied by any of them; and, however his terms are defined in different historical contexts, the broad principles remain inclusive ones. Thus, "in the hearts of the wise, there should be no room for ha-

---

[10] The layout of the dialogue in MS Vat. lat. 3363 was also glossed P for Philosophia, the second speaker (see note 4).

tred" (bk. 4, pr. 4, Slavitt, p. 127); "Love the good, and pity the wicked" (bk. 4, m. 4, p. 128); "If the true causes of something are not understood . . . it can appear to be random and confused. But although you cannot understand the way things are ordered in the universe, you can rest assured that a good governor does indeed keep order and has a plan" (bk. 4, pr. 5, p. 129); "The best kind of government is the inflexible order of causes arising from the simplicity of the mind of God. . . . Nothing happens for the sake of evil, even by the actions of the wicked themselves" (bk. 4, pr. 6, p. 134); "The only way to check [doubts] is with a really lively intellectual fire" (bk. 4, pr. 6, Watts, p. 134). Upon such premises there is no need to rely on divine revelation. The leap of faith required of Boethius's readers is one that authorizes the validity of the processes of logic and makes the power of such reasoning absolute. The momentum of the argument promotes a feeling of exhilaration that may be counter-intuitive but also seems inevitable and impressive. The stimulus for Boethius's statements within the *Consolation* as a whole is conflict with aspects of the external world, such as those which have provoked his suffering as a prisoner. (There is no representation of internal dilemma or spiritual crisis.) The whole text appears to demonstrate how one individual made a last stand for his life's work in promoting fundamental issues according to Greek learning and educational practice.

The single most important message (evident in what Boethius wrote, as well as how) is that reason and argument (alongside the discipline of meter) are a defense against chaos and tyranny: reason and imagination are more powerful than pain. Step by step, the binary oppositions of dialectic establish the principle: "All fortune whether pleasant or adverse is meant either to reward or discipline the good or to punish or correct the bad." The next stage therefore synthesizes agreement "on the justice or usefulness of fortune," leading to the conclusion that "all fortune is good" (bk. 4, pr. 7, Watts, pp. 142–43). Boethius's belief in the self-sufficient, active powers of the mind led him to accommodate several paradoxes; the consoling paradox of gain by loss, for example, is applied in discussion of the advantages of bad fortune.

> Good fortune deceives, but bad fortune enlightens. With her display of specious riches good fortune enslaves (*ligat*) the minds of those who enjoy her, while bad fortune gives men release (*absolvit*) through the recognition of how fragile a thing happiness is. (bk. 2, pr. 8, p. 76; Loeb, p. 224)

He may be making a virtue of necessity, but the greater value applied to enlightenment and truth revealed by adversity, is an important foundation for the consolation of philosophy. Fortune is fickle; nothing remains constant in human life; the complacency induced by wealth, happiness, and success distracts one's mind from painful realities and represents a trap. (One advantage of adversity is the revelation of who one's true friends are [bk. 2, pr. 8].) It may be counter-intuitive again, but Philosophia argues that some suffering may be beneficial since it leads to self-discovery while being attuned to individual capacities: "A wise direction spares the man whom adversity might affect for the worse."

> Providence is the divine reason itself [which] is set at the head of all things and disposes all things. . . .
>
> The relationship between the ever-changing course of Fate and the stable simplicity of Providence is like that between reasoning and understanding, between that which is coming into being and that which is, between time and eternity, or between the moving circle and the still point in the middle. . . .
>
> Providence . . . allows . . . [some people] to be vexed by hard fortune to strengthen their virtues of mind by the use and exercise of patience. (bk. 4, pr. 6, pp. 135, 136–37, 139)

Happiness, as all acknowledge, is the highest good (*summum bonum*), but in adversity a philosopher who believes "there is a God and . . . he watches over his creation" (bk. 1, pr. 6, Slavitt, p. 23) must find opportunities to strengthen his wisdom: virtue is strength (*virtus . . . vires*).[11] However, this virtue must be its own reward; there is no religious consolation offered here, either in terms of an external gift of divine grace or in expectations of reward or punishment after death. In Boethius's situation as a prisoner, such expectations would be inappropriate.[12] His ultimate concerns are moral and ethical; the final message of the *Consolation* emphasizes the necessity to be good, avoid evil, and cultivate virtue, which providence—the vision of divine reason in an ever present eternity—ensures is its own reward (cf. bk. 5, pr. 6, Watts, pp. 168–69).

In the context of the treason charge made against him, Boethius's Prisoner complains:

> It may be part of human weakness to have evil wishes, but it is nothing short of monstrous that God should look on while every criminal is allowed to achieve his purpose against the innocent. If this is so, it was

---

[11] Bk. 4, pr. 7, Watts, p. 144. Cf. "Ex quo etiam virtus vocatur quod suis viribus nitens non superetur adversis." Loeb ed., p. 378. The wordplay is untranslatable.

[12] In bk. 4, pr. 4, the Prisoner asks Philosophia whether she thinks there are punishments for the soul after death. She replies briefly in the affirmative but then deflects the topic entirely saying "that is not the subject I want to discuss just now" (Slavitt, p. 124).

hardly without reason that [a philosopher] asked where evil comes from if there is a god, and where good comes from if there isn't.[13]

Later, at the beginning of book 4, the Prisoner confesses that "the greatest cause of my sadness is . . . the fact that in spite of a good helmsman to guide the world, evil can still exist and even pass unpunished" (p. 116). He has found it even more bewildering to consider, on the basis of his own situation, the inequities of the world.

> When wickedness rules and flourishes, not only does virtue go unrewarded, it is even trodden underfoot by the wicked and punished in the place of crime. That this can happen in the realm of an omniscient and omnipotent God who wills only good, is beyond perplexity and complaint. (bk. 4, pr. 1, p. 116)

In being forced to face such perplexity at first hand, the Prisoner asks the questions he seeks to answer by means of consoling philosophy. Why do the innocent suffer? How can tyrants prevail and the wicked evade punishment?[14]—"this is all turned upside down" (p. 133)—How can God let this happen? What is the point of being virtuous and trying to do good in the world when this disaster wipes out all my good work and destroys me? He speculates: "Surely the confusion of things is due to the fortuitous operations of chance?" (p. 133). Yet, how can one explain the workings of divine providence in these circumstances? And, if God is good and all fortune is good (however we perceive it in this perpetual world), is there any opportunity for man to exercise free will?

In the last two books of the *Consolation*, Boethius raised the largest metaphysical questions and derived a syllogism to accommodate human free will with divine foreknowledge that was widely celebrated throughout medieval Europe. In book 5, Philosophia explains that the common assumption, that God's foreknowledge compromises human free will, is fallacious:

> The cause of this mistake is that people think that the totality of their knowledge depends on the nature and capacity to be known of the objects of knowledge. But this is all wrong. Everything that is known is comprehended not according to its own nature, but according to the ability to know of those who do the knowing. (bk. 5, pr. 4, Watts, p. 157; Loeb, p. 410)

---

[13] Bk. 1, pr. 4, Watts, p. 44. Watts's note indicates that Boethius seems to be thinking of Epicurus, quoted by Lactantius, *De Ira Dei,* 13, 21.

[14] On the theme of tyrants in the *Consolation of Philosophy,* see Gerard O'Daly, *The Poetry of Boethius* (London: Duckworth, 1991), ch. 3.

Because God's existence is beyond time, he is considered able to know everything simultaneously. Providence or divine foreknowledge imposes no necessity on what is going to happen (bk. 5, pr. 6). Such emphasis on the active power of the mind typifies Boethius's assimilation of Aristotelian premises and also characterizes the work's epistemology. For Boethius, philosopher and theologian of natural religion, the rational answer to, Is there any point in striving to do what reason tells us we should do? Have we any real choice in life? Can things ever be made different by our own actions? Is there any point in hope or prayer? and similar questions is yes, because human beings have free will. Philosophia argues that "it would be impossible for any rational nature to exist without it. Whatever by nature has the use of reason has the power of judgement to decide each matter" (bk. 5, pr. 2, p. 149). This freedom is not equal to all; nevertheless, exercise of reason in the pursuit of truth makes man free to know God and choose the path of righteousness. The imprisoned philosopher shows how he learns that "there is no reason at all for hating the bad" (but Boethius's Prisoner does not forgive his enemies):

> For just as weakness is a disease of the body, so wickedness is a disease of the mind. And if this is so, since we think of people who are sick in body as deserving of sympathy rather than hatred, much more so do they deserve pity rather than blame who suffer an evil more severe than any physical illness. (bk. 4, pr. 4, p. 132)

The *Consolation* may be perceived formally as both a process of learning (implying the education of the Prisoner) and a body of wisdom to be shared (implying the education of the reader). Nevertheless, from both points of view the text always operates at different graded levels of difficulty. This is because the author has assumed that his work will be comprehended by its readers according to their ability to grasp it. (This assumption also explains the prosimetric organization of the text.)

Whether Boethius raised questions about good and evil and free will as the result of disinterested reflection on the human condition or in reaction to his own historic situation as Theodoric's prisoner, his solutions to these problems need to be examined in the broader contexts of his intellectual, cultural, and political affiliations. Although these contexts are very specialized and remote from most periods, including the Christian Middle Ages, which have venerated him most, they do not in themselves seem to have distanced readers from the nature of the problems discussed in the *Consolation*. As already shown, the dialectical habits of mind that dominated Boethius's intellectual heritage encouraged him to attempt the resolution of fundamental problems by the application of logic. Yet the products of this kind of reasoning must have been less valuable in periods and cultures that placed a lower value on dialectic. The author's faith in such binary reasoning processes enabled him to argue as if the sufficiency of "one internal proof grafted upon another so that each drew its credibility from that which preceded" was absolute. But the conclusion that, for example, since God who is good and omnipotent can do no evil, therefore "evil is nothing"[15] must always have been more intellectually exciting than philosophically consoling to anyone experiencing real suffering. We may begin to suspect therefore that part of the consolation of philosophy was the intellectual process itself.

## THE ART OF CONSOLATION

It is seldom regarded as sufficient to argue, as Boethius does in the voice of Philosophia, that "the reward we see due to the good must be balanced by a corresponding punishment of the wicked," and to do so simply upon the premises of dialectic that "like good and evil, reward and punishment are *opposites*" (bk. 4, pr. 3, Watts, p. 124, emphasis added). Yet it is always exhilarating and impressive to find evidence that some heroic mind at work in the midst of great suffering could be consoled by such reasoning. Logically the strength of any argument should be independent of the circumstances in which it may happen to be argued: it should be equally valid as proof when repeated by anyone at any time. However, both Boethius and Plato knew that the persuasiveness of any argument is enhanced when emotions are engaged by rhetorical means, including an affecting setting, in the context of someone's actual experience. What more affecting setting for such difficult questions about life and death than the cell of a condemned philosopher? Plato's Socrates had dedicated his last hours to a dialectical proof of the soul's immortality. Who could have greater interest and authority in resolving such questions in such a situation? This is a fundamental part of the appeal of all prison writing.

The Platonic conception of the duality of man's nature passed into early Christian thinking through the works of Philo and through pagan intellectual traditions that had shaped the minds of many early Christians, including the church fathers of the fourth century. Boethius inherited a double tradition—pagan and Christian—that not only rejected the mortality of the soul but also devalued mortal flesh and blood as the earthly prison of the free spirit.[16] Philosophia's discourse on human free will in book 5 clarifies

---

[15] Bk. 3, pr. 12, Watts, pp. 112–13.

[16] Within the context of discussion in book 2 about the relative "immortality" of fame, it is assumed that the death of the soul at the death of the body is "a belief which our reason forbids us. But

this Platonic concept of the body as the prison of the aspiring soul. A series of parallels (matched in binary oppositions that have echoes throughout the text) juxtaposes divine and human, souls and bodies, the free and imprisoned, light and darkness, the higher and the lower, proper reason and ignorance:

> Celestial and divine beings possess clear sighted judgement, uncorrupted will, and the power to effect their desires. Human souls (*humanas animas*) are of necessity more free when they continue in the contemplation of the mind of God and less free when they descend to bodies, and less still when they are imprisoned in earthly flesh and blood (*cum terrenis artubus colligantur*). They reach an extremity of enslavement (*servitus*) when they give themselves up to wickedness and lose possession of their proper reason.[17]

This prison metaphor proved popular with other prison writers. If metaphysical imprisonment is a necessary condition of mortal man, then actual imprisonment is not extraordinary; it merely reflects a special case of ordinary life. For Boethius, actual imprisonment was less dangerous for a virtuous man than the figurative "enslavement" of the wicked, who voluntarily become "prisoners of their own freedom" to make moral choices and then lose that freedom. Thus, if actual prisoners preserve their moral integrity, they remain "free" and can resist tyranny by demonstrating its limits.[18]

Freedom in confinement is a paradox based on the idea that the mind is autonomous and can be overcome only by its own weakness: emotions such as joy and fear, or hope and despair, which bind the mind in chains of its making. For Boethius the theologian, man's mind is made in the image of God (bk. 2, pr. 5, p. 67), and man finds his freedom in contemplation of the mind of God. For Boethius the Christian Platonist, man's aspiring mind is ever seeking wings to escape from the body and effect its release into the heavenly world of light and truth. (This became a powerful metaphor in devotional poetry by all kinds of prisoners.) Boethius regarded himself as liberated mentally (in his higher self) while remaining physically bound and constrained (in his lower self) both by his ordinary mortal existence and by his particular situation as Theodoric's prisoner. Oppressors can con-

---

if the mind stays conscious when it is freed from the earthly prison and seeks out heaven in freedom, surely it will despise every earthly affair," such as the praise which gives rise to fame (bk. 2, pr. 7, Watts, p. 75).

[17] Bk. 5, pr. 2, Watts, p. 149; Loeb, p. 392. Cf. bk. 3, m. 10, p. 104, Loeb, pp. 284, 286; bk. 4, m. 2, p. 123, Loeb, p. 330.

[18] Bk. 5, pr. 2, p. 150; "sunt quodam modo propria libertate captivae" (Loeb, p. 392). Cf. the value of misfortune in freeing the mind from the shackles of pride and ambition (e.g., bk. 2, pr. 7 and pr. 8, reiterate the imagery of confinement that continues the all important contrast between the free mind and the imprisoned body).

trol only physical externals. By contrast, the inner mental life that in Boethius's philosophy denotes both conscience and consciousness is secret and thus safe. The rational mind of man ensures his essential freedom.[19] Boethius, in the voice of Philosophia, argues:

> The only way one man can exercise power over another is over his body and what is inferior to it, his possessions. You cannot impose anything on a free mind (*libero animo*), and you cannot move from its state of inner tranquillity a mind at peace with itself and firmly founded on reason. (bk. 2 pr. 6, Watts, tr. p. 70; Loeb, p. 210)

This philosophy can liberate any prisoner: the self-possession it implies and promotes makes one unassailable (bk. 2, pr. 4, p. 63)—herein lies its chief consolation for an actual prisoner. The paradox of freedom in confinement and the imagery of mental flight recur in prison writings from many different language cultures and historical periods.

Yet philosophy is not the only escape route. The prisoner's retreat into his inner mental world requires the operation of memory and imagination besides cogitation. The *Consolation of Philosophy* places emphasis on memory as evidence of the inner life and as a repository for evidence of the operations of divine providence in the merely perpetual, outer world. While experience shows that nothing in life is constant—change is inevitable—the memory of happier times is lasting and may be recalled to mitigate present miseries: all troubles are relative, and it pays to count one's blessings. Boethius, in the voice of the Prisoner, who perceived his family as his greatest source of happiness, acknowledged on the one hand that grief at particularly his wife's suffering was his only reasonable cause for complaint.[20] On the other hand, he also acknowledged that the pride and pleasure he felt at seeing his two sons take their seats in the Senate together as consuls remained: "If the enjoyment of any earthly blessing brings with it any measure of happiness, the memory of that splendid day (*lucis*) can never be destroyed by the burden however great of growing evil" (bk. 2, pr. 3, Watts, p. 59; Loeb, p. 186). Such memories, he argued, will always be life enhancing, bringing light into darkness. Human happiness may be bittersweet, but self-possession, which implies being able to recall one's life, and thus to recollect

---

[19] Bk. 4, m. 3, pp. 126–27, in Philosophia's song about Circe's transformation of Odysseus's men into pigs: "Nothing is left intact, / Their voice and body changed; / Only the mind remains / To mourn their monstrous plight" (p. 126).

[20] "It is the nature of human affairs to be fraught with anxiety; they never prosper perfectly and they never remain constant" (bk. 2, pr. 4, p. 62). But, as Philosophia says of the Prisoner's family: "Your anchors are holding firm and they permit you both comfort in the present, and hope in the future." In the raging seas of tumultuous, mundane existence the Prisoner acknowledges—as many others were to do later in similar situations—that "so long as [these anchors] do [hold firm] we will ride the storm out" (ibid.).

and reconcile oneself, is both a means and an end to a liberated and more stable state of mind. According to Philosophia, a balanced view of adversity is founded on a store of happy memories.

The wide range of literary reference and allusion in the *Consolation* offers further testimony to the qualities of the author's mind, memory, and cultural background.[21] But this literary infrastructure is also typical of the recorded mental and emotional life of other writers in prison whose physical confinement made such imaginative and intellectual resources all the more important. It is a feature of prison writing, first demonstrated by Boethius, that the wider the cultural experience and active recourse to memory, the better chance solitary prisoners have of preserving their personal integrity. Human memory also has a supranatural value. Echoing Platonic metaphysics, Boethius assumed that all human learning was a process of rediscovery: "Man but recalls what once he knew and lost."[22] The preexistence of the rational soul, which had been part of Socrates' last argument in prison, is also part of Boethius's argument for self-possession. Because memory antedates mortality in Platonic epistemology, it offers man opportunities to transcend not only time but also place, including the literal or physical, and figurative or metaphysical, prisons of life. The state of knowledge and wisdom that is lost by a soul once it enters the world can be recovered by mental effort (*anamnesis*). Finding one's way home to God as the source of light, truth, and goodness is a process of remembering for a neo-Platonist. Yet memory is also clouded by the constraints of the earthly prison of the body.[23] So while the mind of man made in the image of God will always be assumed to seek its own good, like a drunken man it cannot easily find its way home.[24] In such a case poetic imagination proves invaluable not only for the Prisoner who has lost his way but also for the writer finding a way to readers, known and unknown, through rhetorical patterns of repetition that depend on short-term memory (including remembered sounds) and striking, memorable images, including this analogy of the drunkard.

Throughout the work, Boethius—the creative writer—brings his literary and logical methods to the attention of readers by giving both his protagonists opportunities to comment on their proceedings. The prose of book 3, section 9, gives one of the clearest indications that Boethius used dialogue

---

[21] For details of Boethius's range of literary allusions, see further L. Bieler's edition, Corpus Christianorum, series Latina, 94 (Turnhout: Brepols, 1957); Lerer's discussion of literary resources, including Senecan drama, *Boethius and Dialogue*, pp. 237–53; and O'Daly's index of citations and quotations, *The Poetry of Boethius*, pp. 246–48.

[22] Bk. 3, m. 11, p. 109, "Quod si Platonis musa personat verum, / Quod quisque discit immemor recordatur." Loeb, p. 296, lines 15–16; cf. Plato, *Phaedo*, 73a.

[23] Cf. bk. 3, m. 9, Watts, p. 97.

[24] Bk. 3, pr. 2, Watts, p. 80.

not only to display the binary oppositions of dialectic (as in Socratic dialogue) but also to represent the speaking voice (as in Senecan drama). Here the balance and distribution of the speakers' parts suggest the interchange of ideas in a real conversation. The Prisoner proposes ideas, and readers can see that Philosophia respects her interlocutor from the way she talks to rather than at him. When the Prisoner says, modestly, "unless I'm mistaken, true and perfect happiness is that which makes a man self-sufficient, strong, worthy of respect, glorious and joyful," she replies encouragingly: "You are blessed in this belief, my child (*alumne*), provided you add one thing" (Watts, p. 96). All it takes is this light hint and within a few lines (in which each speaker addresses the other no fewer than five times), the Prisoner takes the initiative prepared for him. In the next section Philosophia offers to add an inference to a conclusion by drawing on the example of a technique in Greek geometry (bk. 3, pr. 10, p. 102). In the context of the same discussion, the Prisoner asks Philosophia to clarify a question by being more specific. Similar, self-conscious interjections enable the writer to signal the stages of development in complex argument to aid his readers. The Prisoner's questions and comments punctuate some of the longer speeches, which also encourage a reader to pause, reflect, and assimilate the discussion. The unresolved Prisoner of the dramatic dialogue (rather than the resolved one of the retrospective writing) is the reader's representative in this healing and educative process.[25] When Philosophia praises and encourages the Prisoner, Boethius the author offers the same encouragement to his future readers.

One of the most telling demonstrations of Boethius's self-conscious literary method is the remark the Prisoner makes after Philosophia derives her astounding proof that "evil is nothing":

> You are playing with me, aren't you, by weaving (*texens*) a labyrinth of arguments from which I can't find the way out. At one moment you go in where you'll come out, and at another you come out where you went in. Or are you creating a wonderful circle of divine simplicity? (bk. 3, pr. 12, Watts, p. 112; cf. Loeb, p. 304)

The Prisoner's frustration and admiration forestall a reader's objections and emphasize the method of the argument (the metaphor of weaving is also used for textual construction), deflecting attention (for the moment) from its substance, yet simultaneously prompting a positive critical assessment of

---

[25] Cf. bk. 4, pr. 7, p. 143: Philosophia seeks to accommodate her pupil and asks whether it is his "wish . . . that we should draw closer to everyday language to avoid the appearance of having moved too far from common usage." The Prisoner replies that it is up to her ("ut placet"), but their discussion of the "appearance" of their method implies an audience beyond themselves, which must signify Boethius's readers (cf. Loeb, p. 376).

its wondrous circularity and interwoven texture: its artistry. Philosophia's reply sustains this focus on the labyrinthine method of dialectic when she quotes Parmenides (from Plato's *Sophistes*), who explicitly affirmed its validity and hence, implicitly, the validity of the proof synthesized by it: "You have learnt on the authority of Plato that we must use language akin to the subject matter of our discourse" (bk. 3 pr. 11, p. 113; Loeb, p. 306). Boethius's text embodies a mentality and system of values that are also applied in the author's literary tactics. Presumably, further restatement of the logical proof of the paradox—"evil is nothing"—would have achieved nothing for those readers who live with the reality of an illogical world, and continue to face the perennial problem of the suffering of the good. Yet, if Boethius—as a persecuted theologian and rationalist—had wished to affirm the strength of his own faith by such means, then this striking demonstration of the active power of a brilliant mind, operating in dire personal circumstances, might comfort his family (presumed to be his first readers), satisfy his critics, and characterize his reputation for posterity. However, because Boethius's larger purpose (like Plato's) is more objective and altruistic, he pauses at the climax of his interlocutors' debate, and offers readers a poetic exemplum of the contrary position without straining the bounds of logical proof on such a difficult matter as the suffering of the good. At the end of book 3, in her moving song about Orpheus (whose art won him the opportunity to redeem the life of his dead wife), Philosophia explains the duty of all who seek to "loose the bonds (*vincula*) of heavy earth," using the myth as an exemplum for a wider audience: "To you this tale refers, / Who seek to lead your mind / Into the upper day."[26] The poem evokes the tragic emotion of the poet-singer who recovers but then loses his wife from all too human weakness at the last moment of trial by the gods. Just on the edge of darkness, as he is about to leave the underworld, Orpheus looks back at his Eurydice ("love is a law unto itself"), contravening the condition of her release, and she dies again:

> Heu, noctis prope terminos
> Orpheus Eurydicem suam
> Vidit, perdidit, occidit.
> (bk. 3, m. 12, lines 49–51; Loeb, p. 310)

In this way the alternative to the position offered by the enclosed labyrinth of dialectic is made palpable by the song lyric using meter and metaphor to weave an affective antithesis. Whereas dialogue enacts an argument and

---

[26] "Vos haec fabula respicit / Quicumque in supernum diem / Mentem ducere quaeritis" (bk. 3, m. 12, Tester, Loeb, p. 310, lines 52–54; cf. lines 3–4: "Felix qui potuit gravis / Terrae solvere vincula"; the referent is Orpheus, ibid., p. 306).

with it the recovery process—over a period of time—within the Prisoner, the lyric offers instantaneous emotional correlatives by virtue of its combinations of associations in metaphor (darkness and death) and the expressive verbal music of rhythm and meter in the sequence of verbs describing Orpheus's actions (and personal responsibility) for this new loss of Eurydice: "He saw, he lost, he killed."

These twin disciplines of lyric and logic in Boethius's text infer a hierarchy of literary values and cultural assumptions but also recognition of different kinds of understanding that were appreciated by many other writers in prison. At the beginning of the *Consolation* the Prisoner's lyric complaint and Philosophia's reaction had suggested an association between poetry and emotion that would denigrate poetry by contrast with reasoned argument. Yet the actual deployment of lyric within the work shows that this association is too simple; poetry is highly valued, and its different method—its affectivity—is explicitly defined for the sake of the Prisoner and Boethius's reader.[27] Except at the beginning and end of the work, each subsection is marked by a lyric related to the topic of local discussion. The distribution and variety of the lyrics enabled Boethius to create a flexible structure (based on older, mixed modes of Greek Menippean satire), which allowed him to control the development of the overall argument and keep a self-conscious eye on its reception.[28] The formal variety, introducing different stylistic registers and extraneous stories, also enhances the vitality of the text for any reader. Standard imagery recurs: ignorance that separates man's mind from God's is imagined as the effects of clouds on man's view of the stars—symbolic of order in creation, as well as heavenly lights; the calm and the stormy seas are symbolic of the impact of fortune or chance and fate—the action of the sea is perpetual, yet its different conditions (which signify danger or safety to travelers on the journey of life) reflect the mutability of the world.[29] These images punctuate the text and provide subtle points of reference for Boethius's readers, enabling comparisons and contrasts that reinforce arguments, in oblique and metaphorical language that is emotive, impressive, and hence memorable.[30] By contrast, the binary processes of reasoning

---

[27] Cf. the progressive nature of human reasoning in dialectic with the immediacy of divine intelligence and the effects of poetry or metaphor, see Watts, p. 157, n. 5.

[28] As an introduction to bk. 4, m. 6 Philosophia says to the Prisoner: "But I see that you are long since burdened with the weight of this enquiry (*quaestionis*) and tired by the prolixity of the reasoning, and are waiting for some sweetness in song. So take a draught that you may be refreshed by it and go more firmly further on." (Cf. Tester [adapted], Loeb, p. 371.)

[29] Cf. bk. 3, m. 9, lines 23–25; Watts, p. 97 (on clouds/light). Fortune's wheel moves "like currents in a treacherous bay swept to and fro" (bk. 2, m. 1, p. 56); cf. bk. 2, m. 3 and m. 4, and the image of the Prisoner's family as his "anchors."

[30] See further Lerer, *Boethius and Dialogue*, pp. 154–65 on the Orpheus hymn and language of loss; and O'Daly, *The Poetry of Boethius*, ch. 4: "Nature in the Poetry of the *Consolation*."

"from arguments that fit together and lead from one to the next" are drawn out and cumulative (bk. 5, pr. 4, Watts, p. 156). This dynamic formal framework contributes to the appeal of the text.

In the lyrics Boethius offers readers attractive resting places (alongside the Prisoner, listening to the reasoning and singing of Philosophia) that facilitate meditation, understanding, and assimilation of wise teachings. At first, however, it looks as though poetry and logic are at loggerheads because when Philosophia first comes to the Prisoner's bedside, where he is weeping in self-pity, she banishes the Muses of poetry who have been dictating words of complaint to express his misery. The passion in her reaction is ironic: the rational spirit of eternal wisdom who represents philosophy is livid with rage. She rails at the Muses as "sirens" and purveyors of poison. Her abuse focuses on their deleterious effects: since they have "no medicine to ease . . . pains, only sweetened poisons to make them worse. . . . They habituate men to . . . sickness of mind instead of curing them." She is as passionate as the shameful women who destroy the "harvest of fruits of reason" cultivated by philosophy: "Who let these theatrical tarts (*has scenicas meretriculas*) in with this sick man?"[31] Moreover, her comments have general and particular referents. Philosophia's compassion imparts a strong maternal quality to the emotions of this dramatic recognition scene. When she bends over him from a great height and sits by his bed to dismiss the phantoms of Fortune's creation, her protective gestures and no-nonsense approach offer security and may remind anyone of a source of comfort associated with our earliest memories. The Prisoner reports his shocked reaction:

> Seeing that I was not merely silent, but altogether speechless and dumb, she gently laid her hand on my breast and said: "He is in no real danger, but suffers only from lethargy, a sickness common to deluded minds. He has a little forgotten his real self (*sui paulisper oblitus est*). He will soon recover . . . let me . . . clear his eyes of the mist of mortal affairs that clouds them." (bk. 1, pr. 2, Tester, Loeb, pp. 138–39)

As she wiped the tears from his eyes with a corner of her dress, the "darkness then began to lift as the night frayed, / or perhaps my eyes cleared and recovered their powers":[32]

> In the same way the clouds of my grief dissolved and I drank in the light. With my thoughts recollected (*mentem recepi*) I turned to examine the face of my physician. I turned my eyes and fixed my gaze upon her, and

---

[31] Tester, Loeb, p. 134, line 29; cf. "hysterical sluts" (Watts, p. 36); and "these chorus girls" (Slavitt, p. 4).

[32] Bk. 1, m. 3, Slavitt, p. 6.

saw that it was my nurse in whose house I had been cared for since my youth—Philosophy. (bk. 1, pr. 3, Watts, pp. 38–39; Loeb, p. 140)

The text implies an audience to this literally touching scene: Boethius's readers. The Prisoner's recovery begins after this melodramatic conflict between poetry (symbolizing affectivity) and philosophy (symbolizing rationality). Ironically, the therapeutic consolation of philosophy enacted in Boethius's work is not simply that of an abstract intellectual system; it also arises, as other prisoners were to find, from the personal care of a loyal and emotionally committed woman.

When Philosophia speaks about the prisoner as "he"—a third person— she is glossing his situation for her audience's benefit: the Muses of poetry (within the fiction of the text). Yet she does this in a context of personal intimacy where readers might well expect a personal address to her patient as "you." Speaking over his head in this way might be seen within the narrative setting as a means to encourage the Prisoner in a more objective approach to his situation, yet such tactical distancing is also an authorial strategy to instruct readers. Moments earlier Boethius's readers had been encouraged by his literary method to empathize with the sorrowful Prisoner whose first lyric and narrative monologue speak directly to a reader envisaged as beyond the text.

> See how the Muses grief-torn bid me write (*Ecce mihi lacerate dictant scribenda camenae*)
> . . . they were once
> My green youth's glory; now in my sad old age
> They comfort me.
> (bk. 1, m. 1, Tester, Loeb, pp. 130–31)

If we respond, we are also rebuked by Philosophia for conniving at the Muses' ministrations, which we now learn were dangerous. Just as the Prisoner is so overcome by surprise at the appearance and actions of this imperious female that he can "only fix [his] eyes on the ground and wait in silence for what she would do next," so readers must keep their eyes fixed on the page in curious anticipation. What happens next is equally surprising and instructive in an affective way. When Philosophia sits on the edge of the Prisoner's bed and begins to sing, her first words undermine our responses to the Prisoner's lament. She meditates sadly on the Prisoner's situation:

> So sinks the mind in deep despair . . . when
> It banishes its inward light (*propria luce*)
> And turns in trust to the dark without
> (bk. 1, m. 2, Watts, p. 37, lines 1–2, 4–5; Loeb, p. 136, lines 1–3).

Yet her general assessment soon includes any third person, including a reader, who is invited to witness the Prisoner's tragic reversal: his forgetting of himself.

> This was the man who once was free
> To climb the sky with zeal devout
> To contemplate the crimson sun,
> The frozen fairness of the moon—
>     (lines 6–9)

After listing past examples of the Prisoner's intellectual curiosity and achievements, Philosophia returns to the image of his depressed and oppressed state:

> Now see that mind that searched and made
> All Nature's hidden secrets clear
> Lie prostrate prisoner of night.
> His neck bends low in shackles . . .
> And he is forced beneath the weight
> To contemplate—the lowly dust.
>     (lines 22–27)

The poem glosses its opening statement. This tragic action is self-inflicted; the mind is a prisoner, weighed down in darkness because it turned away from its inward light of reason. Philosophia's dramatic exposition of the situation is replete with symbolic imagery and emotive contrasts. Given her former aspersions on such poisonous arts, this is both ironic and paradoxical, since it encourages readers' sympathies and yet presents a new objective assessment of the situation. As readers we learn by experience that we, like the Prisoner, have made a false start. The evocation of pathos is not appropriate to the consolation of philosophy. However, the affectivity of poetic metaphor and harmony is demonstrated as peculiarly attractive and instructive, and is thus valued by Boethius.[33]

The artistic coherence of the *Consolation* has also been important in accounting for the history of its reception. The attractiveness of the artistic whole, as well as Boethius's exploitation of his literary persona, was designed to engage and encourage readers. Boethius rejected pathos when he made Philosophia banish the Muses, but he did not dispense with sympathy for the Prisoner whether in the attitude of Philosophia (within the text) or in

---

[33] At the end of bk. 5, m. 5, Philosophia draws a contrast with the Prisoner's position and state of mind in book 1. In her last poem, as he raises his head to heaven, she also urges him to raise up his thoughts to heaven. See also O'Daly, *The Poetry of Boethius*, ch. 2: "The Poetics of the *Consolation*," pp. 30–69; and pp. 106–38 on nature in book 1.

its appeal to an implied readership. Even within the historic context of Boethius's life, and a political culture that linked late antique pagan values with Christian ones, the focus is broadly inclusive. (Significantly, the Christian message dependent on Jesus—as icon of Christian pathos and focus of divine compassion for man—has no part in this work.) Attention falls on *this* world because Boethius's text is concerned with ethics not eschatology. The potent image of God as a watchful eye on high, eternally present and omniscient, allowed an individual to judge himself by that absolute of perfection that is known by the inner voice of conscience and may be developed by pursuit of truth, wisdom, and virtue, in spite of the suffering these may bring. The feminine image of Philosophia and the concept of God as creator and father of all widen access to the text, which represents the supreme good as the love of wisdom.

Toward the end of the *Consolation*, as the Prisoner recovers his equilibrium and self-possession, the distribution of lyrics and dialogue becomes weighted toward longer, more abstract speeches by Philosophia. As their dialogue of exchange slows down, the dynamic of their relationship changes. Philosophia does not disappear at the end of the *Consolation* because her message has been assimilated by her brilliant pupil: her patient recovers himself and his philosophical vocation. Narrative closure is thus suspended, yet this is often the case in prison writing where the end of the story may be unknown (even if anticipated), or unable to be told. The Prisoner's implied final prayer is unarticulated. But throughout the *Consolation* humanity has been characterized by its capacity for speech and song as well as reason, and by a need to utter and define the self. The structural bias of the text has been designed to externalize rather than internalize argument and expression. The earlier conversational dialogue in the *Consolation* suggests a human need for the recognition and comfort that come from communication with other, sympathetic, intelligent beings. This need may be universal. Yet it seems significant for writers actually in prison that this need should find relief in the creation of dialogue that constructs and represents the kinds of intellectual and emotional stimuli that may be provided by companions (real or imaginary). Boethius's Prisoner laments the effects of his fall specifically in terms of the effects of separation from his family and friends (bk. 2, pr. 4). His choice of dialogue form certainly reflects a generic convention appropriate for philosophical argument in late antiquity but it may also be seen as psychologically appropriate for prison writers in any period. If the consolation of writing dialogic exchanges enables prison writers to recover or create composure it compensates for the deprivations of imprisonment and may also become a means for overcoming the consequences of that deprivation.

## READERS (EDUCATION AND CONSOLATION)

Over the centuries Boethius's Prisoner has been seen as someone readers can admire; in sympathy with his troubles we can either forget our own relatively smaller troubles or find an example to emulate when coping, in different cultural contexts, with life's larger injustices and painful sacrifices. The order and discipline of literary form in the *Consolation* reflects the emotional and intellectual control that enables its final affirmation of human free will to be the Prisoner's triumph of mind, memory, and art and the reader's consolation. The text shows how the tyranny of fear may be banished by the assertion and realization of free will as Boethius's fiction affirms his argument by testing it on himself as a certain kind of civilized man, Philosophia's pupil and patient: altruistic, faithful, self-conscious, and self-sufficient. In deriving his proof that virtue is its own reward (and asserting this freely, persuasively, and memorably while condemned to suffer injustice and violent death in disgrace), Boethius represented the ultimate defense of his concept of civilization. Given the nature of his education and earlier writing, we must also assume that he knew how he might affect readers and how his reputation as an author would be bound up with his perceived situation as a prisoner. In choosing to write a consolation, Boethius drew upon traditional cultural emphases on literature as a significant medium for ethical values. *Consolatio* as a genre of moral medication offers readers examples of personal misfortune to drive out the effects of other misfortune. Since all troubles are relative, to learn about worse misfortunes should mitigate one's own problems. The text therefore both represents a consolation achieved by the combination of reason and imagination and offers this example, explicitly based on Boethius's personal experience, to mitigate fear and sadness experienced by others in different circumstances.

The main formal components of Boethius's text support these altruistic functions of consolation and education: dialogue teaches by enacting a process of discovery, while poetry teaches by moving and delighting audiences drawn by the inherent attractiveness of figurative language and verbal music. At the beginning of book 3, the Prisoner reports that he was spellbound by the enchantment of Philosophia's latest song. When he came to his senses, he told her that she was "the greatest comfort for exhausted spirits":

> By the weight of your tenets (*sententiarum*) and the delightfulness of your singing you have so refreshed me that I now think myself capable of facing the blows of Fortune. You were talking of cures that were rather sharp (*acriora*). The thought of them no longer makes me shudder. (bk. 3, pr. 1, Watts, p. 78; Loeb, p. 228)

Indeed, poetry has also made the Prisoner accessible to sharper "remedies." Although such a mixture of dialogue and lyric was not unprecedented, its radical use in the *Consolation* shows how Boethius defamiliarized his text to focus on its ethical and political message—by not making it adhere simply to the generic norm of Platonic dialogue in prose. By giving his persona an emotional stake in the outcome of the didactic dialogue, Boethius promoted the authority of his text in the eyes of readers. The authority of this text is derived from readers' responses to the experience of that author.

It has been said that Boethius's reputation and importance in the Middle Ages cannot be overestimated. As the *Consolation* circulated throughout Europe, it helped to regenerate ethical discussion in poetry and fostered humanist sensibilities based on the diffusion of its late antique precepts. Because medieval readers regarded the work as the record of a type of righteous man's resistance to tyranny and persecution, this view of the text valorized resistance.[34] Yet it also reassured and satisfied readers. The history of the reception of this work has been dominated by the idea that the *Consolation* embodied the voice of Boethius's conscience. The first readers of the *Consolation* must have been Boethius's family and friends, who would have venerated the text because it was his, and it implies that these were his last words to them. Later generations of readers, further from the cult of personality configured in Boethius's Prisoner, responded to the precision and clarity of the work's complex ideas, and its eloquence and imagination, as these were perceived and recognized in their own time. The ninth-century cult of Boethius the prisoner, transmitted by Alcuin, among others, established an image of a Christian saint and ancient philosopher, which usefully supported the contemporary aims and values of the Carolingian renaissance. In Anglo-Saxon England, King Alfred's reinterpretation of the *Consolation* reflects his needs as a king with responsibilities for peace and justice in a world endangered by change and disorder.[35] In twelfth-century France Peter Abelard, probably identifying with Boethius as another misunderstood, persecuted philosopher, venerated the author of the *Consolation* as a martyred victim of schism in the church. (According to this view Theodoric as a believer in Arianism had persecuted Boethius for his Catholic orthodoxy.) Jean de Meun and, in the fourteenth century, Dante and Chaucer venerated

---

[34] For the impact of Boethius's text and reputation as a political prisoner and martyr on the prison writing of Thomas Usk, James I of Scotland, and George Ashby, see the separate chapters in Joanna Summers, *Late-Medieval Prison Writing and the Politics of Autobiography* (Oxford: Clarendon Press, 2004).

[35] Janet Bately, "Boethius and King Alfred," in *Platonism and the English Imagination*, ed. Anna Baldwin and Sarah Hutton (Cambridge: Cambridge University Press, 1994), pp. 38–44. Elizabeth I's translation of the *Consolation* into English verse and prose during the 1590s, a period of war, anxiety, and economic depression in England, suggests that she valued its teaching and consolation.

the prisoner Boethius as a tragic poet whose experience had informed his world view and inspired their new poetic sensibilities and ethical themes. Dialogues on love, fortune, and providential order were important elements in many of their most profound works, and Chaucer's translation kept the text accessible to English readers (in printed versions) throughout the sixteenth century. Milton's *Paradise Lost* also grappled with the problems of free will and divine foreknowledge in philosophical ideas made popular in Boethius's *Consolation*.[36] While every interpretation reflects the concerns and values of its own time and place, the length and variety of the literary traditions based on the *Consolation* also indicate the perennial importance of the questions (rather than the answers) it addresses.

Whereas the authority of the message of the text derives from readers' assumed knowledge of the experience of the author as a prisoner unjustly facing execution, the popularity of his text related to its intrinsic qualities as moving and persuasive literature; it speaks across cultural boundaries. Paradoxically, the constraints of art liberated the actual prisoner from time, oppression, fear, and his own human weakness, demonstrating how the power of intellect and imagination can transform life; its long reception history also ensured the continuity of its author's fame, showing how memorable writing can transfigure death, reflecting another aspect of the paradox of gain by loss.[37] The philosopher's teaching and practical demonstration of virtue in adversity remain after death in his writing: "Some men at the price of a glorious death have won a fame (*nomen*) that generations will venerate; some indomitable in the face of punishment have given others an example that evil cannot defeat virtue" (bk. 4, pr. 6, Watts, p. 139; Loeb, p. 366). The sequence of ideas seems to imply that both ways to death (execution as well as through military glory) are heroic, rather than to be contrasted. Writing the *Consolation* allowed Boethius to construct an indomitable myth of his own heroism for posterity. Because the message of this text replaces the example of the author, and instantiates the principles of his life's work, it also provides a remedy for his persecution in an eternity of fame—"despite all the raging of the wicked, the wise man's crown of laurels will never fall from him or wither away" (bk. 4, pr. 3, p. 124). Boethius established yet another

---

[36] See further H. R. Patch, *The Tradition of Boethius. A Study of His Importance in Medieval Culture* (Oxford: Oxford University Press, 1935); *Chaucer's Boece and the Medieval Tradition of Boethius*, ed. Alastair J. Minnis (Cambridge: D. S. Brewer, 1993); Lodi Nauta, "The *Consolation*: the Latin Commentary Tradition, 800–1700," and Winthrop Wetherbee, "The *Consolation* and Medieval Literature," both in Marenbon, *Cambridge Companion*, pp. 255–78, 279–302; and bibliography cited.

[37] Note the irony of the fame of a man who *wrote* philosophy; cf. the paradoxical definition of who is a philosopher: one who stays not only patient and composed under persecution but also silent in the company of fools (bk. 2, pr. 7, Watts, pp. 74–75). Boethius flatters his readers because he is not silent in their company.

paradox of prison writing: that of the prisoner as hero. Heroes are not perfect, but they are interesting because they are always being tested by fortune in the world.

Although Boethius's Prisoner and Philosophia agree that "fame (*claritudinem*) is the product of praise," they also recognize that not all praise, and hence fame, is deserved. A wise philosopher is naturally suspicious of popular opinion and measures happiness not by his reputation among others, but by the "true voice of his own conscience" (*conscientiae veritate*) (bk. 3, pr. 6, pp. 89–90; Loeb, p. 254). Boethius could neither know nor control how his work would be read and understood, yet, like many prison writers, he shows his desire for a personal reputation as a writer (specifically a poet and philosopher) by constructing the voices of conscience. Whether or not readers share his philosophy, the way he wrote about the representation of his journey toward self-discovery and death provides readers with the means to appreciate different qualities of his thought and expression. We may travel with the Prisoner for the pleasure and interest of the journey whether or not we appreciate his cultural affinities, or his ultimate destination conceived in terms of the tragic personal situation he shared as a condemned philosopher with Socrates or the younger Seneca. As a result, we may better understand ourselves as human beings.

Whether by dint of direct influence as a text, or by the coincidence of its treatment of archetypal qualities as reaction and resistance to imprisonment, Boethius's work prefigures many of the elements found in the forms and themes of other prisoners' writings. The autobiographical lament at the beginning of the *Consolation of Philosophy* may represent a false start philosophically, but it indicates that Boethius knew that a writer's experience of suffering could enhance the reputation of his writing and its ethical value for others. It is a feature of prison literature, first recognized by Boethius when he designated Philosophia's pupil a condemned prisoner, that a writer's views acquire more authority in the eyes of readers when these views are known to be founded on personal experience of the situation they reflect. Boethius's case illustrates this aspect of the paradox of gain by loss with a fine irony. As the expression of a prisoner's reactions to his suffering, the *Consolation of Philosophy* has been more valued by readers than any of the philosophical precepts articulated by this same learned author in the ease and comfort of his library. The philosopher, Boethius, lamented leaving his library to engage with politics in public office; in turn, Boethius, the Master of the Offices, lamented leaving office for prison, yet this was where he found his most potent and influential application for philosophy: adversity sifts out truth. Boethius apparently thought so, and so have the generations of readers who venerated the *Consolation* as his prison book and through it learned to sift out new truths in their own lives, wherein "teaching fans the spark to take new life" (bk. 3, m. 11, Watts, p. 109).

## Dietrich Bonhoeffer, *Letters and Papers from Prison* (1943–45): Christian Ethics and Lyric

Boethius and Bonhoeffer were disciplined and dignified, rational theologians. Their juxtaposition illustrates the continuity of values each man identified independently for his own culture and society with classical humanism, and Judeo-Christian ethics based on biblical traditions. Both prisoners recognized the importance to them of their families. This pairing also exemplifies the basis of their ethical philosophies in empathy and imagination through their intermittent recourse to lyric poetry. The rigor of verse composition, the emotional intensity and diversity of metaphor or simile and other rhetorical figures of brief repetitive forms associated with lyric, complemented the reliance on different types of reason in each of these writers' professional lives. Almost as an aside, Bonhoeffer's friend and biographer drew a parallel between Bonhoeffer and Boethius in marveling at the former's theological insights as a prisoner wherein "he strongly relativized what lay closest to him" by arguing that "the natural, the profane, the rational and the humane had its place" alongside a new conception of the "lordship of Christ" in the real world.[38]

Bonhoeffer's radical developments of Christian theology in response to the moral chaos of Hitler's Third Reich—before World War II and during it—were driven by pragmatic ethical concerns. He was disgusted with the response of the German Protestant churches, which had failed to provide moral leadership in resistance to fascism and in defense of human rights on theological principles. He regarded their acquiescence to Nazi ideology as un-Christian and a form of complicity. His theology was founded on recovery of the central paradigm of Jesus Christ as the suffering God whose active life among ordinary people (during another period of imperial rule) inspired discipleship in a godly life for others. Before the war, Bonhoeffer's Christology had evolved into training programs for ordinands in the illegal Confessing Church (a breakaway movement that in 1934 refused to sign agreements with the National Socialist regime), pastoral and political action to encourage resistance to fascism, and the clear enunciation of arguments that justified resistance to Nazi ideology. His outspoken demands that the church of Christ should support his suffering brothers and sisters

---

[38] Eberhard Bethge, *Dietrich Bonhoeffer: Theologian, Christian, Contemporary*, tr. E. Mosbacher, P. and B. Ross, F. Clarke, and W. Glen-Doepel, under the editorship of E. Robertson (London: William Collins, 1970, rpt. 1977), p. 773.

alienated many contemporary Christians whose latent anti-Semitism was rooted in traditional church teaching. (However, Bonhoeffer's subtle qualification of Lutheran anti-Semitism has not always protected his own reputation from complicity in its theological distinctions between baptized converts and religious Jews.) It soon became apparent to Bonhoeffer and his associates that Nazi ideology was pernicious in all walks of life and was corrupting natural law, German national culture, and European civilization. Hitler's tyranny undermined prospects for ordinary legal means of political resistance at the same time that it risked the peace of Europe. After ten years of Nazi rule, Bonhoeffer and others concluded that Hitler had so corrupted many people's freedom of will to act justly, nothing short of his murder would end this tyranny. Moral resistance and being a Christian in Hitler's Reich required actions that concluded with a last attempt on Hitler's life in July 1944. Bonhoeffer had had the moral distinction of being a thorn in the side of the fascist body politic since 1933. He had known that Christian discipleship was costly but insisted that redemption from man's inhumanity to man could not be foisted upon divine providence. For him the reality of God's suffering in this world was a theological imperative for ethical action in the here and now.[39]

Bonhoeffer was arrested on suspicion of treason in April 1943. He spent most of the next two years imprisoned in Tegel, Berlin's military interrogation center and prison. After the failure of the July bomb plot, he knew that it was merely a matter of time before his role would be discovered. In January 1945 he was moved to Gestapo headquarters, thence to Buchenwald in February, and, finally summarily tried by court-martial during the night of 8 April 1945 at Flossenburg concentration camp, where he was executed, alongside Admiral Canaris and General Hans Oster, among others, at dawn the next morning. During his imprisonment at Tegel, Bonhoeffer had access to books, writing material, and parcels from home, including food and laundry. He had regular visits from his parents and fiancée most of the time he was there and wrote letters. From November 1943 he was able to conduct a clandestine correspondence with his former pupil, Eberhard Bethge, who played a constructively adversarial role within their dialogue by letters that provided Bonhoeffer with the intellectual stimulus he needed to clarify his theology in response to his imprisonment. This chapter demonstrates how the prisoner developed his ideas and put them into literary practice using

---

[39] The standard biography, first published in German in 1967, is by Bethge, as previous note; for a convenient summary of the background, see J. A. Moses, "Bonhoeffer's Germany: The Political Context," in *The Cambridge Companion to Dietrich Bonhoeffer*, ed. J. W. de Gruchy (Cambridge: Cambridge University Press, 1999, rpt. 2008), pp. 3–21; and W. W. Floyd, "Bonhoeffer's Literary Legacy," ibid., pp. 71–92.

the stimulus of dialogue in correspondence, the discipline of various other forms of writing, especially verse, and the resources of happy memories and a well-stocked mind. The moral dilemma he faced, and attempted to resolve in promoting practical ways of living for others, was founded on his observation that all it takes for evil to flourish is for good men to do nothing.

Unlike Boethius, who in writing the *Consolation of Philosophy* put his faith in reason, Bonhoeffer wrote because he had reason to believe; he hoped to be able to aid the reconstruction of Christian life after the defeat of the Third Reich. Everything he wrote at Tegel in the midst of the ongoing crises of his own illegal imprisonment and the shared insecurities of war (including heavy bombing, rationing, the displacement of people, and corrosive effects of fear and distrust) bears the impact of life in his double boundary situation as a prisoner and a man of his time. Two themes predominate: his dialogue with the past by means of his memory, historical imagination, and reading—"This dialogue with the past (*die Auseinandersetzung mit der Vergangenheit*) . . . is the almost daily accompaniment (*Begleitmusik*) of my life here";[40] and the intellectual freedom and consolation he experienced through his engagement with ideas in reading and writing—"What a deliverance it is to be able to think" (*LPP*, p. 311, 29 May 1944).

## THE PRISONER AND HIS BACKGROUND

Bonhoeffer did not write with hindsight and could not have known until July 1944 that he would not survive. He evolved and constructed his consolation of theology and ethics in response to the dangers—moral, political, and personal—of his situation in what he saw as a "religionless" world. Boethius had constructed Philosophia's delivery of the consolation of philosophy as a single event enacted through dialogue within his own literary persona. Bonhoeffer's process of evolving and articulating defensive strategies to ensure the survival of Christian values in postwar Germany had no single literary focus. His cultural, religious, and personal defensive tactics operated piecemeal in several different, often unfinished, surviving prison works, including a four-page "Outline for a Book" that he hoped might "be of some help for the church's future," and several kinds of fiction.[41] His literary leg-

---

[40] *Letters and Papers from Prison, the Enlarged Edition*, ed. E. Bethge (London: SCM Press, 1971, rpt. 1986) [hereafter *LPP*], p. 319 (5 June 1944). See also Dietrich Bonhoeffer, *Works*, vol. 8, ed. J. W. de Gruchy (Minneapolis: Fortress Press, 2010) [hereafter *DBWE*], 8 (2010)], p. 416; cf. *Widerstand und Ergebung*, ed. C. Gremmels, E. Bethge, and R. Bethge with I. Tödt in *Dietrich Bonhoeffer Werke*, 8 (Gütersloh: C. Kaiser, 1998), p. 466.

[41] *LPP*, pp. 380–83. See *Fiction from Prison: Gathering Up the Past*, ed. R. and E. Bethge with C. Green, tr. U. Hoffmann (Philadelphia: Fortress Press, 1981). Cf. *DBWE*, 7, ed. Clifford J. Green, tr. Nancy Lukens (Minneapolis: Fortress Press, 2000).

acy was established through the editorial role of Eberhard Bethge, who had married Bonhoeffer's niece in 1943. Bethge survived investigations of the plot against Hitler's life and became Bonhoeffer's literary executor and biographer. Bonhoeffer's prison writings reflect different aspects of his experience and the wider historic situation, in letters, notes for sermons, poems, plays, and stories. His prison letters alone range over many subjects addressed to family and friends as son, lover, pastor, and mentor or as colleague in pastoral need. The poem "Who am I?" addresses this perceived problem of self-identity directly but through the voice of a poetic persona who typifies the options open to a highly literate, self-aware individual responding directly to imprisonment. The moral and ethical dilemmas he discussed were responses to the violent and debased political world he had confronted and condemned. In response to different events and crises, Bonhoeffer's role in his various forms of dialogue with the outside world changed even in correspondence with a single person. Yet the authority of his experience as a long-standing, radical critic of the Nazi regime, whose victim he became, enabled his ideas to live on and provided principled guidance for a generation of German Christians, so many of whom, he feared, had lost sight of the foundations of their faith and done little or nothing to resist.

Bonhoeffer's family background and his pastoral and academic career as a theologian shaped his moral, social, and political values. His father was professor of psychiatry in Berlin who continued in medical practice, in spite of his advanced years, during the war. This medical background had provided opportunities for the young Dietrich to learn about the lives of others before he had opportunities to travel abroad. His mother was well connected to the patrician culture of old Prussia that had given Germany so many of its political and military leaders. Bonhoeffer's "uncle," Paul von Hase (actually his mother's cousin), the city commandant of Berlin, visited the prisoner whom he was powerless to help except insofar as the personal attention of a man of his rank and distinction might ameliorate the behavior of the prison authorities. On one occasion "Uncle Paul" had the prisoner brought from his attic cell, called for four bottles of wine, and stayed for more than five hours entertaining Bonhoeffer in the company of his official jailers. The ironic subtlety of this message of resistance to tyranny was not lost on its audience. As Bonhoeffer commented (30 June 1944), "Such independence, which would be quite unthinkable in a civilian, was most remarkable" (*LPP*, p. 342). His mother's family also demonstrated strong religious convictions. However, Dietrich was the only one of eight siblings to pursue these in professional life. This large, intelligent, and mutually supportive family also enjoyed a rich musical life together, and Bonhoeffer remembered these occasions with pleasure; he also used the term *cantus firmus* as a metaphor in describing the centrality of the Bible in his life, against which other different themes could be counterpointed.[42] The Bonhoeffers' friends and neighbors were drawn from similarly accomplished families. It is also significant that Dietrich's twin sister had a Jewish husband; when the couple escaped to England before the war, Bonhoeffer drove them to the Swiss border.

Before the rise of Hitler, Bonhoeffer had traveled widely in Europe to theology conferences and held short-term teaching or pastoral appointments in Barcelona and London. He had also studied for a year in New York at the Union Theological College, where he assisted neighboring black congregations and became aware of racial discrimination at first hand. Foreign travel and intense programs of scholarly reading helped to develop his thinking. His independently minded family and professional life stimulated the intellectual and political confidence that had made him an early, active opponent of Nazism. In 1933, when other clergy walked out of his paper on "the Church and the Jewish Question," and when reactions to the election of Hitler split the Protestant churches in Germany, Bonhoeffer had realized how deep-seated was the moral, political, and spiritual malaise in Germany. He concluded that the church should "not just bandage the victims under the wheel but put a spoke in the wheel itself" by active resistance.[43] In 1934 he wrote prophetically to a Swiss friend: "I believe that the whole of Christendom must join with us in praying for the advent of 'resistance unto death,' and that people capable of enduring it will be found."[44] Revisionist studies of German intellectuals in the 1930s have not diminished Bonhoeffer's significance as an early, consistent opponent to Nazi ideology, yet it is also clear that his friendship and sympathy for individual Jews was largely focused on converts to Christianity.[45]

---

[42] Cf. "Where the *cantus firmus* is clear and plain, the counterpoint can be developed to its limits. . . . May not the attraction and importance of polyphony in music consist in its being a musical reflection of this Christological fact and therefore of our *vita christiana*?" *LPP*, p. 303 (20 May 1944). Cf. "Begleitmusik" metaphor earlier.

[43] D. Bonhoeffer, *No Rusty Swords: Letters, Lectures and Notes, 1928–1936* (New York: Harper and Row, 1965), p. 225; cf. F. Burton Nelson, "The Life of Dietrich Bonhoeffer," in Gruchy, *Cambridge Companion to Dietrich Bonhoeffer*, p. 35; and E. Bethge, "Dietrich Bonhoeffer and the Jews," in *Ethical Responsibility: Bonhoeffer's Legacy to the Churches*, ed. J. D. Godsey and G. B. Kelly (New York: Edwin Mellen Press, 1981), p. 63.

[44] To Edwin Surtz, 28 April 1934; *The Essential Writings of Dietrich Bonhoeffer*, ed. G. B. Kelly and F. Burton Nelson (San Francisco: Harper, 1990), p. 434, quoted in *Love Letters from Cell 92*, ed. R.-A. von Bismarck and U. Kabitz, tr. John Brownjohn (London: Harper-Collins, 1994), p. 275.

[45] See further Ruth Zerner, "German Protestant Responses to Nazi Persecution of the Jews," in *Perspectives on the Holocaust*, ed. R. L. Braham (Boston: Kluwer-Nijhoff, 1983), pp. 57–68; Victoria J. Barnett, "The Creation of Ethical 'Gray Zones' in the German Protestant Church: Reflections on the Historical Quest for Ethical Clarity," in *Gray Zones: Ambiguity and Compromise in the Holocaust and Its Aftermath*, ed. Jonathan Petropoulos and John K. Roth (Oxford: Berghahn Books, 2005), pp. 360–71 at 366–68. (A commission at Yad Vashem in Jerusalem has refused to recognize Bonhoeffer as one of the "righteous gentiles" who risked their own lives to save persecuted Jews.)

His marginal marks in his Bible, alongside Psalm 74:8–10, indicating the date of widespread, state-sponsored, violent attacks on Jewish life (the so-called Kristallnacht, 9 November 1938), correlate this text with contemporary life.[46] Bonhoeffer was barred from teaching and invited back to the United States by friends anxious to protect him; but he decided not to seek shelter for himself and returned to Germany to offer spiritual guidance to ordinary Germans in July 1939.[47] By September 1940 he was also banned from preaching but continued to work for the resistance as a double agent, under cover of his civilian membership of the Abwehr, counter-intelligence service (commanded by Canaris), until his arrest with his older sister and her husband, Hans von Dohnanyi, in early April 1943. He was a personal friend of George Bell, bishop of Chichester, who passed information to the British government about plots on Hitler's life received from Bonhoeffer at ecumenical church meetings in neutral Sweden. His international standing enhanced his opportunities for resistance but also exposed him (and his associates) to dangerous public attention.

At Christmas 1942, after nearly ten years of Hitler's rule, Bonhoeffer summarized the moral and religious case for violent resistance on behalf of Dohnanyi, Oster, and Bethge. Their concerns related to the "business of life." Their problems were unique, yet Bonhoeffer, whose ideas were always informed by his historical imagination and experience, asked "whether the responsible thinking people of any generation that stood at a turning point in history did not feel much as we do." He wondered whether "there have ever . . . been people with so little ground under their feet—people to whom every available alternative seemed equally intolerable, repugnant, and futile . . . the great masquerade of evil has played havoc with all our ethical concepts" (*LPP*, pp. 3–4). Even without moral grounding, he argued it was up to "responsible people" to stand fast by higher standards than individual conscience, freedom, or virtue. He was aware of the obvious moral dangers this entailed but would also have recognized that the Reformation had been instrumental in developing resistance theory; according to Bonhoeffer, standing fast as a human being had to involve readiness to sacrifice all the normal but failed resources, including human and moral law, when "called to obedient and responsible action in faith and in exclusive allegiance to

---

[46] "They have said in their hearts, Let us destroy them together: they have burned up all the synagogues of God in the land. We see not our signs: there is no more any prophet: neither is there among us any that knoweth how long. O God, how long shall the adversary reproach? Shall the enemy blaspheme thy name for ever?" See Bethge, "Dietrich Bonhoeffer and the Jews," pp. 74–75.

[47] "I have made a mistake in coming to America. I must live through this difficult period of our national history with the Christian people of Germany. I will have no right to participate in the reconstruction of Christian life in Germany after the war if I do not share the trials of this time with my people." Bonhoeffer to Reinhold Niebuhr; in Bethge, *Dietrich Bonhoeffer*, p. 559.

God." He went on to argue for the necessity of sin: that "the God who demands responsible action in a bold venture of faith . . . promises forgiveness
and consolation to the man who becomes a sinner in that venture" (*LPP*,
p. 6). The actions that culminated in imprisonment and death embodied
this argument. In case such ideas might lead an arrogant elite into an attitude of contempt for humanity, he reminded his fellow conspirators:
"Nothing that we despise in the other man is entirely absent from ourselves"
(p. 10); and yet, with reference to the Christian message, "God . . . did not
despise humanity, but became man for men's sake." However, after ten years
of National Socialism, he concluded that "the air that we breathe is so pol-
luted by mistrust . . . it almost chokes us"; and, "mere waiting and looking
on is not Christian behaviour" (pp. 11, 14). Christians were "called to sympathy and action, not in the first place by [their] own sufferings," but by
those of their "brethren"; he argued that they should live "every day as if it
were our last, and yet liv[e] in faith and responsibility as though there were
to be a great future."

This sense of responsibility for reconstructing the future was an important theme in Bonhoeffer's later theology. He condemned those who regarded it as "frivolous" or "impious" in this time of "catastrophe" to plan
ahead: "It may be that the day of judgement will dawn tomorrow; in that
case, we shall gladly stop working for a better future. But not before"
(pp. 15–16). The practical necessity of the task was beyond question, but
he doubted whether their capacities to resist would be strong enough, "and
our honesty with ourselves remorseless enough, for us to find our way back
to simplicity and straightforwardness," (p. 17). The metaphor of finding
the way back indicates that, like Boethius, Bonhoeffer located the resources
required to build a better life first in values tested by history and only secondly in the religious sphere of God's guidance by revelation. He urged his
friends to make their perceptions of generosity, humanity, justice, and
mercy clearer, freer, and less corruptible (p. 17). He did not doubt their allegiance to a personal God, yet sought to comfort the conspirators by reminding them of the paradoxical benefit in suffering: "We have to learn
that personal suffering is a more . . . rewarding principle for exploring the
world in thought and action than personal good fortune" (p. 17). While
this had been a concern of many philosophical prisoners from Boethius
onward, Bonhoeffer's personal anticipation of imprisonment and death
(should the conspiracy fail) came from his sense of pastoral responsibility
to individuals who were not free to ignore moral and ethical imperatives. It
was never sufficient or responsible simply to obey orders. He was also
acutely aware of the doctrinal paradox of the redemption at the heart of the
theology of the cross. After he was imprisoned, Bonhoeffer's emphasis on

Christology was refined by his own sufferings in which he came to understand that "only the suffering God can help," and only then by virtue of Christ's weakness and suffering rather than omnipotence (pp. 360–61, 16 July 1944). In this world, God's help was exemplary compassion and vulnerability by following the historic example of the Christians' savior. In the liminal situation created by wartime, Bonhoeffer recognized from experience, past literature, and imaginative empathy that feelings of insecurity, which were the daily accompaniment of their lives, could be either destructive or liberating, depending on their point of view: "Fundamentally we feel that we really belong to death already, and that every new day is a miracle." If life was a miracle and precious, that could also make dying worthwhile: "It is we ourselves, and not outward circumstances, who make death what it can be, a death freely and voluntarily accepted" (p. 16). (Boethius's *Philosophia* would have approved of this emphasis on the power of the active mind and intellectual independence.)

## LIFE IN PRISON (HUMAN COMMUNION)—
## "THE DIALOGUE REMAINS INTACT"

A cell of his own enabled Bonhoeffer to continue his intellectual life in Tegel. His family supplied books, and he had access to material from the prison library. He was allowed to write letters every ten days and then at intervals of four days. These letters describe his daily life and reactions to his situation. On the wall of his cell he placed a reproduction from Dürer's *Apocalypse* that he found in a newspaper; he kept photographs and family mementoes alongside symbolic reminders of the church calendar. He paced his cell for exercise and was normally allowed thirty minutes' walk in the prison yard. He began and ended every day with prayers and meditative biblical readings, especially those prescribed for the day, which he knew his fiancée, Maria von Wedemeyer, and Eberhard Bethge would also be reading; in this way his religious observance was also a form of human communion. Before going to sleep he hummed hymns to himself and reported finding, as many others had done, that the Psalms were a special solace in prison.[48] His altruism impressed many of the people around him. Most of the other prisoners and older guards were not ideologues and would sometimes talk to him about their problems; he often received little kindnesses at the discretion of individuals. Occasionally he was allowed access to the sick bay where

---

[48] On Bonhoeffer's prayer life in prison, see G. B. Kelly, "Prayer and Action for Justice: Bonhoeffer's Spirituality," in Gruchy, *Cambridge Companion to Dietrich Bonhoeffer*, pp. 246–68, esp. 252–61. Cf. also R. Zim, *English Metrical Psalms: Poetry as Praise and Prayer* (Cambridge: Cambridge University Press, 1987, rpt. 2011), pp. 80–111.

he heard music on the radio, which was comforting. Although the prison clergy visited his cell, he was not allowed to attend church services or receive Holy Communion. The discipline that he chose to impose on his daily occupations brought him into imaginative and emotional communion with his family and was important in maintaining his mental and physical well-being. Although he was determined to write something that might contribute to the reconstruction of German society and culture, he found it difficult to settle his thoughts during his first year in prison when he made several attempts at prose fiction instead. Bonhoeffer's prison writings provide personal testimony to the ideas and values he regarded as the best defense against systematic corruption of people and government by a degenerate power.

An early short story, "Lance-Corporal Berg: A Narrative," set within a prison, compares different attitudes to heroism, guilt, and military bombast in the reactions of complacent guards to a young man disfigured by battle wounds. It exposes the cowardice (and self-interest) of guards who find Berg's scarred face a daily reminder of their own inner disfigurement. Berg is therefore sent back to the front line where he will be killed: out of sight, out of mind. This theme probes the moral failure of those Germans who turned their backs on the realities of Nazi corruption and barbarity. He also began, but soon abandoned, a play and a novel (both loosely based on childhood memories).[49] These literary genres seem to have liberated his imaginative self-exploration; with less responsibility to factual life-story telling, he had more freedom to develop figurative possibilities for different purposes. It is frequently the case that the first topics for novice writers are autobiographical, but this may also be seen among prison writers, including highly literate and accomplished writers such as Boethius in the opening sections of his *Consolation*.

Reading and writing were part of his daily routine. As each season and religious festival, family anniversary, or celebration approached, he would write letters and meditations with more or less hope that he would be free in time to share it with his family.[50] Recurring themes include the effects of uncertainty in wartime and for a prisoner. The gratitude and affection he felt toward his elderly parents who stayed in Berlin to support him are expressed repeatedly in letters that were exposed to censorship; thus, concern for his parents, coupled with the usual formality of their class and genera-

[49] See also *LPP*, p. 94; the play and novel drafts were published by Renate and Eberhard Bethge in 1978 as *Fragmente aus Tegel*.

[50] Some of Bonhoeffer's writing has been lost. References in letters indicate that several small-scale studies, one on "the feelings of time," have not survived; Bethge destroyed letters he had received after August 1944 to protect himself. The last surviving letter, 17 January 1945, is addressed to his parents.

tion, often make this correspondence seem restrained. There are similar anxieties expressed in letters to Maria von Wedemeyer to whom he became engaged shortly before his arrest, when he was thirty-seven and she was nineteen. This discrepancy in years also seems to have inhibited his freedom of expression; he was afraid that she might be harmed by the association with him and worried that her emotional ties would increase the difficulties of her life in wartime; he felt that he had let her down personally. Because they had known each other for such a short period before his arrest, he found that their relatively small pool of shared memories also made it harder to develop their relationship by correspondence.[51] As a result, the most important, intimate, and productive correspondence for Bonhoeffer as a prisoner was with Bethge, who established the uncensored channel for letters through a prison guard and whom Bonhoeffer regarded as the only person to whom he could write "with a certain matter of factness" (*LPP*, p. 319).

His reading and writing explored ideas of what it means to be free and responsible before God as a way of defending human righteousness and human rights. The frustrations caused by his legal position and the pain of the separations endured were often acute: "This waiting is revolting," he commented to Bethge, after a lawyer had failed to keep an appointment to discuss his case: "Prisoners are like sick people and children; promises with them should be kept" (*LPP*, p. 164, 16 December 1943). He had hoped to be released at Christmas and found that "nothing tortures us more than longing." He was "terribly homesick" and acknowledged that "there is nothing more painful" (p. 167). His self-awareness was also analytical, and he went on to discuss how such feelings can lead one willingly to neglect ordinary routines. This he saw as the first stage of capitulation, since even passive endurance becomes unbearable and positive resistance crumbles. The statement that "through every event, however untoward, there is access to God" who is the Christian's eternal "home" seems a rationalization after the event by a homesick theologian; yet, as we know from Boethius's prison writing, it was a traditional idea in Christian and neo-Platonic literature. Later, the situation in which it was known to be reiterated enhanced the value of such ideas for others. Bonhoeffer used his prison experience as a basis for learning how to live a better life. It was equally typical of his theology that such ethical concern should be adapted from and authorized by the Bible. The "access to God" insight is Bonhoeffer's gloss on Matthew 10:29 (on the fall of a

---

[51] A collection of his letters to Maria was published after her death by her sister, Ruth-Alice von Bismarck, and Ulrich Kabitz, as *Love Letters from Cell 92*, tr. Brownjohn.

sparrow) made in the course of a comment to Bethge that "of course, not everything that happens is simply 'God's will'; yet in the last resort nothing happens 'without God's will' " (p. 167). Both the subtlety and the offhand-edness of this remark were produced by reactions to imprisonment.

The previous day Bonhoeffer had written a more poised and circumspect letter to his parents in which he assured them that essential details of the Christmas story, in particular the birth in a stable, which showed that "God will approach where men turn away," were "things that a prisoner can under-stand better than other people." His appreciation of Christian fellowship that broke the "bounds of time and space" reduced the conditions of his own confinement to "insignificance" (p. 166). He was determined not to be depressed by a lonely Christmas, claiming that he wanted to be able to look back honestly on his imprisonment "not with shame, but with a certain pride. That's the only thing that no one can take from me" (p. 165). His sensitivity to that prospect, even while denying it, was matched by a wryly stoical comment to his parents that imprisonment had taught him that "the unexpected often happens, and that what can't be changed must be accepted with a *sacrificium intellectus*, although the *sacrificium* is not quite complete, and the *intellectus* silently goes its own way." Next day, he wrote to Bethge: "There's no changing it, only it's more difficult to adapt oneself to some-thing that one thinks could have been prevented than to something inevi-table." The balance between God's will and man's freedom that had con-cerned Boethius was especially problematic because Bonhoeffer and the other conspirators had identified complacency and fear in others as major contributions to the failure of effective resistance to Hitler. Before he closed this smuggled letter to Bethge he wrote:

> We must learn to act differently from those who always hesitate, whose failure we know in a wider context. We must be clear about what we want, we must ask whether we're up to it, and then we must do it with unshakable confidence. Then and only then can we also bear the conse-quences. (*LPP*, p. 174, 22 December 1943)

It was this quality of unshakable confidence that was so hard for the intel-lectual and the Christian. He regarded imprisonment as an inevitable "part of being involved in Germany's fate," but he worried that faith might endan-ger his capacity to act and to take risks—in short, to live. "I must be able to know for certain that I am in God's hands, not in men's . . . I don't want the machinations of men to make me waver." He had been reading Thomas à Kempis and closed the letter by quoting a passage he had just come across in which Thomas advises the holy man in his monastic cell—a condition of life

and divine service freely chosen—to "take care" of his cell (the special external conditions of his life), promising that it would take care of him.[52]
Thoughtful acceptance and a positive attitude (rather than submission)
were beneficial. In his loneliness Bonhoeffer had also been surprised to discover new beauty and significance in a seventeenth-century Lutheran hymn
by Paul Gerhardt, which had previously meant little to him. In his reactions
to his different kind of cell, he found himself observing the development of
his own spirituality in appreciation of that "slight flavour of the monastery
and mysticism" that he had previously dismissed (p. 170, Advent IV). He
was consoled by the idea that life in a prison cell might well be compared
with Advent in that "one waits, hopes, and does this, that, or the other . . .
the door is shut, and can be opened only *from the outside*" (p. 135, 21 November 1943).

New perceptions and new practices evolved in his spiritual life as a result
of his imprisonment: a paradoxical gain by loss. No experience was wasted;
every nuance of horror or doubt, pain or outrage aided preparations for a
better understanding and future for humanity in this world. He had found
that making the sign of the cross at morning and evening prayers, a practice
he had only recently adopted in prison, was helpful. This was an act of devotion he knew Bethge would consider superficial religiosity, so he felt he
needed to explain and defend it. He found the practice comforting because
there was "something objective about it," and as he realized, the objectivity
of such a ritual act was what was badly needed in the uncertainty and insecurity of war and imprisonment. "Don't be alarmed," he continued, "I shall
not come out of here a *homo religiosus*! On the contrary, my fear and distrust
of 'religiosity' have become greater than ever here" (p. 135). (Simultaneously, in response to the conditions in Tegel, he was also thinking about reform of the penal system for the benefit of future prisoners.)

Most of Bonhoeffer's new theological work evolved during the second
year of his captivity after he had better come to terms with his situation; the
uncensored correspondence with Bethge provided additional stimulus. Besides notes developing ideas beyond his work on *Ethics,* which had been left
unfinished on his desk at his arrest, Bonhoeffer also sent Bethge copies of
prayers he composed for fellow prisoners in November 1943 and poetry
that he began to write during the last year of his life. During air raids prisoners were sometimes left in their cells or taken to shelter in groups. Bonhoeffer's "prayer in time of distress" was intended to provide spiritual resources

---

[52] "Custodi diligenter cellam tuam, et custodiet te" (*LPP*, p. 175); for source details, see *DBWE*,
8 (2010), p. 237, n. 56, and cf. pp. 230–31, n. 21.

for fellow prisoners; he also wrote short morning and evening prayers that were circulated clandestinely with help from the prison chaplains and made brief extracts from Gerhardt's hymns selected for their relevance to prisoners. Bonhoeffer was anxious to remind Bethge that his new prayers did not make petitions for forgiveness of sins a central concern. Reminding prisoners of guilt (when their accusers were often behaving as less than human) and emphasizing punishment as a sign of God's wrath were, he thought, completely mistaken and inappropriate—hence his professional dissatisfaction with the prison clergy).[53] His prayers for prisoners, himself included, petitioned instead for God's help in praying, using language reminiscent of biblical psalms. His experience of imprisonment led to a reaffirmation of the attitudes and strong feelings in so many psalms, and of the idea that it was beneficial for individual voices to articulate their incomprehension and trust together. The premise of providential order in the world is sustained: "I do not understand your ways / But you know the way for me" (p. 139). The morning devotions offer thanks for the peace of the night, for the new day, for God's goodness (throughout the prisoner's life), and include petitions for help in accepting "what is hard from your hand" at present. As with many other religious prisoners' writing in response to imprisonment, the biblical assurance that God will not lay more on the sufferer than he can personally bear is an important theme in Bonhoeffer's new prayers for his companions in Tegel.[54]

In a new petition to "Lord Jesus Christ," Bonhoeffer placed especial emphasis on the identity of Jesus as a prisoner and a man. By contrast, a petition to the "Holy Spirit" asks for faith to protect the prisoner from despair, passions, and vice; it also asks for love of such quality "as will blot out all hatred and bitterness" (p. 140). Such "spiritual" qualities are seen as being represented by the prisoner Jesus in his human behavior, which was ideal. The petition addresses God as the only objective judge who hates and punishes evil without respect of persons, thereby offering comfort to the sinner and persecuted petitioner. The final plea for mercy in this prayer includes remembrance not only of loved ones and fellow prisoners but also of "all who in this house perform their hard service" by working in it, willingly or otherwise. The absolute value of freedom, physical and moral, is affirmed thus: "Restore me to liberty (*Lass mich in Frieden*), / and enable me so to live now / that I may answer before you and before men." It is clear that real and immediate prospects of facing both divine and human judgment meant

---

[53] Cf. *LPP*, p. 213, 13 February 1944.
[54] Cf. 1 Corinthians 10:13.

that trust and hope were essential: "Lord, whatever this day may bring, / Your name be praised" (p. 141). These new prayers offered fellow prisoners consolation, sympathy, and understanding rather than blame or punishment. As a theologian he presumed that every soul would be answerable before a just God, but as a prisoner undergoing his own spiritual trial who saw clearly what fear, self-interest, and corruption had already done in debasing humanity, he knew that like all his fellows he would first have to come to trial before unjust men; this might prove the harder trial.

Bonhoeffer's poetry also reveals imaginative insights into the problems of a prisoner's life and addresses many of the themes and values adduced in the letters to Bethge, but the emotional perspectives, in "The Past" and "The Friend," also provide impressions of psychological pressures evaded or suppressed. Bonhoeffer began writing verse (for the first time since his teens) as a means of coping with subconscious anxieties about his identity as a prisoner. Like Boethius, the prisoner Bonhoeffer made direct, discursive, and analytical approaches to existential problems in his dialogic prose, alongside more suggestive and indirect approaches to his concerns in meter, rhyme, and metaphor. This lyric impulse seems to reflect responses to the pressures of his situation. "The Past" was probably his first attempt at verse in prison; he sent it to Bethge with the comment that the verses came of their own accord; the whole thing was composed in a few hours, and he did not try to polish or revise it. He was intrigued by the impulse as well as bemused by the result. The poem was generated in the context of discussion about Bethge's parting from his young wife on being sent to the Italian front. He was also conscious of his own remarks as a prisoner:

> This dialogue with the past, the attempt to hold on to it and recover it, and above all, the fear of losing it, is the almost daily accompaniment of my life here; and sometimes ... it becomes a theme with variations. (*LPP*, p. 319, 5 June 1944)

These two themes became conflated in the poem, giving vivid emotional actuality to his comments about the pain of longing. Bonhoeffer wanted to send his poem to Maria but was concerned that it might frighten her. This is partly because it begins as a direct address to the past, which is personified throughout as a second person who is "Anguish, life, blessedness, part of myself, my heart," but rejects the speaker; when a door is slammed, he hears footsteps slowly die away (p. 320). The ambiguity of this personification (and physical imagery of psychological torture) may arise from the conflation of associations it likely had for the poem's first readers: Bethge leaving Renate; Maria leaving the prison after visiting her fiancé.

What now remains for me—torment, delight, desire? (*was bleibt mir?*
  *Freude, Qual, Verlangen?*)
This only do I know: that with you, all has gone.[55]

The next idea develops the speaker's wish to hold on to the substance of this
"all" by clutching violently at the image of the past—"your blood gushes
out"—in a form of destructive appropriation that disturbs the speaker.
When the image of the past vanishes, like some ghostly exhalation, this
physical effort to hold "a life in earthly form, complete" (*du leibliches, ir-
disches, volles Leben*) is frustrated; memory fails as presence and communion become unstable:

As the warm breath dissolves (*Wie der Hauch des warmen Atems*)
in the cool morning air,
so does your image vanish from me, (*dein Bild*)
and I forget your face, your hands, your form (*ich . . . deine Gestalt /
  nicht mehrweiss*).

The humanity of the past takes on sensual qualities as the speaker yearns
"to inhale the fragrance of your being, absorb it, stay with it," like bees in-
toxicated by the heavy blossoms of summer.[56] Yet even before this point
Bonhoeffer's reader has difficulty separating this image of the past from a
representation of Maria von Wedemeyer. When the past turns away from
the speaker, masochistic elements in the simile of physical fragmentation (a
form of medieval martyrdom), parallel earlier attempts at rending and
holding "complete" an earthly form: "I feel as if red-hot tongs were tearing
pieces out of my flesh."[57] In spite of the speaker's desperation, the past cannot be held down by the senses, and he rages, restless and reckless, seeking
new ways to retrieve what is lost. Angry at the futility of trying to grasp the
wind or recapture his memory of the past, the speaker swears that he "hates"
everything lovely that moves him and would requite his loss. Toward evening the speaker welcomes the oblivion of night, and prays for extinction.
The ironic frustration of this misdirected prayer is a turning point. Night,
wiser and stronger than day, gives the speaker all that's past in "sheer abun-
dance. / Unharmed by hostile time, pure, free, and whole," in the form of
dreams. However, "in the dead of night," like so many dreamers of poetic

---

[55] For the German text, "Vergangenheit," see *Von Guten Mächten: Gebete und Gedichte*, ed. J. C.
Hampe (Munich: Chr. Kaiser, 1976), pp. 8–12, at 8. Cf. *DBWE*, 8, pp. 418–21 for textual notes
and variant translation.

[56] "Ich möchte den Duft deines Wesens einatmen, / ihn einsaugen, in ihm bleiben, / wie an
einem heissen Sommertag schwere Blüten die Bienen zu Gast laden," *Gebete und Gedichte*, p. 11. Cf.
*DBWE*, 8, p. 419 n. 3, indicating that the original manuscript text read *Busen* (bosom) for *Wesens*.

[57] English text from *DBWE*, 8, pp. 420–21.

tradition, the speaker suddenly wakes to renewed anxiety and fear that the past has escaped again; therefore he prays. Finally the speaker is promised (by another voice) that his life's most vital part will be restored by his gratitude for the past and by his penitence too.[58] This intrusive voice urges the speaker to learn from past signs of God's help so that he may hope and pray for further signs in the present and future. There is no further comment, the poem thus concludes by endorsing the wisdom of this new external voice. The poem is a record of the speaker's agony for the sake of a testimony, or proof of his relief, for other readers. As Bonhoeffer wrote to each of his first readers, the crucial parts were the last lines of this disturbing but poignant poem. Bethge wisely did not discourage the prisoner, and his poetic output was continued.[59]

The integrity of the self is continually affirmed, clarified, and sustained in relationships with others. The foundation of the dialogue in letters between Bonhoeffer and Bethge was their life at the seminary Bonhoeffer had founded at Finkenwalde, and the memories they shared of their work, including discussion of the problems of human suffering, individual responsibility, and religion in a secular world.[60]

> It's really quite wonderful that the dialogue remains intact, and that I feel it's always the most fruitful I have. I feel that it's one of the laws of spiritual understanding that one's own thoughts, when they are understood by others, at the same time always undergo a transformation and liberation through the medium of the person. To this degree letters are really always "events," as you write.[61]

He asked Bethge to save his theological letters in case he might want to consult them later. "One writes some things more freely and more vividly in a letter than in a book, and often I have better thoughts in a conversation by correspondence than by myself" (p. 347, 8 July 1944). He had felt that his intellectual life was beginning "to dry up" until the correspondence with Bethge allowed that dialogue to resume (p. 160). The second poem, written for Bethge in August 1944, described the importance of friendship. In the friend who is "like a fortress" the "lonely" spirit finds "refuge and comfort and strengthening"; this consolation is liberating.[62] There are no bonds of

---

[58] Meditative prayer was also Philosophia's preparation for the Prisoner's cure in the *Consolation of Philosophy*; see bk. 3, m. 9.

[59] Cf. Philosophia reproving the muses of poetry, in verse, in her first metrum.

[60] Cf. *LPP*, p. 279, 30 April 1944, and *LPP*, p. 161, for coded references to shared memories.

[61] *LPP*, pp. 236–37, 24 March 1944. Cf. p. 223, 1 March 1944 to Bethge: "I'm living in a daily spiritual exchange with you; I can't read a book or write a paragraph without talking to you about it or at least asking myself what you would say about it"; and "after these long months without worship, penitence and eucharist and without the *consolatio fratrum*—once again be my pastor . . . and listen to me" (ibid., p. 128, 18 November 1943).

[62] *LPP*, p. 389; cf. *Gebete und Gedichte*, p. 28.

law to bind them "but counsel from one who is earnest in goodness / and faithful in friendship" promotes "brotherly freedom" (*Freiheit / und Menschlichkeit*). The ending is very personal: "I thought of you in silence and for long," at a moment of danger during an air raid. Later the speaker takes comfort from the idea that thus "danger . . . of every kind shall gently pass you by" (pp. 390–1). It was a consolation to Bonhoeffer to believe that, unlike himself, Bethge was blessed with good fortune and would be safe. He even teased (prophetically) that one day Bethge would be his biographer. Like Philosophia—Boethius's fantasy of another self who reintegrates the Prisoner's dispirited persona and guides him along his chosen path of resistance—Bethge would reconstitute and nurture another image of Dietrich Bonhoeffer. (Until his death in 2000 Bethge dominated the reception of Bonhoeffer's life and theology; he is also acknowledged warmly by later editors and scholars.)

This poem for Bethge reworked ideas articulated in contemporary letters. On 14 August, Bonhoeffer wrote a tribute for his friend's birthday:

> There is hardly anything that can make one happier than to feel that one counts for something with other people. What matters here is not numbers, but intensity. In the long run, human relationships are the most important thing in life. (*LPP*, p. 386)

This realization was one of the paradoxical benefits to accrue from the prison experience of psychological torture and loss. It has been shared by many prisoners, as Boethius had anticipated in *Consolation*, book 2. In "Sorrow and Joy" (*Glück und Unglück*), Bonhoeffer reflected that whereas "Joy is rich in fears; / Sorrow has its sweetness"; both emotions "transfigure" those who encounter them. Everyone is curious about life, "peering / into the portent," but when sorrow is drawn "most of our kind . . . turn away from the drama, disillusioned, / uncompassionate (*enttäuscht und gelangweilt*)." Then the true devotion of "loyal hearts" comes into its own, for "loyal hearts can change the face of sorrow."[63] The pity is that they are so rare.

Bonhoeffer's dialogue with the past was also conducted through his reading. He read the Bible every day but while in prison developed a particular interest in the historical books of the Old Testament, which had an impact on his theology and last poems. He also enjoyed the novels of Adalbert Stifter (1805–68) that he found in the prison library. Such diverse reading matter provided different kinds of stimulus and comfort for the intellectual prisoner. In June 1943 he told his parents that he read some Stifter "almost

---

[63] *LPP*, pp. 334–35; cf. *Gebete und Gedichte*, pp. 13–14: "Glück ist voll Schauer, / Unglück voll Süsse." *DBWE*, 8, p. 44, translates the title as "Fortune and Calamity."

every day": "In this atmosphere, there's something very comfortable about the sheltered and sequestered world of his characters—he's old fashioned enough only to portray likeable people—and it focuses one's thoughts on the things that really matter in life" (*LL*, p. 22, cf. *LPP*, p. 50). This distant past of the novelist's creation offered not only a consoling escape from contemporary reality but also a restorative vision of the values that had sustained a better, albeit imaginary world. (By contrast, as Bonhoeffer also noted, he "could not get on at all with Rilke.") In their different ways, Boethius and Bonhoeffer both concluded that what really mattered most in life came from good, loving human relationships. And, in prison, each writer returned to this foundation for all practical moral philosophy, or ethics, in various forms of dialogue between self and other, and between personal and cultural memories in construction of past and present.

## DIALOGUE WITH THE PAST

The cumulative evidence of his reading and writing confirms Bonhoeffer's statement that the daily preoccupation of his life in prison was "dialogue with the past." By this Bonhoeffer, like Boethius, seems to have meant (in part) his personal history—"the attempt to hold on to it and recover it, and above all, the fear of losing it" (*LPP*, p. 319). This recovery was an obvious way for prisoners to preserve their integrity and personal identity and, for Boethius, Bonhoeffer, and other intellectuals with vocational purposes for their writing in prison, a means to guide a wider public. It was therefore also a vital medium for planning reconstruction in the future. In his isolation Bonhoeffer found himself "forced to live from the past" and engage in creative dialogue with it. Yet, as he wrote to his parents at Christmas, the stability, richness, and one's attitude to the past as a shared cultural tradition, rather than a fleeting personal memory, were decisive factors in being able to continue living in the present.

> It's not till such times as these that we realize what it means to possess a past and a spiritual inheritance independent of changes of time and circumstance. The consciousness of being borne up by a spiritual tradition that goes back for centuries gives one a feeling of confidence and security in the face of all passing strains and stresses. (*LPP*, p. 165, 17 December 1943)

The tender feelings this evoked belonged "to the better and nobler part of mankind," but were no solution to the problems of the present.

The problem for the ethical theologian dedicated to defending these cultural and spiritual traditions was how to make them meaningful in the context of contemporary violence and uncertainty. He contrasted the stability and fulfillment that he believed had once been possible for his parents' generation with the present situation, yet hoped that "this very fragmentariness may, in fact, point towards a fulfilment beyond the limits of human achievement; I have to keep that in mind, particularly in view of the death of so many of the best of my former pupils," more than thirty of whom had already been killed during the war.[64] He concluded that it was the duty of men of faith to resist the "pressure of outward events," which "like bombs falling on houses" split lives into fragments, and to hold fast to the heritage of the past as a key to "building" the future. This building metaphor was significant for Bonhoeffer's future plans.[65] The Christian and "cultured" man cannot split up his life, for "the common denominator must be sought both in thought and in a personal and integrated attitude to life. The man who allows himself to be torn into fragments by events and by questions has not passed the test for the present and the future."[66]

## DELIVERANCE IN THOUGHT

Bonhoeffer escaped external pressures, and safeguarded his integrity through his life of the mind that transcended actual experience. After a few hours absorbed in writing he would often be surprised to find himself back in his cell.[67] "What a deliverance it is to be able to *think* and thereby remain multi-dimensional"; this metaphor of paradoxical deliverance emphasizes relief from negative self-centeredness, or "a single dimension," by contrast with the "polyphony" of the life of imagination and sympathy for others.[68] He acknowledged that his longing to be outside on light, warm evenings (when he could picture himself sitting with Maria by the water in Bethge's garden) was self-torture causing physical pain. "If I were not so 'reasonable,'" he admitted ironically, "I might do something foolish. . . . So I take refuge in thinking, in writing letters, in delighting in your good fortune" (p. 312). Being multidimensional provided an escape from the personal suffering of being torn into fragments, yet also a preliminary to understanding suffering theologically. He distinguished between the inclusive "wholeness of an in-

[64] *LPP*, p. 215, 20 February 1944.
[65] Ibid., cf. p. 219.
[66] *LPP*, p. 200 to Bethge; cf. fragmentation simile in "The Past," and the baptism sermon that he wrote for the Bethges' son (*LPP*, p. 297).
[67] To his parents, 31 August 1943; *LPP*, pp. 100–101.
[68] To Bethge, May 1944; *LPP*, p. 311.

dependent existence" that accommodated "many different dimensions of life at the same time" and being "dissolved into fragments." As the prisoner explained to Bethge,

> One gradually learns to acquire an inner detachment from life's menaces—although "acquire detachment" seems too negative, formal, artificial and stoical; and it's perhaps more accurate to say that we assimilate these menaces into our life as a whole. (*LPP*, p. 310, 29 May 1944)

He had noticed that one of the effects of fear on his fellow prisoners was a resurgence of superstition. Use of the expression "keep your fingers crossed" during air raids, he commented, indicated that "people do not want to feel alone in times of danger, but to be sure of some invisible presence."[69] "Touch wood," he rationalized as "a recollection of the wrath of God on the *hubris* of man, a metaphysical, and not merely a moral reason for humility." But in all such phrases he found no trace of eschatology. This intrigued him, confirming his earlier emphasis on the ethics of a "this-worldly" Christianity. In particular, he worried that a sense of powerlessness in a "boundary situation" had induced a state of panic in the prisoners, which troubled yet also offended him. In one of the earliest uncensored letters to Bethge he had described an air raid. "People here talk quite openly about how frightened they were." At first he had not known how to react to them because from his own patrician background he assumed that "fright is surely something to be ashamed of . . . [While] naïve frankness can be quite disarming . . . even so, there's a cynical, I might almost say ungodly, frankness, the kind that breaks out in heavy drinking and fornication, and gives the impression of chaos. I wonder whether fright is not one of the *pudenda*, which ought to be concealed" or restricted to the confessional.[70] His reasons included a concern that "it might easily involve a certain amount of exhibitionism; and *a fortiori* there is no need to play the hero," implying that such an act degraded faith and reason, besides obscuring truth. Yet, this consciousness of role-playing and attention-seeking, even in adversity, also stimulated a poem about his own image, "Who am I?," sent to Bethge in July 1944, that continued discussion of these concerns in the letter written before Christmas 1943, where he had described the strain of his imprisonment and confessed "things here are revolting." This consciousness caused him to reassess his true identity:

> I often wonder who I really am: the one always cringing in disgust, going to pieces at these hideous experiences here, or the one who whips himself

---

[69] *LPP*, p. 231, 9 March 1944.
[70] *LPP*, p. 146, 27 November 1943.

into shape, who on the outside (and even to himself) appears calm, cheerful, serene, superior, and lets himself be applauded for this charade (*Theaterleistung*)—or is it real? (*DBWE*, 8 (2010), p. 221)

Unable to resolve such questions, he acknowledged that, although he knew less than ever about himself after eight months in prison, there was "something more at stake than self-knowledge" which is the object of many prisoners' writing. The urgency of this ambition to go beyond self-knowledge in the service of others (by offering guidance and understanding, based on personal experience) distinguishes the prison writings of Boethius, Bonhoeffer, Thomas More, and Gramsci as political and philosophical defenders of civilization. Yet each of them was also conscious of his self-impression constructed in writing.

Around this time Bonhoeffer was planning an essay, "What is 'speaking the truth'?," because he recognized that "anyone who tells the truth cynically is lying."[71] He wanted to use experience of the horrors of war, to "make them bear fruit, and not just shake them off." The political and ethical problem was how to create the foundations "for making it possible to reconstruct the life of the nations, both spiritually and materially, on Christian principles."[72] Unbeknown to him, constructions of his Christian identity (as early as 1945, some said a "martyr") and as a theologian in prison were to be important in this rebuilding.[73] Meanwhile, he knew that even within the prison his authority as pastor and theologian was based on public perceptions of his actions that belied his experience: Which was true? The speaker in the poem "Who am I?" tests these different, external views of himself and contrasts these images of a calm, confident, authoritative, and even cheerful self with what he knows subjectively.

Am I really all that which other men tell of?
Or am I only what I know of myself,
restless and longing and sick, like a bird in a cage
struggling for breath (*nach Lebensatem*), as though hands were
    compressing my throat,
yearning for colours, for flowers, for the voices of birds
thirsting for words of kindness, for neighbourliness (*guten Worten,*
    *menschlicher Nähe*),
trembling with anger at despotisms and petty humiliation,

---

[71] *LPP*, p. 163, 15 December 1943. Cf. Socrates and Boethius, p. 24 above.
[72] *LPP*, p. 146, 27 November 1943.
[73] See R. Niebuhr, "The Death of a Martyr," *Christianity and Crisis*, 25 (1945), 6–7, quoted by F. Burton Nelson, "The Life of Dietrich Bonhoeffer," in Gruchy, *Cambridge Companion to Dietrich Bonhoeffer*, p. 22.

tossing in expectation of great events,
powerlessly trembling for friends at an infinite distance,
too weary and empty to pray, to think, to work,
faint, and ready to say farewell to it all?[74]

The poem ends without resolving these questions about the speaker's identity, yet it affirms that they are irrelevant because, whoever he may be, God
knows he belongs to him. Although the lonely prisoner's questions and reported actions articulate the values that help to promote his ethical concerns for others, the question whether there might be within himself the
composure he associates with real faith is left open. This evasion was also
conventional doctrine and might have been affirmed to comfort the poet
and Bethge, his reader, pastor, and confessor. The authority of the spiritual
message of the poem derives from its testimony to lived experience, in
extremis.

Bonhoeffer's concern as a theologian was how far the meaning of the
human suffering of one man on the cross had been pushed to the margins of
life, only to be recalled incoherently and superstitiously in the secular modern world during crises. Reading a book on physics, lent by his brother, made
Bonhoeffer realize that it was wrong to use any form of religion as a "stop-
gap" for the incompleteness of human knowledge. The frontiers of that
knowledge were being pushed back all the time, which only led those who
sought human and physical answers to life's moral problems to see God continually in retreat. From his observations Bonhoeffer regarded this as morally and ethically dangerous. His experiences as a prisoner helped to clarify
his conviction that

> God is no stop-gap; he must be recognized at the centre of life, not when
> we are at the end of our resources; it is his will to be recognized in life,
> and not only when death comes; in health and vigour, and not only in
> suffering; in our activities, and not only in sin.

Religious faith should thus provide an ethical core by which to live all of
life. The ground for this, he explained to Bethge, "lies in the revelation of
God in Jesus Christ. He is the centre of life, and he certainly didn't 'come' to
answer our unsolved problems."[75] A month later Bonhoeffer articulated another aspect of the purpose of this revelation. His reading of the Bible had
taken on new significance in prison. He was intrigued to realize that hardly
anyone is punished in the Old Testament by loss of personal freedom. (He'd

---

[74] *LPP*, pp. 347–48 (adapted); cf. *DBWE*, 8, p. 459; *Gebete und Gedichte*, p. 15; sent to Bethge
9 July 1944. Cf. Boethius's personal myth constructed in his own writing.
[75] *LPP*, p. 312, 29 May 1944.

never thought about it before.) He was most impressed that religion in the Hebrew Bible was a daily, practical, real encounter with the will of God rather than a "boundary" experience.[76] Like the prisoner Boethius, Bonhoeffer was not moved to eschatology. "Belief in the Resurrection," he wrote to Bethge, "is not the 'solution' of the problem of death. God's 'beyond' is not the beyond of our cognitive faculties." He came to believe that God is rather "beyond in the midst of our life," in our ethical relations with others: "That is how it is in the Old Testament, and in this sense we still read the New Testament far too little in the light of the Old."[77]

One further consequence of this insight was his conclusion that the (Jewish) faith embodied in the Hebrew Bible was not a religion of redemption since the redemptions referred to there are "*historical*, i.e. on *this* side of death," rather than transcendental.[78] "It's true," he wrote to Bethge, "that Christianity has always been regarded as a religion of redemption," but he questioned whether this was not "a cardinal error" that separated Christ from Hebraic faith and, instead, interpreted him in terms of myths about redemption from death found in other religions. Because he recognized that Jesus was a Jew, he began to think that Christianity's emphasis on a world beyond death was contrary to the Gospels and St. Paul. From his prison cell, in the midst of air raids, uncertainties, and panic, Bonhoeffer decided: "This world must not be prematurely written off." Instead, he concluded, the Christian hope of resurrection should send "a man back to his life on earth in a wholly new way."

> Like Christ himself ("My God, why hast thou forsaken me?") he must drink the earthly cup to the dregs, and only in his doing so is the crucified and risen Lord with him, and he crucified and risen with Christ. (*LPP*, pp. 336–37; cf. Ps 22:1 and Mark 15:34)

This statement is the core of Bonhoeffer's development of his theology of the cross in prison; it strengthened his commitment to drink the dregs of his own earthly cup with a radiance of spirit that impressed those who witnessed his final days.[79] In another letter to Bethge, dated 18 July 1944 (two days before the attempt on Hitler's life), Bonhoeffer clarified this theme:

---

[76] Cf. *LPP*, p. 134, 20 November 1943.

[77] *LPP*, p. 282, 30 April 1944.

[78] *LPP*, p. 336, 27 June 1944.

[79] For description of Bonhoeffer's movements and the pastoral care he administered to his companions in their final days, see Bethge, *Dietrich Bonhoeffer*, pp. 820–23; and, quoting S. Payne Best (*The Venlo Incident* [London: Hutchinson, 1951], pp. 171ff.), at p. 823. Cf. "Bonhoeffer in his skylit cell / bleached by the flares' candescent fall, / pacing out his own citadel, / restores the broken themes of praise, / encourages our borrowed days, / by logic of his sacrifice. / Against wild reasons of the state / his words are quiet but not too quiet. / We hear too late or not too late." Geoffrey Hill, "Christmas Trees," in *Collected Poems* (Harmondsworth: Penguin Books, 1985), p. 171.

Jesus asked in Gethsemane, "Could you not watch with me one hour?" That is a reversal of what the religious man expects from God. Man is summoned to share in God's sufferings at the hands of a godless world. . . . It is not the religious act that makes the Christian, but participation in the sufferings of God in the secular life. (*LPP*, p. 361)

The day after the failed bomb plot, he explained to Bethge about how, during his year in prison, he had "come to know and understand more and more the profound this-worldliness of Christianity" and, by extension, the moral and ethical prerogatives this entailed: "The Christian is not a *homo religiosus* but simply a man, as Jesus was a man—in contrast, shall we say, to John the Baptist," a separate individual (p. 369). This letter is marked by an unusual clarity and confidence of tone; it suggests that Bonhoeffer had found what he had earlier called the ground lost from under their feet as contemporary German Christians (pp. 3–4). By living "this-worldliness," in the philosophical and ethical "religionless Christianity" he came to evolve in prison, Bonhoeffer believed that "we throw ourselves completely into the arms of God, taking seriously, not our own sufferings, but those of God in the world"—as once the apostles had been asked, but failed, to do. This empathy in participation and watching with "Christ in Gethsemane" was what Bonhoeffer described as "faith." It defined how one became truly human and, more particularly, a Christian or disciple: an active follower of "Jesus who is there only for others," in this "world come of age" that had lost its innocence forever. Under the pressure of the moment and expecting death, he said goodbye to Bethge telling him how he was "glad to have been able to learn this" and that he knew he'd "been able to do so only along the road that I've travelled" (p. 370). These insights, this paradox of gain by loss, had come to him solely as a result of his experiences as a prisoner.

## BEYOND TRANSCENDENCE

Systematic study of the Bible had sharpened Bonhoeffer's focus on the self-lessness of the best human beings. He also found it emphasized his fearful contemporaries' need to recover for themselves the humanity of Christ. Boethius had formulated his consolation of philosophy upon his Christian premise of the goodness of divine providence without reference to Christ. Bonhoeffer's ethical concerns in a period of violent cultural and political transitions led him to formulate his theology in the widest possible terms. Bonhoeffer sought to promote what he called (paradoxically) a "religionless Christianity." In the intimacy of his secret correspondence with Bethge, he derided the superficiality, ritualism, intolerance, and self-regard of what he called *homo religiosus*. So far as Bonhoeffer was concerned there was little to choose between the "hardened sinner" and the man of "bourgeois complacency," for "the one is as far from salvation as the other." "It is only by living completely in this world that one learns to have faith."[80]

A contemporary poem, "Night Voices in Tegel," gives life and form to this prison theology, showing how "participation in the being of Jesus" "is the experience of transcendence" that is expressed in relation to other people and "existence for others."[81] The voices the speaker hears are the thoughts of fellow prisoners:[82]

> Their choir is silent (*Stumm ist ihr Chor*)
> But my ear is open wide (*weitgeöffnet mein Ohr*).

As this prisoner stares at the grey wall of his cell,

> Outside, a summer evening
> That does not know me
> Goes singing into the countryside.

The language of Bonhoeffer's poetry is often abstract and generalized, but such vivid images are affective and occasional or germane to the situation of a prisoner who interprets the outside world by its sounds. Within the poem, sequences of night voices alternate, like antiphonal chanting, with the speaker's voice. A prison is never silent, but too often its inmates are inarticulate.

> I hear my own soul tremble and heave.
> Nothing else?
> I hear, I hear
> The silent night thoughts
> Of my fellow sufferers asleep or awake,
> As if voices, cries,
> As if shouts for planks to save them.
> I hear the uneasy creak of the beds,
> I hear chains.

The speaker eavesdrops as

> sleepless men toss and turn,
> Who long for freedom and deeds of wrath.

---

[80] *LPP*, p. 341, 30 June 1944; p. 369, 21 July 1944.
[81] *LPP*, p. 381, "Outline for a Book."
[82] See *LPP*, pp. 349–56. The German is in rhyming couplets; cf. *Gebete und Gedichte*, pp. 16–22.

When at grey dawn sleep finds them
They murmur in dreams of their wives and children.

He follows the dreams and thoughts of young and old prisoners of the wider
world beyond his actual prison, imagining that he hears them.

Night and silence.
Only the steps and cries of the guards.
Do you hear how in the silent house
It quakes, cracks, roars
When hundreds kindle the stirred-up flame of their hearts?

At midnight "howling, evil dogs" frighten him: actual dogs guarding the
prison as well as metaphorical ones.

The wretched noise
Divides a poor yesterday
From a poor today.
What can it matter to me
Whether one day turns into another,
One that could have nothing new, nothing better
Than to end quickly like this one?
I want to see the turning of the times (*die Wende der Zeiten*),

which will come with the ringing of new bells to restore justice, peace, freedom. The poet knows the bomb plot is primed:

Atonement is near (*Sühne naht*).
. . .
Earth, flourish;
Man, become free, (*Mensch, werde frei*)
Be free!

This thought rouses the speaker to grasp something precious in anticipation
of an earthly redemption: "As if, from a sinking ship, I had sighted land."
The problem is "the impenetrable mass of darkness": night is not dark, "only
guilt is dark." The catalog of guilt and moral failings voiced by the accusers
who assail God's ear matches that in Bonhoeffer's summary description of
German society degenerated after ten years under Hitler.

'We accuse those who plunged us into sin,
Who made us share the guilt,
Who made us the witnesses of injustice,
In order to despise their accomplices.

(*Wir verklagen, die uns in Sünde stiessen,*
*die uns mitschuldig werden liessen,*
*die uns zu Zeugen des Unrechts machten,-*
*um den Mitschuldigen zu verachten.*)

'Our eyes had to see folly,
In order to bind us in deep guilt;
Then they stopped our mouths,
And we were as dumb dogs.[83]

'We learned to lie easily,
To be at the disposal of open injustice;
If the defenceless was abused,
Then our eyes remained cold.
. . .

'The once holy bonds uniting men (*Was Menschen einst heilig gebunden*)
Were mangled and flayed,
. . .

'We sons of pious races,
One-time defenders of right and truth,
Became despisers of God and man,
Amid hellish laughter.

'Yet though now robbed of freedom and honour,
We raise our heads proudly before men.
And if we are brought into disrepute,
Before men we declare our innocence (*vor Menschen sprechen wir selbst*
     *und frei*)

'Steady and firm we stand man against man (*Mann gegen Mann*);
As the accused we accuse!'

The prisoners claim that they are only sinners in the sight of God and that
what they have done was weakness not wickedness:

'Afraid of suffering and poor in deeds,
We have betrayed thee before men (*haben wir Dich vor den Menschen*
     *verraten*).
We saw the lie raise its head.
And we did not honour the truth.

'We saw our brethren in direst need,
And feared only our own death

[83] Cf. Isaiah 56:10 for this simile indicating ineffectual moral guardians of the nation.

We come before thee as men (*Männer*),
As confessors of our sins.'

Their collective prayer is to "see the day break" and until then to "keep us in quiet patience."

'Brother, till the night be past,
Pray for me!'

At the climax of this litany of failure, the collective voice of the accused reveals itself as singular and in need of his brothers' prayers.

When the first light of dawn comes into his cell, the speaker hears a man being taken away to execution. He offers this "brother" support in sympathetic anticipation of their common and inevitable end.

Control yourself (*Dich*), brother; soon you will have finished it, soon,
    soon.
I hear you stride bravely and with proud step.
You no longer see the present, you see the future.
I go with you, brother, to that place,
And I hear your last word:
"Brother, when the sun turns pale for me,
Then live for me!"

The biblical context is always the image of one man's agony in the Garden of Gethsemane that was completed on the cross (cf. St. John 19:30). The agonist who rouses himself from moral torpor to hear the night voices of the prison is another brother of suffering mankind and a condemned prisoner. In the morning Bonhoeffer's speaker addresses his Brother, perhaps Jesus as the brother of mankind, or perhaps a contemporary reader and disciple of truth—his fellow conspirators—seeking atonement for sinful complacency:

Brother, till after the long night
Our day breaks
We stand fast!

In the beginning of the poem the speaker had urged himself with the imperative "stand fast!" but at the end there is a promise (made in common with others) to endure until a certain time. The brotherhood of mankind is not merely a biblical premise; and in spite of several echoes from the Psalms (as well as some generalized symbolism in the imagery of night and day), this poem is not overtly religious in a traditional sense. It is, as Bonhoeffer was striving to articulate in other forms (and as Boethius had done), an ethical and political statement in a theological context, and essentially hopeful: if we resist and stand fast, our day will break.

By contrast, at the end of another poem composed about the same time, "Stations on the Road to Freedom," where the title alludes to the Easter liturgy, the speaker faces death. Yet, in traditional theological terms (shared by Boethius and Bonhoeffer as prison poets), this death is invoked as the means to freedom. As death liberates the soul from its existential imprisonment, it also offers mortals the revelation of that beyond which remains hidden in earthly existence. The "stations" on this road are Discipline, Action, Suffering, but none of these alone; finally Death reveals Freedom in the Lord. By the time he wrote these verses, Bonhoeffer knew that the July plot had failed, Hitler's retribution was looming, and in "daring to do what is right" (as prescribed in his description for Action), he was likely to find freedom only in death: "thou greatest of feasts on the journey to freedom eternal" (*LPP*, pp. 370–71). A week later he wrote to Bethge to clarify his ideas:

> In suffering, the deliverance consists in our being allowed to put the matter out of our own hands into God's hands. In this sense death is the crowning of human freedom. Whether the human deed is a matter of faith or not depends on whether we understand our suffering as an extension of our action and a completion of freedom. I think that is very important and very comforting. (*LPP*, p. 375, 28 July 1944)

Bonhoeffer had recently been reading Dostoyevsky's prison literature, *Notes from the House of the Dead* (1860), which had impressed upon him further the human need for hope and certainty. Certainty for Bonhoeffer was not a matter of logic or intellectual understanding; he did not put his faith in reason. Yet Bonhoeffer exhibits a trust in the logic of a good life lived well in freedom of conscience: righteousness. (The Old Testament, he noted, does not speak about saving souls or a personal salvation after death, but rather about God's promise and its fulfillment in the world.) The spiritual confidence that Bonhoeffer seems to have found in the political catastrophe, as he approached the end, was founded on traditional views of the authority of the Bible as the historic record of God's dealings with humankind.[84]

Two late poems, both written after the failure of the conspiracy, use Old Testament analogues to explore his situation. "The Death of Moses" and "Jonah" were smuggled out of the prison to Maria von Wedemeyer. In early October 1944, when documents relating to the plot to overthrow Hitler were discovered, Bonhoeffer gave up his escape plan fearing retribution

---

[84] See further Henning Graf Reventlow, *The Authority of the Bible and the Rise of the Modern World*, tr. J. Bowden (London: SCM Press, 1984).

against his brother, two brothers-in-law, and Bethge, who had also just been arrested. Soon after writing "Jonah," Bonhoeffer was moved to a bunker at Gestapo headquarters, Prinz-Albrecht Strasse, and his poem's themes of impossible escape and self-sacrifice became the reality he had predicted. (Paul von Hase had already been hanged.)

Bonhoeffer's "Moses, the prophet," stands on the mountain overlooking the Promised Land: "Steady is his gaze and tired his hand" as he faces death, acknowledging that he will not enter this land because he is the Lord's "faithless" servant having disobeyed him (by using force to strike the rock to provide the waters of life for his people, instead of speaking to it as commanded by God). In these final biblical subjects, the theme of the servant of God paying for his specific disobedience has strong personal resonance. Bonhoeffer's Moses, the great redeemer of Israel from slavery, faithlessness, and the distractions of false gods, sees his people "march with freedom" and accepts with pride and regret that he will not share in their future nation building:

> You who punish sin and forgive readily,
> God, you know I have loved this people steadily,
> That I bore its shame and sacrifices
> and saw its salvation—that suffices (*und sein Heil geschaut—das ist genug*).
> Hold me fast! for I lose my stave (*mir sinkt der Stab*)
> faithful God, prepare for me my grave (*bereite mir mein Grab*).[85]

He accepts his destiny, hopeful that, though he bears the guilt of his own sin, he is also consoled by the forgiveness to be granted to his people in their new promised land.

In the covering note to Maria attached to his last Tegel poem, on the theme of Jonah, Bonhoeffer reminded her (in a coded way) of his response to their situation: "The reading for today [i.e., Job 5:12: "He frustrates the devices of the crafty, so that their hands achieve no success"] is very fine" (*Love Letters*, p. 225). The bomb plot had failed, but this had to be accepted as God's inscrutable will. Bonhoeffer's poem drew upon only those elements of Jonah's story relevant to his situation; it begins in the midst of the crisis at sea, as Jonah attempts to escape his mission to warn the sinful people of Nineveh to repent, and the ship in which he flees is struck by a terrible storm. Everyone is in danger, but no one imagines that this situation is chance.

[85] *DBWE*, 8, pp. 531–41, at p. 540 (adapted with reference to E. Robertson). For the German text, cf. *Gebete und Gedichte*, p. 30.

In fear of death they cried aloud and clinging fast,
to wet ropes straining on the battered deck,
they gazed in stricken terror at the sea
that now, unchained in sudden fury, lashed the ship.[86]

Jonah's pagan shipmates ask for their gods' help, or for some sign to reveal who has offended "by secret sin, by breach of oath, or heedless blasphemy, or murder," thereby bringing everyone "to disaster ... to make a paltry profit for his pride [*um seines Stolzes ärmlichen Gewinnes!*]." (The biblical Jonah was not accused of pride or murder, but Bonhoeffer knew that he would be, and had accepted years before that these sins were spiritual risks he had to undertake.) There is no casting of lots to determine the culprit because Bonhoeffer's Jonah confesses:

> Behold,
> I sinned before the Lord of hosts. My life is forfeit.
> Cast me away! My guilt must bear the wrath of God (*Mein ist die Schuld*);
> the righteous shall not perish with the sinner!

At first Jonah's shipmates refused to sacrifice him and made strenuous efforts to save the ship. But Bonhoeffer's Jonah is immediately cast away "with hands that knew no weakness" (*mit starken Händen*) and as an "offender from their midst"; whereupon, "The sea stood still." The story of Bonhoeffer's Jonah ends at this poignant moment of confession, self-sacrifice, and concern for the righteous survivors' future. Continuation of the biblical story in Bonhoeffer's poem would have suggested redemption for Jonah this side of death, after confinement in the belly of the whale; but here there is no redemption for the disobedient preacher whose last hope is that his confession and self-sacrifice may save his shipmates.

The stories of Moses and Jonah traditionally prefigured the doctrinal significance of the life of Christ, but Bonhoeffer made no reference to these interpretations. Neither did he submit rashly to his and his fellow conspirators' final sentence of death. Bonhoeffer's resistance and canny equivocation under interrogation continued at least until his summary trial, hours before the end; in this action too he sought to protect other lives besides his own. At Christmas 1944 he wrote his last surviving poem in the squalid Gestapo cellars where he was held with surviving conspirators as evidence against them was gathered. It has become a familiar hymn in German schools and keeps his name as a martyr alive for succeeding generations: "By Powers of

---

[86] There are several published English translations of "Jonah"; the text in *LPP*, pp. 398–99 echoes the language and rhythms of the English Bible; cf. *Gebete und Gedichte*, p. 31.

Good" (*Von guten Mächten*). The tone is calm, gracious, and faithful. Finally, there is nothing more to be done: "The old year still torments our hearts, unhastening; / the long days of our sorrow still endure," yet he and his fellows are safe in God's hands, "protected with consolation dear" and confidently ready to "wait for come what may," after death if need be: "When we are wrapped in silence most profound." If they are offered the "bitter cup, resembling / sorrow, filled to the brim and overflowing," they will take it "thankfully, without trembling." But if they are granted "joy of this world and bright sunshine," they will once more dedicate themselves to God, and "in our minds we will past times relive" (*dann wolln wir des Vergangenen gedenken, / und dann gehört Dir unser Leben ganz*).[87] It is clear that the speaker in the poem, and his company, only earn the right to surrender to God's kindly powers once they have exhausted all other possible means of action and Christian discipleship by living for others. Within weeks, Bonhoeffer was moved again to a dungeon at Buchenwald. In the message of comfort he had written for Bethge's birthday, he urged him to persevere in quiet meditation on the life, sayings, actions, sufferings, and death of Jesus in order to learn both what God promises and what he fulfills in the world.

> It is certain that we may always live close to God and in the light of his presence, and that such living is an entirely new life for us; that nothing is then impossible for us, because all things are possible with God; that no earthly power can touch us without his will, and that danger and distress can only drive us closer to him.... In these turbulent times we repeatedly lose sight of what really makes life worth living.... But the truth is that if this earth was good enough for the man Jesus Christ, if such a man as Jesus lived, then, and only then, has life a meaning for us. (*LPP*, p. 391)

To the end the prisoner was seeking a meaning for life in an ethical religion for turbulent times. He based his ethics on faith in action and on understanding the historic biblical record of the will of God. These last surviving letters written as a prisoner to Bethge were Bonhoeffer's personal and professional testament as a theologian and a friend. Like the message of Boethius's Prisoner, it was mediated to the remnant of the civilized world, to defend its values and mitigate its turbulence, by the family and friends to whom it was first addressed. Their testimonies have subsequently been received by readers as warranted by the personal experience of exemplary, philosophical prisoners in fulfillment of their vocations in life.

---

[87] *LPP*, pp. 400–401, and *Gebete und Gedichte*, p. 32. Cf. *DBWE*, 8, pp. 548–50 with notes.

# CHAPTER 2

# Creative Dialogues with Textual Partners, Past and Present

Much of the writing produced in prison by European intellectuals originated as reactions to extraordinary crises, yet, as we have seen, their various forms of resistance to these situations demonstrate their clarity and rigor of approach to common concerns. The writer who is a prisoner because he or she is a writer and a humanist (of one sort or another) has a special claim on us. Such writers put their lives, liberty, and happiness at stake for ideas about how people should live. Thomas More and Antonio Gramsci would each have been appalled at the other's philosophy of life and conception of civilization—the author of *Utopia* was never a democrat and Gramsci's pan-European aspirations for a just society had little to do with More's idea of Christendom—but they would each have understood the other's practical policies for improving the quality of a civilized society composed of responsible individuals working together for the greater good. Both men stressed the importance of language skills, logical rigor in thinking, and a historical awareness of the institutions that were used to organize society. Both wrote urgent appeals to contemporary readers and called for unity against the trends they considered responsible for undermining their different conceptions of a best society. Gramsci advocated a tactical Popular Front against fascism as early as the mid 1920s. The strategic aim of all More's polemic against Protestantism was the restoration of the unity of Christendom. They continued to write and examine the problems of their day when each was imprisoned as a dangerous and seditious intellectual. Their determination to resist recent political changes that affected principles of government, and to protect their values by examining these principles afresh on historical and ideological grounds, led to martyrdom. This chapter demonstrates some of the similarities in the political and intellectual methods that generated their prison writing and helped to create their posthumous reputations.

These conceptual changes were partly owing to a shared heritage of classical learning that conditioned how their thought processes are reflected in their forms of expression. The mental habits of both polemicists were formed by their literary training in dialectic: they each made creative use of contrast rather than comparison or similitude. In prison these tendencies were exacerbated, as different forms of dialogue and dialectic enabled each writer to reassess the ideas for which he was being persecuted and to sustain his resolve and humanity in family relationships. Both men were able to defend their different conceptions of the best basis for society by continuing to evolve and articulate themes from their earlier polemical writings. In defending their own philosophies of life and formulating their ideas in writing, for the sake of others, each prisoner was also able to resist his oppressors' persecution. More's and Gramsci's prison writings therefore engage with existential themes and the politics of authority (historically defined), yet at the same time they reflect the warmth and importance of family relationships in the dialogic forms of personal correspondence. Their prison writings have been crucial to the political impact of their lives.

## Thomas More, *A Dialogue of Comfort against Tribulation*: A Political Guide to the Dilemmas of Religious Conscience (1534–35)

In the summer of 1535, the Catholic king of England, Henry VIII, shocked the intellectual and diplomatic elites throughout Europe by executing a frail, old man, John Fisher, bishop of Rochester, and Sir Thomas More, former Lord Chancellor of England and one of the best-known, learned laymen of his generation. They had conscientiously objected to an oath that implied recognition of Henry's new supremacy over the church in England. As is well known, Henry had hoped to secure the succession to the crown by remarrying and producing legitimate, male heirs. However, the pope (at that time under the political control of Catherine of Aragon's nephew, the Holy Roman Emperor Charles V), would not invalidate Henry's longstanding marriage to Catherine. So, after years of debate and procrastination the king had taken control of clerical jurisdiction, divorced his wife, and married a Lutheran, Anne Boleyn. Thomas More had made his disquiet at the submission of the English clergy to Henry's plans evident when he resigned the lord chancellorship in May 1532 and subsequently refused to attend Anne's coronation. As a former speaker of the House of Commons and privy councillor, More was reputed a wise and witty counselor of state; he was also a prolific author of spiritual guides for the laity and polemical works against Protestant schismatics whose ideas he saw spreading dissent and disorder in northern Europe. He had worked for reform of abuses in the English legal system, promoted humanistic learning, and defended the cultural and doctrinal traditions of the universal church, believing that the traditions of the church and the collective decisions of its leaders in an apostolic succession from St. Peter, should not be overturned by any short-term, personal, or national interests. Humanistic learning was about restoring the best of the past along the way to the kingdom of God in heaven. More was a radical reformer of English society conceived in terms of a consistent, conservative ideology.

His personality and principled opposition in resigning the highest public office made his stance difficult to ignore; anything he did attracted attention and was seen as a political act. The Act of Succession in March 1534 declared the king's new marriage "consonant to the laws of Almighty God" and required the whole population to "make a corporal oath" to support "the whole effects and contents of this present act."[1] When shown the wording of the oath by Archbishop Cranmer and a commission of privy councillors at Lambeth Palace in April 1534, More claimed that, while he would not deny Parliament's power to determine the succession, he could not swear to the oath without risk to his eternal soul. He was the only prominent layman who refused the oath, and even though it was required under duress (since refusal of the oath constituted misprision of treason), he would not equivocate and was regarded as dangerously obstinate.[2] He gave the commissioners no further explanation of his reasons. This created a political impasse that Cranmer tried to negotiate by suggesting to the king's secretary that More and Fisher should be offered a modified form of the oath. The king who was already exasperated with More in particular, would not allow this expedient, believing it would be taken as criticism of his marriage which had overturned papal jurisdiction. After More was imprisoned, a stalemate ensued until the Act of Supremacy explicitly made Henry head of the church in England; in November 1534, separate acts of attainder making More and Fisher *civiliter mortuus* (thereby denying their civil rights) were passed by Parliament. More knew from his career in common law that direct opposition to the supremacy would render him liable to a treason charge but that if he remained silent the crown would have no admissible evidence upon which to convict him of a capital charge. This premise was a crucial factor in all his prison writing.

During his fifteen months in the Tower of London before trial, More's writing was concentrated on devotional or spiritual didactic themes. His letters are very carefully worded; he consistently refused to discuss his decision

---

[1] For the background and details of the act, see S. E. Lehmberg, *The Reformation Parliament, 1529–1536* (Cambridge: Cambridge University Press, 1970), pp. 182–216; *"The King's Good Servant" Sir Thomas More 1477/8–1535*, ed. J. B. Trapp and H. Schulte Herbrüggen (London: National Portrait Gallery, 1977), p. 123; and Seymour Baker House's life of More in *The Oxford Dictionary of National Biography* (Oxford: Oxford University Press, 2004, and online updates).

[2] For reports of Henry's view that More had been "the occasion of much grudge and harm in the realm and that [he] had an obstinate mind," see St. Thomas More, *Selected Letters*, ed. E. F. Rogers (New Haven: Yale University Press, 1961, rpt. 1967), p. 250.

not to acknowledge Henry's supremacy, with anyone, and he repeated his own claims that he had not "meddled" with anyone's conscience by attempting to influence, or comment upon, their decisions. He also sent contemporary reports of oral interrogations to his family to safeguard his legal defense and personal reputation. At his trial, on 1 July 1535, he was convicted on the perjured evidence of the solicitor general, Richard Rich, who claimed that two weeks earlier when he had helped to remove More's books and papers from the Tower, the prisoner had treasonably rejected Henry's supremacy. His colleague, the attorney general, also interpreted More's silence as "a sure token and demonstration of a corrupt and perverse nature, maligning and repining against the statute."[3] After the guilty verdict was given, More dropped his defense strategy and repudiated the royal supremacy that had separated England from the universal church, the mystical body of Christ, and was (he claimed) "directly repugnant to the lawes of God and his holye Churche."[4] He told the court that history and the rest of the world agreed with him.[5] In his last reported words from the scaffold, More affirmed he remained the king's good servant but God's first. In 1935, the four hundredth anniversary of their martyrdom, Fisher and More were canonized. More is also now officially recognized by the Vatican as the patron saint of politicians.

## MORE'S ROLE IN THE POLITICS OF TUDOR THEOLOGY

More's prison writings show his spiritual concerns for himself and others but also make repeated reference to the contemporary political crisis facing the English church, albeit by coded, literary means. Biographical interpretations of his writing in prison tend to emphasize his fears of bodily suffering and determination not to depart from his conscientious resistance. Yet 1534 seems too late for such a careful, prescient man to have been working out his position in such extensive texts as he composed in the Tower.[6] A spiritual biographical emphasis also risks obscuring continuities between More's earlier guides to the laity, characterized by the traditional Christocentric piety

---

[3] *Oxford Dictionary of National Biography*, quoting Nicholas Harpsfield, ca. 1557, *The Life and Death of S[i]r Thomas Moore, Knight*, ed. E. V. Hitchcock, Early English Text Society, original series, 186 (London: Oxford University Press for EETS, 1932), p. 185.

[4] Ibid. p. 193.

[5] "And for one Councell or Parliament of yours (God knoweth what maner of one), I have all the councels made these thousande yeres. And for this one kingdome, I have all other Christian Realmes." Ibid. p. 196.

[6] G. E. Haupt (*Complete Works*, 13 [New Haven: Yale University Press, 1976], p. li) emphasized the "dominantly public nature" of More's *Treatise Upon the Passion* (datable early 1534), and *De Tristitia Christi* (unfinished by June 1535). For a study of More's prison writings, with a leaning toward spiritual biography, see L. L. Martz, *Thomas More: The Search for the Inner Man* (New Haven: Yale University Press, 1990). On fear, see further discussion.

he shared with friends at the London Charterhouse, and his last works. The *contemptus mundi* theme in his last written prayers had also been anticipated in his English writing on eschatology. The language of the spiritual life echoed devotional forms and wide-ranging themes found in biblical psalms that provided the nucleus for all Christian liturgies and in gospel accounts of the exemplary life and human suffering of Jesus.[7]

Like Boethius, he used the cultural resources of his prison writing to reach the widest audience in politically significant ways. The imitation of Christ, whose faith had been severely tested in adversity, was expected to encourage conscientious individuals to follow their master, into martyrdom if necessary. In prison More continued the creative dialogues he had had with biblical and contemporary textual partners. *A Dialogue of Comfort against Tribulation* sustains a teleological argument on the analogy of classical philosophy (as Boethius had done) to persuade More's readers to follow shared doctrinal and spiritual traditions so that they might resist tribulations of many kinds, especially religious persecution. In *De Tristitia Christi,* More engaged in intertextual dialogue with a late medieval harmonization of the gospel narratives and wrote in Latin—the language of the universal church—for an educated reader. Like Bonhoeffer he contemplated the human agony of Jesus, who, knowing he would soon suffer a horrible death by execution, had prayed alone in the Garden of Gethsemane. More's text addresses future readers in direct forms of speech that project the voice of an anonymous commentator.[8]

Finally, in the real-life dialogue of letters to his daughter, More drew upon the support of his loving family and reciprocated by offering them the consolation of his writing. This literary exchange refined his earlier creative performances of self-impression, and configured a mask of personality that was consistent with his existing reputation. In all these different kinds of writing, he never stopped looking out at the world beyond the Tower even as he thought about relinquishing it. More, no less than later Protestant martyrologists who knew his work, would have recognized the political and spiritual value of writing that articulated ideas about faith, fear, and persecution in the context of martyrdom. This chapter emphasizes his concern for others, his moral leadership in defending his religious conception of culture and society, and his doubts (like Bonhoeffer's), about playing the hero.

---

[7] On More and the Psalms, see R. Zim, *English Metrical Psalms: Poetry as Praise and Prayer, 1535–1601* (Cambridge: Cambridge University Press, 1987, rpt. 2011), pp. 82–85, and introduction to *Thomas More's Prayer Book: A Facsimile Reproduction of the Annotated Pages,* ed. L. L. Martz and R. S. Sylvester (New Haven: Yale University Press, 1969, rpt. 1976). On More's earlier spiritual works, see *Oxford Dictionary of National Biography* and references cited.

[8] Cf. "Reader, let us pause for a little at this point..." (*Complete Works,* 14, ed. C. H. Miller [New Haven: Yale University Press, 1976], p. 113).

*A Dialogue of Comfort*, written in the early part of his imprisonment, uses the fictional (yet historic) setting of the Hungarian city of Buda under siege (as it had been in 1526) by the army of Suleiman the Magnificent. The disputants in this *Dialogue*—Anthony, a sick old man, and his anxious young nephew Vincent—seem to represent different aspects of the same personality. There is little to distinguish either speaker beyond the decorous hierarchy implied by their respective ages and family relationship.[9] Anthony tends to cite learned sources, and Vincent prefers a pragmatic approach, yet they always argue from the same premises—an absolute Christian faith; they never agree to disagree, but the older man's confidence often seems qualified by his nephew's need for reassurance. Anthony does not have the unreserved superiority of Boethius's alter persona, Philosophia, and there is more give-and-take between More's speakers. Toward the end of the *Dialogue* their identities seem to converge, as Vincent is consoled by his uncle's "talking cure" while remaining troubled by his recognition that "al the pinch is in the pain" and "all the wisdom in this world can never so maister payne, but that payne wil be paynefull, spite of all the witte in thys world."[10] Anthony acknowledges that reason cannot change the nature of pain but can mitigate it by demonstrating its inevitability and relative transience. Finally, Vincent learns that consideration of the joys of heaven should make anyone threatened by the Great Turk "endure any paynfull deth." The explicit purpose of their dialogue, to offer comfort in tribulation, is confirmed when both speakers express their satisfaction in a religious consolation based on St. Paul's promise of the joys of heaven for those who earn them by suffering and by faithfully remembering the death of Jesus. If the Turk, as the devil's agent,

> threatten us with captivitie: let us tell him agayne, better is it to be thrall unto man a while for the pleasure of God, then by displeasing God, be perpetuall thralle unto the devill. If he thrette us with impriesonment: let us tell hym we will rather be mannes prisoners a whyle here in earth then by forsaking the fayth, be his prisoners ever in hel. (bk. 3, ch. 27, p. 353)

Vincent's last speech expresses his desire to put Anthony's advice into remembrance (by writing) and to translate it for others to read. Anthony's modest response is that Vincent should have consulted "some wyser man" if

---

[9] Cf. Boethius's merging of voices of Prisoner and Philosophia. In the prologue to book 2, Anthony apologizes for not letting Vincent take a larger part in their discussion, drawing attention to the decorum of the literary form that he cites as an analogy for their "real" conversation: "I wysshed . . . that wee hadde more often enterchanged words, and parted the talkyng betwene us, with ofter enterparlying upon your parte in suche maner, as learned menne use, beetwene the persones whom they devyse, disputing in their fayned dialogues" (Everyman ed., London: J. M. Dent, 1910, rpt. 1946), p. 183; i/j, u/v regularized. The Yale edition (*Complete Works*, 12, ed. L. L. Martz and F. Manley, 1976) is similarly based on the 1557 edition of More's *English Works*.

[10] Bk. 3, ch. 24 (Dent's Everyman ed., 1946, as earlier, and in quotations hereafter), p. 336.

that was his intention, but, until better men come along, he prays that God will breathe "his holy spyrite into the readers breste, whiche inwardely may teache hym in harte without whom, little avayleth all that all the mouthes of the worlde, were able to teache in mennes eares" (p. 356).

Boethius's therapeutic dialogue between his Prisoner and mentor, Philosophia, was a favorite precedent quoted by More.[11] Like Boethius, he claimed to shun the false consolations of flattering fortune and was skeptical that Henry would restore his favor:

Aye, flattering Fortune, look thou never so fair,
... smile,
As though thou wouldst my ruin all repair,
During my life thou shalt not me beguile!
Trust I shall God to enter in a while
His haven of Heaven.[12]

More's dialogue of comfort offers religious consolation, whereas Boethius chose philosophy, but they shared a faith in logic and a pragmatic political skepticism.

At the beginning of the *Dialogue,* the positions and attitudes of Anthony and Vincent suggest those of More and his daughter, Margaret Roper, reflected in their correspondence during More's imprisonment. The prologue focuses less on Anthony's tribulations (even though he is not expected to live much longer) than on Vincent's and on the family that will soon have to endure the Great Turk's religious persecution without Anthony's counsel. Vincent says:

here shal you leave of your kinred, a sorte of sory coumfortlesse Orphanes, to all whom, your good helpe, coumfort, and counsell, hath long been a great staye, not as an uncle unto some, and to some as one farther of kinne, but as though that unto us all, you had been a naturall father. (p. 126)

The text is playing with a punning emphasis on "father." For any reader aware of the writer's situation—in the first place, More's family—these references to "here" and "now" and "this country," all signify England in 1534 and More's situation, defying the king who would be supreme head of the

---

[11] See *Correspondence of Sir Thomas More,* ed. E. F. Rogers (Princeton: Princeton University Press, 1947), p. 519, for quotation from book 2, prose 6, in More's speech reported in letter 206 [August 1534]; cf. *Selected Letters,* pp. 146–47 for letter to his "school," including his own children [in 1521] recommending bk. 5, m. 5.

[12] More's verses written in the Tower, after a visit from Master Secretary Cromwell, according to William Roper's *Life of Sir Thomas More,* in *Two Early Tudor Lives,* ed. R. S. Sylvester and D. P. Harding (New Haven: Yale University Press, 1962), pp. 242–43.

church in England. As Vincent says, "there is no borne Turke so cruell to christen folke, as is ye false christen that falleth from the fayth" (p. 128).

The unity and welfare of Christendom had been the theme of More's polemic against the Reformation in his *Dialogue concerning Heresies* and *The Confutation of Tyndale's Answer*. Christendom was both a religious and political concept: it embraced the whole of the civilized world, representing a state ordained by God's law and guided by the heirs of St. Peter. More was concerned that reformers would break up this world order that had been sustained for fifteen hundred years. He saw little difference between those who denied the doctrine of the real presence in the sacrament and those who had betrayed the historic figure of Jesus in the Garden of Gethsemane. In the *Dialogue of Comfort*, Anthony and Vincent also lament the disunity of Christendom and pour scorn on such doctrines as salvation by faith alone.[13] Anthony implies that in the past he would have disputed with the "newe men" who deny that penance is a sacrament, but now he is too old to study their arguments. Nevertheless, he assures Vincent that the Bible "is verye playne agaynste them, and the whole corps of Chrystendome in everye Christen regyon . . . and al the olde holy doctours have ever more taught agaynste them, and all the olde holye enterpretours, have construed the scripture agaynst them" (bk. 2, ch. 7, pp. 196–97). So it is unlikely that these new men are right and everyone else has misunderstood the matter, but if they are not wrong and have found an easy way to heaven, without the sacrament of penance, then (Anthony concludes), "I am not he that wyl envye theyr good happe. But surelye counsayle dare I gyve no man, to adventure that waie with them" (p. 197). Anthony believes they are damned, and talking to them about the comfort of penance in tribulation is useless. The situation of Anthony and Vincent living on the edge of civilization, under threat of persecution, reflects Protestant threats to that concept of Christendom, which More discussed in his other Tower works (especially *De Tristitia Christi*) and had defended in polemic since 1523.

However, the text is not such a simple allegory as its early pages imply. The *Dialogue* refers explicitly to many different kinds of tribulation, and More cannot be identified exclusively with Anthony's voice, even though the text flirts with their association in several places.[14] The message of the

---

[13] See bk. 1, ch. 12, where Anthony notes that "some men have of late brought up some such opinions" and spread them abroad, bringing Christianity into disrepute, but they disagree among themselves and change their minds, so: "Stryve wyl I not with them for thys matter now" and he cites the beliefs of "all Chrysten people" for the past thousand years to contradict them instead (Dent's Everyman ed., pp. 151–52). Vincent also mentions that many deny the existence of purgatory.

[14] Anthony adopts the punning self-deprecation associated with More's literary personae in ear-

text is comprehensive, as well as occasional and particular—hence the credibility of Vincent's elaborate promise to publish Anthony's counsel. As John Fowler explained to readers of the 1573 edition,

> The invention ... of the Authour seemeth to respect some particular cases. . . . But under this particular case of Turks persecution he generally comprehendeth al kinds of afflictions and persecutions both of body and mind, that may any way be suffred.[15]

The convolutions in the original title's claim that it was "made by an Hungarien in Laten, and translated oute of Laten into Frenche, and oute of Frenche into Englishe," were intended to appease (and possibly ridicule) a censorious reader, yet they also imply and advertise its wider appeal.

Conflict, challenge, opposition, defiance, and an occasional *reductio ad absurdum* characterized More's habitual modes of creativity. He would have practiced adversarial techniques of extended debate and written forms of argument from his school days. These were then honed in his legal career and in Parliament. The ordinary sense of "dialectic" in More's lifetime was logic, or formal verbal reasoning. Its purpose was to investigate the truth of a proposition by articulating arguments for and against a proposition, in an art of critical examination. Early modern humanists placed great emphasis on rhetoric, but anyone resisting oppression and seeking to clarify his or her own stance might find this kind of verbal reasoning useful. For More, dialectic was more than a critical tool; it was essential to his creative thinking and also mirrored his world view of perpetual conflict between positive and negative forces. More believed that humanity's only hope of transcending this conflict was the possibility of eternal salvation by the sacrifice of Jesus Christ, which redeemed sin; all temptation was the work of the devil. What More called "tribulation"—misfortune, suffering, any kind of pain, disease, or distress—was rationalized as a common weapon of the forces of good, as well as evil. Tribulation was thus not merely a punishment for sin (or failure to resist the devil); it was also a form of preventive medicine instituted by God to provoke and test the faithful, thereby enabling them to increase their merit.

---

lier works, including *Utopia*, when he observes how easily men make jokes and tell idle tales as relief from solemn matters: "and of trouth cosin, as you know very well, my selfe am of nature even halfe a gigglot and more. I would I could as easily mende my faulte as I well knowe it, but scante canne I refraine it as olde foole as I am: howbeit so parcial wil I not be to my fault as to praise it" (bk. 2, ch. 1, p. 185). The repetitions of "I" and the word play on "more" and "fool" (cf. *morus*) represent the same kind of coded allusion as seen above in the first pages of book 1.

[15] *Complete Works*, 12, pp. 485–86.

## DIALOGUE AND DIALECTIC

*A Dialogue of Comfort against Tribulation* (like the *Consolation of Philosophy*) is a dialectical structure of reasoned argumentation, built upon the premise of an absolute faith: God is faithful and has promised that individuals will not be tempted or challenged beyond their capacity to resist.[16] In More's dialectic, tribulation is opposed by comfort; both are then redefined as a consequence of their opposition, and finally the new synthesis, a revised conception of tribulation, is celebrated as a means to the truest comfort available to mankind: spiritual consolation. Since the text proceeds as statement and objection, point by point, it both justifies the spiritual value of trial by tribulation and mirrors the adversarial process. Creative tension permeates the text even at the level of rhetoric. Anthony makes a virtue of this adversarial necessity when he explains (paradoxically) how

> the mo[re] we be tempted, the gladder have we cause to be ... for there is in this world sette up as it wer a game of wrestling, wherin the people of God come in on the one side, and on the tother syde come mighty stronge wrestlers and wylye, that is to wyt, the divels ... the spiritual wicked gostes of the ayre.
>
> But as God unto them that on his part give his adversari the fal, hath prepared a crown, so he that wil not wrestle, shall none have [i.e., man cannot come to glory by opting out, it has to be earned]. For as S. Paul saieth: *Qui certat in agone non coronabitur nisi legittime certaverit*: Ther shal no man have the crowne, but he that doth his devour [i.e., duty] therefore according to the law of the game. And then (as holi S. Bernard saith) how couldest thou fight or wrestle therfore, if ther were no challenger against the[e] that would provoke thee therto? (bk. 2, ch. 9, pp. 198–99)

Even the biblical metaphors of challenger and spiritual warfare justify, as they represent, the terms of the larger argument. Since the proof of More's argument is always dependent on the authority of the Bible (as evidence of God's dealings with mankind), interpreted, as here by the church fathers, its premise anticipates its conclusion.

Beyond this metaphor of the "challenger," resistance is built into the work chapter by chapter, especially in the first part of the *Dialogue*, where Anthony offers to prove that comfort and wealth are spiritual dangers mitigated by tribulation. He calls several external textual authorities as witnesses to the thesis that since one cannot have a good time in this world and the

---

[16] 1 Corinthians 10:13.

next, it is better to suffer briefly now than for eternity later. He concludes with a corollary that those who enjoy life should have "greate cause of feare and of discomforte" since their prosperity, health, and happiness may be signs that they have "fallen oute of Gods favour, and stand depe in hys indignacion and displeasure" (p. 155). This argument too is paradoxical, and Vincent, while agreeing with the general thesis, advances his own objections: "Yet me thinke that you say verye sore in some thynge concerninge suche persons as are in continual prosperity."[17] He asks, if tribulation is so necessary for salvation, why does the liturgy encourage people to pray that God will send them perpetual health and prosperity? No one goes to visit the sick, he continues, to congratulate them on their tribulation but, rather, to wish them a full and speedy recovery. Anthony's sophistry is counterintuitive, and Vincent prefers the evidence of what he calls "playne experience" that shows him "manye a man is ryghte welthy and yet therewith righte good: and many a miserable wretche as evel as he is wreched." Thus, he continues, it cannot be true that the good things in this life are always a sign of God's displeasure and "a token of eternal dampnacion." He concludes this local argument: "And therfore, it semeth hard, good uncle, that betwene prosperitye and tribulacion the matter shoulde go thus" (p. 158). In a later chapter Anthony answers these objections by qualifying the terms of his own argument, thereby creating a new synthesis. Chapter by chapter, they debate many of the usual topics in popular didactic works on religious consolation, using set forms of verbal reasoning that evoke the drama and creative conflict associated with argument in the literature of ancient moral philosophy, including works by Plato, Seneca, and Boethius. More engaged with a literary form and method of intellectual resistance that placed him, a persecuted prisoner of conscience, in a venerable tradition. The text also witnesses to his dialogue with the past for the sake of his present defense of righteousness, and for its future safeguarding in this world, always with an eye on salvation in the next.

The local dialectic in these chapters is mirrored in the larger tripartite structure of the *Dialogue*. Book 1 expounds the theory of comfort. Book 2 is less abstract and schematic; the literary model changes from scholarly argument (by statement, objection, and resolution) to a mixed mode akin to Menippean satire, in contrast with the careful logic of book 1 (however, there is no verse). Digressions, embedded fables, and hints of personal references to More's friends and family suggest the chaos apparent in the real world and give this second book a richer feel, making it easier for readers to engage with; its prologue speaks of providing relief from threats, danger,

---

[17] Bk. 1, ch. 13, p. 156.

and difficulty. One of Anthony's "merry tales" introduces a nun and her brother, a doctor of divinity, meeting after a long separation:

> Forthwith began my Lady to geve her brother a sermon, of [th]e wretchednes of this world, and the frayltie of the flesh, and the subtil sleightes of the wicked fiende, and gave hym surely good counsel (saving somwhat to[o] long) how he shold be well ware in his living and maister well his body for savynge of his soule.

She begins to find fault with him and Anthony impersonates her direct speech:

> In good faith brother, I do somewhat mervayle that you [tha]t have bene at lerning so long . . . dooe not nowe at oure metinge (while we mete so seldom) to me that am your sister and a simple unlearned soule geve of your charitie some fruiteful exhortacion . . . your selfe. (bk. 2, prologue, pp. 183–84)

His pithy reply is that he cannot, "for your toungue hath never ceased, but sayde ynoughe for us bothe." This is a prelude to Anthony's apology for hogging the debate in book 1; he therefore aligns himself (ironically) with the garrulous woman. Vincent's rejoinder is a tale about Anthony's kinswoman (thereby inviting speculation about her identity) whose husband dined out a good deal, which discontented her. In extenuation, she is told that his host allows her husband all the table talk; this she shrewdly misinterprets, revealing why her husband prefers better company:

> Al the wordes quod she? Marye that am I content, he shall have all the woordes with good will, as he hath ever hadde. But I speake them all my selfe, and geve them all to hym, and for oughte that I care for them, so shall he have them styll: but otherwyse to saye that he shall have them al, you shal kepe hym still, rather than he geat the halfe. (p. 184)

The playful wit that caricatures her depends on her being sharper than she seems, after all. The strong hint that this tale implies affectionate teasing of More's wife, Dame Alice, is supported by similar stories about shrewd wives including a brief digression within Anthony's narrative of Mother Mawde's tale in chapter 14 when a "wife" coming home from confession announces that she will leave off all her old shrewdness and begin again, intending to turn over a new leaf but letting her shrewder husband understand that she will renew her old behavior. Anthony and Vincent acknowledge that they both knew the couple were joking (p. 211).[18] Book 2 therefore, in its vitality

---

[18] Cf. the reference to a young girl whose kinsman had begun to teach her physic and was able

and hints of anarchic worldliness, can be seen as the antithesis to the literal sophistication and abstraction of book 1.[19]

Book 3 is different again, although it contains another story that may have had a private meaning for More's family and would have encouraged their application of the message of the text to themselves. This last part of the *Dialogue* returns the focus to the historical situation of Anthony and Vincent in the besieged city of Buda. Book 3 resolves the tensions between the two earlier parts by creating a synthesis composed of generalized abstraction within the context of the Great Turk's persecution, as Anthony suggests that God will use "these infidels that are his open professed enemyes" to create "the sorowefull scourge of correccyon" for faithless Christians who are "his falselye professed frendes" (p. 265). Vincent laments that people are beginning to get used to the idea of the Turks' power and that "some of our owne here among us" are "more gladde to fynde faultes at every state of christendom, priestes, princes, rytes, ceremonies, sacramentes, lawes, and customes spirituall, temporall, and all" (pp. 263–64). Anthony concurs drawing attention to their own situation "here in dede, and that but even now of late." The coded reference to Hungary scarcely covers the immediate application of their discussion to England since the passage of the Act of Succession:

> For since the title of the crowne hath comen in question, the good rule of this realme hath verye sore decayed as lytle whyle as it is. And undoubtedly Hungary shall never do wel, as long as it standeth in this case, that mens myndes hearken after noveltie, and have theyr heartes hangynge uppon a chaunge, and muche the worse I like it, whan their woordes walke so large towarde the favoure of [th]e Turkes secte, which thei wer ever wont to have in so greate abhominacion, as everye true minded christen man and chrysten woman to[o], must have. (p. 264)

Finally therefore, discussion of this specific problem of religious persecution and forced conversion mirrors More's view of the dilemma facing English Catholics: whether to die for one's Christian faith and so save one's eternal soul, or be forsworn, as the Turk will require, and so save one's mor-

---

to identify Anthony's tertian fever from her reading of Galen's *De differentiis febrium*. Vincent suggests that he thought at the time that she might have been lying, simply to show off: "because she would you shold take her for cunning." But Anthony replies that by chance she found a copy of Galen "ready to be solde in the boke sellers shoppes" and was able to show him the chapter in her source. Harpsfield's biography of More indicates that this story became part of the family's folklore and described his foster daughter, Margaret Giggs (later Mrs. Clement), who studied Greek and medicine within More's household. The moral function of this story within the *Dialogue* is to show how one should both express sorrow and be joyful in tribulation. Bk. 2, ch. 4, p. 190.

[19] Cf. on the medicinal value of laughter in book 2, A. L. Prescott, "The Ambivalent Heart: Thomas More's Merry Tales," *Criticism*, 45 (2003), 417–33.

tal life. The larger didactic purpose of the *Dialogue* presents opportunities for individuals to consider the problems inherent in this situation. The dilemma is not without spiritual danger, as the "fault of saint Peter" who "made a proude promise, and sone hadde a foule fall" should remind everyone (p. 267); but, on the whole, Anthony concludes, since we are weaker than the martyrs of old, everyone has much more need to anticipate their response:

> While the thyng shal not appeare so terrible unto them, reson shal better enter, and through grace workyng with their diligence, engender and set sure, not a sodayn sleight affeccion of sufferaunce for goddes sake, but by a long continuance, a stronge depe roted habitte, not lyke a reede ready to wave wyth everye winde, nor like a rooteles tree scante set up on end in a lose heape of light sand, that wil with a blast or two be blowen down. (bk. 3, ch. 3, p. 274)

Reading the *Dialogue* may teach everyone how to encourage strong deep-rooted habits that can resist persecution and reconcile them to the consequences, should it take hold.

The topics discussed in this final part include responses to the loss of land, property, gifts of fortune, riches, flattery, and status in the world that would later be experienced by many English recusants.[20] Anthony sums up the relative worthlessness of such worldly goods, pointing to "the povertye that our Savyoure wyllingly suffred for us ... to make us ryche in heaven" (p. 302). The remainder of book 3 returns to the theme of St. Peter's lapse of faith in the context of human fears of bodily pain, captivity, forced exile, imprisonment, and a shameful death. Anthony's empathy with the faithful soul's resistance to these threats is channeled through his evocation of the "greate horrour and feare that oure Saviour hadde in his owne fleshe againste [i.e., before] hys painefull passion." He recommends dealing with the temptation to submit to fear by meditation on the agony in the Garden of Gethsemane; one should also remember St. Paul's promise to the Corinthians that "God ... suffereth you not to be tempted above that you maye beare, but giveth also with the temptation awaye out."[21] According to Anthony a fearful martyr should remember the courage of Jesus, and also that there are many mansions in the house of God who

> exalteth not every good man up to the glorye of a Martyr, but foreseinge theyr infirmitie, that though thei be of good wil before, and peradventure

---

[20] Cf. M. Questier, "Catholicism, Kinship and the Public Memory of Sir Thomas More," *Journal of Ecclesiastical History*, 53 (2002), 476–509.
[21] Bk. 3, ch. 17, pp. 304, 305; cf. ch. 20, p. 326.

of right good corage to[o], woulde yet play saint Peter, yf they were broughte to the point, and thereby bring their soules into the peril of eternal dampnacion. (p. 304)

In such cases, he continues, it is comforting to learn that God makes other provision to save their souls, as the biblical histories of St. John the Evangelist, and St. Peter demonstrate. In discussing imprisonment, Anthony also cites the biblical precedents of Joseph and Daniel, each of whom gained from such adversity, and when he returns to the theme of "our saviour" who was taken prisoner "for our sake" (ch. 20, p. 327), he repeats the word "prisoner" nine times, in one sentence, to emphasize the folly of fearing as shameful anything experienced by Jesus.

Anthony argues at length that the very nature of imprisonment is relative, being "nothinge els but the retainyng of a mans person, wyth in the circuite of a certaine space, narower or larger as shal be limited to him, restrainynge hys lybertye fro the further going into any other place" (bk. 3, ch. 19, p. 313). Yet we deceive ourselves if we imagine ourselves free merely because we do not perceive the limits that always constrain us; no one is wholly free to do what he likes, and in respect of the bondage of sin, he concludes, the condition is universal. Anthony cites the "good remedye" of Seneca's moral philosophy: "Endevour thy selfe evermore, that thou do nothing against thy wyl, but the thynge that we se we shal needes do, let us use always to putte our good wyll thereto." Vincent's characteristically pragmatic response is that this is easier said than done.[22] Here More seems to recall Boethius's argument for the mind's autonomy, but with a crucial difference since (in bk. 3, ch. 19) Anthony concludes that everyone, everywhere, is a prisoner "in this large prison of the whole earth" (p. 320). All aspects of life are curtailed in some way: "Upon our prison we bild" our prisons, some of gold, lands, goods, livelihoods, or vice. Vincent regards this argument as "a sophysticall fantasy," but Anthony goes on to call God our chief jailer (perhaps recalling Boethius's image of the divine panopticon—the great eye in the sky—from the closing pages of the *Consolation of Philosophy*) and, to comfort Vincent, insists on the relative nature of our imprisonment.[23] He cites the voluntary confinements of nuns and monks, who love their enclosed life, to argue that "the lothnes of lesse rowme, and the doore sh[u]t upon us . . . is but an horrour enhaunced of our owne fantasy" (ch. 20, p. 325). This horror of being shut in and suffocated is vividly represented in a digression about a woman Anthony knew who came to visit a prisoner whom she found confined

---

[22] Ch. 18, p. 310; cf. Seneca, *Ep. Mor.*, 61.2.
[23] Ch. 19, p. 316; cf. 319, 321, and ch. 20, esp. pp. 321–24 on the existential prison of the world.

in a chamber (to say [th]e trouth) metely fayre, and at the leastwise it was strong inough, but with mattes of straw the prisoner had made it so warme, both under the foote and round about [th]e walles that in these thinges for the kepynge of his health, she was on his behalf gladde and very well coumforted, but amonge many other displesures that for his sake she was sory for: one she lamented much in her mind, that he should have the chamber doore upon him by nighte, made fast by the gayler that should shette him in. For by my trouth quoth she, if the dore shold be shet upon me, I would wene it wolde stoppe uppe my breth. (p. 325)

The repeated reference to "truth" and the use of direct speech here seem to suggest another coded allusion to More's actual situation.[24] The prisoner laughs to himself at her ambivalent reaction because, as Anthony comments, "he stoode in awe of her" and was maintained by her charitable alms. Besides, this prisoner knew well enough that she also used to shut her chamber door and windows every night, and "what difference then as to the stoppyng of the breth whether they wer shet up within or without?" (p. 325). More's first readers, his family, would likely see further affectionate teasing of Dame Alice in this poignant and astute psychological commentary on the prison visitor's empathy. Anthony does not deny the "grief" of this prisoner's "hard handling," but, as Boethius and More understood, "our feare may ymagine them much greater grief then they be. And I say that such as thei be, many a man endureth them, yea and many a woman too, [tha]t after fare ful wel" (p. 326). If More makes Anthony comment here on his own attitude to his circumstances, then one may see him mitigating them for the sake of others. The final chapters of the *Dialogue of Comfort* continue discussion of this theme that willpower controls the impact the senses have on a person's attitudes to fear, including fear of death. Vincent acknowledges the initial premise of the dialogue that faith is prerequisite to the receiving of comfort; and Anthony (echoing Boethius), refines this by adding "reason grounded upon the foundacion of fayth" (ch. 22, p. 333). If the cumulative experience of reading all three parts of the *Dialogue* is greater than the sum of these parts, it is because the creative tension in their dialectical relationship changes our understanding of the questions and dangers being debated. This structure suggests More's strategy to describe and teach readers how to find spiritual consolation in a specific historic situation, yet it also applies more widely for any reader who defines the human condition as imprisonment by the world or the flesh.

---

[24] There is no documentary evidence for the specific conditions of More's imprisonment, but the traditional site, the Lower Bell Tower, does not have a chimney or fireplace, so keeping warm would have been difficult. The only natural light in this chamber comes from five unglazed arrow loops. (I am grateful to David Tomback for the opportunity to visit the Lower Bell Tower.)

Like Bonhoeffer, More was faced with a choice between his definition (or understanding) of conscience and an expedient compromise that many other religious people at that time felt able to make. These historic parallels between them are limited and generic, yet the ability to function as an intelligent, sentient human being in these kinds of circumstances (when resistance must also risk falling victim to monumental hubris) was aided in each case by their theological recourse to contemporary understanding of the suffering human figure of the prisoner Jesus and by recognition of the value of strong family ties.

## AFFECTIVE PIETY

The last chapter of the *Dialogue* informs readers that "consideracion of the paynfull death of Christ, is sufficient to make us content to suffer paynfull death for his sake" (ch. 27, p. 349). Yet, as Bonhoeffer and Boethius both realized, emphasis on the four last things, and death in particular, may be inappropriate for prisoners. More discussed martyrdom in several of his Tower works and focused on the human fear (rather than death) of Jesus. More's theological understanding of fear was bound up with how it might compromise a man's faith which protected his soul like a shield and was the gift of God's grace.[25] His concern with bodily fear and mental anguish seems personal but was not peculiar to him. In the *Dialogue of Comfort,* Anthony does not belittle Vincent's "feare that forceth mine harte to tremble" because, as he says, "the greate horror and feare that oure Saviour hadde in his owne fleshe" are authoritative precedents for such forms of human weakness, especially in contemplating the pain of dying. Since the Bible indicates that Jesus overcame his fear, Anthony tells Vincent, and More tells his readers: "I maye wel make you take that comforte to[o]" for, in spite of "grudging felte in your sensuall partes," "your reason shal [not] give over, but resist it and manlie maister it," as Jesus did.[26] In More's discussion of the fear of fear, which might weaken a strong man in his final earthly trial, there are recurrent references to this exemplary behavior of Jesus at Gethsemane, and

[25] Cf. More's application of the metaphor from Ps. 90 [91]: 4, see bk. 3, ch. 16, p. 303; cf. ch. 27, p. 352. John Fisher's appeal from the scaffold for the prayers of others also revealed his fear of fear: "Hitherto I have not feared death. Yet I know that I am flesh and that St Peter from fear of death, three times denied his Lord. Wherefore help me, with your prayers, that at the very instant of my death's stroke, I faint not in any point of the Catholic faith for any fear"; see R. W. Chambers, *Thomas More* (London: Jonathan Cape, 1938, rpt. 1957), p. 334 and note; William Rastell was an eyewitness.

[26] Bk. 3, ch. 17, p. 304. Cf. "For in man reason ought to reign like a king, and it does truly reign when it makes itself loyally subject to faith and serves God." *De Tristitia, Complete Works,* 14, p. 509.

St. Paul's consoling promise that God would not allow anyone to be tested beyond his capacity to resist.

*De tristitia tedio pavore et oratione Christi ante captionem eius*, translated by More's granddaughter as "Of the sorowe, werinesse, feare, and prayer of Christ before hys taking," explores the psychology of suffering, and demonstrates the efficacy of prayer by the afflicted, in an extended commentary on the gospel narratives.[27] The text is unfinished but appears to be very nearly complete, if we assume that More intended to comment on the whole of the last biblical verse he quoted, and was always expected to end, as the title in More's handwriting confirms, with the arrest of Jesus, rather than the crucifixion, or later.[28] More developed a series of affective meditations, based on the gospel narratives, with extensive dramatic speeches by Jesus to his followers, both the original disciples and later Christian readers. There are also speeches, in the anonymous voice of a commentator (presumed to incorporate aspects of More's identity and interests) who addresses his reader as well as Jesus and digresses from the biblical scenario of the agony in the Garden to remark (often heatedly) upon the doctrinal innovations of "new men" who lead people astray. Thus, those "of a certain sect" who deny the real presence of Christ in the sacrament are compared with Judas because they too "betray" Jesus "into the hands of sinners";[29] and those who "boast that they are 'autodidacts' (to use St Jerome's word) and [believe] that, without the commentaries of the old doctors," anyone can fathom the mysteries of God's word in the Bible for themselves, are compared to swarms of wasps or hornets. The writer's exasperation, scorn, and intellectual snobbery are motivated by concern for those who, by opposing the Catholic faith, risk "their eternal ruination" as well as the unity of Christendom. Such digressions reveal More's didactic purpose and continued involvement in anti-Protestant polemic. He seems to have found these anxieties and criticisms easier to express in Latin than in English. As a lay theologian he was also careful to defer to appropriate authorities and identified his principal source for *De Tristitia* as a harmonization of the gospels by the Parisian theologian Jean Gerson (d. 1429); More's extended biblical commentary therefore represents an intertextual dialogue with the evangelists and a popular theologian.[30]

---

[27]  Cf. Matthew ch. 26, Mark 14, Luke 22, John 18.

[28]  *Complete Works*, 14, pp. 738–40; More's holograph manuscript, with textual revisions also in his hand, survives at the Royal College of Corpus Christi in Valencia where it has been since the sixteenth century. Mary Basset (née Roper)'s English translation is reprinted in *Complete Works*, 14, pp. 1022–1165.

[29]  Ibid., p. 355.

[30]  G. E. Haupt regards the harmonization as "the textual symbol of an affirmation of Christian unity" (*Complete Works*, 13, p. xlviii). Cf. also the dialogic text representing the debate of John

The emotional range in More's characterization of Jesus, evident from the tones of voice More invests in his direct speeches, draws the reader's sympathy, confidence, and approval. As in other spiritual guides and devotional aids of this kind, the rhetorical intention is to move the will and to persuade readers to feel loved, consoled, and encouraged. More's rhetoric is more carefully attuned to the drama of the human voice than to visual evocation of an affecting scene as Jesus echoes several different biblical texts. The reader is invited not only to hear the words of Jesus as if they were addressed to oneself (in the second person singular) but also to consider one's physical proximity to Jesus who understands human fear having experienced it before and after his imprisonment:

> You are afraid, you are sad, you are stricken with weariness and dread of the torment with which you have been threatened. Trust me. I conquered the world, and yet I suffered immeasurably more from fear, I was sadder, more afflicted with weariness, more horrified at the prospect of such cruel suffering drawing nearer and nearer . . . follow my leadership; if you do not trust yourself, place your trust in me. See, I am walking ahead of you along this fearful road. Take hold of the border of my garment.[31]

The exemplary didactic functions of these speeches to encourage the weak and console the afflicted are found in contemporary devotional works, exhibiting similar devotional sensibilities, where imitation of this paradigm of human suffering was considered empowering for afflicted or dejected souls, especially those afraid of dying.[32] By contrast, when glossing the biblical words of Jesus to the soldiers who take him prisoner—"This is your hour and the power of darkness"—More's Jesus also powerfully rebukes his enemies, and all the other faithless who will follow them through history, imagined "as a brief power of darkness [that] will be given to other governors and other caesars against other disciples of mine" (p. 543). More laced *De Tristitia Christi* with digressions on the doctrinal and spiritual conflicts of his own age. Thereafter, whatever Thomas More was known to say on such topics in the Tower of London was bound to have greater resonance and impact on his readers. His warnings should seem more authoritative because, like Jesus's account of his agony (known only to him in his solitude, as More

---

Colet and Erasmus on the same biblical theme of the agony in the garden (*Complete Works*, 14, p. 742); Miller suggests that More wrote for an educated rather than a learned or expert reader.

[31] *Complete Works*, 14, pp. 101–5; see further on this passage R. Zim, "The Reformation: The Trial of God's Word," in *Reading the Text: Biblical Criticism and Literary Theory*, ed. S. Prickett (Oxford: Blackwell, 1991), pp. 64–135, at 76–81.

[32] Cf. Haupt's discussion of the devotional literature that explains the Christocentric emphasis of More's Tower works (*Complete Works*, 13, pp. lxxxv–xciv).

noted), they arose from the fruits of bitter personal experience that had been carefully analyzed for the benefit of others.[33]

Like many political prisoners, More used references to his society's problems to warn others to be vigilant. The application may be limited, in More's case to English Catholics, but it is notable that he argued for an ethical imperative, not to stand by while others are in danger, that has universal value: "How could it be anything but disgraceful" to contemplate such apathy? "If we are perhaps unmoved by the misfortunes of others because they are at some distance from us, let us at least be moved by our own danger. For we have reason to fear that the destructive force will make its way from them to us" (p. 339). The "plague" of "contagion" he saw "creeping" toward England was already destroying his idea of Christian civilization. Since it was about to destroy him too, he used his intellect and rhetorical powers to warn others to defend themselves and their values. The Tower works may have helped More to reevaluate his spiritual position, but they also enabled readers to appreciate what was at stake in a wider context. Some twenty years after his death, the reception of his texts in England was controlled by his family who promoted his image as a prisoner and martyr for the faith in the large folio edition of his *English Works,* printed in 1557, by his nephew. (This included his granddaughter's translation of *De Tristitia.*) By this date it would have seemed that Catholic England had returned to the papal fold under the rule of Mary Tudor.

An English prayer written in the upper and lower margins of his prayer book was among his last compositions in the Tower of London. It begins adjacent to a large woodcut illustrating the nativity of Jesus and ends adjacent to one of him carrying the cross to Calvary.[34] In this context, and by his own handwriting, More indicated that he was attempting to follow his master. The *imitatio Christi* message is encoded in this layout rather than the words of the text; it was thus accessible only through this book, to himself and his family, who could be expected to value his prayer book and its inscriptions as evidence of his spirituality. All the ideas are conventional in early Tudor Catholic devotion. The petitioner asks ("Gyve me...") for

---

[33] Cf. the commentary writer's review of the evidence for Jesus as his own recording witness: *Complete Works*, 14, pp. 189–99.

[34] See facsimiles and transcription in *Prayer Book*, pp. 3–20 and 185–87. The text was included in William Rastell's edition of More's *English Works* (1557), where it is entitled "A godly meditacion, written by sir Thomas More knyghte whyle he was prisoner in the tower of London, in the yere of our Lord, 1534." [i.e., 25 March 1534–24 March 1535]. On the conflicting evidence for dating, see also G. E. Haupt's conjecture that the liturgical context of its position, added to pages from the Office of the Virgin and the Hours of the Cross, might indicate that More wrote the prayer to coincide with the Visitation of the Virgin commemorated in the church calendar on 2 July. Haupt suggests 2 July 1535, the day after More's trial. Martz and Sylvester link the themes of More's prayer to his Latin psalter annotations.

God's grace to renounce the world, for help "to be content to be solitary," to consider his sins, "patiently to suffre adversite" and "to be joyfull of tribulations"; he hopes by leaning on God's comfort, "to bere the crosse with christ." More first wrote "my" after "bere" but deleted it as he wrote to replace it on the line of writing with the impersonal definite article.[35] The last lines of the prayer explain the uses of adversity, citing Joseph who was betrayed and sold into captivity by his brothers. The layout of the text separates it from a short coda added on the facing page as a commentary, commending the petitioner's intentions more widely: "These myndys are more to be desired of every man than all the treasure of all the princes & kynges christen & hethen were it gathered & layed to gether all uppon one hepe." The cult of the prisoner More was evidently started by More himself as he inscribed this meditation in the margins of his prayer book.

## FAMILIAL PIETIES AND A REPUTATION FOR POSTERITY

The day before his execution, More wrote his last letter explaining why he was ready to die: "I woulde be sorye, if it shoulde be any lenger than to morrowe, for it is S. Thomas evin and the utas of Sainte Peter and therefore to morowe longe I to goe to God, it were a daye very meete and conveniente for me."[36] According to the English church calendar, 7 July commemorated the translation of the body of St. Thomas Becket to a new tomb in Canterbury Cathedral upon his canonization in 1220. More's namesake, Thomas Becket, was another defender of Christendom against the secular power of another King Henry. This conjunction of More's own appointment with the judgment of God, the translation of Becket's body to his tomb, and the biblical St. Peter's feast was a very personal consolation.

When More had acknowledged his fears of weakness in contemplating pain, he compared his experience with that of St. Peter who "so cowardly forsook his master" but repented in time to die a martyr. In the dialogue between More and his daughter Margaret Roper, which is part of her letter to Alice Alington, the prisoner More tells Margaret that he knows well "the naturall faintnes" of his own heart: "Yet if I had not trusted that God shoulde geve me strength rather to endure all thinges, than offend hym by sweringe ungodly against mine owne conscience, you may be very sure I wold not have come here" [i.e., to prison] (p. 516). The king may have deprived him of his liberty but he had thereby brought him "so great good by the spirituall profytt that I trust I take . . . that . . . upon my faith my prison-

<hr/>

[35] Cf. the double memorial portrait of More, illustrated in *The King's Good Servant*, p. 140, showing him, as Lord Chancellor, wearing his gold collar of esses and, as martyr, carrying his cross.

[36] *Correspondence*, p. 564; the "utas" refers to the octave of the feast of St. Peter (29 June).

ment" is the chief of all the king's "great benefites" already bestowed upon Thomas More. He continued, "I cannot . . . therefore mistrust the grace of God. . . . And therfore mine owne good daughter, never troble thy minde for any thinge that ever shall happe me in this worlde. Nothing can come but that that God will" (p. 531). This letter contains some of the most personal and carefully worded arguments for More's position, yet his words are embedded within a larger literary dialogue between his daughter and her foster sister. The mask of More's personality and self-impression is regressive but, in the context of his themes as a prison writer, paradoxically more credible than ever, in this safer dramatized form. More's recurrent expressions of his fear of fear were, like Fisher's, associated with St. Peter's fear. Finally, as he tells his daughter, he will trust the grace of God:

> Though I shoulde fele my feare even at poynt to overthrowe me to[o], yet shall I remember how S. Peter, with a blast of winde, began to sinke for his faint faith, and shall doe as he did, call upon Christ and praye him to helpe. And than I trust he shall set his holye hande unto me, and in the stormy seas, holde me up from drowning. Yea and if he suffer me *to play S. Peter* ferther, and to fall full to the grownd, and swere and forsware too . . . yet after shall I trust that his goodnes will cast upon me his tender pyteous eie, as he did upon S. Peter, and make me stande up againe and confesse the trouth of my conscience afresh, and abide the shame and the harme here [i.e., in prison] of mine own fault.[37]

In all the most important Tower works—the *Dialogue of Comfort*, the Latin gospel commentary, and letters to various correspondents—these themes of the agony of Jesus, St. Peter's betrayal through weakness, and St. Paul's promise that no fearful martyr will be tested disproportionately are welded together in a dialectical relationship. If reason based on faith and love was the thesis More proposed in the Tower works, and fear was their antithesis, then martyrdom was the synthesis that should witness to the soul's rebirth into a higher nature.

Establishing a dialogue with loved ones outside prison was not only a means to prevent that personal, moral degeneration that More imagined as "playing" St. Peter. As the letter to Alice Alington indicates, his attempts to teach and protect his family were also part of his defense of a wider Christian society, since the family is also a microcosm of the nation. More's iden-

---

[37] *Correspondence*, pp. 514–32 at p. 531 (August 1534); my emphasis. The Yale editors of the *Dialogue of Comfort* (where More also refers to St. Peter) consider the letter to be "primarily More's own composition" (*Complete Works*, 12, p. lxi); Rastell's edition attributes the letter to Margaret Roper and then adds "But whether thys . . . wer written by syr Thomas More in his daughter Ropers name, or by her selfe, it is not certaynelye knowen" (More, *Workes* [1557], p. 1434).

tity as a father figure as well as a prisoner has been important in the construction of his reputation. The range and depth of More's communicable feelings for his family are most evident in his prison letters addressed to his firstborn, Margaret Roper (1505–44).[38] Yet these too had public and political significance, at the time, and later in print. It appears that Margaret was allowed to write to her father and to visit him in the Tower because members of the Privy Council hoped that she would act as an *agent provocateur*, or she may have presented that option as a means to gain access to him. In her first letter she seems to have attempted to persuade him to subscribe to the oath which he had refused on grounds of conscience. This provoked an apparently pained but firm reply:

> If I had not ben, my derely beloved doughter, at a firme and fast point (I trust in God's great mercie), this good great while before, your lamentable letter had not a litle abashed me, surely farre above all other thynges. . . . But surely they all towched me never so nere, nor were so grevous unto me, as to se you, my wel-beloved childe, in such vehement piteous maner labour to perswade unto me, that thinge wherin I have of pure necessite for respect unto myne owne soule, so often gyven you so precise answere before. (p. 508)

Later, he was able to tease her about being a temptress—"Mistress Eve"— who for the "favour" that she bore him wanted to save his life and, therefore came to "labour to make hym sweare against his conscience, and so sende hym to the devill."[39]

If being a prisoner means being cut off and kept apart from the secure continuities of normal life, however that is defined, then the ability to retain contact with family and the outside world enables one to continue to recognize oneself. More's relationship with Margaret was affectionate and close. It is difficult to compare the dynamics of early modern family relationships with modern ones, but from their letters there is no doubting the strong bond between them, the subtlety of their mutual understanding and More's pride in her. In his last letter he thanked her for kissing him in the street after the trial, "for I love when doughterly love and deere charitie hathe no laisor to looke to worldely curtesye" (p. 564); toward the end of the sixteenth century, this scene was translated into a timeless, classical myth in Antoine Caron's painting where the soldiers of the prisoner's escort wear

---

[38] See M. Bowker's article on Roper in the *Oxford Dictionary of National Biography*. The centrality of her role in transmitting the image of More that is seen in the letter to Alington and other correspondence may be compared with the role of Eberhard Bethge in the transmission of Bonhoeffer's legacy. Cf. "Father, I have many tymes rehearsed to mine owne coumfort and divers others, your fashyon and wordes ye had to us when we wer last with you" (*Correspondence*, p. 539).

[39] Cf. Margaret Roper to Alice Alington, *Correspondence*, p. 515.

ancient Roman armor.[40] He called her variously "mine own good daughter," "Margaret," "Meg," "my dearly beloved child," using such terms of endearment to address her directly and frequently, in letters that substitute for conversation. Margaret affirmed this explicitly in a letter where she began every other sentence with the vocative, "Father...," and concluded: "Father, I am sory I have no lenger laysure at this time to *talke* with you, the chief comforte of my lyfe, I trust to have occasion to *write* again shortly."[41]

Although there are many similarities between the themes of More's letters and his devotional and didactic writing in the Tower, the tone and style of many of his prison letters offset the ideological concerns in these other works. It is not simply that the warmth of the relationship in the dialogues with Margaret projects a more humane and sympathetic image of the man than his sarcasm and vituperation in polemic or his irony and evasiveness in learned wit. Both father and daughter were aware that Thomas Cromwell and his officials scrutinized their correspondence looking for incriminating evidence of More's position—perhaps as much to trap him into conceding to the terms of the Act of Supremacy as into opposing them (hence More's reiteration of his refusal to "meddle" in the matter of any man's conscience, coupled with his hope that others would do the same). The politics of resistance also partly explains why More sent Margaret Roper information about his interrogations. On the one hand, he wrote to reassure his family: "For asmuche, deerly beloved doughter, as it is likely that you either have hearde or shortely shall heare that the Counsaile was here this daye, and that I was before theim, I have thought it *necessary* to send you worde howe the mater standeth."[42] On the other hand, these letters were his opportunity to record his version of events and might have been admissible evidence at his trial should the prosecution have attempted to twist his testimony given during these interrogations. Two letters (written 2 or 3 May 1535 and 3 June 1535) contain detailed reports of interrogations, either in indirect speech or in the direct speech of formal dialogue. This he reserved for his own answers to the most crucial questions put to him about the Act of Supremacy.

> On Fryday the last day of Apryle in the afternone, Mr Leuetenaunt [of the Tower] cam in here unto me, and showed me that Mr Secretary [of the Privy Council] wold speke with me. Whereuppon I shyfted my gowne, and went owt with Mr Leuetenaunt into the galery to hym. Where I met many, some knowen and some unknowen in the way. And

---

[40] See illustration of the original painting, ca. 1591 (Musée du Château de Blois), in *The King's Good Servant*, p. 131; More also praised his son's "natural fashion" in kneeling at Tower wharf for his father's last blessing.

[41] *Correspondence*, p. 539 (my emphasis).

[42] 3 June 1535. ibid. p. 555 (my emphasis).

in conclusion commying in to the chamber wher hys Mastershyp sat with Mr Attorney, Mr Solicitor, Mr Bedyll and Mr Doctour Tregonnell, I was offred to syt with them [i.e., a mark of respect], whych in no wyse I wolde. (p. 551)

More shows his appreciation of the psychology of interrogation and strengthens his resistance by not accepting either the kindness or the flattery he was offered in the invitation to be seated. The formal switch here from reported to direct speech is also tactical and significant. He reports that the first question Cromwell put to him was whether he had seen the new statutes: "Whereuppon Mr Secretary shewed unto me, that he dowbted not, but that I had by such frends as hyther had resorted to me sene the new statutes made at the last syttyng of the Parlyament."

> Wherunto I answered: ye verely. How be yt for as much as beyng here, I have no conversacion with [a]ny people, I thought yt lytle nede for me to bestow mych tyme uppon them, and therefore I redelyverd the boke shortly and theffect of the statutes I never marked nor studyed to put in remembraunce. (pp. 551–52)

The irony of what he has obviously "studied to put in remembrance" about his interrogation (rather than the statutes), and the characterization of himself as a kind of bumbling hermit with no need to cultivate current topics for polite conversation, are typical of More's self-impression in earlier fictional dialogues, such as *Utopia*. This letter is a double dialogue in defense of humanity, civility, and his conception of his integrity. The dramatic dialogue within the letter, between More and Cromwell to which Margaret is made a witness (or audience), is part of More's legal defense of himself: that is, he still has nothing to say about the new statutes. The second dialogue of the correspondence with Margaret also reveals the character of a man under pressure and the human needs of the prisoner. In writing to Margaret, More was literally addressing an image of his posterity—his grown-up child—but specifically also writing for a different kind of posterity, the public image of himself as a wise and witty *pater familias* that would continue to embody his reputation. This image was largely self-made in the various forms of literary dialogue he conducted with himself and his daughter from the isolation and insecurities of his prison cell.

As prisoners, philosophers, and fathers, Boethius and More each wrote to console their families, addressing those who must have been their first readers. But like all prisoners who write, it is clear that Bonhoeffer and More also wrote to console, defend, and preserve themselves. Bonhoeffer testified to the value of his writing when he echoed the assurance of Boethius's Philosophia that no one could control a free mind, and when he affirmed what a deliverance it was from the condition of confinement to be able to think and pursue his thoughts freely in disciplined forms of writing. More seems to have been able to read and write until his books and papers were removed from his cell shortly before his trial. After this, he is supposed to have blocked out the daylight and to have explained to his jailer: "Now that the goods and implements are taken away, the shop must be closed."[43] This story is part of the political myth constructed after the death of a martyr. More's early biographer saw this retreat from the world as a sign of the prisoner's need to focus on his personal spiritual readiness for the coming crisis. The implication is that there was to be no more commerce with the world, but therefore that his writing until this point had been oriented toward the external world of other people, and for them.

More referred repeatedly to the importance of resisting all kinds of pressure to surrender principles and convictions upon which one had established a position of leadership, or moral influence, in public life. As Anthony tells Vincent, the question of whether to die for the faith has to be thought about well in advance—"while the thyng shal not appeare so terrible"—because later, when the point of decision arrives, it will be more difficult to think clearly. Thereafter, the decision should be kept in mind and periodically looked over so that one may get used to it (bk. 3, ch. 3, p. 274). In much the same way, the prison writer's intellectual and imaginative anticipation of moral disintegration under pressure can be seen as a safeguard against it. The creative antagonism inherent in More's thought processes, and the adversarial forms of dialogue in which they were expressed, also became a primary defense against personal disintegration. Four hundred years later Gramsci made very similar use of dialogue and dialectic in order to preserve his functions in public life by writing from prison to focus willpower and resistance, and to create order from chaos.

## Antonio Gramsci, *Prison Letters* (1926–37): Dialogue in Dialectic

Like Boethius, More, and Bonhoeffer, Antonio Gramsci continued his life's work and defended it by writing in prison. A founding father and leader of the Italian Communist Party, Gramsci regarded himself as a prisoner of conscience with a duty to defend his own conception of a higher world order. His Great Turk figure was Benito Mussolini; yet, like More, Gramsci

---

[43] Stapleton's "Life of More," quoted in Miller's introduction to *De Tristitia, Complete Works*, 14, p. 738.

also wrote about wider cultural matters as well as the causes and the consequences of repression. And, like Bonhoeffer, but without his conceptual base of a biblical and Christian moral code, Gramsci attacked the new political heresy of the day—fascism—in universal terms.

Gramsci was arrested (illegally, and despite his parliamentary immunity) when communist deputies were proscribed (with other opposition parties) on 8 November 1926, the eve of a parliamentary session called to approve legislation that would suppress antifascist publications, dissolve all opposition parties and organizations, establish special new courts, and reinstate capital punishment. Like More, Gramsci had relied on his legal standing as a "licensed" polemicist and as a law maker rather than law breaker. The regime had difficulty finding evidence for charges against Gramsci; and it was twenty months before he was eventually tried (alongside twenty-two other party members) by Mussolini's new "Special Tribunal for the Defense of the State"—effectively a court-martial and political show trial—from 28 May to 4 June 1928. He was accused of "conspiracy, of instigation to civil war, of justifying criminal acts, and of fomenting class hatred."[44] Shortly before the trial he had attempted to reassure his mother and explain his view of his actions:

> I am a political prisoner and . . . I have nothing to be ashamed of, and will never have anything to be ashamed of. I would like you to understand that in a certain sense I have myself wished to be imprisoned and condemned, because I would not change my opinions . . . and for this reason I am bound to be at peace with myself. . . . Dearest Mother, I really would like to hold you very close . . . and . . . to console you for this great grief which I've caused you . . . sons must sometimes cause great grief to their mothers if they wish to preserve their honour and their dignity as men.[45]

He was originally sentenced to more than twenty years' imprisonment. The circumstances of Gramsci's actual imprisonment, from November 1926 until his death on 27 April 1937, only days after the expiry of his commuted sentence, meant that he was unable to produce any extended, finished compositions. He was not allowed writing materials in his cell until January 1929.[46] His thirty-two prison notebooks contain fragmentary notes and

---

[44] See G. Fiori, *Antonio Gramsci: Life of a Revolutionary*, tr. T. Nairn (London: NLB, 1970), pp. 226–30; and the full discussion of Gramsci's imprisonment, his chronic bad health that antedated his arrest but was severely exacerbated by imprisonment, and his final days (still under guard) at a clinic in Rome, in Antonio Gramsci, *Prison Notebooks*, vol. 1, ed. Joseph A. Buttigieg, tr. J. A. Buttigieg and A. Callari (New York: Columbia University Press, 1992), pp. 1–64; see also Buttigieg's invaluable chronology of Gramsci's life, pp. 65–94.

[45] Fiori, *Life*, pp. 290–91 (10 May 1928).

[46] See ibid., pp. 235–36, on his prison writing habits.

some fuller drafts and outlines of essays and articles—even books—which he proposed to write later, whenever he might be freed and have access to a library. He was allowed to receive books and journals in prison, but did not have access to the kinds of resources that aided Bonhoeffer; however, Gramsci was supported throughout his years in prison by his sister-in-law, Tatiana Schucht (1887–1943), and by the generosity of the economist Piero Sraffa (1898–1983), who paid for an account at a Milan bookshop in Gramsci's name that enabled him to keep reading and thinking. Gramsci was determined to make the best of his situation and, even when suffering chronic illness, worked to define and defend his principles for the benefit of others. Imprisonment, as he wrote to his sister-in-law, was an opportunity to settle down and write something of lasting value for posterity. He found that he was "haunted," as he said many prisoners were, by the idea that he must use his time wisely to work on some special project "für ewig."[47] The opportunity to write was also an opportunity to forget or displace his own pain and loneliness. Although he found it difficult to study at first, he read widely and complained that the monotony of his life in prison was otherwise unrelieved. To settle his mind he began by translating German fairy tales and drew up several schemes of study, including an essay on Dante's *Inferno*, canto 10, in which he commented on the intense anguish of the poet Guido Cavalcanti's father, who mistook the use of a past tense verb to infer that the son he was separated from—Dante's friend—was also dead.[48] However, in the main the work he undertook as a prisoner was analytical, abstract, and polemical.

### THE EXPRESSION OF A "LICENSED" POLEMICIST

Gramsci set out first to understand the world he had been separated from by analyzing different phases in the history of Italian culture and society. In particular he examined the role of intellectuals, such as Machiavelli and Benedetto Croce (whom he came to consider the philosophical apologist for fascism, but whose ideas remained a bedrock for his own), in influencing the world view of their contemporaries and successors. This analysis became a prelude to the creative redevelopment of his political philosophy. Thus, from his study of Machiavelli and from engagement with critical debate about Machiavelli, he formulated his own idea of the modern Prince as a dramatic myth: a modern revolutionary movement in action. Gramsci's modern Prince was seen as a collective mass of individual living cells.

---

[47] *Gramsci's Prison Letters*: Lettere dal Carcere: *A Selection*, tr. and ed. Hamish Henderson (London and Edinburgh: Zwan and the *Edinburgh Review*, 1988), p. 45.
[48] *Prison Notebooks*, vol. 2, pp. 246–58 and 595–602.

Such an organism has already been produced by history, it is the political party. . . . The modern Prince must be, and cannot fail to be, the protagonist and organizer of intellectual and moral reform—that is, he proposes the terrain for a further development of the collective national-popular will towards the construction of a superior, all-embracing form of modern civilisation.[49]

The Communist Party had a duty to promote intellectual and moral reform because there was no point, he believed, in handing power to the working classes without first providing them with the cultural and political self-consciousness to use that power responsibly. As a modern humanist, he shared the belief of his early modern counterparts, including Thomas More, that education created new types of humanity. Gramsci therefore proposed to continue the aims of his earlier political journalism published in the left-wing Turin weekly review and (from January 1921) daily newspaper, *L'Ordine Nuovo*. Among the regular features he had written and published to help educate the industrial work force of Turin was a review column on contemporary Italian theater. As a philosopher and cultural historian he knew that man does not live by bread alone; yet, as a Marxist, the traditions of the universal church, which had nourished him in youth, were repugnant. During one especially acute bout of delirium and delusions caused by narrowing of the arteries, he (like Socrates on his last night) "spent a whole night [7 March 1933] discoursing on the immortality of the soul, in a realistic and historical sense, that is as a survival of all our useful and necessary acts, and their incorporation into the universal historic process regardless of our own wishes."[50]

Since his imprisonment, his life had been entirely controlled by external forces and "the boundaries of [his] liberty shrank until they enclosed only [his] own inner life." This language of confinement and his sense of the self as a residual core beyond this state resembles that of Boethius. In Gramsci's case, his will had been reduced to "nothing but the will to resist."[51] Prison life had "cut deeper" into him than any other cause of uncertainty, or isolation from his family, and, in observing the "spiritual deformations" he said he diagnosed in other long-term prisoners, he began to doubt his "own power to watch over" himself (pp. 86–87). He realized that he was dying slowly, yet he formulated his own vision for the future which he defined historically as "an integral new culture which will have both the mass character of the Protestant Reformation or the French Enlightenment and the

[49] Fiori, *Life*, p. 245; cf. *Selections from the Prison Notebooks*, ed. and tr. Q. Hoare and G. N. Smith (London: Lawrence and Wishart 1971, rpt. 1986), pp. 129, 132–33.

[50] Gramsci, quoted in Fiori, *Life*, p. 276.

[51] *Prison Letters*, p. 266.

classical cultural character of Greek civilization or the Italian Renaissance."[52]
Gramsci remained appreciative of the ways in which political history in
Italy and elsewhere had been shaped by the institutional organization of the
church since the Middle Ages, but he wanted this new "integral" culture to
contain a radical grass-roots element—a "Jacobin" element—which he
thought the Catholic Church had prevented from developing in Italian society. He also wanted to see the development of a democratic elite that
would welcome a socialist hegemony; he associated this elite with classical
culture. A fluent and confident command of the standard form of the vernacular language was crucial to the development of both Jacobin and elite
elements.

Because Gramsci's university education had been based in historical lin-
guistics, he created and defended his concept of civilization on the basis of
universal language skills and associated the "mass character" of the Reformation with use of the vernacular languages in Europe, rather than Latin.
Like Boethius, he identified the classical culture of Greek civilization with
the self-consciousness of members of class groupings and their political
power in the city- or nation-state. Every language, he believed, contained
the elements of a conception of the world and of a culture. The only question was which language and conceptions:

> Someone who only speaks dialect, or understands the standard language
> incompletely, necessarily has an intuition of the world which is more or
> less limited and provincial, which is fossilised and anachronistic in rela-
> tion to the major currents of thought which dominate world history.

He argued that at the very least it was "necessary to learn the national language properly," in order to command, through translation, if need be, a
"world-wide means of expression" and so to gain access to the "historic richness and complexity" of other great cultures—in short, of civilization.[53]
Normally, he considered, a prisoner's obsessive "chewing over the past" re-
sulted from the impossibility of his making plans for the future, and such
"constant searching of the past becomes comfortless and unprofitable."[54]
However, like Bonhoeffer's and Boethius's engagement with personal and
cultural histories, Gramsci used his thinking about history in his attempt to
make something of value for the future of society. He was as critical of
Croce's idealist philosophy (which he considered too abstract and disembodied) as he was of the opposite tendency that he saw developing in the

---

[52] Cf. Fiori, *Life*, p. 241.
[53] "The Study of Philosophy," note III; see *Selections from the Prison Notebooks*, p. 325.
[54] *Prison Letters*, pp. 133, 94.

antihistoricist materialism of post-Leninist, Marxist thought.[55] He therefore dismissed Croce's positivist philosophy as akin to "theological speculation" but argued against the equation of realism with any kind of materialism. (Gramsci scholars speculate that if Mussolini had not locked him up, Stalin would have had to shoot him.)

While the ordinary forms of dialectic in the philosophical cultures of Boethius and of More implied logic and verbal reasoning by challenge, and a dialogue of adversative rhetoric, for Gramsci, an adherent of Hegel's philosophy (especially as it influenced Marxism), dialectic also described a historical process of development by the continuous unification of opposites. Such contradiction and conflict (in historic time) was what made the world go forward and, so far as Gramsci was concerned, would also make it a better place, since the Hegelian synthesis created a higher truth. For Gramsci therefore dialectic became a feature of his habitual thought processes that mirrored the progress of historic development generally and were based on the conflict of opposing terms. These tendencies were exacerbated by the experience of imprisonment and by the "real psychology of a prisoner," which (as he explained to his sister-in-law) reflected his being subject to the "administrative machine" as "an object without will or subjective personality." "If to this machine and its irrational jerkings is added the irrational and chaotic flurryings of one's own relations, the prisoner feels himself absolutely crushed and pulverised." This condition might lead even a patient, educated man "capable of a great deal of self-restraint [to] become obstinate, and assert 'his own will' . . . just to prove to himself that he's still alive."[56]

Gramsci's dialectical habits of mind were strong and deep-rooted. As noted earlier, it was his reflections on the concept of Machiavelli's renaissance Prince that had challenged Gramsci to create his own idea of the Communist Party as the "modern Prince," or the "protagonist and organizer of intellectual and moral reform." In response to the combative thrust and pressure of what he called Machiavelli's "armies of words," Gramsci debated with himself in the prison notebooks for 1933–34:

> The active politician is a creator, an initiator; but he neither creates from nothing nor does he move in the turbid void of his own desires and dreams. He bases himself on effective reality, but what is this effective reality? Is it something static and immobile, or is it not rather a relation of forces in continuous motion and shift of equilibrium? If one applies

[55] See especially Buttigieg's section on "Gramsci's method" in his introduction to his 1992 Columbia edition of the *Prison Notebooks*, vol. 1, pp. 42–64, developed from analysis of Gramsci's entry (made between July and October 1929) on "Cuvier's little bone."

[56] *Prison Letters*, p. 188.

one's will to the creation of a new equilibrium among the forces which really exist and are operative—basing oneself on the particular force which one believes to be progressive and strengthening it to help it to victory—one still moves on the terrain of effective reality, but does so in order to dominate and transcend it (or to contribute to this).[57]

Among these "forces" he included the insubstantial realities of prejudice, and the effects of the historic role of the church in Italian society. The "superior ... form of modern civilization," which this active politician and intellectual historian (Gramsci now, rather than Machiavelli as the starting point for an argument with himself) attempted to create from within his prison cell, derived from the antagonism between his interpretation of "reality" and his own will to change that reality. Thus the past became identified with liberal-democratic premises of early twentieth-century society standing for an initial thesis of dialectic. The effects of a dominant political will—such as his own, or the Communist Party's—operating in the present was to be identified with the antithesis. Finally, the emergent synthesis—the "new equilibrium" or the "superior form of ... civilization" in the future—would "transcend" each of these antagonistic forces, even as it comprehended unquantifiable elements of both. The revolutionary outcome was to be a new consensus growing from the grass roots of a culturally homogenized society, rather than a violent insurrection that could be sustained only by terror.[58]

The literary substance of this kind of argument structure is evident throughout his prison notebooks since Gramsci tended to generate ideas from criticism of, and reaction to, the books he was reading. These processes give many of his notes and fuller expressions of his ideas a spontaneous quality. As readers, we gain the impression of a man thinking aloud and share the intellectual experience of that process as we follow the logic of his reactions to his adversaries. The argument seems to grow under his hand, but at the same time its logical rigor makes the line of development seem inevitable; such spontaneity and inevitability combine paradoxically. Sometimes Gramsci made himself a component in the initial antagonism; at other times he drew conclusions from the stimulus provided by his juxtaposition of different authors' views. Thus he was able to construct an argumentative dialogue either with contemporary reviewers of new books or with the theorists whose ideas had influenced his modern world: Croce, Bukharin, Machiavelli, Hitler. Thus:

[57] "The Modern Prince," *Selections from the Prison Notebooks*, p. 172.
[58] See J. M. Cammett, *Antonio Gramsci and the Origins of Italian Communism* (Stanford: Stanford University Press, 1969); and James Joll's succinct account of Gramsci's political theory in his *Gramsci*, Fontana Modern Masters series, ed. F. Kermode (Glasgow: Fontana/Collins, 1977).

In *Mein Kampf,* Hitler writes: "The founding or the destruction of a religion is an action of immeasurably greater importance than the founding or destruction of a State: not to speak of a party...." Superficial and acritical. The three elements—religion (or "active" conception of the world), State, party—are indissoluble.

Gramsci's initial reaction was forthright and combative; he then moved on to create a new idea in developing his reaction:

> In Machiavelli, in the ways and language of the time, an understanding of this necessary homogeneity and interrelation of the three elements can be observed. To lose one's soul in order to save one's country or State is an element of absolute laicism, of positive and negative conception of the world (against religion, or the dominant conception). In the modern world, a party is such ... when it is conceived, organised and led in ways and in forms such that it will develop integrally into a State ... and into a conception of the world.[59]

Gramsci developed his own ideas about how the party and the state reacted with and modified each other so that he might transform contemporary "ways of thinking and acting," which might then impinge (again) on state and party anew. He then considered what kinds of inflexibility and "fanaticism" would be likely to hinder this growth. The nature of the political argument and the literary form it takes mirror each other as dialectical structures. This correspondence between form and content also reveals the mental habits of the author that were exacerbated or intensified by his experiences of hardship and isolation in prison. These experiences drove him farther into a life of the mind. The rules of formal logic, he said, were like grammar: assimilated from practice in a "living" way. This intertextual dialogue in the prison notebooks and Gramsci's intellectual self-reliance generated new ways by which he hoped to build and refine society in the future.

## WOMEN, LETTERS, AND SELF-IMPRESSION

Such argumentative habits of mind were not restricted to Gramsci's prison writings on political philosophy, or Dante's poetry, or on the role of intellectuals in generating new forces in the world, as if in deference to some principle of rhetorical decorum for theoretical debate. This mode of thought by challenge and reaction had become ingrained in him and thus also affected the development of his closest personal relationships which during

---

[59] "Religion, State, Party" [1933], *Selections from the Prison Notebooks,* pp. 266–67.

his long imprisonment were mostly sustained (or sometimes partially suspended) by the exchange of letters. Shortly before he was imprisoned, Gramsci's Russian wife, Julia Schucht, retreated to Moscow (with their two young sons), where she suffered recurrent mental illness. Letters were their only means of direct communication, but as she was unable to write as often or fully as he required—she wrote about forty letters in ten years—their relationship gradually atrophied even though expressions of love, anxiety, and mutual dependence on each other continued from time to time.[60] They never met again. Her unmarried sister, Tatiana, who remained in Italy, looked after Gramsci's welfare as best she could and became their go-between.[61] In a letter from the prison at Turi (near Bari), Gramsci explained why he wanted to wait for Julia to write to him before he wrote to her again; his explanation seems an elaborate form of excuse, but it is nonetheless self-consciously revealing.

> I don't want to write to Julia yet; I want to receive one of her letters first . . . maybe it's because all my intellectual training (*formazione*) has been of a polemic nature; also it's even difficult for me to think "disinterestedly" likewise [to] study for the sake of study. Just occasionally, but rarely, I happen to forget myself during the course of a systematic order of considerations and seek out, as it were, in the things themselves, that which is of special interest to me personally in order to devote myself to their analysis. Usually, it is necessary for me to set myself a point of view formulated through dialogue or dialectic (*un punto di vista dialogico o dialettico*), otherwise I don't feel any intellectual stimulus. As I once told you, I don't like to pitch stones into the darkness. I want to have the sense of a real interlocutor or adversary; also, I want to create a dialogue in personal relationships. Otherwise it would seem to me that I was writing an epistolary novel, or whatever, and [that would be] to create bad literature.[62]

---

[60] "I always read your letters with immense interest, and they give me a few hours of serenity and happiness." To Julia Schucht, 29 August, 1932; *Prison Letters*, p. 233. Cf. "My darling, I'm so isolated that your letters are like bread for the starving. . . . So why do you measure the ration so cannily?" 24 November 1936; ibid., p. 272.

[61] See Antonio Gramsci, *Letters from Prison*, 2 vols., ed. Frank Rosengarten, tr. Raymond Rosenthal (New York: Columbia University Press, 1994), I, xviii–xx (on Gramsci's Schucht family correspondents), and pp. 8–9 (on Julia and Tatiana). Gramsci wrote about 476 prison letters to family and friends, more than half of these were to Tatiana who also passed some on to other friends, e.g., Sraffa (pp. 9–12).

[62] To Tatiana Schucht, 15 December 1930; cf. *Lettere dal carcere*, ed. S. Caprioglio and E. Fubini (Turin: Einaudi, 1965), p. 390. I owe this reference to Jonathan Steinberg. Cf. also *Letters from Prison*, I, 369. In October 1930 Gramsci had complained to Julia that they had never managed to get a "dialogue" going in their letters which were therefore lacking in "correspondence"; *Prison Letters*, p. 123.

While both More and Gramsci were polemical thinkers and writers before their imprisonments, in prison both men continued to defend their different conceptions of civilization by using combative, dialectical thought processes and the literary forms associated with these, including the dialogue of correspondence. In prison, these academic and scholastic tendencies to dialectic and dialogue were extended to family correspondence and reinforced and sharpened by personal reactions to their different circumstances. Gramsci wrote: "What I had not allowed for was the other prison which has been added to the first: it consists in being cut off not only from the life of society, but from family life as well."[63] Like More, he referred repeatedly to the importance of resistance to pressures that might compromise the integrity upon which he had established a position of influence and leadership in public life; and he expressed his fear of personal disintegration. Like More, Gramsci feared a failure of will at some crucial point in his imprisonment that might undermine important principles and annihilate some essential element of selfhood through a failure of resistance; this would effectively make him into a different person.

In March 1933, after nearly seven years in prison, and in particular after eighteen months of what he described as "a kind of continuous catastrophe," including the onset of his final tubercular disease, Gramsci wrote to Tatiana Schucht expressing his fears about what he might do, or become in prison, if such corrosive pressures continued. He discussed his situation in terms of a meaningful analogue that reveals his horror at the prospect of a failure of willpower. He told her the story of a small group of survivors from a shipwreck—another kind of catastrophe—that ends with some of the survivors eating human flesh. "If you had enquired of each of them beforehand, whether they would prefer to become cannibals or die, they would have answered in complete good faith, that—if such really were the alternatives—they would choose to die." But when the time came, and "when the choice forced itself upon them in all its practical immediacy," some of them changed their minds. In that case, asked Gramsci, "are they truly the same people as before? . . . they are not," he concluded.[64] As he applied this analogy, Gramsci decided that successive years of imprisonment—reaction to its pain, depri-

---

[63] To Tatiana Schucht, 19 May 1930, *Prison Letters*, p. 115; cf. *Letters from Prison*, I, 331. (Where available I have preferred the style of Henderson's translations.) Cf. "Have I bored you? Do you know, writing is now my substitute for conversation; I really feel that I am speaking to you when I write." To Tatiana Schucht, 19 March 1927, *Prison Letters*, p. 46.

[64] To Tatiana Schucht, 6 March 1933; cf. *Letters from Prison*, II, 278–79; and Fiori, *Life*, p. 275. Buttigieg notes that on 20 March "an independent doctor examined Gramsci in prison" and concluded that he could not "survive long under [his] present conditions." The doctor recommended urgent transfer to hospital, but Gramsci "refused to ask for a pardon which would have allowed him to leave prison and seek treatment under better conditions" (*Prison Notebooks*, vol. 1, p. 92). He considered that asking Mussolini for mercy would be a form of suicide (Fiori, *Life*, p. 277).

vations, and uncertainties—would cause a new personality to emerge; speaking impersonally, he concluded, "men of good faith" would be undermined by catastrophe and "transformed." The new synthesis created under this pressure would represent a horrific degradation of civilized man. Thomas More, the Christian humanist and theologian, had imagined himself playing St. Peter and denying his master, in which case he would no longer be a man of "good faith." Gramsci imagined this personal disintegration, in an equally appropriate metaphor for a dialectical materialist, as eating one's own kind. Maintaining the will to survive as oneself under the pressure of persecution, fear, and hardship became another way of defending civilization that More and Gramsci each achieved in the dialogue of their personal correspondence with intelligent, sensitive, and devoted women.

Gramsci enjoyed writing and regularly used his full allowance on letter writing days in prison. He scolded members of his family if they did not respond or left him without news: "You just can't manage to get any sort of picture of what it's like to be in prison, and of the importance which correspondence takes on—how it fills up the blank days, and continues to give a certain savour to life."[65] He was afraid of losing not only the intellectual stimulus of an interlocutor but also the capacity to feel human. After two years as a prisoner, he had written to his wife: "I'm always afraid of being overcome by the prison routine, a monstrous machine which crushes and grinds with definite method."[66] Letters from home gave him what he called "the direct living impression" that enabled him to resist the power of the prison machine to deform and destroy those within its control. In this respect, the correspondence, or dialogue in letters, with Tatiana Schucht, who also visited him regularly, was Gramsci's lifeline.

Tatiana was his sparring partner; although she had a natural sciences degree from the University of Rome, she did not consider herself his intellectual equal, but she was creatively provoking (intentionally and unintentionally) and fully aware of his need for dialogue. Writing letters gave her significant opportunities to stimulate a wide range of lively responses in her correspondent, which all helped to promote his welfare (although he frequently became frustrated and angry at her interference, as he saw it, when she used her own judgment). When she told him about lectures on Greek

---

[65]  To his mother, 24 August 1931, *Prison Letters*, p. 157; cf. *Letters from Prison*, II, 58. See also my note 60. Contrast his stoicism to Tatiana (9 November 1931): "These particular five years are a swathe out of the most important and productive period in a man's life. But there's nothing to be done about it: they've passed by, and I have no desire to tot up the profit and loss, or to cry my eyes out over this stretch of my life that has gone to the devil...I can't manage to concentrate my attention on any subject; I feel myself as stultified intellectually as I am worn out physically" (*Prison Letters*, pp. 180–81; cf. *Letters from Prison*, II, 98–99).

[66]  To Julia Schucht, 19 November 1928, *Prison Letters*, p. 87; cf. *Letters from Prison*, I, 233. See also my note 56 for this same metaphor used in January 1932.

philosophy that she had attended recently, she provoked a mixture of academic gossip and pedantic footnotes from Gramsci. In his response, he also joked about the inappropriateness of her proposal to send him Sardinian-style yogurt (*gioddu*) as a reminder of home. It would be pointless since if it did not contain a certain necessary "dose of dirt in shepherd and environment . . . [and] one cannot fix this element with mathematical accuracy," it would not be genuine; she was therefore advised to give up this idea of "playing Amaryllis or Chloe in some dainty Arcadian painting."[67] His deployment of a literary Greek pastoral theme echoed her comments about the lectures she had attended. Although Gramsci often seems patronizing to his sister-in-law, his most characteristic tone in response to her questions, comments, and speculations in many different letters was a mixture of affectionate teasing and exasperation. Yet he could also respond frankly and seriously to her comments about life. Thus, in this same letter he quoted the comments she had offered in her previous letter, which he then used as a starting point for his own meditation, since, "joking apart," he explained, "I have devoted a great deal of thought to the questions you raise, and about which you get impassioned." This was a real dialogue; yet he had also considered his own responsibilities and actions, and went on—as if to himself—to raise new questions about duty in human relations: "But there is a further question: giving and receiving may balance up in the general reckoning, but do they balance up in single individual cases?" While talking on paper about his own situation and the emotional costs of high principles, Gramsci here adopted an impersonal style:

> When one has harnessed one's whole life to a certain end, when one concentrates towards the achieving of that end the whole sum of one's energies and one's will . . . a man may perhaps discover that he seems egotistic to the very people that he would never have thought could see him in that light. And he discovers the origin of the error, which is weakness—the weakness of not having dared to remain alone, of not having refused to permit himself ties of love, obligations, close relationships, etc. (7 April 1931)

But even this terrible train of thought ended in self-conscious mockery of its logical conclusion: "I have hopes that in a few more years I'll be completely mummified." This letter also contains a teasing plea that *carissima Tatiana* should not be tempted to take herself too seriously either. Even as he contemplated the awful prospect of denying his own humanity, the external pressure of maintaining a dialogue in correspondence that became, as that

---

[67] 7 April 1931 (*Prison Letters*, pp. 141–42; cf. *Letters from Prison*, II, 25–27, at 26).

of More and Margaret Roper had been, "a substitute for conversation" provided a counterbalance that, he was happy to acknowledge, helped to keep him fully alive. This irony has also helped to soften his reputation, keeping his humanity to the fore, and complementing the image of the political philosopher seen in the prison notebooks.

Gramsci's need for dialogue in his personal correspondence places the confidence, intellectual rigor, and objectivity of the remorseless logician against a background of self-doubt, humor, and compassion. His letters give Gramsci—the stern and cerebral ideologue—the human face of a family man of letters: a secular martyr, as fearful of his own potential to sacrifice his integrity as More had been of his potential to let his soul go to the devil. Both sides of each man have been important in convincing readers that these prisoners' ideas and values had been tested by experience. Their dialogues in letters from prison may not have had the primary purpose of their didactic and polemic writings. The prison letters of More and Gramsci are neither a defense of civilization in the abstract nor an argument for organizing the way of the world, yet they provided testimony for others of practical ways to live a human(e) life. Furthermore, when seen here in conjunction with each other, their different responses to their situation, as prisoners, can modify perceptions of them as philosophers, politicians, and men. Alongside Gramsci, we see more clearly in More the political aspects of his resistance as a Christian martyr. Next to More, we glimpse the devout vocation of the Italian communist: Gramsci the new renaissance humanist and witty, ironic, family man. Finally, although their concepts of humanity and civilization in different times, cultures, and languages were not mutually compatible, the problems and dangers each faced and wrote about, as prisoners of conscience and state, can make abstract contradictions merge into a higher synthesis that may comprehend us all. "In human life," wrote the prisoner Gramsci, asserting the authority of experience, "it may happen ... that the more an individual is compelled to defend his own physical existence, the more will he uphold and identify with the highest values of civilisation and of humanity—in all their complexity."[68] More's defense of the church was matched by Gramsci's concern for the state. Each of these prisoners recognized that to practice and anticipate one's reactions before or during a crisis may mitigate the effects of fear and actual persecution by enabling the writer to synthesize a stronger or clearer sense of self-worth. The political tactics of

[68] "The Modern Prince," 1933–34, 1st version 1931–32, *Selections from the Prison Notebooks*, p. 170. For a summary of trends in the reception of Gramsci's ideas, and examples of their recent applications, see *Gramsci and Global Politics: Hegemony and Resistance*, ed. M. McNally and J. Schwarzmantel (London: Routledge, 2009), esp. pp. 1–16 (Schwarzmantel's introduction), and Will Leggett, "Prince of Modernisers: Gramsci, New Labour and the Meaning of Modernity," pp. 137–55.

each dialectician were complemented by their personal correspondence with loyal and intelligent women. Both prisoners defended their highest values for the good of themselves, their contemporaries, and future generations when stimulated to engage in the dialogues implicit within these family letters.

Each of the subjects in this section, the philosopher, the theologian, the lawyer, and the political theorist, addressed himself first to a specific political and ideological conflict against a repressive power and founded his tactics of resistance, in prison writing, upon reason and creative argumentation. In each case, however, the prisoner also used his writing to promote an image of himself that upheld and represented his values for the sake of readers. The need to account for and to preserve their personal histories, and thus images of themselves, led many prisoners to write personal confessions as literary memorials. Boethius, it should not be forgotten, began the process of enacting the *Consolation of Philosophy* within a framework of personal memoir. The next section examines this application for writing as a primary strategy by prisoners who argued their own cases and sought to preserve literary memorials to themselves, in various kinds of life-writing or autobiographical modes of literary self-impression.

# PART II

# Preservation of Self

# CHAPTER 3

## Memory and Self-Justification: Images of
## Grace and Disgrace Abounding

I can speak of memory and I recognize what I speak of. But where else do I
recognize it except in my memory itself? Can it be that the memory is not
present to itself in its own right but only by means of an image of itself?
(Augustine, *Confessions*, X, 15.)

The first part of this section explores the use of confessional modes of writing. It argues that the stories John Bunyan and Oscar Wilde told themselves
and their readers about their different situations were forms of self-
justification based on personal memories of past events that had either
caused or directly contributed to their imprisonment. Yet, as in any life-
writing, the construction of a readable image of self had to be shaped by received conventions derived from other writers' cultural (as well as personal)
memories in order to be accessible to others. This act of creation was therefore never purely personal in terms of either its resources or its textual out-
comes.[1] In addition, writers who specifically ask readers to recognize them
as writers in prison always have a range of motives beyond those expected of
authors in other circumstances. If a writer seeks to bare his soul, and offer its
representation as a literary construct for the judgment of others, what are
the public or political risks and gains in deploying affective tactics to evoke
sympathy and understanding in controversial cases? In prison, Bunyan and
Wilde each sought to construct a rhetorical self-image as a martyr by exploiting shared cultural hierarchies of earlier texts. Their resources are literary and contingent, just as their personal memories were presumed to be,
and, as in any of the various forms of life-writing, the hybridity of forms and
modes used in their prison writing to shape and preserve textual impressions of self had wider significances. For the purposes of this chapter, "justi-

---

[1] For assessments of recent theoretical discussion of many of these problems (without reference
to Bunyan's or Wilde's life writings), see Max Saunders, *Self Impression: Life-Writing, Autobiografiction, and the Forms of Modern Literature* (Oxford: Oxford University Press, 2010).

fication" implies showing good reason for an action and declaring an act, person, or situation as righteous, acceptable, and therefore forgivable. The literary choices made by Bunyan as a godly nonconformist in Restoration England and by Wilde as a late-Victorian aesthete suggest that they likely chose to write in prison to justify themselves in the midst of their personal turmoil and crises of identity caused by imprisonment. Yet, in publishing (or envisaging publication) of their literary confessions as justified sinners of different kinds, they wrote to persuade others to remember them as well as to learn from them. In each case, the prisoner made constructive use of his local public image as a radical dissenter and social dissentient. The later reception of those self-impressions in writing has ensured that these new textual versions of the prisoners' selves have overwritten and outlived other versions created by the English legal system that punished each of them by imprisonment.

Bunyan's *Grace Abounding to the Chief of Sinners* describes his spiritual life story, in particular his experience of the discovery of God's grace, by means of what appear to be random interactions with biblical texts. The narrative is episodic in form as well as content, being composed of numbered sections of prose, some occupying a page or more of printed text and others only a few lines. Bunyan's prison writing was explicitly designed to substitute for his preaching; in this respect, it shares some of the political functions of prison writing in the previous section. While the themes and the forms of his writing are explicitly personal, in the context of seventeenth-century ideas of the spiritual life and of the importance of realizing and circulating this kind of self-image, they are not exclusive. The main sections of spiritual autobiography are framed by descriptions of Bunyan's arrest, trial, and various discussions of his case, which provide explanations for his political stance and its consequences that were borne by his family as well as himself. Bunyan knew that his effectiveness and personal authority to edify the faithful (as an unlicensed preacher) depended not only on his being personally assured of the grace of God but also on his being recognized as a justified sinner by others—hence, the publication of his text during his imprisonment. His experience of the life of the spirit and the condition of the prisoner of conscience were presented to readers within the same work to preserve his public self-image as a dissenter and to authenticate the message of his text.

Wilde's confessional writing adopted the literary form he and his readers associated with religious martyrs' pastoral care for others. Like Bunyan's readers, Wilde knew that the Pauline epistles were shared vehicles for authoritative teaching on the life of the spirit. His letter from prison (*De Profundis*) was addressed in the first instance to one individual and made detailed reference to shared memories of their relationship, which he offered to interpret for their mutual benefit, claiming a superior understanding from the "privilege" of suffering that he associated with the Christian message in the Greek Bible. Yet Wilde also envisaged later readers who had witnessed his humiliation and degradation as a public figure sentenced on criminal charges. Certainly the social significance and often the conditions of imprisonment were far worse and more strictly applied in Wilde's England than Bunyan's. It seems clear that the prisoner Wilde wrote his letter from prison in the hope that it might reconfigure his situation of "disgrace abounding" and reclaim for posterity the reputation of a wise and insightful critic of life and art. To these ends, the prisoner revised his life story, exploiting biblical themes, language, and role models, as well as drawing on classical literary genres and models. The established authority of these texts, acknowledged by contemporary readers, would be instrumental in helping the prisoner to engage the attention and respect of his readers (in the context of other worthy or valuable teaching), on the basis of personal experience. Both Wilde and Bunyan claimed paradoxically, in common with other prison writers, that they had been privileged in their suffering because their struggles to understand how they came into prison granted them spiritual rewards and new insights. These were then communicated to readers, who were encouraged to respond to the new authority of carceral experience reflected in each prisoner's writing.

In both texts, the recording consciousness of a prisoner explains the reasons for his imprisonment; the narrative is therefore restricted to events and interactions that changed the author's past life and created his literary persona's new responses to them: self-knowledge. The protagonist of each narrative is thus a doubly displaced persona—not only a literary construct but also a shadow from the past—and no longer a separate consciousness except insofar as this is represented by the converted prison writer's quotations of his reprobate self's speech or thoughts. The memorial testimony of the prisoner connotes the experiences of his narrative's shadowy protagonist but specifies different perceptions of these experiences; in this way, each prisoner offers his recollections of personal memories as expert interpretations of historic actions, and description or analysis is coupled with dramatic dialogue. Each of these life stories is mythic. Wilde's memorial reconstruction of his personal story insists that suffering defines life as a vale of soul making, whereas Bunyan's deconstruction of eternally deferred meanings of suffering insists that life is a process of soul discovery. For the sake of the present argument, the soul may be defined by each writer as an essential, true, and secret inner core of his unique, but not necessarily exceptional, personal identity. In very different situations of public disgrace, their literary strategies as prison writers were orientated toward restoring their displaced status as authors and authentic authority figures; the status each was thought to have lost as a prisoner—relatively, a greater loss for Wilde—he regained as a writer. This observation leads to another paradox of prison writing: readers' sympathies create proximity in, and approximations to, situations that actually separate the outcast writer from the world of his reader—even the contemporary reader—who is not a prisoner. Both writers also appealed directly to established religious traditions of charity toward prisoners.

## John Bunyan, *Grace Abounding to the Chief of Sinners* (1666): Writing the Eternally Present Self

After the Restoration of the monarchy in 1660, and the (re)establishment of the Anglican Church, many nonconformist preachers were persecuted or their activities suppressed. John Bunyan was imprisoned in November 1660, charged that he had "devilishly and perniciously abstained from coming to church," and that he was an upholder of "unlawful meetings and conventicles, to the great disturbance and distraction of the good subjects of this kingdom."[2] The sentence upon conviction should have been three months in prison. Bunyan might have secured his freedom by promising to forswear his unlicensed public preaching, but this he repeatedly refused to do, saying that his "conscience" would not "suffer" him to do it, and "I dare not but exercise that gift which God hath given me, for the good of the people" (*A Relation*, pp. 103, 114). He was imprisoned in the county jail at Bedford where he remained a prisoner for the next twelve years until the Declaration of Indulgence in 1672 brought a period of religious toleration.[3] Bunyan's imprisonment was not continuous; like other early modern English prisoners, he was able to "wander" (under supervision), released occasionally for short periods to visit family and friends; he even addressed meetings locally and in London. New charges were laid in 1662 that a recent visit to London had been made "to plot and raise division, and make insurrection." After

---

[2] *A Relation of the Imprisonment of Mr John Bunyan*, first published in 1765 from Bunyan's manuscript and since reprinted with editions of *Grace Abounding*. See John Bunyan, *Grace Abounding with Other Spiritual Autobiographies*, ed. J. Stachniewski with A. Pacheco (Oxford: Oxford University Press, 1998, rpt. 2008), pp. 97–122, at p. 106. All quotations from this Oxford World's Classics edition unless indicated.

[3] For the life of Bunyan in historical contexts, see R. L. Greaves's article in *Oxford Dictionary of National Biography* (2004 and online revisions); and his *Glimpses of Glory: John Bunyan and English Dissent* (Stanford: Stanford University Press, 2002). As Michael Davies notes in the context of the persecutions that followed the passing of the First Conventicle Act (1664): "Far from being simply the confessions of a solitary, private 'I' . . . *Grace Abounding* bespeaks a powerful spirit of solidarity" with a community under increased threat ("*Grace Abounding to the Chief of Sinners*: John Bunyan and Spiritual Autobiography," in *The Cambridge Companion to Bunyan*, ed. A. Dunan-Page [Cambridge: Cambridge University Press, 2010], pp. 67–79, at 78).

this, Bunyan reported, "my liberty was more straitened than it was before; so that I must not look out of the door" (p. 121). The political implications of his actions were such that at any time after the initial three months' sentence Bunyan was at risk of transportation for his continued refusal to conform. It is also clear from his own account of his imprisonment that during one early period of depression, "being but a young [i.e., inexperienced] prisoner," he feared the death penalty: "I was also at this time so possessed with the thought of death, that oft I was as if I was on the Ladder, with the Rope about my neck."[4] He wrote that he consoled himself at that time with the idea that, in addressing the multitude he thought would come to see his execution, he might "convert one soul by [his] very last words" and thus not lose his life in vain (§268, pp. 91–92).

His attitude to his imprisonment seems ambivalent. He wrote movingly about how "the parting with my Wife and poor Children hath oft been to me in this place, as the pulling the flesh from my bones" evoking the same image of torture that was later used by Bonhoeffer (§260, p. 89). Absence from his family caused distress and acute hardship. At one point in *A Relation of the Imprisonment of Mr John Bunyan*, Bunyan represented his wife's speech to Justice Hale: "I have four small children, that cannot help themselves, of which one is blind, and have nothing to live upon, but the charity of good people" (*A Relation*, p. 119). The present-tense, direct-speech forms enhance the pathos of her position. In the same dialogue Bunyan indicated that she suffered a miscarriage when her husband was arrested. Although Bunyan's authorial persona naturally regretted the plight of his wife and children (the suffering of his blind daughter was an especially emotive topic), there are also signs that this regret was tactical. He wrote that he was "not altogether without hopes, but that my imprisonment might be an awakening to the Saints in the country, therefore I could not tell well which to chuse," liberty or imprisonment (p. 105). As a prisoner of conscience who might have obtained his release by outwardly conforming with the law that prohibited unlicensed preaching, Bunyan, like Gramsci, must have felt a measure of personal responsibility for his family's hardships: "O I saw in this condition I was as a man who was pulling down his house upon the head of his Wife and Children; yet thought I, I must do it, I must do it" (§262, p. 90). He would also have felt a personal need to justify the position he had taken in such circumstances—hence, his reconstructions of them in writing.

---

[4] *Grace Abounding*, ed. Stachniewski, §§266 and 268, p. 91; this edition of the text and layout follows the first edition of 1666, with correspondences to the section numbering of the enlarged, third edition indicated in square brackets.

To support his family, the prisoner made and sold long-tagged laces and wrote devotional verse for publication, including the blatantly politicized title *Prison-Meditations, Directed to the Heart of Suffering Saints and Reigning Sinners* (1663). These prison meditations identify the poet as a prisoner who asks that his "Friends write to me, that I would hold / my Head above the Flood," emphasizing the importance of letters in maintaining the welfare and resistance of the prisoner, as seen in other prison writing. (These lines were omitted in the second edition, which was also published while Bunyan remained a prisoner, but possibly a more confident one.)

> I am (indeed) in Prison (now)
> In body, but my Mind
> Is free to study Christ, and how
> Unto me he is kind.
>
> For though men keep my outward man
> Within their Locks and Bars,
> Yet by the Faith of Christ I can
> Mount higher than the Stars.
>
> Their Fetters cannot Spirits tame,
> Nor tye up God from me.[5]

Bunyan reiterated a classic theme of resistance in celebrating the freedom of the mind; his consolation in prison was that he had preached "Grace and Faith" to sinners in power, which was his "comfort" (p. 43). In prison Bunyan also wrote a conduct manual, a polemical defense of his refusal to use the Book of Common Prayer (both printed in 1663), and an exegetical work expounding symbolism in the book of Revelation (1665). These were published during his imprisonment to further his "business" of saving souls. His best-known prison writings are *Grace Abounding* (1666), and the first part of *The Pilgrim's Progress* published in 1678, after his release.

In *Pilgrim's Progress,* the allegory of Christian's journey from this world to "that which is to come" is presented "under the similitude of a dream" in the first sentence; the narrator describes himself as lying in "a den," which is glossed in the margin: "The gaol."[6] There is no further intrusive reference to this situation, but the prison context established at the beginning might help to explain the intensity of the imaginative, introspective world created by the author. Although the pilgrim figure only represents the narrator and

---

[5] John Bunyan, *The Poems*, ed. G. Midgley (Oxford: Clarendon Press, 1980), pp. 42–51 at 42–43, text of first edition as indicated by Midgley's apparatus and notes.

[6] John Bunyan, *The Pilgrim's Progress*, ed. R. Sharrock (Harmondsworth: Penguin, 1968), p. 39; a facsimile of the 1678 title page is included as p. 29.

the author (insofar as they share the universal allegory of Christian's spiritual journey through life), some of the most memorable episodes in *Pilgrim's Progress* represent despair by exploiting images of imprisonment. Thus, in the Interpreter's House despair is seen "as a man sat in an iron cage" who cries that he cannot get out, and in Doubting Castle Christian and Hopeful are imprisoned in "a dark dungeon, nasty and stinking" by the Giant Despair. When Christian and Faithful are paraded in chains and put in the cage in Vanity Fair, they are beaten and mocked for disturbing the peace and deluding the men of the Fair, which may be seen as imaginative reworkings of a situation parallel to Bunyan's, as well as existential conceptions. After their trial, Faithful is executed ("Hanging is too good for him," said Mr Cruelty), but Christian is remanded in prison until he finally escapes.[7]

*Grace Abounding* develops a different approach to the problems of the Christian's spiritual identity and destiny.[8] Instead of a generalized allegory (as in *Pilgrim's Progress*), which may be interpreted in different ways by individuals searching for paradigms of Christian experience, in *Grace Abounding* Bunyan was seen to offer an account, "or, a brief and faithful relation," as the 1666 title page claims, of his own spiritual experience.[9] This narrative is offered "for the support of the weak and tempted People of God." The title-page epigraph speaks alongside the psalmist, inviting readers, *"Come and hear, all ye that fear God; and I will declare what he hath done for my soul,* Psal. 66.16." In *Grace Abounding,* the narrator and authorial persona of Bunyan *is* a pilgrim, but, his journey being incomplete, he is more appropriately represented as the protagonist in a series of battles. At the end of the work, Bunyan wrote: "Many more of the Dealings of God towards me I might relate, but these out of the spoils won in Battel have I dedicated to maintain the House of God, 1 Chron. 26. 27" (§272, pp. 92–93). The emphasis throughout is thus on process, "dealings," rather than progress; the argument of *Grace Abounding* is not, as in *Pilgrim's Progress,* an exposition of the ends that await Christian and Faithful (and why might these differ), but rather how one may recognize the "treasure of ... experience of the grace of God" and the "merciful kindness and working of God" upon one's

    [7] Ibid., pp. 65–67, 152, 128, and 134.

    [8] For a convenient survey of twentieth-century, critical approaches to *Grace Abounding*, see T. Spargo, " 'I being taken from you in presence': *Grace Abounding to the Chief of Sinners* and Claims to Authority," in her *The Writing of John Bunyan* (Aldershot: Ashgate, 1997), pp. 43–67. For later trends, see the summary analysis in Beth Lynch, *John Bunyan and the Language of Conviction* (Cambridge: D. S. Brewer, 2004), pp. 1–9; and *The Cambridge Companion to Bunyan*, including the reception of Bunyan's texts and reputation.

    [9] See facsimile and transcript in Roger Sharrock's 1962 Clarendon Press edition of *Grace Abounding*, p. xxxiii and facing p. 1. Cf. Kathleen Lynch, "Into Jail and into Print: John Bunyan Writes the Godly Self," in *Prison Writings in Early Modern England*, ed. W. H. Sherman and W. J. Sheils, *Huntington Library Quarterly*, 72 (2009), 273–90.

soul, by reference to another's account of his spiritual experience, both before and during his actual imprisonment.[10] *Grace Abounding* is concerned with demonstrating to Bunyan's contemporaries what it feels like to believe one is either a sinful reprobate or elected for salvation, and how one may recognize a spiritual "awakening," if, and when, it comes. Two-thirds of the way through the text, Bunyan addressed the reader, summarizing the argument so far:

> Having thus in few words, given you a taste of the sorrow and affliction that my Soul went under by the guilt and terror that this my wicked thought did lay me under; and having given you also a touch of my deliverance therefrom, and of the sweet and blessed comfort that I met with afterwards, (which comfort dwelt about a twelve-month with my heart, to my unspeakable admiration) I will now (God willing) before I proceed any further, give you in a word or two, what, as I conceive, was the cause of this Temptation; and also after that, what advantage at the last, it became unto my Soul. (§190, p. 67)

The narrative action of his account was completed before his imprisonment, but the memorial image of that action, created for his readers, is subtly colored by the writer's contemporary status as a prisoner.

## AUTHENTIC SUFFERING

Bunyan's sufferings as a prisoner of conscience are an intrinsic part of his message in *Grace Abounding*; they help to authenticate the narrative of his discovery of faith and demonstrate the effects of the gift of grace that identify him as one of the elect. In his brief account of his call to the ministry, the prisoner speculated that his experience served "to confirm the Truth by way of Suffering," by contrast with his previous method (as a free man) "in testifying of it according to the Scriptures, in a way of Preaching" (§232, p. 79). Here Bunyan embarks on a circular argument. He saw his ability to survive persecution as a mark of God's grace which (according to his theol-

---

[10] Cf. the contemporary spiritual *Memoirs* of Thomas Halyburton, where he recounts the "Lord's gracious conduct toward me . . . in a way that shall tend to the conviction, consolation, and edification of the reader . . . and . . . be a great use to my own confirmation," quoted by V. Newey, " 'With the eyes of my understanding': Bunyan, Experience, and Acts of Interpretation," in *John Bunyan Conventicle and Parnassus: Tercentenary Essays*, ed. N. H. Keeble (Oxford: Clarendon Press, 1988), pp. 189–216, at 191. A. H. Hawkins ("John Bunyan the Conflictive Paradigm," in *Archetypes of Conversion: The Autobiographies of Augustine, Bunyan and Merton* [Lewisburg: Bucknell University Press, 1985], pp. 73–99) quotes Halyburton's assertion that "the work of the Lord, in substance, is uniform and the same in all; and 'as face answereth to face in a glass,' so does one Christian's experience answer to another's, and both to the word of God," citing G. A. Starr, *Defoe and Spiritual Autobiography* (Princeton: Princeton University Press, 1963), p. 14.

ogy) is freely given to the elect soul and may be recognized as faith and hope. However, this faith was confirmed by his own choice to prolong the persecution of a long and tedious imprisonment, rather than conform. The leap of faith required to break this hermeneutic circle is inferred at the end of *Grace Abounding* when Satan asks the inexperienced "Prisoner" considering martyrdom, "What evidence have you for heaven and glory, and an inheritance among them that are sanctified?" (§§266–69, pp. 91–92).[11] There is no answer; but the preacher considers:

> That it was for the Word and the Way of God that I was in this condition [i.e., prison] . . . God might chuse whether he would give me comfort . . . but I might not therefore chuse whether I would hold my profession or no: I was bound, but he was free. (§§269–70)

The nature of the charge against Bunyan was enough to bind the actual prisoner to his "duty to stand to [God's] word." In justifying his spiritual life story by recollecting his experience, Bunyan similarly made his choice to assume that he had no choice. His authorial persona—the older, experienced prisoner—recalls the reasoning of his younger self:

> Wherefore, thought I, the point being thus, I am for going on, and venturing my eternal state with Christ, whether I have comfort here or no; if God doth not come in, thought I, I will off the Ladder even blindfold into Eternitie, sink or swim, come heaven, come hell; Lord Jesus, if thou wilt catch me, do; I will venture for thy Name. (§270, p. 92)[12]

His venture is his risk of execution by hanging. Such "blindfold" faith is an incalculable risk. But writing about it for others was more calculated.

Bunyan's idea of his authority on spiritual matters, including the value of his assessment of the nature of God's dealings with his soul, was also more calculated. He foresaw that his authority would be founded on his record of that spiritual experience composed in the midst of his captivity and, paradoxically, that evasion or escape would be detrimental. He described his rationalization of the value of his arrest, trial, and punishment in the following terms:

---

[11] Cf. Thomas More's satisfaction at the conjunction of significations drawn from the date of his execution.

[12] Richard Greaves believed that Bunyan's concern with eschatological themes was "a direct outgrowth of his incarceration," but this is not a prominent concern of prison writing, and I suggest that, like Bunyan's exposition of millenarian themes in his commentary on Revelation, *The Holy City* (1665), this was more a sign of the times than his situation as a prisoner. Cf. R. Greaves, "Conscience, Liberty, and the Spirit: Bunyan and Nonconformity," in *John Bunyan and English Nonconformity* (London: Hambledon Press, 1992), pp. 51–70; see further, J. R. Knott, *Discourses of Martyrdom in English Literature, 1563–1694* (Cambridge: Cambridge University Press, 1993).

Therefore thought I, if I should now run, and make an escape, it will be of a very ill savour in the country. For what will my weak and newly converted brethren think of it? But that I was not so strong in deed, as I was in word. Also I feared that if I should run now there was a warrant out for me, I might by so doing make them afraid to stand, when great words only should be spoken to them. Besides I thought, that seeing God of his mercy should chuse me to go upon the forlorn hope in this country; that is, to be the first, that should be opposed, for the Gospel; if I should fly, it might be a discouragement to the whole body that might follow after. And further, I thought the world thereby would take occasion at my cowardliness, to have blasphemed the Gospel, and to have had some ground to suspect worse of me and my profession, than I deserved. (*A Relation*, pp. 98–99)

Bunyan seems to have been aware that a reader's interest in *Grace Abounding* would be focused on its testimony to a common humanity, especially a vivid inner life, as well as on his particular spiritual experience, which he offered to others as a model and guide. This influenced how he wrote while in prison and why he added dramatic incidents and enhanced pathos in later editions published after his release.

## MEMORY AND THE PRISONER

At the beginning of *Grace Abounding,* Bunyan states that he wrote to justify his perception of the gift of grace, for the sake of honoring God for this gift—not to explain it. Furthermore, he intended to use his memory of how he personally arrived at this perception of grace for the sake of reminding others to consider what God had already done for them. (The work is dedicated to those "children" whom "God hath counted him worthy to beget to Faith, by his Ministry in the Word"[ p. 3]). The injunction to remember is a recurrent motif in the preface to *Grace Abounding* and in the work at large: "call to mind the former days . . . 'remember also your songs in the night' (Psalm 77:5–12)."

It is profitable for Christians to be often calling to mind the very beginnings of Grace with their Souls. . . . Remember, I say . . . remember . . . remember also . . . (preface, pp. 4–5)

An important precedent for Bunyan's spiritual exercise as a prisoner is the "accustomed manner" of St. Paul, who "when tried for his life, Acts 24" would "open" or layout "before his Judges the manner of his Conversion:

He would think of that day and that hour, in the which he first did meet with Grace: for he found it [a] support unto him" (p. 4). According to Bunyan's theology, the central act of Christian worship is an act of remembrance of the Lord's Supper: "*Do this in remembrance of me,*' Luke 22.19" (§207, p. 72). Bunyan showed his awareness of the importance of memory and re-enactment when he demonstrated, as well as described, the inner struggles that had characterized the testing of his faith. Among the different voices represented in this reenactment are those of his soul, Satan (or the Tempter), and Scripture. These internal conflicts are typical of nonconformist, spiri-tual autobiography but also resemble the dialogic expositions of similar metaphysical problems by other Christian writers in prison, including Boe-thius and Thomas More. The vivid representations of Bunyan's authorial persona are also typical of the imaginative resources used by different kinds of prisoner to bring their known past and uncertain future into a consoling dialectical relationship; this enables them to make sense of their liminal state as prisoners, cut off from free association and sensory perceptions of the external world.

When he first embarked on "the business of Faith," the authorial persona pitying his shadow—the protagonist of the past narrative—explained to readers that he had no practical knowledge of it.

> But, alas, poor Wretch! so ignorant and brutish was I, that I knew to this day no more how to do it, than I know how to begin and accomplish that rare and curious piece of Art, which I never yet saw nor considered. (§38, p. 18)

What he *knew*, in the past, *to this day*, in the present, indicates the fusion of the different stages in a process that creates a historic present for the sake of enlivening the experience. In this "business" of faith, experience, even that of memories made manifest in writing, is knowledge, yet significantly the descriptive metaphor involves the productions of rare fine art. This attitude to writing as knowledge had been assumed when he considered the value of recollecting a particular moment,

> wherefore I said in my Soul with much gladness, Well, I would I had a pen and ink here, I would write this down before I go any further, for surely I will not forget *this*, forty years hence. (§74, p. 28)

What the protagonist had hoped to remember about his spiritual experi-ence, the prison writer recollected in order to "lay down the *thing* as it was," in the "plain and simple" language conventionally prescribed for matters related to salvation (preface, p. 5). The problem here is that the style of the memory made manifest, as well as the truth of the spiritual experience, must be made substantial; the "thing" must be physically "laid down."[13] Bunyan used two principal methods to fix his memories, making them communicable and credible.

The first is a simple variant on the ancient arts of memory in which details are recalled by the evocation of place: passing in the field, on the street in Bedford, sitting by the fireside at home. The second is more intrinsic—it defines and structures his experience—and follows his own advice to readers in the preface to *Grace Abounding*: "Remember also the Word." Just as the Bible is the record constructed by human scribes of God's dealings with mankind, so *Grace Abounding* is presented to its readers as the record of God's dealings with John Bunyan. But whereas the authority of Scripture in his society was absolute and final, that of *Grace Abounding* is contingent and peculiar, or personal, to him. Bunyan therefore sought to define himself by borrowing the authority of Scripture to authenticate the process of his discovery of God's grace—the long labor of his rebirth—which is enacted by his struggles with biblical texts. The Bible validates his story because it substantiates it and because *history* may be construed from it.

As Bunyan's authorial persona—the prisoner—recalls the chief events of this life story, they all seem to have occurred in response to the agency of scriptural texts. Some of their actions are murderous ("this was that which kill'd me, and stood like a Spear against me"); but the prisoner also reports a wider range of direct and indirect actions. Thus, they did *visit* his soul and *brought comfort*; at other times they did *seize upon* his soul, *fell upon, tear and rend* his soul; he was either *refreshed* or, more likely, *given a justle* when they *bolted in upon* him; or did *pinch* him *very sore* just as *their visage changed*; "for they looked not so grimly" as he previously thought they did.[14] The physical effort expended in these encounters was remarkable. Sometimes, he reported, a text would cry out as if running after him:

> And sometimes it would sound so loud within me, yea, and as it were call so strongly after me, that once above all the rest, I turned my head over my shoulder, thinking verily that some man had behind me called to me, being at a great distance. (§75, p. 28)

(And again, "that Scripture fastned on my heart . . . even as if one had clapt me on the back" [§157, pp. 57–58].) These visitations of scriptural texts

---

[13] Cf. John Locke's metaphor for "memory" which "is as it were the storehouse of our ideas," *An Essay concerning Human Understanding*, II.x.2, quoted by Sharrock in "Spiritual Autobiography: Bunyan's *Grace Abounding*," in *John Bunyan and His England, 1628–88*, ed. A. Laurence, W. R. Owens, and S. Sim (London: Hambledon Press, 1990), pp. 97–104, at 99, n. 9.

[14] Cf. §§179, 169, 167, 139, 183, 85, 158, 136, 177.

caused the different phases of the campaign to occur; they enabled these phases to be identified and interpreted; and so allowed the whole inner process to be represented in communicable ways to others. This succession of voices and physical actions recalled from the past also enabled the protagonist to track his spiritual development and make sense of his own thought processes or consciousness.

> §166. And I remember one day, as I was in divers frames of Spirit, and considering that these frames were still according to the nature of the several Scriptures that came in upon my mind; if this of Grace, then I was quiet; but if that of *Esau*, then tormented. Lord, thought I, if both these Scriptures would meet in my heart at once, I wonder which of them would get the better of me. So me thought I had a longing mind that they might come both together upon me; yea, I desired of God they might.

> §167. Well, about two or three dayes after, so they did indeed; they boulted both upon me at a time, and did work and struggle strangly [*sic*] in me for a while; at last, that about *Esaus* birthright began to wax weak, and withdraw, and vanish; and this about the sufficiency of Grace prevailed, with peace and joy. And as I was in a muse about this thing, that Scripture came home upon me, *Mercy rejoyceth against Judgment.* (pp. 60–61)

The actions of Scripture construe a personal history that, like memory, both represents and heals, or reintegrates the divided self by meeting in his heart. Life writing is similarly a means to integrate and save the subject self. Interpretation and selection of ideas to make a life in writing can make the flux of life seem stable and coherent.

The value of biblical texts in *Grace Abounding* as agents of the protagonist's spiritual development reflects traditional incentives for personal meditation on the Scriptures as the Word of God that may be seen in Augustine's *Confessions* and in a wide variety of Christian literature. Nevertheless, these incentives were especially prominent among early Protestants who tended to rely on the authority of the Bible for all aspects of everyone's religious life. Many nonconformist Protestant sects of the period advocated and practiced applications of Scripture similar to Bunyan's; some even made such accounts of religious conviction a requirement for membership. *Grace Abounding* demonstrates one specific example of how these traditional incentives for Bible study could be applied. But there is more to Bunyan's account of his past relationship with the Bible, which has to do with *Grace Abounding* being a prisoner's book.

Bunyan is explicit at the end of *Grace Abounding* that his relationship with the Bible was radically changed by imprisonment. In the "here" and "now" of the Bedford prison, his authorial persona claims the spiritual rewards of new insights and a new closeness to the numinous.

> I never had in all my life so great an inlet into the Word of God as now: them Scriptures [*sic*] that I saw nothing in before, are made in this place and state to shine upon me. Jesus Christ also was never more real and apparent then now; here I have seen him, and felt him indeed . . . in this my imprisoned condition. (§254, pp. 87–88)

The rewards are such that he would not have been without "this trial," or challenge. Paradoxically, he feels that he has been privileged in his place of suffering because it has revealed his conviction of God's mercy and support: "I have had sweet sights of the forgiveness of my sins in this place. . . . I never knew what it was for God to stand by me at all turns." Four biblical texts in particular, he reports, "have been sweet unto me in this place: I have seen that here, that I am perswaded I shall never, while in this world, be able to express" ( (§§255–56, p. 88). These texts marked the process of his historic development to faith, which Bunyan recalled in prison and considered the most rewarding companions of his imaginative life in prison. Reading and remembering biblical texts that he associated so actively with the specific and personal, were ways of recollecting his past in order to make sense of the present. As keys to past experience these texts were thus also ways of reintegrating the isolated prisoner into his known, more comfortable world. The crises of imprisonment—its loneliness, anxieties, uncertainties, humiliations, and physical hardships—may provoke any prisoner to look inward for the emotional comfort and intellectual stimuli necessary to sustain himself or herself, and those with well-stored memories, or any capacity to live in the mind and transcend the actual, fare better than those with fewer imaginative or mental resources. In Bunyan's case, the world he usually wrote about was metaphysical. The visitations of Scripture come from memory, which, as Augustine had recognized, is present only by means of an image of itself. In recollecting or organizing these memories of the Word of God, Bunyan was able to construe a particular history, in universal paradigms and communicable forms that made sense of his suffering as a prisoner.

## THE PARADOX OF SELF-PRESERVATION

*Grace Abounding* is introspective, self-justifying, confessional, and emotionally intense. It demonstrates a process of personal discovery and recovers that process by mixing narrative and dialogue (with the personification of temptation, Satan), to create a memorial reconstruction of spiritual encounters. This is the honest deception of all fiction that consciousness can be realized and transmitted by literary forms. Satan's voice uses a free-direct-speech form as he interacts with the historic mental processes of the narrator whose thoughts he overhears.

> Then hath the Tempter come upon me also with such discouragements as these: You are very hot for mercy, but I will cool you; this frame shall not last alwayes; many have been as hot as you for a spirt [i.e., short time], but I have quench'd their Zeal (and with this such and such who were fallen off, would be set before mine eyes) then I should be afraid that I should do so too: but, thought I, I am glad this comes into my minde; well, I will watch, and take what heed I can: Though you do, said Satan, I shall be too hard for you, I will cool you insensibly, by degrees, by little and little; what care I, saith he, though I be seven years in chilling your heart, if I can do it at last; continual rocking will lull a crying Child asleep: I will ply it close, but I will have my end accomplished. (§90, pp. 32–33)

> . . . yet, thought I, I will pray, but said the Tempter, Your sin is unpardonable. Yet, said I, I will pray. (§156, p. 57)

Even as the writer recalls this memory, he controls its realization. As his speakers' voices intermingle, their battle of wills evokes its temporal frame. Satan promises to cool the soul's fiery enthusiasm for God's mercy "by degrees," over the space of seven years, if need be. Satan's analogy of the crying child seems sympathetic and constructive at first. Any reader would assume that it was a good idea to soothe a crying child until it sleeps peacefully; but this sleep is deadly to the spirit. The chilling of the heart hovers ominously between a physical and a spiritual meaning, and both imply death. Yet, over time, the writer's imagination shapes a record of his remembered thoughts; his writing presupposes a new figurative afterlife of literary fame.

Whereas the circumstances of Bunyan's imprisonment—his separation from his family, his sense of responsibility for their hardships and his consideration of martyrdom—might suggest that the intensity of soul-searching discovered in the text served an urgent personal need, there were ancient and contemporary models for the interpretation of the experiences it relates as self-memorial. Augustine's confessional mode had established a pattern for Christian conversion narratives and descriptions of the processes of God's dealings with men's souls. If the emotional intensity of Bunyan's representation of his persona's introspection may often go beyond that in other Puritan spiritual autobiographies, such intensity, including that demonstrated by the dialogic forms of his account, also characterized many other prison writers' parables of self-justification. It might be thought that the external value of the work, in reassuring others engaged in soul-searching, would be limited by the extraordinary condition of Bunyan's status as a prisoner, yet Bunyan was well aware that there were authoritative examples of prisoners' writings. The example of St. Paul would have been especially meaningful to him; in 1 Philippians 7:17, Paul wrote from prison that it was "to defend the Gospel that I am where I am," and in 7:20, Paul continued, "I shall have no cause to be ashamed, but shall speak . . . boldly." The speaker in Bunyan's *Prison Meditations* also proclaims that it is not disgraceful to be in prison, which is the "School of Christ" and a vantage point from which to look out on this world, and the next: "Gaols are Christ his Schools, / In them we learn to dye."[15] Insofar as these arguments have biblical precedents, Bunyan's first readers would not have seen their articulation as merely a form of special pleading. Yet Bunyan's own sense of his need to make his account more meaningful to others may be inferred from a comparison of the first edition of *Grace Abounding*, published in 1666, with later ones "corrected and much enlarged by the Author," after his release.[16]

Bunyan's revisions are almost all additions and tend to elaborate his narrative to achieve enhanced rhetorical effects (and greater clarity) as well as variety, giving readers more details and explication of his experiences; they also change the character of the work in subtle ways. The additions dissolve the first edition's sharper focus on the protagonist within the historic narrative and generate more digressions from the personal account. The first edition—the prisoner's contemporary work—is thus briefer and more rigorously focused on asserting and describing his gift of grace, and the isolation of its authorial persona, the prisoner Bunyan. In three new sections created between 10 and 11, Bunyan added four dramatic escape stories in order to emphasize God's protection from drowning and snake bite, among other threats.[17] Various additions provide vivid examples of the prisoner's former way of life, including neighbors' reactions to his conversion and to his renunciation of bell ringing as well as dancing. These incidents, created between the first edition's sections 27 and 28, distract readers from the principal event leading to his conversion: his meeting and discussion with the group of poor women in Bedford. The prominence and special qualities of this encounter are compromised by later more colorful additions, especially those that disturb the sequence of the narrative. Similarly, the addition of a new, page-long digression after 132 complicates the main narrative and dis-

---

[15] *Poems*, p. 45, lines 102–3.
[16] Ca. 1672–74 and 1680; see *Grace Abounding*, ed. Sharrock, pp. xxxiv–xxxv.
[17] Cf. clarity in layout of text from different editions, in the Oxford World's Classics edition.

tracts readers. More damagingly, the tension that builds up to a crisis in which the protagonist is tempted to deny Jesus is broken by the addition of sections after 104 referring to his later discovery of Luther's commentary on Galatians.[18] The least of the additions are rhetorical enlargements of earlier, simpler details.[19] Chief among the rhetorical effects added later are repetitions to delay and so enhance the affective quality of the narrative and exclamations designed to evoke pity (such as, "Oh! none knows the terrors of these days but my self").[20] By contrast, Bunyan's prison version of *Grace Abounding* offers readers little respite from the tensions that develop in the continuity of a narrative resolutely centered on the protagonist's state of mind. Repeating cycles of despondency and hope (as the process of remembered soul-searching progresses by the equivalent of two steps forward and one step backward), strengthen a reader's sense of involvement in the introspection and self-centeredness of this first edition.

## WRITING THE ETERNALLY PRESENT SELF

Any literary self-impression reinvents the past in reworking selected incidents construed as the past by memory and imagination which are contingent and non-essential. Yet, as we have seen, Bunyan was aware that the partial evidence of memory may be fixed by writing. His authorial persona assumes that his history is meaningful for others not because it is his but because he believes it is true. The nature of that truth—its spirituality—justifies and exonerates the self-centeredness of his narrative. Bunyan's autobiography presupposes eternity or, from a moral point of view, the future, which also accounts for the absence of such accidentals of life as external descriptions of place and persons. When he addressed readers (in the preface to *Grace Abounding*) as "my dear children," he revealed his intentions toward his posterity literally, and especially figuratively in a pastoral sense. The mundane record of his experience in the temporal world of books also, paradoxically, assumes the metaphysical truth of a timeless state in eternity. The written record of the authorial persona's past interprets, constructs, preserves, and validates the history of his immortal self, the soul, which he can regard as eternally present.

---

[18] Less relevant digressions that also disturb the coherence of the personal narrative (and are reminiscent of More's digressions on contemporary "heresies") are those on Ranters, Quakers, and their "errors," after section 33 and in the middle of section 101.

[19] Other minor interruptions include additional commentary and reflection, such as, "But, I observe..." in the third edition as section 83 (p. 25) and self-defensive remarks, which may stem either from readers' responses or his own later assessments, such as, "These things may seem ridiculous to others... but to me..." added in the fifth edition's section 184 (pp. 52–53).

[20] Cf. ibid., pp. 28–29 and 43.

Bunyan's sense of the divisions between mortal and immortal aspects of the self finds its correspondence in his literary method. Inner conflict, between extremes of hope and fear, or doubt, is a dominant theme of the narrative and intermittent dialogue in *Grace Abounding*. This conflict represents the soul of John Bunyan, the protagonist whose self-division into the old natural and new spiritual man is the working premise for the work's literary tactics. His method is interpretative, it recollects the spiritual trial and error of the protagonist's historic attempts to understand the writer's spiritual status: elect or damned, saint or sinner. In Bunyan's theology the soul is passive and must await the action of God's will. It was the Calvinist's duty to search his soul diligently for signs of God's grace, mediated through the Word of God in Holy Scripture. In *Grace Abounding* the protagonist's relationship with sacred writing is a form of intertextual dialogue in which the agency of both God and Satan are communicated to him through his reflections on biblical texts and then represented to others, in the same record of God's dealings with humankind. (By contrast, More's theology prioritized the soul's work in progress to deserve the gift of grace.)

Autobiographers always seek to influence what other people think about them and hope to inscribe their preferred self-images for posterity. When this image is inscribed as personal memory, it is equivalent to the writer's memorial. For Bunyan this image reflected his understanding of the status of his immortal soul. The discrepancy between past and present implies a turning point that justified the historic sufferings of the distressed sinner by juxtaposing them with the later spiritual assurance of the authorial persona, who may be a prisoner but reveals himself as no reprobate. The separation of the authorial persona from his counterpart within the narrative past allowed Bunyan to assess the actions and reactions represented as his former life. This site of personality, the prison writer's self-impression, amalgamates different states of being. The inexperienced protagonist is represented as tormented and pulled in opposing directions; he is seen as weak-willed, irresolute, and sinful by the prison writer. By contrast, the authorial persona—the prisoner of conscience—connotes a whole personality, one renewed and strengthened by resolution of the conflicts of interest indicated by his testimony, and thus always past. The prisoner's wisdom and calm assurance exemplify the spiritual value of the experiences stimulated by his new theological assurance. As he describes the old insecurities, obsessions, and emotional states, the form and quality of his writing bring readers into a vicarious relationship with this shadow from the past. The dramatic treatment of conflict in several episodes that include direct speech make this written memorial of religious rebirth especially moving, even if, as readers, we know nothing of this process from our own lives. Alongside the representation appropriate to the stages in the protagonist's spiritual conflict as a divided self, *Grace Abounding* develops the theme of an individual literally separated from the world, which also defined the author's actual situation in prison. Yet the question remains how far even this authorial self is either a representative or an exclusive construct of personality.

Bunyan's use of prison or confinement metaphors to define the alienated protagonist symbolizes pain and longing arising from a sense of separation from God. These feelings are resolved when the newborn Christian is "enclosed," or embraced by the "arms of grace so wide," in a gesture of paternal protection that includes others besides him (§159, p. 59). At the end of *Grace Abounding*, the protagonist feels a renewed sense of community as he declares the "joy" of his final assurance of grace to his wife ("O now I know, I know!") and his desire "for the company of some of God's people that I might have imparted unto them what God had shewed me" (§216, p. 75). This restoration and reintegration into community is in sharp contrast to the situation maintained or repeated in *Grace Abounding* as a whole, where signs of physical inaction and incapacity to move signify the protagonist's doubt. His spiritual paralysis is likened to a physical dislocation, or bondage: "I could not feel my Soul to move or stir after grace and life by Christ; I was as if my loyns were broken, or as if my hands and feet had been tied or bound with chains" (§214, p. 74). He remembers that he was oppressed for several days by a "great cloud of darkness" until rescued by the sensible perception of a phrase from Scripture "that came bolting in upon [him]" as he sat by the fire—a significant source of light and revivifying warmth (§215). Such visitations are Bunyan's favorite means of releasing the afflicted soul from its despondency or chains of guilt: when "thoughts would so confound me, and imprison me, and tie me up from Faith, that I knew not what to do" (§142, p. 53); (here, as in the larger allegory of *Pilgrim's Progress*, imprisonment represents despair and confusion). In other references, too, the authorial persona resorts to the simile "as it were a prison to me" when his tormented shadow self experiences something "grievous."[21] The chains and shackles within the narrative are metaphysical; Scripture therefore can either persecute or liberate the sinner, and one biblical sentence may liberate him from persecution by other texts:

> Now did my chains fall off my Legs indeed, I was loosed from my affliction and irons, my temptations also fled away: so that from that time those dreadful Scriptures of God left off to trouble me; now went I also home rejoycing, for the grace and love of God. (§184, p. 66)

---

[21] Cf. *Grace Abounding*, §§150, and 230, for liberty and chains imagery.

In such "was . . . now" formulations, the prisoner recollects his past, mixing the grammatical markers of past and present to relive personal experience in terms of vivid images that may be shared more easily by his readers. Bunyan's authorial persona reported that he had been particularly oppressed by the text of Hebrews 12:16–17, which refers to the rejection of Esau after he sold his birthright: "*When he would have inherited the blessing, he was rejected. . . .* These words were to my Soul like Fetters of Brass of my Legs, in the continual sound of which I went for several months together" (§§113–14, p. 40). Here, although we know very little about the actual circumstances of Bunyan's imprisonment, the sensory element in this simile suggests a more than rhetorical value, since the "continual sound" can be read literally as that of brass fetters rather than oppressive biblical words.[22]

Similarly, metaphors of darkness and of separation from the world of light by a wall or a door characterize some of the most vivid and affective representations of the sinner's search for signs of salvation, especially the influence of his meeting with the poor women of Bedford. In sections 41–42, *Grace Abounding* describes the contrast between their happiness and the protagonist's miseries in allegorical terms: "I saw, as if they were set on the Sunny side of some high Mountain, there refreshing themselves with the pleasant beams of the Sun, while I was shivering and shrinking in the cold, afflicted with frost, snow, and dark clouds" (§41, p. 18).[23] The prisoner takes no responsibility for his protagonist's consciousness: the images seen "in a dream or vision" are given to him; other interpretations of them are possible ("as if they were . . ."); and he reports that even at the time, he had felt separate from his dream-vision self. The prisoner expounds the allegory thus: "the Mountain signified the Church of the living God; the Sun that shone thereon, the comfortable shining of his mercifull face on them that were therein" (§43, p. 19); such traditional metaphors are part of a pattern of associations, including storms and floods, that represent the relative situations of the faithless and the saved according to Bunyan's theology. The image of a "wall that did compass about this Mountain" and the protagonist's longing to penetrate this wall to comfort himself "with the heat of their Sun" reinforce his sense of exclusion from the company on the sunny side of the mountain (§41). In his dream memory he walked the wall "again and again,

---

[22] Cf. Thomas Wyatt's epigrammatic verse epistle written, as would appear from verbal echoes of his "Defence," in the Tower of London, 1541: "Sighs are my food, drink are my tears, / Clinking of fetters such music would crave; / Stink and close air away my life wears, / Innocency is all the hope I have; / Rain, wind, or weather I judge by mine ears; / Malice assaulted that righteousness should have: / Sure I am, Brian, this wound shall heal again, / But yet the scar shall still remain." *Collected Poems*, ed. J. Daalder (Oxford: Oxford University Press, 1975), p. 209.

[23] Cf. Vera J. Camden, "John Bunyan and the Goodwives of Bedford: A Psychoanalytic Approach," in *Cambridge Companion to Bunyan*, pp. 51–64.

still prying as [he] went," searching for a place of entry. This striving for inclusion becomes an image of rebirth, as the dreamer delivers himself from the darkness and breaks into the world of light, warmth, and companionship. The only way through the wall is

> a narrow gap, like a little door-way . . . thorow which I attempted to pass: but the passage being very straight, and narrow, I made many efforts to get in, but all in vain, even untill I was well nigh quite beat out by striving to get in: at last with great striving, me thought I at first did get in my head, & after that by a side-ling striving, my shoulders, and my whole body; then was I exceeding glad, and went and sat down in the midst of them, and so was comforted with the light and heat of their Sun. (§42, p. 19)

As the prisoner expounds this allegory, the wall is "the Word that did make separation between the Christians and the world: and the gap . . . was Jesus Christ, who is the way to God the Father" (§43, p. 19). However, as with the sound of the fetters of brass, the dreamer's strivings and labor to deliver himself into the company of the godly people of Bedford seem to figure more prominently than the allegory of the born-again Christian might require. It is as if the prisoner had also been dreaming of rejoining his family and friends among the actual godly people of Bedford. Elsewhere, the prisoner's narrative contrasts the comfort and safety of those "whom God had hedged in . . . within his care, protection, and special providence" with the memory of his protagonist's sense of exclusion as "a reprobate" fallen into "the snare" of temptation (§123, p. 43). On another occasion, he recognized that his reprobate's heart was shut up "against the Lord" by its own action of physical exclusion when his "unbelief" set, "as it were, the shoulder to the door to keep him out." Then he had cried out urging God to use violence to break open his hardened heart and, in the words of Psalm 107:16, "*cut these bars of iron asunder*" (§68, p. 25). The emotional impact of such traditional imagery is made yet more striking for readers who remember Bunyan's situation as an actual prisoner.

By his own account, the Bible was literally and metaphorically Bunyan's salvation in prison. In reviewing his long campaign between faith and doubt, and writing about it, Bunyan was able to revisit his past imaginatively and thereby make the present imprisonment both comprehensible to himself and useful to others. The emotional intensity of his past and present reactions to his experience of the Word of God suggests that Bunyan was highly imaginative and that, as a prisoner of conscience, he needed to remind himself how, and why, he fell into that predicament, as well as assess the value to himself, and others, of continuing in it. Bunyan's expectation that he might suffer execution could have been colored by his access in prison to John Foxe's *Acts and Monuments*, popularly known as the "Book of Martyrs."[24] In the context of Christian martyrdom, such spiritual reassessment of his situation would validate the past and, hence, justify the present (perhaps mitigating its consequences) for the sake of future benefits in eternity. Also at stake was Bunyan's personal authority to preach and edify the faithful, which depended on his being perceived as a particular kind of Christian: assured of the grace of God. As a nonconformist, without the sanction of holy orders (and a legal license to preach), it was important for Bunyan to be recognized as such by others. The representative memorial self-image created in *Grace Abounding* ensured that he might continue to fulfill his idea of his vocation and be remembered for this image. The tactics of Wilde's prison writing were similarly motivated.

## Oscar Wilde, *De Profundis* (1897): A Pastoral Letter of Disgrace Abounding

Wilde's prison writing, like Bunyan's, takes the generic form of a pastoral letter addressed to others for their edification and instruction, but his contemporary readership was intended to be more limited. Wilde's authorial persona identifies himself as a prisoner and indicates that his experience of imprisonment provided the opportunity for a reevaluation of life that stimulated new writing. Building upon his earlier public role as artist and writer, Wilde's authorial persona assumes the voice of a moral teacher or philosopher who has analyzed his life story, as one—newly wise—who had suffered into truth and learned "there is no truth comparable to sorrow."[25] The prisoner wrote to proclaim the wonder of his belief that he had "been placed in direct contact with a new spirit working in this prison through man and things," which had helped him "beyond any possibility of expression in words" (p. 125). He wrote to evangelize this message in reconstructing his self-image.

During April and May 1895, Oscar Wilde was tried twice on charges of committing "acts of gross indecency with other man persons." He was found guilty and, to the surprise of many at the time, sentenced to the maximum

---

[24] See *Grace Abounding*, ed. W. R. Owens (Harmondsworth: Penguin, 1987), p. 126n. citing a seventeenth-century source.

[25] See *The Complete Works of Oscar Wilde*: vol. 2, *De Profundis, "Epistola: in carcere et vinculis,"* ed. Ian Small (Oxford: Oxford University Press, 2005), p. 106; all quotations are taken from this edition. I have silently preferred the manuscript readings as the prison text (recovered from Small's apparatus) where these differ from the unexpurgated text printed by Wilde's son, Vyvyan Holland, in 1949. A facsimile of the manuscript (London, British Library, Additional MS 50141A), edited by Merlin Holland, was published by the British Library in 2000.

penalty of two years' imprisonment with hard labor, some of which he served in solitary confinement. The charges against Wilde arose after the collapse of his case for criminal libel against the Marquis of Queensberry, father of his friend and lover Lord Alfred Douglas. Wilde had initiated the legal process that led to his conviction and sentence.[26] In January 1897 he was given permission to write to Douglas; he began an account of the events and emotions that had destroyed his life. This letter included statements of how the public disgrace of his conviction by the courts, coupled with the emotional and physical hardships of his sentence, had affected his personal and intellectual development in prison. The letter was completed by late March 1897 but returned to Wilde by the prison governor at his release from Reading Prison in May 1897. It had not been sent to Douglas because Wilde had included a note, against prison regulations, to another friend, Robert Ross, in which he had asked him to copy the letter to preserve it for wider circulation in the future.[27] The 55,000-word letter to Douglas had been written on single leaves of paper folded into four smaller pages, which should have been passed to the prison authorities when completed in return for fresh ones. Nevertheless, it seems that completed sheets were made available for reference or revision, and the holograph manuscript contains hundreds of local revisions and interlinear corrections or additions.[28] The historical arrangement of events recollected, together with the emotional intensity and concentration of the writer's focus on his inner life give the work coherence, so that the image of the memory created appears remarkably consistent. In this way Wilde's account of his past and evaluation of his new spiritual development in prison resemble a conversion narrative: not grace, but disgrace abounding.

The prisoner hoped his letter would make Douglas feel shame and remorse such as the writer confessed to feeling. These motives were explained in the note to Ross; Wilde had asked him to copy the letter because it was the "only document that really gives any explanation of [his] extraordinary behaviour." He told Ross that when he read the letter he would "see the psychological explanation of a course of conduct that from the outside seems a combination of absolute idiocy with vulgar bravado. Some day the truth

---

[26] For details of the trials, see H. Montgomery Hyde, *The Trials of Oscar Wilde* (New York: Dover, 1973); cf. H. Pearson, *The Life of Oscar Wilde* (London: Methuen, 1946; rpt. Twickenham: Senate, 1998), pp. 326–32; and R. Ellmann, *Oscar Wilde* (London: Hamish Hamilton, 1987), pp. 409–92, "Disgrace." Cf. Jason Haslam, *Fitting Sentences: Identity in Nineteenth- and Twentieth-Century Prison Narratives* (Toronto: University of Toronto Press, 2005), pp. 87–108 especially for contemporary newspaper reports.

[27] For Wilde's letter (1 April 1897) of instructions to Ross, whom he appointed his literary executor, see *De Profundis*, ed. Small, pp. 308–10.

[28] For a discussion of dating and the composition, which may have gone through three phases, see Small's introduction (ibid., pp. 4–11); on the subsequent textual history, see also pp. 11–21.

will have to be known: . . . I don't defend my conduct. I explain it."[29] In showing Douglas the consequences of his behavior and moral failings, the prisoner anticipated some tender response that would demonstrate pity for the disgraced writer, "though the world will know nothing of whatever words of grief or passion, of remorse or indifference you may choose to send as your answer" (p. 37). Bunyan had also acknowledged the encouragement he received from friends' letters at the beginning of his *Prison Meditations*, and the importance of letters to prisoners of all periods and conditions is already well attested by the experience of More, Gramsci, and Bonhoeffer. Letters as a form of dialogue that enable prisoners to continue in communion with normal life are usually a source of comfort.[30] When Wilde wrote of two lives, "of the past and of the future, of sweet things changed to bitterness and of bitter things that may be turned into joy" (p. 37), he wrote not without hope. He diagnosed Douglas's "one really fatal defect of character" as a "terrible lack of imagination" (p. 66); without imagination, there is no memory and no moral sense: "Life is quite lovely to you," he wrote to Douglas.

> And yet, if you are wise, and wish to find Life much lovelier still, and in a different manner, you will let the reading of this terrible letter—for such I know it is—prove to you as important a crisis and turning point of your life as the writing of it is to me. (p. 70)

He anticipated that writing about their shared past and offering forgiveness would have a cathartic effect:

> I don't write this letter to put bitterness into your heart, but to pluck it out of mine. For my own sake I must forgive you. One cannot always keep an adder in one's breast to feed on one, nor rise up every night to sow thorns in the garden of one's soul. (p. 94)[31]

Echoes of a biblical idiom (in pluck it out, rise up to sow thorns in a garden, and the parallel phrasing) may represent a decorum of style associated with pastoral letters (such as St. Paul's), but, like Bunyan, Wilde was also clearly exploiting ancient and authoritative traditions in writing of his own experience according to such paradigms. One of the first books offered to Wilde in prison had been *Pilgrim's Progress*. He was also allowed the Bible and

---

[29] Letter to Ross, 1 April, 1897, see ibid., p. 308.

[30] Wilde rebuked Douglas for his neglect and compared the comfort he had received from knowing that people wrote to him even if delivery of their letters was rationed to every three months: "I know that they are there. I know the names of the people who have written them. I know that they are full of sympathy, and affection, and kindness. That is sufficient for me. I need to know no more. Your silence has been horrible" (ibid., p. 91). Cf. Gramsci's pleasure on receiving letters.

[31] Cf. Jeremiah 4:3 and 31:12 (ibid., p. 243n. for biblical idiom).

Book of Common Prayer with the lyrical poetry of the Psalms. One of the first books Wilde requested in prison was St. Augustine's *Confessions*.[32] He also represented himself as paradoxically privileged by his sufferings as a prisoner and considered that insights born of adversity and bred in captivity were important lessons for others beside himself—hence the shift from "I" to the impersonal "one" (a tactic also used by Gramsci), as the writer's vantage on himself shifts to a new position of moral superiority. The imagery he repeatedly used of eradicating obsessive emotions suggests that he regarded writing as a form of spiritual therapy (like the *consolatio* of Boethius's prisoner), yet the language used to describe his past pain and compulsions is also symbolic of the writer's current concerns.

If Bunyan's autobiographical mode was a hermeneutic process of self-discovery (implying interpretation and representation of an eternally completed action), Wilde's may be described as a process of creating a new self to displace the old. However shallow or selfish the image of his past life appears in the account of the authorial persona who admits moral weakness and pride, there is always a contrast drawn with Douglas's even worse behavior and vanity. This relative context can make Wilde's acknowledged weakness appear more pathetic, yet it may also be calculated, aesthetically, to mitigate it. The appeal to Ross seems to assume that if readers are persuaded by his analysis of the situation they will exonerate Wilde's persona to the same extent that they condemn Douglas. The letter is a multilayered text which represents the prisoner talking to Douglas in an expository, reflective mode of extended monologue, yet simultaneously looking over Douglas's shoulder at other readers in order to create a public monument to the reputation and fame of Wilde: a self-justifying testimony to be read after his death, since "some day the truth will have to be known—not necessarily in my lifetime or in Douglas's but I am not prepared to sit in the grotesque pillory they put me into, for all time."[33]

## "THE ETHICAL EVOLUTION OF CHARACTER" AND "MY REAL IMPRESSION"

When Wilde instructed Ross how his text was to be copied he suggested, in a semi-humorous vein, it might be called *Epistola: in carcere et vinculis*, fully

---

[32] See H. Montgomery Hyde, *Oscar Wilde: A Biography* (London: Eyre Methuen, 1976), p. 296, for the prison chaplain's offer of *Pilgrim's Progress*; cf. R. B. Haldane, *An Autobiography* (London: Hodder and Stoughton, 1929), pp. 177–79 on Augustine. See further Thomas Wright, *Oscar's Books* (London: Chatto & Windus, 2008), pp. 319–22, for a "List of Books Requested by Wilde, 1895–97," collated from lists in *The Complete Letters of Oscar Wilde*, ed. M. Holland and R. Hart-Davis (London: Fourth Estate, 2000). I am most grateful to John Stokes for these references.

[33] Letter to Ross, in *De Profundis*, ed. Small, p. 308.

aware of the pretension implied by a Latin title.[34] However, when Ross published extracts from this *Epistola,* in 1905 (in his capacity as Wilde's literary executor), it was given the title *De Profundis.* In selecting this Latin cue for the penitential psalm, Ross presented Wilde's letter as a lyrical cry for forgiveness from the inner depths.[35] In Wilde's own telling of his story, he made the discrepancy between what he was "in old days" and what he is "now" (as he sat in "humiliation and disgrace") the source of its tragic dimension (p. 94), and implied that the greater the fall from grace, the greater its tragedy. Comparing himself to Byron, albeit as a superior "genius" symbolic of the age, Wilde said that he took full responsibility for his actions and admitted that "nobody great or small can be ruined except by his own hand" (p. 94). Yet he also made an implicit comparison with "one whose life is without stain of any kind [who] can forgive sins" (p. 94). Wilde thus fashioned himself into the Christian image of a man of sorrows for his own age which had already "created myth and legend around" Oscar Wilde (p. 95). It has been said that "autobiography may only be the acceptable face of megalomania"; but also that at the end of Augustine's *Confessions* prototypical autobiography, the rhetorical register rises "from the personal to the generic, from the historical to the philosophical, from the experiential to the metaphysical."[36] Wilde's authorial persona assumes a similar paradigm for his text. Yet, unlike Bunyan, Wilde could not rest his case for posterity upon the recollection of a gift of grace abounding; his very public disgrace necessitated a fresh start. His observations about charity toward prisoners were colored by the English class system to the detriment of his "own rank": "The poor are wiser, more charitable, more kind, more sensitive than we are."

> In their eyes prison is a tragedy in a man's life, a misfortune, a casualty, something that calls for sympathy in others. They speak of one who is in prison as of one who is "in trouble" simply. It is the phrase they always use, and the expression has the perfect wisdom of love in it. With people of our own rank it is different. With us, prison makes a man a pariah. (p. 93)

Wilde therefore constructed his new image upon the premise that "where there is sorrow there is holy ground." Like Augustine, whose works were available in prison, he sought to raise the stylistic register of his own confes-

---

[34] Ibid. p. 310.

[35] Cf. Vulgate Ps. 129/ Book of Common Prayer Ps. 130.

[36] See J. Sturrock, *The Language of Autobiography* (Cambridge: Cambridge University Press, 1993), p. 13; cf. A. Fleishman, *Figures of Autobiography* (Berkeley: University of California Press, 1983), p. 69.

sional rhetoric and build a tragic view of life based on his insights as a prisoner.

> I have said of myself that I was one who stood in symbolic relations to the art and culture of my age. There is not a single wretched man in this wretched place along with me who does not stand in symbolic relation to the very secret of life. For the secret of life is suffering. (p. 106)

The value of "art and culture" implies a moral purpose: suffering reveals the way to a better life. Wilde claimed that this revelation came directly from the experience of imprisonment and disgrace; it raised his text from the personal to the ethical and from the experiential to the metaphysical. It converted his soul and gave him, as artist, friend, and world teacher, a new message and a reformed identity.

Like Bunyan's narrator, Wilde's prisoner looks at the world quite differently from his alter ego, the protagonist of the narrative past. The gap between the attitudes of these personae is not measured merely in time; Wilde's pastoral letter and spiritual autobiography, unlike Bunyan's, affirm essential changes as well as specific turning points. The distinctions between Wilde's personae are cognitive and judgmental as well as temporal; they affect the prisoner's premises, values, personal history, and his place in the world: "here" and "now" cancel "there" and "then." Wilde does not discover his "true" self, as when Bunyan recognizes his unchanged, essential self to be one of the godly elect rather than a sinful reprobate. Wilde's text describes a historical process of displacement and validates this new development in the creation of a "personal myth."

> And exactly as in Art one is only concerned with what a particular thing is at a particular moment to oneself, so it is also in the ethical evolution of one's character. I have got to make everything that has happened to me good for me . . . the silence, the solitude, the shame—each and all of these things I had to transform into a spiritual experience. There is not a single degradation of the body which I must not try and make into a spiritualising of the soul. I want to get to the point when I shall be able to say quite simply, and without affectation, that the two great turning points in my life were when my father sent me to Oxford, and when Society sent me to prison. (p. 99)

This personal myth is based upon the paradox implied in the last sentence: the benefits he received from each experience were similar, and they were different from those intended or expected. Like all martyrs, he claims his suffering as privilege. The penitential attitude of the prison writer in disowning the displaced protagonist's pride, and his indifference to suffering endorses later nineteenth-century ideas about the function of imprisonment: to reform the criminal by a regime of discipline and punishment.[37] Wilde's *Epistola* evinces a bitter irony but does not subvert this principle of reformation, which it supports vigorously.

When the prisoner described events and conversations between himself and Douglas, he emphasized the psychological significance of each episode and construed each man's character in relation to the other. He recollected images of their shared past, accompanied by his descriptive commentary and, often, a new exposition of his earlier inferences. These are punctuated by repetition of the statement "I remember," yet they are often drawn in terms of a universal comment on life or art, or the relationship between life and art. He made their particular experiences representative (or in some way typical) of human nature, thereby extrapolating objective truths. The particular here reveals the paradigmatic.

Wilde's epistolary narrative maintains its double focus on the workings of Douglas's mind (as mirrored in Douglas's behavior), and his own mind, before and after this crisis of imprisonment. The authorial persona assumes that Wilde's earlier premises for action were more carefully considered than those of Douglas, whose youth encouraged vanity, opportunism, and thoughtlessness. Yet Wilde began his exposition with details of their actions and words that he took as the only external guide to their conscious or unconscious minds. As a former dramatist, Wilde's authorial persona infers character in a realistic manner for a moral purpose and sought to teach Douglas about human nature and the deficiencies of Douglas's nature in particular. This assertion of his moral purpose is complicated by the covering note to Ross in which self-defensive aspects of Wilde's writing are given clear priority. Whereas Ross's title, *De Profundis,* and the full psalm cue (*De profundis clamavi*) emphasize the subjective nature of the text in relation to its associations with biblical, penitential lyric, Wilde's title—*Epistola in carcere et vinculis*—emphasizes genre and context: a letter by a prisoner writing in prison and literal chains. Although Wilde may have mocked his intellectual pretension, the Latin title's associations with ancient and medieval epistles (such as Cicero's, St. Paul's, and Peter Abelard's) help to preserve his moral authority as a writer who offers to teach about abiding, universal values. If Ross's title makes the penitent's cry from meta-

---

[37] There is an extensive bibliography on the subject; among the studies I have found most useful are: C. Harding, B. Hines, R. Ireland, and P. Rawlings, *Imprisonment in England and Wales: A Concise History* (London: Croom Helm, 1985), and P. Priestley, *Victorian Prison Lives: English Prison Biography, 1830–1914* (London: Methuen, 1985). Cf. M. Foucault, *Discipline and Punish: The Birth of the Prison*, tr. A. Sheridan (London: Penguin, 1979); Haslam, *Fitting Sentences*.

phorical depths seem merely personal—a lesson of disgrace abounding and pathos—the significances of both titles were also supported by Wilde's choice of literary method and strategy.[38] His letter claims to offer readers a revelation worthy of general attention, yet this higher claim is mediated through the partiality, bitterness, and egocentricity of his authorial persona—the prisoner. If readers cannot sympathize with the empathy the prison writer feels for this shadow of his past self, they are unlikely to respond to the story he relates and expounds as Wilde had anticipated and expected. His premise as a writer—to sympathize is to understand—required that he move readers to respond to an illusion of reality rendered with the intensity and persuasiveness of rhetorical art. His premise as a prisoner is that to understand is to forgive. No one knew this better than the dramatist Wilde, yet the prisoner described the material letter he was writing—its "blots, corrections and all"—as proof of its having a "definite meaning behind every phrase. There is in it nothing of rhetoric." Like Bunyan he appealed to a stylistic decorum for truth (Augustine's *sermo humilis*) in the possibility of some "absolute expression of [his] thoughts" and claimed to be "seeking to render my real impression to find for my mood its exact equivalent." Yet, even as he did so he borrowed an idiom drawn from art and instrument that undermined such a naive purpose: "Language requires to be tuned, like a violin" (pp. 145–46).

## MEMORY AND ITERATION

Prison writers' memories, recalled in response to given stimuli, and recollected by imagination, become their insistent companions. Remembrance is a selective but also a regenerative process that may console when completed to the satisfaction of the writer's needs. But whereas Bunyan's memories of his spiritual struggles—safely past—endorsed his conception of himself, and therefore—as he said—comforted him in prison, the images of Wilde's memory were tormenting shadows:

> the memory of our friendship is the shadow that walks with me here: that seems never to leave me: that wakes me up at night to tell me the same story over and over till its wearisome iteration makes all sleep abandon me till dawn: at dawn it begins again: it follows me into the prison yard and makes me talk to myself as I tramp round: each detail that accompanied each dreadful moment I am forced to recall: there is nothing that happened in those ill-starred years that I cannot recreate in

---

[38] Ironically, the most personal elements of Wilde's cry from the depths were excised by Ross's editions of the text published in 1905 and 1908.

that chamber of the brain which is set apart for grief or for despair. (pp. 64–65)

Wilde also referred to "the cell of one's heart" (p. 107) and seems to reiterate the allegorical equation of despair with imprisonment that had found its greatest English literary presence in *Pilgrim's Progress*. Bunyan's work would have taken on a new significance for Wilde whether or not he took the opportunity to reread it in prison; he probably also knew *Grace Abounding*, which relates an obsessive inner life to symbolic locations.[39] He was conscious of being imprisoned within himself and, in the covering note to Ross, Wilde anticipated that on the day of his release he would be "passing from one prison into another." Like More, but independently evoking a tradition of prison writing, Wilde acknowledged that the whole world seemed "no larger than [his] cell," yet far from being the consolation that More had offered to his readers through this conceit, Wilde found that idea was "as full of terror" as his cell (pp. 308–9).

The obsessive circle within the chamber of the brain becomes the metonymy of a memorial process reflected in the text. This shadow which is the image of memory "makes" him talk to himself. Yet the prisoner's shame is mitigated by the writer's pride in his powers of imaginative reconstruction that are repeated in his text.

> The thing that you personally have long ago forgotten . . . is happening to me now, and will happen to me again to-morrow. Remember this, and you will be able to understand a little of why I am writing to you. (pp. 82–83)

Even the cyclical patterns of time, visible in the seasons and the diurnal movement of the earth, were suspended to converge in perpetual twilight upon the internal and external constants—the heart and the cell.

> Outside, the day may be blue and gold, but the light that creeps down through the thickly-muffled glass of the small iron-barred window beneath which one sits is grey and niggard. It is always twilight in one's cell, as it is always twilight in one's heart. (p. 82)[40]

[39] Cf. Gramsci's description of the prisoners who "obsessively chew over the past." *Gramsci's Prison Letters*, ed. H. Henderson (London and Edinburgh: Zwan and the *Edinburgh Review*, 1988), p. 133. O. D. Edwards's article on Wilde in the *Oxford Dictionary of National Biography* emphasizes the clerical background of his immediate family in discussing his boyhood and education, which were subject to evangelical Protestant influences. On the cross-class appeal of Bunyan's works and the value placed on Bunyan as a "political and spiritual guide" in the nineteenth century, see Emma Mason, "The Victorians and Bunyan's Legacy," in *Cambridge Companion to Bunyan* (2010), pp. 150–61, esp. 153–56 (there is no mention of Wilde).

[40] Cf. Gramsci's description: the "light which gets through to the cell is halfway between the light of a cellar and that of an aquarium." *Prison Letters*, ed. Henderson (1988), p. 77.

The impersonal pronoun signifies not only this writer in prison but also any kind of prisoner whose mind, lacking external stimuli and oppressed rather than consoled by memory, is doubly trapped: in time and space. "Suffering is one very long moment. We cannot divide it by seasons. We can only record its moods, and chronicle their return." Time and change, the normal indicators of life's progress, seem restricted in imitation of this experience.[41]

> With us time itself does not progress. It revolves. . . . The paralysing immobility of a life every circumstance of which is regulated after an unchangeable pattern, so that we eat and drink and lie down and pray, or kneel at least for prayer, according to the inflexible laws of an iron formula . . . makes each dreadful day in the very minutest detail like its brother. (p. 82)

The qualification ("or kneel at least . . ." which emphasizes the inner life of the spirit as the distinguishing, but also unknowable, feature of personhood) restores some individuality to the prisoners. When Wilde uses plural pronouns, he identifies himself with other prisoners and invites his readers' understanding and sympathy for them all. New insights gained from the pain of such introspection are the defining characteristics of his new authorial persona: the actual and existential prisoner:

> We who live in prison . . . have to measure time by throbs of pain, and the record of bitter moments. We have nothing else to think of. Suffering—curious as it may sound to you—is the means by which we exist, because it is the only means by which we become conscious of existing; and the remembrance of suffering in the past is necessary to us as the warrant, the evidence, of our continued identity. (p. 51)

(Other warrants and evidence had also created their identities as convicts.) This prisoner had become conscious of earlier weakness in his relationship with Douglas, which he now regarded as pathetic: "Prison life with its endless privations and restrictions makes one rebellious" (p. 108).

While the prison writer's memory is a key agent in the production of this strand of self-representation, it is not the only one. Wilde's letter refers repeatedly to differences between what he was, what he is at the time of writing, and how he wished to be remembered in the future, through his writing. By analogy with the Augustinian pattern of guilt-ridden self-exposure (described by Fleishman as fall, exile and wandering, crisis, epiphany, and conversion, followed by salvation), Wilde's authorial persona sites his epiph-

---

[41] Cf. Wilde's use of historic present tenses in his narrative: "You send me a very nice poem . . . I reply . . . I compare . . . Society is thrilled . . . I produce . . . the Crown takes it up: the judge sums up on it . . . I go to prison for it at last" (*De Profundis*, p. 59).

any in the prison yard and hoped to find his salvation as a writer. As the weak-willed protagonist, he may be represented as sinner and tragic hero whose story should arouse pity and fear as it progressed to its inevitable catastrophe. Yet, as prisoner, he modeled himself in the shape of a penitent, both remorseful and wiser for having endured his long moment of suffering. Wilde made a virtue of necessity by insisting on sorrow as the catalyst to his enlightenment that led him to cast off the shadows of the past (including moral complacency and intellectual pride), together with the obsessive relationship with Douglas, which he regarded as their tragic product. The prisoner explains how his sense of disgrace abounding taught him to value pain as a paradoxical privilege. This in turn allowed him to create an authorial persona who is a martyr redeemed by his experience of suffering into a new life, made visible by the text, that enables his claim to the immortality of fame as his salvation. The text displaces infamy since it constructs a new literary image as prison writer that can stand as his memorial in the afterlife of publication.

Whereas Bunyan had relied exclusively on the Bible's cultural value in constructing his reformed self-impression, Wilde used a variety of literary resources.[42] In particular, he relied on Greek tragedy, as well as the Gospels, to shape the prisoner's consciousness of his conversion experience and communicate this sense of spiritual enlightenment. These literary choices reflected the high moral value the writer placed on his conversion and anticipated the responses of any reader familiar with their values in the prevailing literary culture (and later).

## PARADIGMS OF CONFLICT AND TRAGEDY

Wilde's autobiographical account reflects a series of psychological conflicts. As in *Grace Abounding,* the representation of the power of the adversary is an important aspect of the authorial persona's struggles toward self-awareness and self-definition. The narrative defines Douglas as the adversary, or tempter, as well as temptation or the projection of the obsession that precipitated the protagonist's fall. Because the prisoner's pride does not allow him to consider that Douglas's power over his past self was greater than his own weakness permitted, the recollected image of their relationship is always an unequal one between the paradoxically large but weak, and small but strong. Douglas is like a small stinging "thing" that infests a man's

---

[42] Wilde's range of literary reference in this work included Dante and Shakespeare but also Goethe, Wordsworth, Byron, Arnold, Baudelaire, Coleridge's "Rime of the Ancient Mariner," Emerson, Pater, Tacitus, and Verlaine. Wilde's intertextual allusiveness frequently drew upon his own works, including *The Picture of Dorian Gray.*

clothing: "Of course, I should have got rid of you. I should have shaken you out of my life as a man shakes from his raiment a thing that has stung him" (p. 44). He is also like an affectionate lion cub inhabiting the house of a "great lord" that grows up to fulfill its nature and destroys everything. The story of the lion cub, attributed to "the most wonderful of all [Aeschylus's] plays," is accompanied by quotations in Greek, thereby enhancing the tone of the local English story with the authority deemed to inhere in classical tragedy as a repository of universal wisdom.[43] Wilde's choice of the word "raiment" also evokes associations with the language of the English Bible; and both of these images depicting relationships between men and animals seem familiar from the traditional literary stock of parable and fable. Their ancient symbolic qualities make the struggle between the two men seem less specific to them; it has happened before and may even be inevitable. Although Wilde's authorial persona acknowledges past failures of willpower as his "fault," the associations of these literary analogues impute this tragedy to universal laws of nature.

> You wore one out. It was the triumph of the smaller over the bigger nature. It was the case of that tyranny of the weak over the strong which somewhere in one of my plays I describe as being "the only tyranny that lasts." And it was inevitable. In every relation of life with others one has to find some *moyen de vivre*. In your case, one had either to give up to you or to give you up. There was no alternative. (p. 43)[44]

In the penultimate sentence, the repetition of words in the rhetorical figure of chiasmus mimics the self-involved, obsessive, repetitive patterns of behavior that characterized their relationship. The outcome of this conflict, defined as "tyranny" or "triumph," suggests an issue of absolute force and political (or public) importance; and, again, the impersonal pronoun "one" removes the authorial persona of Wilde, the prisoner, from too close an association with the protagonist (who is his shadow) in this tragedy.

A second conflict of interest and judgment emerges from within the text as the newly disgraced but thereby enlightened persona—the prison writer—displaces the actions of the protagonist with his new literary constructions. Ironically, these written images of his memories condemn the action in the past at the same time as they exonerate their agents, making them better understood in references to tragic suffering. The register of Wilde's emotive style mitigates the unattractive, singular qualities of the action,

---

[43] See *De Profundis*, p. 45, and Small's note, pp. 210–11, for quotation from Aeschylus, *Agamemnon*, lines 717–28.

[44] See also Small's note, ibid., p. 208, for quotation from *A Woman of No Importance*, act 3, lines 112–13.

and moves ordinary readers closer to an appreciation of its pathos and archetypal qualities. In recollecting the critical moment when Wilde began criminal libel proceedings against Queensberry (goaded on by Douglas, who hated his father), Wilde's wiser authorial persona, the prisoner, acknowledges: "My judgment forsook me. Terror took its place. I saw no escape. . . . Blindly I staggered as an ox to the shambles" (p. 43). The pace of the psychological action is reflected in the rhythm of short sentences mounting to a climax in the simile of the ox led to slaughter. The ox knows nothing of his fate, but the onlooker anticipates his pain. As the narrative persona staggers on to his figurative "shambles," the disgraced writer in prison interpolates exegesis into his retrospection; his persona resembles the pitiful hero of a morality play, whose intellectual pride anticipated a fatal moral apathy:

> I had made a gigantic psychological error. I had always thought that my giving up to you in small things meant nothing: that when a great moment arrived I could myself re-assert my will power in its natural superiority. It was not so. At the great moment my will power completely failed me. (p. 43)

Like some Faustian figure the protagonist had recognized too late that by deferring his judgment in exercising his will, he had finally lost his power to resist the adversary. In retrospect the prisoner understands how this miscalculation led his shadow self to the libel action, which led immediately to criminal charges against himself and thence to prison. However, the prisoner abstracts general truths about humanity from this experience that both corrects his former self's assumptions and testifies to his newfound wisdom, gained in adversity and disgrace. Thus, the writer stands between his readers and his protagonist as a moral arbiter. "In life there is really no great or small thing. All things are of equal value and of equal size. My habit—due to indifference chiefly at first—of giving up to you in every thing had become insensibly a real part of my nature" (pp. 43–44). For the particular reader ("you" refers to Douglas), the prisoner may remain a flawed antagonist who now sees his own "habit" differently; but for an ordinary reader the paradox of gain by loss enables the prisoner to be a new kind of hero and philosopher, one who identifies norms that relate the particular to general paradigms (whether in life or art) and mediates between images of past and present recollected by memory. The prison writer's intellectual actions of interpretation and re-creation may also be consoling because they separate him from the narrative action, raising him above it, and thereby distancing the inferior protagonist from readers' sympathies. Wilde's narrative strategy is both assertive and defensive; its circularity is also evident as the particular case is defended by reference to the archetypal, which is then asserted as paradigmatic (reinterpreting the individual's experience as representative of the human condition) and offered to a wider readership as instructive and important. Yet, as the prisoner wrote, ostensibly for the benefit of others, he also mitigated the harm heaped on his personal reputation. Like Bunyan's *Grace Abounding*, Wilde's *Epistola* offers its readers a chaotic sequence of episodes that develop a narrative of consciousness by dialectical patterns of opposing binaries, or conflict. These dramatic encounters are then interpreted by the authorial persona as parables of soul-searching and self-justification. Moral writing displaces social disgrace.

Quotations from Aeschylus are part of a larger pattern within the *Epistola* drawn from literary traditions that had shaped Wilde's perceptions and defined his values as an artist. References to tragedy (or the tragic) not only confirmed the prisoner's sense of his former greatness and evoked pathos. Wilde also relied on the affective quality of his writing to convince readers of this assessment of his life. In speaking of the bitter illusions he had formerly entertained, the prisoner complained, "I thought life was going to be a brilliant comedy... I found it to be a revolting and repellent tragedy" (p. 64). The reversal of his fortunes in a life of penal servitude led him to identify Douglas as "the true author of the hideous tragedy" which had made a once brilliant comic dramatist—a hero free from common restraints and attitudes—into a disgraced "spectacle" (p. 71). Phrases such as "the tragedy of my life" or the "fatal errors of life" (pp. 49, 67) may be merely coded gestures toward a sad story with a catastrophic ending; yet, when he considered authorship and spectacle Wilde also raised questions about his responsibility toward his public and, hence, the perceived morality of his life as art. When he designated Douglas as the "author" of this tragedy, the prisoner associated himself with any *audience* standing outside the action, watching in fear and pity. Wilde regained control of his life story from Douglas in order to continue the construction of it: "It is only by realising what I am that I have found comfort of any kind" (p. 99). This realization involved new perceptions and their expression in new writing. It also involved exercising the paradox of gain by loss to convert "degradation" into spiritual value. He argued that just as the physical body "absorbs things of all kinds, things common and unclean," "and converts them into swiftness or strength" (signifying power and beauty),

> so the soul... has its nutritive functions also, and can transform into noble moods of thought and passions of high import what in itself is

base, cruel, and degrading... and can often reveal itself most perfectly through what was intended to desecrate or destroy. (p. 100)

He could never forget that he had been in prison, yet without reconfiguring that experience he would always be "haunted by an intolerable sense of disgrace" (p. 100). His life was his intellectual property. It was therefore important for the autobiographical narrative to assess alternative, conceivably better, courses of action in recounting decisive moments in the plot, because, "if one is ashamed of having been punished, one might just as well never have been punished at all" (p. 100). This narrative of disgrace abounding is more abundantly discursive and morally reflective in its parables of "justification" than those dramatic encounters with biblical texts in the narrative of Bunyan's discovery of grace abounding; but memory, iteration, and symbolic action were just as important in shaping Wilde's narrative as Bunyan's.

The most traumatic experience of Wilde's imprisonment appears to have been the most public one: his exposure and humiliation at Clapham Junction, handcuffed and dressed in prison uniform, while being transferred to Reading Prison in November 1895. "When people saw me they laughed. Each train as it came up swelled the audience. Nothing could exceed their amusement." He was conscious that those who had laughed with him (at fictional representations of society's foibles and hypocrisies in his comedies) were now laughing at his particular situation: "For a year after that was done to me I wept every day at the same hour and for the same space of time" (p. 128). And then he consoled himself by writing about it instead. His first concern was to illustrate a generalization about life and modern art, but thereby also to acknowledge the development of his own ideas in response to imprisonment.

> I remember that I used to say that I thought I could bear a real tragedy if it came to me with a purple pall and a mask of noble sorrow, but that the dreadful thing about modernity was that it put tragedy into the raiment of comedy, so that the great realities seemed commonplace or grotesque or lacking in style. It is quite true about modernity. It has probably always been true about actual life. It is said that all martyrdoms seemed mean to the looker-on. The nineteenth century is no exception to the rule.[45]
> (p. 127)

It especially offended his vanity and taste that everything about his "tragedy" had been "hideous, mean, repellent, lacking in style" (p. 127). Its "meanness" qualified him, in his own eyes, as a spectator of his tragic per-

---

[45] For references in this passage to Wilde's *The Critic as Artist* (part 2) and Ralph Waldo Emerson's comment on martyrdoms, see Small's notes, *De Profundis*, p. 274.

sona, for martyrdom or self-sacrifice in testimony to noble ideals. Secondly, the prisoner relived his disgrace at Clapham Junction because it was common and undignified and offended an aesthetic rather than a moral concept of self-consciousness in being "grotesque" and common. Finally, the penitent prisoner also reflected on the moral and ethical applications of his experience for its several audiences: his fellow passengers at Clapham whose amusement had diminished their humanity; then, Ross and Douglas; and, eventually, the unknown readers of his posthumous publication.

> Well, now I am really beginning to feel more regret for the people who laughed, than for myself. . . . They should have known also how to interpret sorrow better . . . to mock at a soul in pain is a dreadful thing. Unbeautiful are their lives who do it. In the strangely simple economy of the world people only get what they give, and to those who have not enough imagination to penetrate the mere outward of things, and feel pity, what pity can be given save that of scorn? (p. 128)

If the differences between objects of mockery and of scorn are indecipherable on the basis of a superficial glance, the writer in prison with a penetrating and transforming imagination can console himself by redirecting the "unbeautiful" audience's laughter. In life, as in art, he noted, there is nothing intrinsically tragic or grotesque; and, it may be argued, it is important for a writer's affective rhetoric to rouse emotional reactions in those who lack the imagination to respond appropriately to human suffering.

The idea of a "real tragedy" is a paradox which assumes that, if life imitates art, it follows the generic course determined by its author. The prisoner acknowledged that when he had been at the peak of his creative powers he used to treat "art as the supreme reality and life as a mere mode of fiction" (p. 95). Now real life was taking its revenge on art, yet the particular was still being represented in terms of a general paradigm. Related to these references to tragedy are evocations of ancient religious beliefs about retribution and the powers of indifferent gods to make misfortune into forms of divine punishment. To Shakespeare's Edgar, the gods administer only poetic justice:

> The gods are just, and of our pleasant vices
> Make instruments to plague us
> (*King Lear*, V, iii, 170–71).

As Wilde's authorial persona assimilated and applied this allusion, it was their cruel indifference that perverted humanity in order to "scourge" it:

> The Gods are strange. It is not of our vices only they make instruments to scourge us. They bring us to ruin through what in us is good, gentle, hu-

mane, loving. But for my pity and affection for you and yours, I would not now be weeping in this terrible place. (p. 58)

Emphasis on the strangeness and mystery of these powers is a familiar and convenient way of registering incomprehension and lack of self-knowledge:

> The strange Doom you seem to have brought on me in all things ... makes me feel sometimes as if you yourself had been merely a puppet worked by some secret and unseen hand to bring terrible events to a terrible issue.... To be entirely free, and at the same time entirely dominated by law, is the eternal paradox of human life that we realize at every moment. (p. 62)

The experience of imprisonment made him realize, with a bitter irony, that the paradox was irresolvable: "One of the many lessons that one learns in prison is, that things are what they are and will be what they will be" (p. 80).[46] Thus, no man is entirely the author of his own life in reality, but insofar as art reflected the grotesque tragedy of modern life, a writer could authorize his life's story by drawing on the best literary traditions to console himself in new writing. When Boethius attempted to reflect on the inequities of his own grotesque situation, he also validated his life's work in terms appropriate to his identity as a philosopher and theologian, by seeking to reconcile man's free will with God's foreknowledge.

## REDEEMING THE PAST IN BIBLICAL PARADIGMS

Wilde assessed his actions and suffering by values derived from art rather than a Christian tradition based directly upon the Bible, as More and Bunyan had done, yet the model life of Jesus also came to have a special significance for Wilde in prison. At Christmas (1896) he acquired a Greek Bible and began to read a little every day, from the Gospels.[47] Even though he read at random and claimed that he had no formal religious faith, the prisoner acknowledged that he derived new insights from his reading: "When one returns to the Greek, it is like going into a garden of lilies out of some narrow and dark house." The imagery suggests relief from repression and confinement—the prison house of the *English* Bible—and sensual pleasure in the ancient language of the Gospels, which he associated with light

---

[46] Cf. Bonhoeffer: "There's no changing it, only it's more difficult to adapt oneself to something that one thinks could have been prevented than to something inevitable. But when facts have taken shape one just has to fit in with them." *Letters and Papers from Prison, the Enlarged Edition*, ed. E. Bethge (London: SCM Press, 1986), p. 167.

[47] See *De Profundis*, p. 118: "the four prose poems about Christ"; Wright, *Oscar's Books*, p. 320.

and beauty, as well as a channel that connected Christian and pagan philosophy. He also preferred the Greek text because he assumed that Jesus and the apostles, who "like the Irish peasants of our own day, were bilingual," had spoken Greek.[48]

Wilde's use of English biblical language and ideas operated on at least two levels. First, he exploited the rhythms and imagery of a prose style associated in contemporary culture with eternal verities; this seems to have been for the sake of enriching his own prose with the flavor of authoritative patterns of speech and venerable metaphors that would be recognized by English readers. The prisoner reflected on the conduct of his inner life in a biblical landscape. Previously he had gone "down the primrose path to the sound of flutes" (p. 109).[49] And yet, he told Douglas, "I knew that if I allowed myself to hate you that in the dry desert of existence over which I had to travel, and am travelling still, every rock would lose its shadow, every palm tree be withered, every well of water prove poisoned at its source" (pp. 74–75). Yet it is Nature, he wrote, that "will cleanse me in great waters, and with bitter herbs make me whole" (p. 152), and will atone for "the misery that puts ashes on its head, the anguish that chooses sackcloth for its raiment and into its own drink puts gall" (p. 108). The best of human nature is also redemptive. The memory of Ross's kindness to the prisoner "unsealed ... all the wells of pity: made the desert blossom like a rose, and brought me out of the bitterness of lonely exile into harmony with the wounded, broken, and great heart of the world" (p. 85).[50] Secondly, he used the Gospels to develop ways of understanding his position as an outcast and prisoner. In rereading St. John's Gospel especially, he claimed to find confirmation that imagination was the basis of the artistic life as well as human(e) sympathy: "I see the continual assertion of the imagination as the basis of all spiritual and material life, I see also that to Christ imagination was simply a form of love" (pp. 118–19). Some of these ideas about the life of Jesus and that of the artist had been developed earlier, in *The Soul of Man under Socialism*, and Wilde referred to his work in affirming these connections— "Christ's place indeed is with the poets"—in the *Epistola* (p. 110).[51] How-

[48] See *De Profundis*, p. 118. Cf. Small's note, pp. 266–67, citing Isobel Murray's findings on the likely source of Wilde's misapprehension.

[49] Cf. Small's note, ibid., p. 250, quoting *Hamlet*, act 1, scene 3, lines 47–51; cf. also the biblical metaphor in Matt.7:13–14. Wilde's language here is Shakespearean.

[50] Cf. Great-heart, Bunyan's historic allegory of his professional life in *Pilgrim's Progress*. Wilde originally wrote "heart of the great." Ross had waited in the crowded corridor when Wilde arrived from prison in handcuffs at court for bankruptcy proceedings and raised his hat to acknowledge his friend, Wilde commented: "Men have gone to heaven for smaller things than that" (*De Profundis*, p. 85). Cf. Thomas More's appreciation of the natural kindness of Margaret Roper's greeting of her father in the street following his trial.

[51] See *De Profundis*, p. 110, and Small's note, p. 251.

ever, what was apparently new, and came to him specifically, as he said, in response to the experience of imprisonment, was a perception of the value of suffering in the creative act of expression. Like Bunyan and others who responded to the paradox of gain by loss, Wilde recognized the prison as a vantage point on the world, and beyond; but his beyond was the "eternity" of art:

> During the last few months I have, after terrible difficulties and struggles, been able to comprehend some of the lessons hidden in the heart of pain. Clergymen and people who use phrases without wisdom sometimes talk of suffering as a mystery. It is really a revelation. One discerns things that one never discerned before. One approaches the whole of history from a different standpoint. What one had felt dimly, through instinct, about Art, is intellectually and emotionally realised with perfect clearness of vision and absolute intensity of apprehension. I now see that Sorrow, being the supreme emotion of which man is capable, is at once the type and test of all great art. (p. 105)

Wilde, the prisoner, defined humility—a personal virtue especially valued in Christian doctrine—as the basis for this revelation and as a buried treasure that he had just discovered within himself: "It is the last thing left in me, and the best: the ultimate discovery at which I have arrived, the starting-point for a fresh development" (p. 96).[52]

Wilde's sense of the prison as a "House of Pain" and of suffering as a revelation was to transform all other perceptions; like a profound religious experience, it proved to be the starting point for a new life. His choice of language was highly suggestive; he wrote of his *Vita Nuova* (p. 96), implying a displacement of the old spirit (with an important allusion to Dante's prosimetrical text, which he had access to in Italian and in English translation).

> Pain, unlike Pleasure, wears no mask... Truth in art is the unity of a thing with itself: the outward rendered expressive of the inward: the soul made incarnate: the body instinct with spirit. For this reason there is no truth comparable to Sorrow. There are times when Sorrow seems to me to be the only truth. Other things may be illusions of the eye or the appetite, made to blind the one and cloy the other, but out of Sorrow have the worlds been built, and at the birth of a child or a star there is pain. (pp. 105–6)

---

[52] Cf. also note, ibid., p. 244 for biblical sources of Wilde's language here in Jeremiah, and Matthew.

The key locking these ideas together was Wilde's meditation on the life and death of Jesus in considering "the true life of the artist." (He proposed "just two subjects" for any future writing in the sense of "artistic work": "Christ as the precursor of the Romantic movement in life"; and "the artistic life considered in its relation to conduct.") The emphasis in the Gospels on the ministry of Jesus among the oppressed and inarticulate fascinated the prison writer: "With a width and wonder of imagination that fills one almost with awe, he took the entire world of the inarticulate, the voiceless world of pain, as his kingdom, and made of himself its eternal mouthpiece" (p. 114). What Jesus made of himself, in order to give others, relates the theology of the Incarnation to artistic creation. As in the ancient world of epistemological dualisms, this language proclaiming the prisoner's new faith in one true revelation of the meaning of pain echoes that defining Eucharistic communion. Wilde as prisoner and artist creating his own memorial image in writing— "the unity of a thing with itself"—was particularly drawn to the potential of this Christian type.

> Those . . . who are dumb under oppression and "whose silence is heard only of God," he chose as his brothers. . . . His desire was to be to the myriads who had found no utterance a very trumpet through which they might call to heaven. And feeling . . . that an idea is of no value till it becomes incarnate and is made an image, he made of himself the image of the Man of Sorrows [cf. Isaiah 53:3]. (p. 115)

> Out of his own imagination entirely did Jesus of Nazareth create himself. . . . That is why he is so fascinating to artists. (p. 117)

Such an idea was especially valuable to the writer in prison searching for a new identity in the process of reconstructing the image of his past life.

This knowledge became the basis for a new life-story. The prisoner had begun by reiterating his self-blame, in parallels that echo the translatable structures of Hebrew biblical poetry: "As I sit here in this dark cell in convict clothes, a disgraced and ruined man, I blame myself. In the perturbed and fitful nights of anguish, in the long monotonous days of pain, it is myself I blame. I blame myself for . . ." (p. 38). Somewhat later, in the context of his consideration of the Gospels, and adopting a more detached and impersonal style of expression, he affirmed: "Of course the sinner must repent. But why? Simply because otherwise he would be unable to realise what he had done" (p. 123). Using the example of the parable of the prodigal son, Wilde's authorial persona argued further that "the moment of repentance is the moment of initiation": "More than that: it is the means by which one alters one's past." As soon as the prodigal son "fell on his knees and wept," he made the sins of his old life into "beautiful and holy moments." This realization was a critical part of the prison writer's new start. In this revisionist approach to history, the old sins become opportunities for renewal and are thus creative. Wilde's authorial persona acknowledged the relevance to his own life of the "mystery" of such suffering as holy moments, saying: "It is difficult for most people to grasp the idea. I dare say one has to go to prison to understand it. If so, it may be worth while going to prison" (p. 123). At the end of the *Epistola,* Wilde represented himself as both teacher and pupil within a "terrible school," the prison, in which he was sitting at his "task," "chosen" (perhaps) to teach "the meaning of Sorrow, and its beauty" (p. 338).[53] The justified sinner took on a pedagogic function in this pastoral letter for Douglas and spiritual autobiography for posterity.

The final challenge for the prisoner's epistle was to redeem the time. "Do not be afraid of the past," he told his reader:

> If people tell you that it is irrevocable, do not believe them. The past the present and the future are but one moment in the sight of God, in whose sight we should try to live. Time and space, succession and extension, are merely accidental conditions of Thought. The Imagination can transcend them, and move in a free sphere of ideal existences. Things, also, are in their essence what we choose to make them. (p. 338)[54]

Such ideas and their formulation are a staple of European prison writing, as Wilde's own title, *a letter in prison and chains,* acknowledges most appropriately. Boethius would have understood Wilde's authorial position and his incentives to find consolation in a spiritual and intellectual understanding of his own predicament, with an opportunity to teach others and to affect unknown readers. Wilde's pastoral letter, like Bunyan's, evokes its author's struggles to *reform* his life by imaginatively recalling his past, but unlike Bunyan's letter Wilde's *Epistola in carcere* was written from the depths of his consciousness of disgrace abounding. His work's final and abiding concern, therefore, is with the image of the new persona created by (re)vision of the old. Like the prodigal son (and without irony), the prisoner tells himself and his friends:

> What lies before me is my past. I have got to make myself look on that with different eyes, to make the world look on it with different eyes, to make God look on it with different eyes. (p. 338)

---

[53] Cf. my note 15, Bunyan's image in his *Prison Meditiations* of the prison as "the School of Christ."

[54] Cf. Boethius's image of the eye of God.

The analogues of spiritual revision, initiation, and regeneration reveal the literary resources behind the construction of Wilde's textual memorial. The way one alters one's past for oneself and the world is by writing about it; writing in the context of the crises of imprisonment speaks to the future more authoritatively than any other self-impression considered by readers to be the product of easier, more comfortable, less pressing circumstances.

After his release, Wilde went into a self-imposed exile in France and completed just one new literary work before he died in Paris on 30 November 1900. "The Ballad of Reading Gaol," like Bunyan's *Pilgrim's Progress*, revisits in more detached and universal allegorical forms the fruits of a prisoner's experience and introspection. The ballad narrates in affective verse the life and death of a fellow prisoner, hanged for murder, whom Wilde had never met. This ordinary man's story gave him the opportunity to win, by artistic means, the sympathy of his readers for a more "wretched man" than himself and to coax from them a more generous human(e) response than he felt he had received from society at large. He also wrote directly to the *Daily Chronicle* to challenge public complacency and ignorance about conditions within English prisons (on the basis of specific abuses he had witnessed in Reading Prison) and to call for further investigation and reform.[55] In this respect Wilde wrote to defend in practical ways a concept of civilization based on religious traditions of Christian charity. He argued that the life of Jesus taught mankind how love, not hate, made the world a fairer place, with imagination and sympathy in outlook informing higher standards of human behavior. But those who had jeered and spat at the prisoner waiting at Clapham Junction seemed to intensify their incivilities when they recognized Oscar Wilde. Therefore, in the final analysis his situation was personal. His pastoral letter was addressed beyond its initial readers as not only an explanation of his conduct but also a re-creation of his reputation as a writer and social critic. His understanding of Bunyan's and Augustine's spiritual life-writings that depict the symbolic reconstruction of a converted sinner consoled this Victorian prisoner, suggesting an agenda for new writing quite unlike his previous works. Wilde was adamant that he was not prepared to sit in the pillory for all time.

## "IT IS BY UTTERANCE THAT WE LIVE"

Like Bunyan's persona in *Grace Abounding*, Wilde's authorial persona recollected the past, mentally circling (again and again) his conflicts with the

---

[55] See *De Profundis*, pp. 323–29, 27 May [1897], signed; pp. 330–34, 23 March [1898], signed "The Author of the 'Ballad of Reading Gaol.'"

adversary, in order to reinvent the past, accommodate himself to its image, and finally inscribe that image in a new form. Few examples of prison literature in this self-memorializing mode show such marked separation of authorial from narrative personae as Bunyan's and Wilde's. In each case the prison experience was a catalyst for recalling and writing about events that had culminated in imprisonment. However, the crisis in Bunyan's story arose earlier in his life, with the circumstances of his imprisonment providing both the incentive and the opportunity to describe and to recover its significance. Thus, whereas Bunyan's prison writing confirms (and authorizes) his new self-awareness as testimony of the gift of divine grace, Wilde's prison experience has a different relationship to his writing. Bunyan could expect his first readers to admire his sacrifices, since they testified to conflict between eternal forces of good and evil that had already been resolved in his case. In Bunyan's *Prison Meditations,* prison is sweet because the prisoner is at peace with his conscience and his God. However, Wilde's narrative is of events and emotions that led to what was seen by himself and others as a spectacular fall from moral and social grace. Thus, at the time, his inner turmoil arising from a consciousness of personal weakness in a sordid conflict of interests with another human being could only be considered pitiful. Yet, in relation to contemporary ideas and practices of penal servitude, Wilde's statements from within the confines of a "penitentiary," that his sufferings as a prisoner among prisoners had precipitated new self-knowledge and spiritual reformation, were as politically "correct" for his own time as Bunyan's different statements, confirming his sense of God's grace abounding, were for his first readers. Haunting memories make a virtue of necessity:

> For me the world is shrivelled to a handsbreadth, and everywhere I turn my name is written on the rocks in lead. For I have come, not from obscurity into the momentary notoriety of crime, but from a sort of eternity of fame to a sort of eternity of infamy. (pp. 101–2)

Nevertheless, when confession inscribed that self-knowledge which period convention required from the testimony of a penitent, imagination could displace sorrows and transform disgrace abounding into a famous literary monument. When Robert Ross finally published his edition of Wilde's prison writing, as *De Profundis* in 1905, he drastically cut down the original manuscript by eliminating any personal matter that might provoke a new libel case. By the same means, he hoped that the text would "give many readers a different impression of the witty and delightful writer," who knew himself to have been ruined by "the effect of social *débâcle* and imprisonment"

(p. 312).[56] Wilde's claim that "prison life makes one see people and things as they really are" provided him with the opportunity to reform and change his own outlook and, more importantly, to resist and change the world's view of him: "I need not remind you that mere expression is to an artist the supreme and only mode of life. It is by utterance that we live"—in the present, and hereafter in writing (p. 311).

[56] Ross printed part of the covering note to himself in which Wilde offered the text to those who were interested in his "mental development in prison, and the inevitable evolution of [his] character and intellectual attitude towards life that has taken place" (ibid., p. 311).

# CHAPTER 4

# Memorial Narratives as Salvation for the Feminine Self

Marie-Jeanne Roland (1754–93) and Anne Frank (1929–45) wrote memorial narratives to preserve details of their lives because they believed that writing about their ideas, experiences, and feelings would help to sustain them in the exceptional circumstances of confinement. While they wrote, their lives were subject to arbitrary violence, uncertainty, injustice, and the danger of imminent death. Subsequently, both writers have become popular heroines: their prison writings have been continuously in print since shortly after their deaths. Yet their personal memoirs of different kinds have been read and valued as historic witness accounts of wider, catastrophic events: the French Revolution and the Holocaust. Both writers were conscious of their roles as historic witnesses, but this chapter seeks to refocus attention on their ideas of themselves as writers and the primary functions of their texts as literary testimony to unique personal identities rather than the historic victims of terror they came to represent for later readers. At the end of the eighteenth century Roland was conscious that writing one's own words could be subversive signs of identity and agency for a woman; Frank, in the mid-twentieth century, was also conscious of her potential as a female writer and saw her writing, which was formally directed to a female (albeit fantasy) reader, as a departure from more traditional roles for women. Writing well about one's self has always been an especially potent form of self-defense and resistance.

Oscar Wilde considered that his mother's standing as an authority on the men and manners of her day ranked historically with Madame Roland's reputation as the author of astute political memoirs.[1] Nineteenth-century readers were encouraged to see Roland as a political heroine because she had dedicated her writing skills to her husband's career, and because she died on the scaffold, a tragic victim of the revolutionary violence she had helped to unleash.[2] She was celebrated for her virtue as a wife and her self-consciousness

---

[1] *De Profundis,* ed. Ian Small (Oxford: Oxford University Press, 2005), p. 134. (Wilde's remarks flatter his mother, who was never credited with the authority of experience that readers have always valued in Roland's work.)

[2] Goethe's (1820) view saw her works, situation, and character as inherently linked; by contrast,

as a writer and witness of *sans-culotte* barbarism. This reputation derived from her self-impression projected through her prison memoirs written in the knowledge that she was likely to be killed. Yet her self-consciously feminine authorial persona was also suffused with a self-confidence in political affairs that was traditionally characterized as virile. She had insisted on a decorous subservience to her husband's career in public service; yet she also subverted contemporary gender roles by proclaiming her intellectual independence as a patriot and political analyst. When it seemed clear that her political cause and life were lost, she insisted on reclaiming the attribution of her work that had previously passed as her husband's, and on recording for "history" that she had been a dominant influence on the early revolutionary movement. As she wrote about her role behind the scenes, Roland's energy and confidence also came to characterize her literary self-impression. She finally declared her aspiration to the reputation of a preeminent historian: specifically, a French Macaulay, or even a contemporary Tacitus who had recorded and analyzed her world turned upside down by corruption, violence, and anarchy.[3] Her friends' efforts to save and publish her prison writing ensured that her life and eloquence in resisting defeat were remembered. She represented her courage, commitment, and insight in several kinds of prison writing. *Notices historiques* records her impressions of events and personalities, including Danton, Marat, and Robespierre, who had come to her home to meet her husband and others, but then betrayed their cause in promoting the Terror. She presented herself as an eyewitness whose judgment of men was wise and true. Finally, as she sensed the end approaching, she wrote her autobiographical *Mémoires particuliers* to commemorate her life. She hoped thereby to leave her young daughter with an interpretative key and substantive link to her mother's identity. She also more narrowly defended herself against the slanders of her husband's enemies, who continued to attack her character in scurrilous publications, even after her imprisonment, calling her a "Circe" of the Republic. Writing gave Roland a sense of the power she lacked as a prisoner. The paradox embodied in her memoirs is her freedom as a prisoner finally to be herself and to make her own image in writing for posterity.

Anne Frank's diary addressed her present and future concerns because she had no past to speak of as a young person. Unlike Roland she had no pretensions to the status of the historic witness she became through her

---

Carlyle focused on the image of perfect female victim; cf. Paul de Roux's introduction to his edition of *Mémoires de Madame Roland* (Paris: Mercure de France, 2004), p. 40.

[3] Catharine Macaulay's eight-volume *History of England* was first published between 1763 and 1783; a French translation appeared in 1791–92; *The Memoirs of Madame Roland*, tr. and ed. Evelyn Shuckburgh (London: Barrie & Jenkins, 1989), p. 47, n. 2.

writing, to the impact of the Nazi occupation of Amsterdam on a group of eight Jewish civilians forced into hiding to avoid deportation and death. Frank wrote about the confinement of her family as it reflected on the wider repercussions of the politics of hatred and the confines of family life, as she sought the freedom to construct her own identity and voice. In the first instance, and like Roland, she recognized her need to write not only to comfort herself but also to find and express her individual voice. In the second instance, her story of confinement is also a fragment of a larger history of her time, but one that impresses readers because of the energy, vitality, and thoughtful candor of her personal eloquence. Under constant pressure from danger and uncertainty, writing defused feelings of hope and hopelessness alike. Yet, also like Roland, she revised her recorded experience in terms inflected by literary sources and with a view to the creation of personal testimony to historic events. She had hoped to use her diary to write a book, after the war, about her experiences as a prisoner in hiding, and she also began to revise her early entries for later readers after she heard about plans to create an archive of the Dutch experience of war that would include personal letters and diaries. All the observations she made were addressed to an imaginary correspondent and confidant. The letter form of her diary enabled her to construct one side of the ideal, sympathetic dialogue she craved with a personal friend, beyond her confinement, who was also an ideal surrogate reader.

All subsequent readers have known that these writers endured cruel deaths at the hands of their persecutors. Roland was executed by guillotine within hours of her sham trial; Anne Frank died from typhus shortly after she was deported to a concentration camp when the families in hiding were betrayed and arrested. Our knowledge that neither prisoner survived is an important part of what we bring to their texts as readers and helps to enhance the authority readers attribute to each writer's responses to her experience. Death was a constant threat. Yet, Roland and Frank reported finding solace in writing their memoirs. As this chapter also shows, Roland and Frank believed that they were preempting criticism of their behavior and ambitions in resisting their societies' expectations of women and girls. This chapter finds an affinity between them based on more than the writer's representation of her rebellious self. Nevertheless, the history of the transmission of their texts, which were published by devoted survivors, illustrates a special form of a general problem already seen in Wilde's case and affecting most of the personal testimony that is published posthumously. Editorial control leading to censorship of personal or politically sensitive writing is almost always a symptom of sympathy and well-meaning intervention by friends and relations rather than of hostility. Women writers' works are often subject to social expectations that may be different for the work of male authors.[4] It is clear that some of Roland's and Frank's personal and sexual candor was excised from early editions of their texts because it was considered indecorous by their male editors. Yet each of these female authors considered her account of her emergent sexuality to be an important part of her self-revelation. Madame Roland saw herself as a social being committed to ideas of democratic progress and concerned to realize her own potential in relationships with other people. She idolized the works of Rousseau, cultivated a refined sensibility, and frequently proclaimed her self-possession. She also repeatedly subverted contemporary patterns of gender roles and, shortly before her arrest, informed her husband that she had formed an emotional attachment to another man. The lives of these writers were oppressed and extinguished because of who they were—a Jew; a wife—rather than for any actions of their own, as each of them recognized. They therefore chose to defend themselves by insisting on an honest appraisal of the truth, as they saw it, of their lives and circumstances. Since they were both resolutely determined to be themselves and leave their mark on the world through writing, this required a constant focus upon the personal in both the adult woman's retrospective memoir and the adolescent's diary of contemporary experience.

## Marie-Jeanne Roland, *Memoirs* (1793): Writing History Herself

Marie-Jeanne Roland (née Phlipon) would have been a controversial public figure in her own time simply on account of her left-wing Girondist politics; she became a romantic heroine for many in the nineteenth century, and in the later twentieth century she became a feminist icon (albeit an ambiguous one).[5] When she was arrested in June 1793, at the height of the Terror in Paris, she realized that she was unlikely to survive, and therefore wrote (and rewrote) her copious memoirs with astonishing speed. She was executed on 8 November 1793, leaving her prison writing, including many personal letters, in the hands of friends.[6] Her first subjects were a series of historical narratives including pen portraits of men she had seen in action as colleagues of her husband, who was a Girondin minister of state for the Inte-

---

[4] Cf., however, the editorial substitution "being" for "bosom" in Bonhoeffer's poem "Who am I?"

[5] For a wide-ranging and well-judged study of Roland's writing and critical reputation, see Mary Trouille, "The Circe of the Republic: Mme Roland, Rousseau, and Revolutionary Politics," in *Literate Women and the French Revolution of 1789*, ed. Catherine R. Montfort (Birmingham, Alabama: Summa Publications, 1994), pp. 81–109; cf. Lisa Beckstrand, *Deviant Women of the French Revolution and the Rise of Feminism* (Madison: Fairleigh Dickinson University Press, 2009), pp. 42–73.

[6] The standard edition remains *Lettres de Madame Roland*, ed. Claude Perroud, 4 vols. (Paris: Imprimerie nationale, 1902–15). They are not discussed here.

rior until the fall of the early revolutionary government. Her second writing project was the intimate self-portrait she wrote for her daughter, Eudora, whom she knew would grow up without a mother. (There was some overlap between these memoirs since she began to rewrite the *Notices historiques*, first written in June and July, as *Portraits et anecdotes* in August, mistakenly believing that her earlier notebooks had been destroyed by fire.) All her prison writings, whatever their subject matter, generate the image of a vibrant and self-sufficient human being.

## "I ASPIRE ABOVE ALL TO BE FRANK"; "I SHALL DO MYSELF STRICT JUSTICE"

Among the political papers Roland had drafted on behalf of her husband was the celebrated letter of protest addressed to Louis XVI on 10 June 1792, which had precipitated his fall. She was proud of her fluency and power in writing, as well as self-satisfied, opinionated, and judgmental in her political assessments. She considered that her husband "lost nothing by being interpreted through" her writing skills and saw herself as the ideal political wife who enhanced his career by her actions behind the scenes. They were an effective couple; she wrote with him just as she ate with him and regarded the one as natural as the other: "Roland without me would have been no less good an administrator... but with me he has made more mark (*plus de sensation*)."[7] She derided those women who lacked the intelligence and interests to be good company for their husbands and argued that it was tiresome for women to be preoccupied with "domestic trifles": "I know of nothing... better calculated to make a man look elsewhere for his pleasures."

> In my opinion a woman ought to be able to keep her linen and wardrobe in good condition, or have it done for her, feed her own babies, manage her own kitchen or even do the cooking herself without complaining about it, and (*avec une liberté d'esprit*) at the same time to think and talk about other things and give pleasure by her presence as a woman (*par les grâces de son sexe*). (p. 218; cf. French pp. 465–66)

She appears to endorse social expectations of the bourgeois married woman, yet could never understand "how an active and organised woman" could find herself "fully occupied by household duties, however large her estab-

---

[7] Quotations from Shuckburgh's translation (amended to enhance literal fidelity or with parallel text to indicate significant lexical choices and substantive detail not accessible from the translation), compared with De Roux's edition (2004) for further clarification; see English, p. 92, cf. French, pp. 233–34.

lishment" and not have time to read and also to write regularly (as she had done since the death of her mother in 1775). However, she thought that taking the time to read and develop one's mind was the best way to be a companion for a man, and that there was no point in a woman becoming known as a writer, because "men do not like it" and other women were always critical: if a woman's writing was any good people would always assume it was not her own, and if they acknowledged her authorship, they soon "turn[ed] to picking holes in her character, her morals and her talents. All her personal faults are set in the balance against her wit" (p. 218).

> I delighted in writing pieces for him [i.e., Roland] which I thought would be useful, and when I saw them in print it gave me greater pleasure than if I had been known to be the author. I am avid for happiness and I find it most in the good which I can do; I have no need for fame (*gloire*). (pp. 92–93; cf. French p. 234)

After she was imprisoned, she changed her mind about such indifference to her personal reputation. Only as a prisoner did she feel free to be herself and to reveal these earlier stratagems. She had appeared disinterested only to disavow any political ambition or action of her own. She now became scathing in assessments of her husband's colleagues: "I can never resist the temptation to prick their vanity (*rabattre leur suffisance*) by failing to notice the merits of which they are so proud" (p. 93; cf. French p. 237). She declared that she had been arrested merely because her husband was a man of integrity in a corrupt age and that his enemies attacked her as his proxy.

In prison Roland also defined her femininity by contrast with the qualities she observed in other women, including her daughter, maid, prison keepers' wives, other politicians' wives, and other prisoners. She described her twelve-year-old daughter as "charming" but lamented that "nature has made her cold and indolent." This was a great disappointment as she had expected her daughter to resemble her, since she had nursed her as a baby and hoped that she had been a memorable example to the child.[8] Nevertheless, the girl had a different temperament, and her mother therefore found her deficient:

> Her dullness (*son âme stagnante*) and lack of spirit will never give me the joy [my heart was promised] . . . [although] her existence will be a consolation to her father. She will never know my lively affections nor my pains

---

[8] Cf. "Remember your mother . . . farewell, beloved child, you whom I have nourished with my own milk and whom I would wish to imbue with all my feelings" (18 October 1793), in *Last Letters*, ed. O. Blanc, tr. A. Sheridan (New York: Noonday Press, 1989), p. 23.

nor my pleasures. And yet, if I was to be born again and allowed to choose my qualities (*dispositions*), I would not want to change; I would ask the gods to make me again exactly as they have done. (p. 38; cf. French p. 59)

Her abrupt change of subject, from her daughter to a reconsideration of her own attributes, suggests a moment of self-doubt. She was, in effect, comparing herself with her offspring as if with a second version of herself "born again." A reader may recognize that Roland's situation on the brink of personal extinction prompted a need to reassess the totality of her life and an opportunity to consider not only who she was but how she might wish to be remembered. Thus, after years of repression Roland's determination to control her destiny through her writing, as an independent woman with a vivid inner life stimulated by reading, became a principal concern.

Like other prisoners, including Bonhoeffer, she seems instinctively to have resorted to organizing the space around her as a first step toward maintaining control of her inner life; like Boethius, she gained consolation from the idea that the mind is its own place and that the opportunity to write for posterity would become a powerful means to resist persecution and slander. As she wrote, she imagined her reader as a surrogate visitor to whom rhetorical questions might be addressed and whose reactions and judgment might be anticipated, as if in a real-life dialogue. She therefore explained that she also wrote to defend her reputation, as if anticipating a charge of vanity should she talk about herself without claiming some higher purpose, such as an appeal to justice: "I would never have thought of devoting the short time that remains to an account of my own life had I not been the object of scurrilous attack by my enemies (*si la calomnie ne m'avait traduite*)" (p. 217; cf. French p. 464). In anticipating a violent death, she changed tack from thinking that her "chief ambition (*besoin*) was to please people and to do good" to acknowledging herself as someone bound to obey a higher calling to truth: "Now that my character has been hardened by political adversity and other troubles I aspire above all to be frank." She claimed that she no longer cared what her contemporaries might think; in the future, regardless of what might be desirable or decorous, she wanted to be known as she alone truly knew herself: "I shall do myself strict justice, painting the good and the bad with equal freedom" (p. 126; cf. French p. 307). Roland's conjunction of justice, equal freedom, and painting must stand for her intentions in writing. She insisted that she was sustained in the present crisis by her clear conscience and asked only for the peace of the just (p. 192).

In prison Roland showed her acute self-awareness as both a witness to history and an individual in distress.

I am now in prison and may at any moment suffer a violent death. I have known happiness and adversity. I have seen history in the making (*j'ai vu de près la gloire*) and have endured injustice. . . .

What can you do better in prison than re-live the past and imagine yourself back in happier days? You can certainly enrich your experience by reflecting on the past and I hope that it may make the present easier to bear. . . . I shall now write my memoirs. I think it will help to distract me, at a time when I am particularly distressed, if I talk a little about myself. (pp. 125–26)[9]

Preservation of an image of self might be thought merely selfish, but Roland (like Rousseau in his *Confessions*) also claimed an altruistic purpose in her self-exposure: "My idea here is to present truths which are applicable to others besides myself. I suppress nothing because I believe that the details all serve to create a convincing whole (*leur enchaînement serve à leur démonstration*)" (p. 217; cf. French p. 464). This included personal matters that she had never discussed with anyone before, including her earliest sexual awareness, the indecent behavior of her father's apprentice, and her disappointment in marriage: "All this throws light, I think, on the workings of the human heart and should be an object lesson to sensitive souls" (p. 246; cf. French p. 512). "Possibly, too, those who seek to understand the human heart (*les philosophes*) through a novel or a play may find something worth studying in my story" (p. 156; cf. French p. 363). On this basis, the authority of lived experience, as well as the intrinsic interest of her character, would, she thought, make her narrative more impressive and educational than any fiction. She believed that her particular experience was generally relevant and useful. She also conceived of the interest and sympathy of some unknown "sensitive soul" in the future and was consoled by the idea that another prisoner might apply her prison writing—that "perhaps one day these artless pages (*mes récits ingénus*) may lighten the darkness of some other unfortunate captive (*charmeront les instants de quelque infortunée captive*), helping him [or her] to forget his own misery [*son sort*/destiny] in thinking of mine."[10] This is part of the appeal of prison writing: remembrance of another may help to mitigate one's own troubles.

---

[9] Cf. "Je me propose d'employer les loisirs de ma captivité à retracer ce qui m'est personnel depuis ma tendre infance jusqu'à ce moment; c'est vivre une seconde fois que de revenir ainsi sur tous les pas de sa carrière, et qu'à-t-on de mieux à faire en prison que de transporter ailleurs son existence par une heureuse fiction ou par des souvenirs intéressants? Si l'expérience s'acquiert moins à force d'agir qu'à force de réfléchir sur ce qu'on voit et sur ce qu'on a fait, la mienne peut s'augmenter beaucoup par l'entreprise que je commence . . . je vais faire des *Mémoires*; et, m'accommodant avec prudence à ma propre faiblesse dans un moment où je suis péniblement affectée, je vais m'entretenir de moi pour mieux m'en distraire"; pp. 305–7.

[10] English, p. 156; cf. French, p. 363. Cf. Gramsci to Tatiana Schucht, 30 January 1933: "The

## PERFORMING ON PAPER: THE SELF AND ART

If she envisaged readers, she also recognized that writing was not "artless." Roland's prison memoirs convey the impression of a lively mind performing on paper, consciously involved in a rhetorical process that reveals its classical Latin and contemporary French models, without undermining her credibility as a frank witness to public and private histories. The strongest literary influences behind her self-portrait and sensibility were the works of Rousseau and of Diderot.[11] Yet the organizing principle of her work was her personal response to crisis, and there are frequent changes of stylistic register that often mirror the writer's episodic representations of emotional reactions. Thus, she would interrupt her political narrative to lament the national situation and express her own disgust at the behavior of the monstrous government that her actions had helped to create, but which now "destroys everything it touches and devours itself" (p. 154; cf. French p. 358). Her frustration and aggressive disappointment at the political ineptitude of contemporary Girondins and Jacobins led her, eventually, to consider suicide: she despaired at the failure of their ideals. There was no justice, liberty, equality, or fraternity in the chaos of the Terror. This thought prompted her address to the historical figure of Brutus, "whose bold right arm freed the corrupt Romans in vain from tyranny," acknowledging to him that "we have been mistaken, as you were! (*comme toi*)" (p. 155; cf. French p. 359).[12] The horror she felt at the violence she had witnessed, coupled with her own fears and misery in prison, led her to claim that she was rendered inarticulate. She wrote that she had laid down her pen, yet we know this only because she had done nothing of the kind. Her coy self-consciousness of her role as a storyteller recurred as she found herself enjoying the act of writing for an audience: "And what did you write about? . . . everything" (p. 165). In this rhetorical aside, or brief dialogue with an imagined reader, or prison visitor, she also described her regular correspon-

---

only remedy is to contrast one's own fate with a fate that's even worse, and console oneself with the thought of the relativity of human fortunes." *Gramsci's Prison Letters*, ed. H. Henderson (London and Edinburgh: Zwan and the *Edinburgh Review*, 1988), p. 252.

[11] Note also her obsessive rereading of Rousseau's *Julie ou la nouvelle Héloise,* which she first encountered at the age of twenty-one when mourning the death of her mother. Not enough consideration has been given to the impact on Roland of the underlying literary allusion in Rousseau's title to Heloise, the original twelfth-century intellectual woman who in her own account of her life renounced a forbidden love but suffered for her sublimated desire from within the convent she established and ruled as a place of safety, learning, and prayer, beyond other worldly vicissitudes.

[12] L. J. Brutus became a hero of antimonarchical revolution; but cf. also, possibly (on account of his "error") the descendant of this Brutus, i.e., the murderer of Julius Caesar. See further Harold T. Parker, *The Cult of Antiquity and the French Revolutionaries* (Durham, NC: Duke University Press, 1965).

dence with a former school friend.[13] Similarly, when she had described her mother's pet name for her as a child, Roland interrupted her narrative to announce:

> Yes, she called me Manon. I am sorry to disappoint the romantic reader [*j'en suis fâchée pour les amateurs de roman*, i.e., lovers of novels], for this is not a noble name and hardly fits a heroine in the grand style. But after all it is what I was called and I am writing history (*c'est une histoire que j'écris*). (p. 129; cf. French, p. 311)

Playful and tongue-in-cheek though this apology appears, it shows that Roland was also thinking about her self-constructed image in terms of different kinds of literary models and readers (even as she gently mocked them) who might have expectations of literary heroines in the grand style.[14] She simultaneously rejected these models and exploited the expectations they had stimulated in their readers. In real life too, it seems that Roland often defined herself by contrast with period norms: her unique self was a counter image to resist and revise social expectations.[15] According to the eyewitness whom she commissioned to report on her death, she went to the guillotine with courage and dignity, showing compassion for the distraught male stranger with whom she shared her final journey.[16]

The freshness and immediacy of Roland's personal testament are best seen in her extended account of events on the night of her arrest. The details she selected and her usual literary forms—narrative interspersed with direct speech or dialogue—reveal her pleasure in creative writing. As she recollected scenes, she interpreted and most likely sought to enhance the impact of her own words and actions. She would have known that readers of ancient historical writings accepted, and expected, that an author would use literary license in recreating the speeches of different characters. Roland's rhetorical command of different speech idioms comes to the fore in representations of her conversations with various people. Upon the failure of her

---

[13] On the implied reader/friend and dialogue, cf. Elissa Gelfand's description of Roland's "noble interlocutor. . . . This reader/redeemer," *Imagination in Confinement: Women's Writings from French Prisons* (Ithaca: Cornell University Press, 1983), p. 140.

[14] Roland may allude to the Abbé Prévost's penitent courtesan heroine, redeemed by love, in his novel *Manon Lescaut* (1731).

[15] Cf. Gelfand sees Roland's *Mémoires* as "an extreme example of women's victimization by cultural contradictions," and contrasts responses to her testimony and criticism of revolutionary excess with those of André Chénier who was in the same situation (ibid., pp. 150–52).

[16] She also commissioned paintings and drawings of herself; cf. A. Labille-Guiard (Musée des Beaux–Arts, Quimper), reproduced as De Roux's cover image; and portrait by unknown artist (Musée Lambinet), as Shuckburgh's cover. Sophie Grandchamp was asked to watch the tumbril pass by from the corner of the Pont Neuf and to write an account of her death; see Shuckburgh's postscript (pp. 259–60), and Paul de Roux's introduction (cf. pp. 37–38), for description of Roland's death.

second attempt to deliver a letter of protest addressed to the Convention which had replaced the legislative assembly, Roland was shocked to find that the session had ended. Her text sets the scene and communicates her frustration (and disgust) by drawing the reader into the situation and asking a series of rhetorical questions without pausing for comment:

> A day of insurrection, when the sound of the tocsin had scarcely ceased to rend the air, when two hours previously 40,000 armed men had surrounded the Convention and petitioners were threatening members at the bar of the house. Why [is] the Convention not in permanent session? [Is] it then ... entirely subjugated and [has it done] all that it was told? [Is] the *revolutionary power* now so mighty that the Convention dare not oppose it [and is it redundant]?

She then represents her own words of enquiry, while posing as sympathetic to the enemies of the Convention, addressed to a group of citizens standing by a cannon. In creating this dialogue, she gave verisimilitude to the citizens' speeches in demotic obscenities. This touch of naturalism was probably intended to denigrate them in the eyes of her readers.

> Citizens, I said to a bunch of *sans-culottes* standing around a cannon, did everything pass off well? Marvellous well, they replied. They were all embracing one another and singing La Marseillaise, over there under the tree of liberty. Then were the men of the right reconciled (*le côté droit s'est apaisé*)? I asked. Faith (*Parbleu!*), they had no choice, they had to see reason. And the Commission of Twelve? Kicked into the ditch (*Elle est f ... dans le fossé*). And the Twenty-Two? The municipality is to arrest them. Good! has it the power to do that? [Jarnigué,] isn't it sovereign? Just as well too, so it can sort out the traitors (*redresser les b ... de traîtres*) and defend the Republic. But what about the departments, will they be content to see their representatives treated so? What do you mean? Paris does nothing without the consent of the departments; they said so in the Convention. [That's not so certain, because] to know their opinion there should have been primary assemblies. What about the tenth of August? Didn't the departments approve what Paris did then? They'll do the same again. [It's Paris that'll save them. Be] their ruin, more like. (pp. 34–35 amended; cf. French, p. 55)

As the dialogue developed, Roland dropped the speech markers (I said, they replied) but maintained the verb tenses of direct speech. This makes the dialogue seem more immediate and resembles the techniques of period fiction. Her own fearlessness is evoked in her dramatic persona's linguistic command of this rapid exchange (she is asking the questions and directing the scene).

In the next section of the text, as she described finding a cab to take her home, the mood changed, and the dominant image, characterizing the scene, changes from a cannon to a small dog that rubbed against her legs.

> Is the poor creature yours? asked my coachman, with a gentle tone (*un accent de sensibilité*) rare in his sort, which struck me particularly. No I don't know him, I replied gravely as if we were speaking of a person. I was already thinking of other things.

The friendliness of the dog, by contrast with the surly *sans-culottes*, also brings out the gentleness of the cab driver, which Roland remarks upon as if it were morally, as well as socially, significant "in his sort." Her own distraction in speaking of the dog as if it were human might suggest preoccupation with her husband's fate. That evening had been one of momentous crisis and emotion, but her immediate concerns, as she wrote later, became focused on the symbolic value of the dog: fidelity.

> We had not gone twenty paces when the cab stopped. What is it? I asked. He's escaped, stupid animal, said the driver. I wanted him for my little boy to play with. Here, come here, little one, he called. I remember that dog; it was comforting to have a friendly man, a father and a good fellow, as my driver at that hour. [Try to] catch him, I shouted, you can put him in the cab and I will hold him for you. The man was delighted. He caught the dog, opened the door and put it in with me (*me donne compagnie*). The poor beast seemed to feel that [it] had found [protection and] a refuge; I was much licked and fawned upon (*Je fus bien caressée*). (p. 35; cf. French, p. 56)

Here the narrative plays with different tropes of captivity and the paradox of a refuge in confinement. Roland comments that she was reminded of the fable of a man, "tired of people and disgusted by their passions" who withdrew to a forest where he "found amongst the animals an affection and gratitude for his attentions which he had never had from his fellow men." After this interlude in the action during which Roland and the coachman have collaborated simply as human beings, in the interests of a child and a dog, another tense moment develops with suspicious guards at the checkpoint by the Samaritaine.

> [Sit tight], said my driver very quietly, turning on his seat, it's the usual thing at this time of night. The sergeant came up and opened the door, Who's there? A woman (*Une citoyenne*)—Where have you come from?—

From the Convention.—That's right muttered the coachman, as if he was afraid they would not believe me. Where are you going?—Home.—Have you no baggage?—Nothing, look.—But the session's over.—I know, unfortunately for me (*Oui, dont bien me fâche*), I had a petition to present. But a woman (*une femme*), at this hour? It's impossible (*inconcevable*). Most imprudent! it is undoubtedly unusual; it's certainly not pleasant for me. I had the strongest possible motive.—But, Madame, all alone!—How alone, Monsieur? Do you not observe *Innocence* and *Truth*? What more is necessary?—I must accept your explanations.—And you do well to do so. I said in a softer tone, for they are true (*bonnes*). (p. 36 adapted; cf. French, pp. 56–57)

Roland insists on her moral integrity without irony but with an improbable attempt at literary allegory by presumably pointing to her real traveling companion, the recently recaptured little dog. There is also a hint that a universal fable may be evolving as the alliance between the coachman and the lady reveals a new basis for society in the natural protection of the weak by the strong. Whether any such improbable words were actually spoken to the sentry can never be known. Her tactic in self-representation and self-defense is nevertheless clear. Her language appeals beyond the sergeant's expectations of what women may do in real life to her own literary model of innocence and power; yet she develops the status of herself from *citoyenne* to *femme* to *madame*. The way she tells her adventure story also endorses her powers of persuasion and reveals her optimistic political premise that truth and innocence have value in the world and may be recognized by anyone.

Roland wrote this passage during the early period of her imprisonment when she still thought it worthwhile to write irate letters of protest at the injustice she had suffered to the National Convention and to the newspapers. (Later, she became resigned to the arbitrary persecutions and violence of the Terror.) She dramatized her heroism in naturalistic terms, yet derived this image of her courage from types of nobility found in ancient history or neoclassical tragedy (such as Racine's Andromache, perhaps): highly articulate, morally superior, gracious (even stately), proud, passionate, and acutely self-conscious, but also energetically fearless in defense of noble ideals.

I have always found, when misfortune has struck, that my immediate grief is soon swallowed up in determination to oppose and overcome the forces arrayed against me. I screw up my courage and try to do good in return for evil. I shall not allow events to overwhelm me. Tyrants may persecute me but they shall never get me down. Never! (*Les tyrans peuvent me persécuter, mais m'avilir? Jamais, jamais*). (p. 126; cf. French, pp. 306–7)

They shall not prevent me from living to the full, right up to the last moment, I told myself. If they come they will find me much happier with my clear conscience than they are [moved by their anger]; I shall meet them face to face and go to death as if it were to sleep. (p. 47; cf. French, p. 72)

She had no time left to realize her goals and so used her new identity and situation as a prisoner to realize her ideal self. She described how, after only one night in prison, she had accepted her situation stoically and settled into her new quarters, giving priority to her books and writing: these were so important to her that she would eat off a corner of the mantelpiece, "so as to keep my work-table clean and orderly" (p. 47). At her arrest she happened to have had in her pocket a copy of James Thomson's *Seasons*; she soon ordered new books and planned to improve her knowledge of English by reading David Hume's English history with the help of Sheridan's *Dictionary*.[17] However, first among the other books that she asked to be brought to her cell was Plutarch's *Lives*, which she claimed she used to take to church instead of her prayer book, "but had not seriously looked into since" the age of eight.[18] Plutarch's series of parallel lives of great Greeks and Romans provided a link between her precocious childhood, her projected historical narrative that included character sketches of the great men of the French Revolution, and her literary project to construct her personal history. In explaining her choice of this work of ancient history and biography, Roland hinted at her need for an exemplary ethos and authority, which she typically sought from pagan, classical models, as well as from her beloved Rousseau.

The charade of release and immediate rearrest on specific charges in late June prompted Roland to analyze her defensive tactics. She wrote: "I was not daunted by the new calamity that had befallen me, but I was outraged by their particular cruelty in letting me taste freedom and then binding me with new chains, their barbarous device for cloaking my detention with legality." Nevertheless, the shock had unsettled her, and she became conscious of being temporarily overwrought and agitated: "j'ai besoin de me posséder, parce que j'ai l'habitude de me régir" (p. 113; cf. French p. 272). Her self-control was habitual. In taking charge of the situation, she wrote about her own thought processes in the same free indirect forms that had allowed her to drift in and out of retrospective narrative and dramatic speech in recreating memorable scenes.

---

[17] Cf. "La raison de Shaftesbury fortifiait la mienne, ses pensées favorisaient la méditation; la sensibilité de Thompson [sic], ses tableaux riants ou sublimes, pénétraient mon cœur et charmaient mon imagination. Je dessinais ensuite jusqu'au dîner"; *Mémoires*, ed. De Roux, pp. 272–73.

[18] However, this is likely a memory of life writing rather than life. Rousseau (*Confessions*, bk. 1, sec. 4) also said that he read Plutarch at about the same age; J.-J. Rousseau, *Confessions*, tr. Angela Scholar (Oxford: Oxford University Press, 2000), p. 8. See Roland, *Mémoires*, ed. De Roux, p. 464.

Why pay my persecutors the compliment of being upset? All they had done, after all, was to add to their own crimes; they had not substantially altered the conditions which I had already learned to endure. Had I not books here, as at the Abbaye [Prison]? Had I not leisure (*du temps*)? Was I not still myself (*n'était-je plus moi-même*)? I began almost to be annoyed at having been disturbed, and resolved to make use of my time and my faculties with the detachment worthy of a strong character (*d'une âme forte*) under duress. That is the way to defy (*trompe*) one's enemies. (pp. 113–14; cf. French, p. 272)

The mature prisoner looked back on her initial shock in order to tell her implied reader how she had debated with herself and resolved to preserve her integrity and self-worth as the basis of effective resistance.

Fortitude (*fermeté*) does not consist simply in rising above circumstances by an effort of will; one must sustain it with a suitable regime and way of life. True wisdom is the sum of all the individual steps one takes to act wisely and to preserve one's sanity. (p. 114; cf. French, p. 272)

Roland claimed that she preserved her equilibrium and "fortitude" in prison by organizing time, as well as space, for her studies. Writing sustained her self-respect and generated her ideal image of ladylike dignity, philosophical wisdom, and (in due course) pragmatic philanthropy. When she believed that the early manuscript of her *Notices historiques* had been burned, she wrote (8 August 1793):

I must admit that I would rather have been thrown in the fire myself. This loss caused me more distress than anything else I have suffered.... My end is very near (*la crise approche*); any day I may be slaughtered, or hauled before some tribunal where the tyrants get rid of troublesome people. These papers were a [pillow on which I rested the justification of] my memory and the memory of so many [interesting] people. (p. 75; cf. French, pp. 147–48)

Then she had reminded herself that "one must never give up" (*il ne faut succomber à rien*) and settled down to replace that memoir with a more random selection of "portraits et anecdotes," hoping that if she survived she would be able to reconstruct the "lost" manuscript. Nevertheless, she confessed that its loss was especially regretted because its text was stylistically superior to the new one, and she presumed that "whatever might happen to me, this would be my moral and political testament" (p. 75; cf. French p. 147).

Despite her assertions of principle and energetic political activism as a left-wing democrat, in practice Roland's haute-bourgeoisie sensibilities often made her seem snobbish, elitist, and intolerant. She nevertheless inspired the devoted friendship of many men and women. She believed her personal dignity and thoughtfulness also endeared her to her jailers, whom, she reported, accorded her many privileges merely from their own sensitive appreciation of her refinement and exceptional character; these qualities, she seems to have believed, were greater than her (unexceptional) ability to pay for those same privileges. At Sainte-Pélagie, her second prison, she described how she became the special pet of the keeper's wife, Madame Bouchard, who (apparently) recognized how "difficult" it was for "the virtuous wife of a distinguished public figure," with such refined sensibilities, to share "a damp stinking hall" with "the dregs of humanity," including prostitutes and murderers.[19] Bouchard therefore moved Roland to a single room, and for a short period she was no longer forced to "fight" her way through "crowds of . . . disgusting neighbours." Bouchard is praised for treating the prisoner like a guest, so that she was able to study and even to make her own music in this home from home and thus to "forget" her captivity.[20] (Roland makes no mention of money changing hands here.)

However, Roland soon became aware that conditions for less wealthy prisoners were inadequate and she blamed herself as if she were still her husband's proxy, since while he was minister of the interior M. Roland had reduced the daily allowance for prisoners' expenses to two livres. She set about trying to reduce her own expenditure in order to supplement the rations of other prisoners, yet her motives were not exclusively altruistic. Now that the Commune had control of her person, it seemed even more important for her to reassert control over her imprisoned body. She cut down her daily food intake and declared her intention to experiment to see how far she could reduce this basic human need by sheer willpower. Roland could have paid for her normal meals since "one is free in theory to add whatever one likes to one's expenditure," but this restricted diet had a "moral purpose" and, besides, she added, "I have no use for pointless economy." She therefore described how she set aside "a sum of money for the unfortunate down-and-outs (*les malheureux à la paille*), so that when I ate my dry bread in the morning I should have the pleasure of knowing that thanks to me [these

---

[19] Cf. irony that as the Terror increased, the prisons filled up with the kinds of females Mme Roland was "not ashamed to know" (p. 121). For disorder in prison, see the French text, pp. 285–86.

[20] Cf. pp. 115–17; and French, p. 278. Shortly afterward, in the interests of equality, she was forced back into the squalor and dangers of the main corridor without privileges (p. 120; and French, p. 289).

poor devils] could add something to theirs at night." She said that she hoped to earn "some blessings incognito" from these practical expressions of solidarity with other prisoners (p. 51; cf. French p. 79). She also felt obliged to compensate the prison staff for the loss of income they incurred from her self-denial and explained, as if in conversation with her reader:

> Anyone who is (*on est*), or appears to be, severely economical in his own expenditure must be generous to others, and particularly to those who are dependent for their livelihood on his spending . . . I must pay for not making use of these people. My own independence—and their affection—must be bought (*il convient donc que j'achète l'indépendance où je me mets d'eux; c'est la rendre plus parfaite et me faire aimer en sus*). (pp. 51–52; cf. French, pp. 79–80)

Charity towards prisoners was thus not simply a religious or humanitarian duty; such actions also helped this prisoner to live at peace with her conscience and provided further objective signs of her resistance.

## WRITING HISTORY HERSELF: "AN OBJECT LESSON TO THE REPUBLIC."

Whereas Roland's "voice" in her memoirs frequently shows alertness to how her interactions with others were perceived at the time, her writing also demonstrates how she sought to influence the judgment of posterity by the power of her pen. When neither her outraged nor more muted complaints in letters were accepted in her defense, she resolved to go over the heads of the increasingly dominant Paris Commune to address what she called the judgment of history, or fame. This, she realized, would require the application of a more subtle, yet imponderable literary strategy of resistance.

Her epigraph for the first memoir dated from the Abbaye Prison, June 1793, "On the throne today; tomorrow in irons," confirms the reversal of fortune that since Boethius had been deemed the "common lot of the virtuous in time of revolution" (p. 27; cf. French p. 45). In this memoir Roland wrote as a political philosopher, offering readers timeless advice from her own experience and classical learning, about the fate of the "wise" and "virtuous" in all periods who help the people resist oppression but then become their victims. Yet, having earlier misread the forces of revolutionary history that she had helped to unleash, and been shocked at her former allies' betrayal of principles, she would have felt obliged to reassess her situation, for her own sake in the first instance. It was also politically astute to gather her thoughts for a counter-attack on her enemies and, while she still had the opportunity, to testify to her own role in recent events, previously subsumed under her husband's name.

The earliest parts of her narrative therefore defended her husband's actions. She called him Roland, in a detached objective way, yet offered her readers intimate details about his motives and the reasoning behind specific actions which had led to his resignation from a government that had lost power to the Commune as France slipped into anarchy. She likely began with her husband's image because she was already identified so closely with him, and her own expression occasionally shows that she had internalized that view: "Once we were out of office . . . I thought it quite right that Roland should avoid the fury of the mob" (p. 37); "our knowledge and our opinions were, so to speak, held in common" (p. 62; French p. 106). She was also likely to reflect on the irony of their respective situations since Roland had succeeded in escaping to a secret refuge near Rouen, while she was arrested, having delayed leaving Paris. The family had decided to split up, assuming that Roland's freedom of movement would be greater if he were alone. But Madame Roland's emotional commitment to another man had complicated her motives for retreating from Paris. She was fiercely loyal to her husband's political reputation with which she was inextricably bound, yet sufficiently disloyal to their personal relationship to nurture this attachment to another married man, which probably compromised her ability to escape.[21] Her view of her own courage also meant that she tended to be apologetic about escape plans. She even claimed that she saw a function for the terrible violence in that it might shock other leaders in regional government: "The degradation (*l'avilissement*) of the Convention, its daily acts of cowardice and impotence upset me so much that I found the recent excesses almost preferable; they might at least wake up (*éclairer*) the departments and force them to take a stand" (pp. 30–31; cf. French, pp. 49–50).

Such bravado is a recurrent theme in her prison writings. Roland seems especially eager to frustrate her contemporary readers' expectations of appropriate feminine responses to murder, mayhem, and individual suffering. It was also vital to the makeup of her self-impression that she had studied classical history and politics: "When I was a child of twelve, I wept that I had not been born in Sparta or in Rome; and in the French Revolution I thought I saw the unexpected triumph (*l'application inespérée*) of principles upon which I had been nourished" (p. 49; cf. French, p. 75). She modeled

---

[21] For her view of François Buzot, "dont les principes purs, le courage, la sensibilité, les moeurs douces, m'inspiraient infiniment d'estime et d'attachement," see the French text, p. 87, and the biographical note (in Shuckburgh's translation, p. 19). She wrote letters to Buzot ("Celui de tous qui m'était le plus cher") from prison; see her statement in the French text, p. 277.

her personal behavior on patterns of stoic forbearance in adversity and stated proudly that the commissioners responsible for her first arrest had praised her dignity, telling her, as they took her into custody, that she had "more character than many men" (p. 40; cf. French p. 63). Even in the midst of the most violent stage of the French Revolution she claimed to have admired an unsentimental attitude to the political expediency of murder, which she associated with the ruthless politics of Seneca's Rome. On the death of Mirabeau, she remembered thinking, that "this was timely for his reputation (*sa gloire*) and for the cause of freedom" to which he became a martyr; "but subsequent events," she continued, "have taught me to regret him more. We needed the counterweight of such a man to oppose the depredations of a pack of curs" (p. 79; cf. French, p. 192).

Fear of assassination had been one of the reasons for Jean-Marie Roland's decision to leave Paris, yet his wife claimed she had already calculated the political utility of his death and considered the impact of his murder in different circumstances. As she recollected in prison,

> my feeling was that to violate the private home (*l'asile*) of a public figure was a very grave step for a criminal to take, and that if there were villains capable of attempting such a crime it might not be altogether a bad thing for the enterprise to succeed (*il n'était pas inutile qu'il se consommât*); . . . I thought the minister [i.e., Roland] ought to stay at his post. Death at his post would cry out for vengeance and provide an object lesson to the Republic; whereas an assassination in the by-ways, though of equal value (*profit*) to the perpetrators, would have less impact on the public and give less glory to the victim. (p. 37 adapted; cf. French, p. 58)

Sensing that such comments would expose her to charges of unfeeling cynicism, she continued, "I realise that this [reasoning] will sound absurd to anyone who values his life above everything; but in time of revolution anyone who attaches importance to his own life is likely to attach none to virtue, honour or his country." This dichotomy was her response to classical literary traditions and a political reality recognized by many other dissidents forced by oppression to choose between their principles and their continued existence. (Some compromises, as Gramsci's cannibalism metaphor also recognized, changed the purpose and value of life beyond recognition. One cannot live with oneself if one no longer recognizes one's own identity.) Thus Roland both justified her own reasoning (in anticipating criticism) and derived a general truth from history in order to validate her reactions and affirm her superior political wisdom. Her style here reflects her interpretation and assimilation of heroic roles from antiquity, and what it meant to be a contemporary *philosophe* with a highly developed moral understanding and mental power. She relished holding opposing ideas in balance in order to assess the value of an action to the perpetrators and to the victim, and proudly contemplated the viewpoint of "villains," describing their "crime" euphemistically as an "enterprise" in thinking what she knew ought to have been unthinkable by a woman of feeling and a wife. She personified death in imagining its "cry" for vengeance, yet discussed the male victim impersonally and contrasted the importance and value of her husband's life (the actual subject) with such abstractions as "republican virtue," "honour," and "country." She acknowledged the human instinct for self-preservation, yet prioritized acting according to an ancient honor code over loyalty to relationships in real life, which she was aware made her calculation seem "absurd."

This is ironic in the context of her writing memoirs designed to represent her life, and to maintain an image of it after death, while facing the probability of her own imminent murder. She wished to be remembered on her own ideal terms. Not surprisingly therefore she reports that she also considered the political value to France of her own arrest and death at the hands of the radical Jacobins she had accused of undermining the Revolution.

> I reckoned that if they had any sense of shame and wanted to respect the formalities, interrogate me and stage a trial, I would have no difficulty (*je ne serais pas embarrassée*) in confounding them; indeed it might give me a chance to enlighten people. (p . 37; cf. French, p. 59)[22]

Her naive premise is that anarchists would respect the rule of law, allowing her to make a judicial defense of her husband in court and that her powers of argument and rhetoric would be effective against slander. However, it would seem that there was no irony intended here because even after arrest and imprisonment she failed to qualify the idealism upon which this assessment was based. If the street violence and massacres of the previous September were renewed, she not only would be proud to become their victim but also envisaged sacrificing her life to save Roland's: "I would rather die than witness the ruin of my country; I should consider it an honour to be counted amongst the heroic victims (*les glorieuses victimes immolées à la rage du crime*)" (p. 37; cf. French, p. 59). Thus Madame Roland anticipated both the circumstances of her death and the general consequences of the Terror, yet underestimated the impact on Roland of his wife's death. When news of her execution reached him in the countryside, he committed suicide.

---

[22] Cf. Bunyan's fantasy of converting souls from the scaffold, and larger theme of paradox of gain by loss more widely.

Her desire to die a prisoner, rather than witness the ruin of France, anticipated her own suicidal despair when the Commune became more violent
and powerful than the National Convention. At the beginning of October
1793, the Convention indicted the remaining Girondin deputies; in response to this news, Roland stopped writing her memoirs in prison and
began a hunger strike intending to commit suicide.

> I cannot go on writing in the midst of these horrors which are tearing my
> country apart. I cannot live amongst (*sur*) its ruins. I prefer to be buried
> beneath them. Nature, open your arms to me (*ouvre ton sein*)! Righteous
> God, receive me (*Dieu juste, reçois-moi*)!
>
> At the age of thirty-nine. (p. 252; cf. French, p. 520)

Self-preservation and self-control were not necessarily complementary. Yet
by 14 October she was in the prison hospital and receiving food again because she had decided to postpone her suicide in order to make what she
hoped would be a more affecting and therefore effective political protest.
She knew the trial of the Girondin deputies would be a sham, but she
planned to swallow poison in open court after delivering a passionate speech
from the witness box. When this plan failed because no defense witnesses
were called, and Louis-Augustin-Guillaume Bosc (a loyal friend since 1780)
refused to procure the poison, she wrote about her suicidal intent which she
justified on the grounds that her own trial and execution were imminent.
Her last prison meditation begins under the heading (in English) of a line
adapted from Hamlet's soliloquy:

> *To be, or not to be: it is the question.* The question will soon be answered
> for me (*Elle sera bientôt résolue pour moi*). (p. 253; cf. French, p. 527)[23]

As a daughter of the French Enlightenment, she considered that whereas life
was a blessing there were also conditions attached which she valued as much
as the gift of life itself: "We are born to seek happiness and to serve the happiness of our fellow mortals (*d'autrui*). The social order (*l'état social*) extends
the range of this objective and indeed of all our faculties; it adds nothing
new" (p. 253). She thought that so long as one could see a prospect of doing
good and setting a good example one should find the courage to persist in
spite of misfortune. It is highly significant that she recorded her own new
enthusiasm for the works of Tacitus while a prisoner of the Terror: "J'ai pris
dans ma prison une véritable passion pour Tacite" (p. 521). As a student of
Tacitus, she concluded that "when a term has already been set to [one's] life-

---

[23] Cf. P. de Roux and her knowledge of English: she also quoted from Thomson's *Seasons* (more
extensively), see the French text, pp. 353–54.

span by our enemies," an individual was "entitled to shorten" that life-span, "particularly when nobody on earth will gain anything by our battling on (*surtout si la force de subir son dernier effet ne doit rien produire d'avantageux à personne*)" (p. 253; cf. French p. 527). Yet, finally, she did battle on by going to the guillotine with great dignity and fortitude three weeks later, and in the memorial impression of her life preserved by her prison writing.

## "PASSIONATE FOR MY COUNTRY"—POLITICS, RHETORIC, AND LIBERATION

A most satisfying way to resist and defy one's enemies, she had decided in the early stages of imprisonment, was to write down the taunts and curses against them that it would have been impossible to utter aloud. In a direct address to the Commune from her cell in the Abbaye Prison, Roland expressed her outrage by writing diatribe:

> My blood boils when I hear the Parisians praised for not wanting another 2 September massacre. Good God (*justes dieux*)! Nobody needs you, citizens of Paris, for another massacre. All you have to do is to sit tight, as you did last time. Your help was necessary for collecting the victims and you lent yourselves complacently to their arrest. . . . Do not come now boasting that you defend the Convention; you are the ones who bind the Convention in chains, standing by like cowards as its most virtuous and talented members are led to execution. . . . [24] France will hold you accountable for all these crimes. You serve our enemies; you are preparing the disintegration of France! Do you think that proud Marseilles and wise Gironde will forgive the affronts committed against their representatives? Do you think they will ever again co-operate with your crime soiled city? You are the destroyers of your city; when you find yourselves standing in its ruins you will regret your infamous cowardice. (p. 31 adapted)

The fury, frustration, and disappointment as she harangues the citizenry in this monologue suggest her anticipation of an audience for whom she maintains her self-appointed role as a political analyst, in goading and warning the citizens of Paris to face reality. As seen earlier in her dramatic representation of the dialogue with *sans culottes* by the cannon, the force of her speech reflects the imagination and rhetorical talents that had been her most characteristic contribution to revolutionary politics. While at liberty she had

---

[24] At this point in the French text (see p. 50) she mentions Algernon Sidney (1622–83) as an exemplary exponent of republicanism who was killed by his enemies.

claimed to be content with a ventriloquized voice in politics as her husband's proxy; finally, this same literary voice, excited yet reasonable and analytical, was entirely her own and reveals her existential liberation as a prisoner.

Roland was especially forceful and energetic in voicing (in the direct speech of dramatic monologue) her antipathy to Danton whose ruthless manipulation of the mob she blamed for the recent violence.

> O Danton! This is the way you (*tu*) sharpen the knives against your victims! Strike! One more murder will hardly add to your crimes. You cannot escape eternal infamy for what you have done. Cruel as Marius, more frightful than Catiline, you surpass their crimes without having their greatness. History will spew up (*l'histoire vomira*) your name with horror when it records the butcheries of September and the savagery of 2 June. (p. 113 adapted; cf. French, p. 271)

Her sense of history and imaginative correlation of ancient Rome with contemporary Paris make her assessment accessible and meaningful to a wider range of readers beyond her own time and place. The names of Marius and Catiline are important coordinates on a scale of brutal tyranny that would have resonated with any educated reader of her time.[25] She also reported finding such rhetorical resistance pleasurable and reassuring: "I rather enjoyed composing vigorous tirades under the very noses of the brutes who would have murdered me if they had heard a single phrase" (p. 119).[26] Writing in this situation was not only cathartic but also a consolation. In such language that might still provide others with inspiration to resist the persecution of tyrants, she was cheering herself up, strengthening her resolve, and making a subversive, preemptive strike against the anarchy and repression that were about to destroy her. Thus she not only fashioned a literary image of her own fame for posterity but also ensured that Danton would never escape his infamy in the judgment of her history.[27] Judgment and understanding were crucial. The contemporary problem, as she defined it, was a lack of leadership and vision: there were no real men around: "France seemed to be entirely drained of men (*epuisée d'hommes*) ... nothing but pygmies are to be seen. ... Where do we find a complete man (*l'homme supérieur*), combining true understanding of the present with a far-sighted vision of the future? Hardly anywhere" (p. 86; cf. French, p. 227). She returned again and again to this *ubi sunt* trope and the frustration it induced.[28]

---

[25] Cf. her praise of her husband as "an Aristides in justice, a Cato in severity" (p. 41) and her lover, Buzot, who "professait la morale de Socrate et conservait la politesse de Scipion" (p. 150). See further Parker, *The Cult of Antiquity*.

[26] Cf. "sous les yeux ... des misérables qui m'auraient massacrée" (p. 287).

[27] See further on Danton, French text, pp. 208–13.

[28] E.g., of Baron Luckner, commander in chief of the army, she wrote: "I have never seen any-

Naturally, those qualities that she most valued and admired were also those she thought she detected in herself: "I burned with zeal (*pénétrée du désir*) for the prosperity of my country. Public affairs had become a torment to me, a moral fever which left me no rest" (p. 89; cf. French p. 231). "Je ne crains rien du monde" (p. 53).

If writing about the events and personalities of the French Revolution became her chief consolation in prison, she also recognized that it was her only effective, long-term form of self-defense. In this respect her title, *Notices historiques*, is misleading since Roland's actions, judgment, and opinions are the principal subjects of all her prison writing. However, the frankness and assertiveness that characterize these different literary forms of self-preservation were considered unflattering by their first editor. Although Bosc collected and preserved Roland's manuscripts after her death and hid them during the Terror, the work he published in 1795 as her *Appel à l'impartiale postérité* was heavily edited to conform to his own ideas of taste and appropriate literary form. Bosc made substantial cuts and rearranged her texts to make them appear better organized and more balanced; he also rewrote passages in an attempt to "correct" her style in ways that her modern editor, Paul de Roux, has described as clumsy.[29] De Roux followed Claude Perroud's critical edition (1905) and reinstated the authority of Roland's manuscript texts in which she had deliberately inscribed her self-impression and political judgments for readers in the future by recollecting and recreating the past.

Before her imprisonment Roland had written mainly letters of various kinds. She enjoyed and perhaps (like Gramsci) needed the prospect of dialogue with a specific correspondent that this literary form entailed. In the prison memoir she wrote for her daughter, she commented on the long letters she had written to her old school friend, Sophie Grandchamp (née Cannet): "My sensibility was such that I really needed I will not say an imaginary recipient (*une chimère*), but a principal target for my confidences" (p. 179; cf. French p. 402). Writing was also a discipline that enabled her to think more effectively and efficiently: "With a pen in my hand I was able to control my imagination and follow my reason, whereas without it I too often found myself just dreaming" (p. 218). She described herself as having

thing so second rate [*si médiocre*] in my life. An old soldier, half besotted, witless, spineless, a sort of nobody whom the most primitive monkey could lead by the nose!" (p. 97). Her judgment of Le Brun was more wittily epigrammatic: he "passed for a wise man because he had no enthusiasms of any sort and for an able man because he was a competent clerk" (p. 100).

[29] *Mémoires*, pp. 38–39. For information on how Roland's small manuscript notebooks were dismembered and smuggled out of the prison by her visitors, see pp. 33 and 401; cf. Shuckburgh's translation, p. 178n. Approximately seven hundred closely written pages of her notebooks are now in Paris, Bibliothèque nationale. Bosc also hid Jean-Marie Roland for several weeks in the country.

been a lonely and studious child whose best companion was her mother, and at the age of twenty-one, after her mother's death, as she recorded in her prison memoir, she began to write about her studies as well as her feelings of grief: "My only thought was to get my various opinions down on paper so that I could compare them later on and form a sort of conspectus of my intellectual progress.... I never had the slightest intention of becoming an author" (p. 218). Her prison writing was different in that she intended her *Notices historiques* to be read widely as both witness testimony to political events and her own moral and political testament. She also yearned for "some enduring place in the minds of future generations" (p. 192). This incentive was so strong that when she thought her early manuscripts had been lost she immediately began to rewrite them, reverting to the consolations of writing to construct a memorial to her own life and opinions, and seeking distraction when she was so "particularly distressed" by talking to others on paper about herself (p. 126). She was well aware that this was her last chance to secure an afterlife of literary fame.

Anne Frank's diary and stories, written in confinement during another period of violence, persecution, and terror, served her in similar ways. Anne Frank may be seen as Roland's literary daughter, and perhaps as the kind of daughter—lively, opinionated, ambitious for self-fulfillment, shrewd, observant, and personally outspoken in her writing—that Roland might have cherished and appraised more highly than her own daughter. Anne Frank expressed disappointment in her relationship with her mother, whom she thought passive and deficient in her understanding of her daughter. Anne also recognized a strong histrionic streak in herself and yearned to do more than she considered women of her mother's generation had been able to achieve. Writing well was her ambition; she already had some of the fluency and confidence on paper of a more mature writer. Like Roland she was conscious that she also needed to write in order to think and was comforted by doing so. Her imagined reader was the diarist's female alter ego, Kitty. Writing for this fantasy figure prompted Anne to re-create conversations and texts of other letters, sketch pen portraits of her companions, describe their surroundings, and reflect upon changes in her ideas and state of mind, as tensions among the group in hiding increased. Letters to Kitty enabled the fast maturing Anne to construct a dialogue between her past and present selves; rereading and revising her diary allowed her to trace the signs of her own development, and to fashion a literary persona. She was a studious, well-read child and dreamed of a future career as a writer, which she proposed would start with a memoir of her experiences in hiding during World War II: her own version of "historical notes," filtered through a direct impression of persecution and captivity, with a personal account of her inner life. In the end, two years after her death, her writing was edited and published by a devoted, male reader according to his own ideas of tact and decorum: her father. She has since been defined by the reception of her writing as an important witness to devastating historical events and as a literary personality whom we think we know intimately from the variety and liveliness of her self-representation.

## Anne Frank, *The Diary* and *Tales from the Secret Annexe* (1942–44): Life Writing

Anne Frank was given a blank book in which to write a diary on her thirteenth birthday, 12 June 1942. Within a month her family had been forced into hiding, in German occupied Amsterdam, initially to protect her older sister Margot from a deportation order. Dutch Jews were being systematically rounded up and deported to death and slave labor camps in Germany and Poland causing some twenty thousand to go into hiding. The Franks were a middle-class Jewish family, originally from Frankfort-am-Main, who had lived in the Netherlands since Anne was four years old. Her father Otto, a businessman with premises at 263 Prinsengracht in an old house facing the canal, had prepared a suite of rooms at the top of the house, toward the rear, as a retreat. Their neighbors at home were told that the family had gone abroad after the Franks moved into the annex to the offices and warehouse premises. They were joined a week later, in July 1942, by three others, the van Pels family, and, later still, in November by Fritz Pfeffer, a single man. (Anne's intention to publish a book based on her diary led her to list pseudonyms for her companions and helpers; these names were substituted for the real ones in Otto Frank's postwar edition of his daughter's diary. The van Pels family and Pfeffer were renamed the van Daans and Albert Dussel.)[30] They were protected and supplied with food and news by a small group of Otto Frank's non-Jewish business associates, who thereby risked their lives and those of their families. Access to the "Secret Annex" was restricted to those times when the building was otherwise unoccupied; the doorway to the annex was carefully hidden by a sliding bookcase. Although they had

---

[30] See *The Diary of Anne Frank: The Critical Edition, Prepared by the Netherlands State Institute for War Documentation*, ed. David Barnouw and Gerrold van der Stroom, tr. Arnold J. Pomerans and B. M. Mooyaart-Doubleday with introductions by the editors and Harry Paape, and a summary of the report on the original manuscript, by the Netherlands State Forensic Science Laboratory, compiled by H.J.J. Hardy (London: Viking, 1989); this essential diplomatic edition from the original manuscripts was first published in the Netherlands in 1986. Quotations here are taken from this edition using the first version "a" or, where it exists, "b" text of the *Diary* as the latest version revised by Anne Frank. There are substantive differences between each of the three versions of the text represented in this critical edition. (The "c" text is the more widely known version edited by Otto Frank.)

chosen their own confinement as a form of protection, their only other option was deportation to the concentration camps. From July 1942 until they
were betrayed by persons unknown, this little group lived in hiding, unable
to go out of the building or to venture farther than other rooms of the house
at night. After their arrest by the Gestapo and deportation to Auschwitz in
August 1944, one of the family's helpers, Miep Gies, retrieved the notebooks and loose leaves of Anne's diary from debris strewn over the floor, and
kept them locked away (unread), intending to return them to their author.
When it was clear that Anne had died, she handed the diaries to Otto Frank,
the only survivor of the group, in 1945. He published an edited version of
his daughter's diary in 1947; it was later translated into many languages and
helped to inform the world, and especially young people, about the persecution of Jews and the Holocaust. Since the death of Otto Frank, the full text
has been published in the original Dutch and in many translations; it exists
in two states from the hand of Anne who revised her early entries for possible publication, not necessarily in diary form, at some future date and thus
envisaged readers.

Anne's epigraph to her diary, which she signed and dated 12 June 1942,
indicates her aspirations and ultimate achievement through this book:

> I hope I shall be able to confide in you completely, as I have never been
> able to do in anyone before, and I hope that you will be a great comfort
> to me. (*Diary*, p. 177)

Within a few days, this personification of the book as confidant and consolation had crystallized into an imaginary friend: "I want this diary, itself to
be my friend, and I shall call my friend Kitty" (20 June 1942, p. 181, "a"
text). Thereafter, the form of Anne Frank's diary is an irregular sequence of
personal letters addressed to her "friend"—"Dear Kitty" occasionally "Dearest Kitty" (*Beste Kitty*)—and signed, either, "Yours, Anne," or, with her full
name. The fiction of this friendship is established from the first entry in letter form, which is prefaced by Anne's favorite photograph of herself, a brief
autobiography, and her vivid summary of the restrictions on Dutch Jews
imposed since May 1940. "No one will grasp what I'm talking about if I
begin my letters to Kitty just out of the blue so I'll start by sketching in brief
the story of my life, much as I don't like to" (p. 182). This figure of Kitty was
clearly not the only reader Anne envisaged by this introduction. "It's an odd
idea for someone like me, to keep a diary. . . . Still, what does that matter? I
want to write, but more than that, I want to bring out all kinds of things that
lie buried deep in my heart. There is a saying that paper is more patient than
man" (20 June 1942, "b" text, p. 180). She imagined that what she would

need to write might try the patience of anyone else. Kitty is always "patient" (p. 297), and Kitty was her alter ego: "Who besides me will ever read these letters? From whom but myself shall I get comfort?" Like Madame Roland, she found that the discipline of writing (or "talking") about herself as if addressing others, as honestly as possible, provided emotional catharsis and a valuable distraction as well as consolation in troubled times. The creation of her personal narrative was thus necessary and therapeutic. However, after the Dutch authorities in exile broadcast an appeal for private papers including letters and diaries as historical resources, in March 1944, Anne started to revise her diary for submission to this archive.[31] These letters were therefore also intended as her "historical notes."[32]

Like Roland in her youth, Anne Frank also wanted to be able to retrace her intellectual and emotional development by reviewing her writing and used the diary to take stock of what happened within the secret annex. When she read over her own entries and commented on her changing attitudes and feelings, the diary can be seen as one side of a dialogue constructed between her past and present images of self.[33] Yet she was also interested in learning how to observe and analyze what she saw around her, since she came to regard the diary as source material for a later book, to be called *Het Achterhuis*, literally the house in the back, which became the title for the published *Diary*. She wanted to become a professional writer and journalist.[34] She therefore practiced writing regularly and was self-conscious about why she was writing. In addition, Anne wrote short stories for herself and often as birthday presents for other people. Several of these stories overlap closely with the ideas and feelings recorded and explored in the diary. As she continued her schoolwork, she also read more widely and was engaged in writing notes and essays of several different kinds. Writing and reading were her chief occupations in confinement; writing the diary in the form of letters to Kitty became her most necessary and pleasurable pastime; it was also her chief means of realizing herself by constructing a literary self-impression and thinking about her life.

---

[31] *Diary* entry for Wednesday, 29 March 1944: "Bolkesteyn, an M.P., was speaking in the Dutch news" (via BBC radio broadcasts) "from London, and he said that they ought to make a collection of diaries and letters after the war. Of course they all made a rush at my diary immediately" (p. 578, "b" text).

[32] For discussion of this theme in a literary theoretical context and alongside a summary of the reception of Anne Frank's diary, see also Rachel Feldhay Brenner, "Writing Herself against History: Anne Frank's Self-Portrait as a Young Artist," *Modern Judaism*, 16 (1996), 105–34.

[33] See the entry for Saturday, 25 March 1944, in which Anne considers: "When you change you only notice it after you have changed. I have changed and radically so, wholly and in every way. My opinions, ideas, critical outlook; outwardly, inwardly everything is changed and I can safely say, since it is true, for the better . . ." (*Diary*, "a" text, p. 567).

[34] See *Diary*, 11 May 1944, "a" text, p. 647.

## "IT IS ALMOST IMPOSSIBLE TO ESCAPE"

As the family prepared to go into hiding, Anne packed her diary first; she understood that the consequences of discovery and deportation would be fatal and occasionally discussed these anxieties and their implications. On 9 October 1942 she wrote about what happened to her friends when they were taken away by the Gestapo, "without a shred of decency, being loaded into cattle trucks and sent to Westerbork" (the holding camp in the eastern Netherlands from where more than 100,000 Dutch Jews were deported to Auschwitz).[35]

> It is almost impossible to escape....
>
> If it is as bad as this in Holland whatever will it be like in the distant and barbarous regions they are sent to? We assume that most of them are murdered. The English radio speaks of their being gassed; perhaps that is the quickest way to die. I feel terribly upset. I couldn't tear myself away while Miep told these dreadful stories.[36]

Even at this very early date in the development of the camps as killing factories with gas chambers, a thirteen-year old in hiding in Western Europe was under no illusions about the realities of what became known as the Final Solution to the "Jewish Question." By 19 November she had heard about house-to-house searches to round up those Jews who remained at liberty in Amsterdam, and from the top of the Prinsengracht house she saw the brutal consequences with her own eyes.

> In the evenings when it's dark, I often see rows of good, innocent people accompanied by crying children, walking on and on ... bullied and knocked about until they almost drop. Nobody is spared, old people, children, babies, expectant mothers, the sick, each and all join in the march of death. ("b" text, p. 316)

Mixed in with this historic eyewitness testimony is Anne's personal struggle to accommodate these acts of terror with her own desire to continue living. The first consequences of her empathy with her Jewish neighbors and friends being marched away were feelings of guilt at her inability to help them, and then fear.

---

[35] *Diary*, "b" text, p. 272. On conditions at Westerbork from July 1942, see *An Interrupted Life: The Diary and Letters of Etty Hillesum 1941–43*, tr. A. J. Pomerans (London: Persephone Books, 1999).

[36] *Diary*, "b" text, pp. 272–73. BBC news broadcasts began to refer to the gassing of Jews, in Poland, in June 1942. Miep Gies (see obituary, *The Times*, 13 January 2010, pp. 57–58) was Otto Frank's secretary.

I feel wicked sleeping in a warm bed, while my dearest friends have been knocked down or have fallen into a gutter somewhere out in the cold night.

I get frightened when I think of close friends who have now been delivered into the hands of the cruellest brutes the world has ever seen. And all because they are Jews. (19 November 1942, "b" text, p. 316)

There is no more variety in our thoughts than there is for ourselves, everything goes round and round like a roundabout—from Jews to food and from food to politics. By the way, talking of Jews, I saw 2 Jews through the curtain yesterday, I could hardly believe my eyes; it was a horrible feeling, just as if I had betrayed them and was now watching them in their misery. (12 December 1942, "b" text, p. 328)

None of the adults around her seemed to have better ideas about how to cope with the brutalities of German occupation, yet Anne was able to articulate, recognize, and clarify their dilemma by writing about it to Kitty. Dread and distress were turning their hiding place into a "Secret Annex of Gloom"; Miep became afraid to pass on bad news about acquaintances and, according to Anne, concluded that it was best not to say very much. Her mother and Mrs. van Pels wept at the news brought by Miep; Anne thought,

Must I keep thinking about those other people whatever I am doing and if I want to laugh about something, should I stop myself quickly and feel ashamed that I am cheerful? Ought I then to cry the whole day long? No, that I can't do and, besides, in time this gloom will wear off. (20 November 1942, "b" text, p. 317)

Their "gloom" did not diminish, but the occupants of the secret annex learned to live with it, and some days were better than others. Like Roland, when Anne found herself "surrounded by too great a void" of terror, in a world-turned-upside-down, she turned her thoughts inward to keep "unhappy things" at bay and wrote.[37] Anne Frank's self-consciousness as a writer sustained her during confinement and persecution; after her death this writing provided the basis for the literary fame that has preserved her self-image among readers.

After a year in confinement, "some of it . . . quite indescribable," she set about describing an ordinary day in the routine of the secret annex, ending with verbal sketches of her companions around the dinner table.[38] Their characters intrigued and amused her so she made several attempts to repre-

---

[37] *Diary*, "b" text, p. 318. Cf. 13 January and 30 January 1943.
[38] Wednesday, 4 August 1943, "b" text, pp. 381–84, at 381.

sent them all on paper. A few days earlier, after a paragraph (venting her frustration) in denigration of Mrs. van Pels, she commented wryly to herself (and Kitty): "I could write whole chapters about Madame, and who knows, perhaps I will some day" (pp. 378–79). When she wrote up these events, under the title "Anne in theorie" among her *Tales from the Secret Annexe (Verhaaltjesboek)*, she added a note, distancing herself from the action, as if she were the editor of her text, and apologizing to the reader for the author's attitude: "Will the reader take into consideration that when this story was being written, the writer had not cooled down from her fury!"[39] Three weeks later she wrote a story about "the communal duty of the day: potato peeling!," indicating that she was consciously composing different types of narrative alongside the fiction of the correspondence with Kitty. The vitality of this scene derives partly from her use of direct speech in representing dialogue and partly from the shrewd details she had selected after close observation of her companions.

> Pf. begins, does not always scrape well, but scrapes incessantly, glancing right and left. "Does everyone do it the way he does? No! Enne, zee here; I take ze knife in mein hand like zo, scrape from ze top downvards! Nein, not like zat—like zis!"
> "I get on better like this, Mr Pf.," I remark timidly.[40]

The simple narrative detail in the first sentence here is followed by an omniscient narrator's anticipation of the character's motives, which effectively and economically links the description with the dialogue in the later sentences. If Anne's text mocks Pfeffer's German accent, it would also remind the group in hiding about their origins as native German speakers and the irony of their linguistic kinship with the corrupted culture they had been forced to flee. Such qualities of liveliness and perception enabled the writer to interpret, enhance, and preserve an intrinsically inconsequential, yet significant and representative aspect of their actual lives.

Anne eagerly read whatever she could lay her hands on in Dutch, German, or English; her companions passed library books among themselves, which they discussed together; they also bought books for each other as birthday presents.[41] She read widely and considered history, art, and ancient

[39] See text and note with diary entry for 29 July 1943, *Diary*, p. 379. Otto Frank incorporated this sentence as a postscript implying "Kitty" as the reader; see "c" text, p. 379.

[40] "Pf," i.e., Fritz Pfeffer, aka Mr. Dussel in the "c" text. "Tales from the Secret Annex," extract, Friday, 6 August 1943, reprinted in *Diary*, p. 395. Otto Frank incorporated Anne's story into the "c" text of the diary for 18 August 1943.

[41] Sylvia Patterson Iskander, "Anne Frank's Reading: a Retrospective," in *Anne Frank Reflections of Her Life and Legacy*, ed. H. A. Enzer and S. Solotaroff-Enzer (Urbana: University of Illinois Press, 2000), pp. 100–109, especially the appendix of books mentioned in the *Diary* (pp. 106–9), which

mythology her favorite subjects. Nevertheless, as the pressures inherent in this life of confinement (dominated by a sometimes morbid fear of discovery) grew more difficult to cope with, Anne reported to Kitty how her earlier enthusiasm for escaping the present in reading about other lives seemed diminished. She was upset to find herself so sensitive to the moods of her companions, and she was similarly affected by her reading. "If I read a book that impresses me I have to take myself firmly in hand before I mix with other people" (8 November 1943, "b" text, p. 415).

In late October and early November 1943, she described the tensions induced by a kind of prison neurosis that she was experiencing, using an ancient literary image of freedom. The simile of a songbird in a cage suggests that she found expressive analogues for her experience in her reading, yet the image of a real bird may also have come to mind and influenced the development of her new image of self-identity.[42] The atmosphere was especially tense on Sundays when the city was so quiet: "You don't hear a single bird singing outside, and a deadly sultry silence hangs everywhere, catching hold of me as if it would drag me down deep into an underworld."[43] Paradoxically as Anne wandered freely about the empty house, in the absence of the warehousemen and office workers, she was more aware than ever of her confinement. She described herself listlessly, "feeling like a songbird who has had his wings clipped and who is hurling himself in utter darkness against the bars of his cage." Knowing that she had no energy to effect any compensatory escape through reading or writing, she slept to make both the time "and the stillness and the terrible fear" pass, "because there is no way of killing time."[44] Here the caged bird image which traditionally represents the human soul trapped within the body emerges from her memory of literature to represent her sense of repression or suffocation through "a deadly silence." Even the birds not singing outside are signs of disturbance and disruption in the natural world, and of a lack of harmony within nature and between the human and the natural world. The motif is a familiar one in representations of prisoners, literal and figurative. The bird bridges spaces in Anne's imagination that represent the freedom (through flight) she lacked in confinement, and as a rebellious girl with aspirations beyond those of her mother's generation. Some of the inmates of the secret annex had been quarrelling anxiously. In wanting to "kill" the abstractions of stillness and fear that tormented her, she expressed the anticipation of discovery and death that dom-

includes Alphonse Daudet's *La Belle Nivernaise* (in French), Wilde's play *An Ideal Husband* (in English), and John Galsworthy's *The Forsyte Saga* (revised in a Dutch translation printed in 1934).

[42] Cf. in a similar context Bonhoeffer's poem "Who am I?"

[43] Cf. Boethius's application of this trope in his Orpheus metrum (loss of Eurydice).

[44] Sunday, 17 October 1943, "b" text, p. 411.

inated the adults' waking hours and conversation. About this time she reported vivid dreams of being "alone in a dungeon," anticipating the destruction of the secret annex while its occupants, "you," are being taken away at night: "I see everything as if it is actually taking place and then still have the feeling that it could all happen to you very soon!" (8 November 1943). She yearned for escape from confinement and its uncertainties, even by anticipating disaster, and distinguished her dream self from her dreamer self; just as when she remembered her carefree life before the war, it now seemed "as if another person lived it all, not me" ("b" text, p. 146). New life experiences caused this new identity to develop, yet it was being realized and analyzed in writing.

## "COURAGE IS REBORN"—"I WANT TO GO ON LIVING EVEN AFTER MY DEATH"

Anne Frank's diary persona, like Roland's self-representation, indicated that her initial reaction to her situation of confinement was full of excitement and nervous energy. The new experiences—even of unpredictable terror—were stimulating, but later, in the wider contexts of worsening external situations, both writers became so severely demoralized that they appear (temporarily) to lose the will to resist and survive. For Anne, these feelings of hopeless resignation were fleeting but they affected her view of writing, which had come to signify more than the immediate solace of a private confessional memoir: Kitty could always be relied upon "to keep a secret."[45] After twenty months in confinement she was determined that writing would be her salvation; she decided that she was also the best critic of her own work and that, because of its importance to her, she would go on writing for herself even if no one else shared this view of her talent.

> I don't want to have lived for nothing like most people. I want to be useful or give pleasure to all the people around me yet who don't really know me, I want to go on living even after my death! And therefore I am grateful to God for giving me this gift, this possibility of developing myself and of writing, of expressing all that is in me. (24 March 1944, "a" text, p. 569)

Literary strategies of resistance were immediately beneficial to her: "I can shake off everything if I write; my sorrows disappear, my courage is reborn![46] "Anyone who doesn't write doesn't know how wonderful it is."[47] In this way

---

[45] Thursday, 6 January 1944, "a" text, p. 440.
[46] Ibid., p. 588. Cf. Roland's assertion: "je ne crains rien."
[47] 5 April 1944, "a" text, p. 587.

she was revived in the present and consoled by imagining how she might live on in the future through the writing she hoped would substitute for her life. She had also started to think more objectively about the confines of her own life by writing stories of different kinds.

In the aftermath of a crisis at the secret annex, caused by a burglary in the house followed by a police search, there were anxious recriminations. Anne wrote to Kitty as usual to tell the inmates' story, and then commented:

> None of us has ever been in such danger as that night. God truly protected us, just think of it—the police at our secret cupboard, the light on right in front of it, and still we remained undiscovered . . . Debates are going on all the time now in the "Secret Annexe."
>
> We have been pointedly reminded that we are in hiding, that we are Jews in chains, chained to one spot, without any rights, with a thousand duties. We Jews mustn't show our feelings, must be brave and strong, must accept all inconveniences and not grumble, must do what is within our power and trust in God.
>
> Some time this terrible war will be over. Surely the time will come when we are people again, and not just Jews. ("a" text, pp. 599–600)

From describing one personal experience and the tense review of all aspects of life in the secret annex that this necessitated, Anne went behind these events to focus hard on the underlying moral and political implications in a series of pointed rhetorical questions. Her resentful tone became reflective and meditative.

> Who has inflicted this upon us? Who has made us Jews different from all other people? Who has allowed us to suffer so terribly up till now? It is God that has made us as we are, but it will be God, too, who will raise us up again. If we bear all this suffering and if there are still Jews left, when it is over, then Jews, instead of being doomed, will be held up as an example. Who knows, it might even be our religion from which the world and all peoples learn good, and for that reason and that reason only do we have to suffer now. We can never become just Netherlanders or just English or any nation for that matter, we will always remain Jews, we must remain Jews, but we want to, too. ("a" text, p. 600)

She would never know the words "Shoah," or "Holocaust" with its tendentious applications in late twentieth-century historiography and theology, but here, anticipating so many fundamental questions, was a thoughtful teenager not only surviving but also resisting in the midst of catastrophic events. This same diary entry for 11 April 1944 concludes with the earnest expression of a desperate historical determinism and new personal resolutions prompted by the crisis in the secret annex.

> Be brave! Let us remain aware of our task and not grumble, a solution will come, God has never deserted our people; right through the ages there have been Jews, through all the ages they have had to suffer, but it has made them strong too, the weak are picked off and the strong will remain and never go under! ("a" text, p. 600)

As she remembered waiting in the dark for the police to find them, expecting to die, she assimilated the language and ideas of a different kind of nationhood and the heroism that she associated with combatants in war:

> I was prepared, as the soldier is on the battlefield. I was eager to lay down my life for the country, but now, now I've been saved again, now my first wish after the war is that I may become Dutch! I love the Dutch, I love this country, I love the language and want to work here. And if I have to write to the queen myself, I will not give up until I have reached my goal! ("a" text, p. 601)

The excitement and her relief are represented by fluent changes from analytical observation to philosophical questioning, and to performative oratory in the apostrophe "Be brave!" Anne's literary personality is emotional, thoughtful, enthusiastic, and young in years, but every word testifies to the pressures of experience and the need to escape and assimilate in order to survive.[48]

The lessons extrapolated from that experience in such an urgent, simple way have a strong ethical direction, based on religion. Anne Frank knew that she had grown up:

> I am becoming still more independent of my parents, young as I am, I face life with more courage than Mummy; my feeling for justice is immovable, and truer than hers. I know what I want, I have a goal, an opinion, have a religion and love. Let me be myself and then I am satisfied. I know that I'm a woman, a woman with inward strength and plenty of courage!
>
> If God lets me live, I shall attain more than Mummy ever has done, I shall not remain insignificant, I shall work in the world for mankind!

---

[48] Cf. Bonhoeffer's letter to Bethge on the same day (11 April 1944) in which he confirms that he has no regrets about returning to face the crisis of war in 1939 and that he is thankful for "an uninterrupted enrichment of experience.... If I were to end my life here in these conditions, that would have a meaning that I think I could understand; on the other hand, everything might be a thorough preparation for a new start and a new task when peace comes." *Letters and Papers from Prison*, ed. E. Bethge (London: SCM Press, 1986), p. 272.

And now I know that first and foremost I shall require courage and cheerfulness!

Yours, Anne M. Frank ("a" text, p. 601)

As soon as she had a pen in her hand, she started to think and express opinions as if in conversation with Kitty. She pondered the social and economic injustices of the world in a series of exasperated rhetorical questions, after describing food shortages and the irrationality of governments spending on "still more gigantic planes ... still heavier bombs and then prefabricated houses for reconstruction."[49] She then concluded, in an equally energetic and engaged style, that war was inevitable because there was "an urge to destroy, an urge to kill, to murder and rage," and, over time, "everything that has been built up, cultivated and grown, will be cut down and disfigured," after which people will have "to begin all over again." There was no point blaming others: "I don't believe that the big men, the politicians and the capitalists alone are guilty of the war, oh, no, the little man is just as guilty, otherwise the peoples of the world would have risen in revolt long ago!" (p. 628). Like Roland, revolutionary, mother, and political tactician, this "frank" daughter of another age of terror, violence, and hatred was forced into consideration of larger problems by her historic circumstances, and not only in these musings but also at other more vulnerable, yet honest moments.

Three weeks later Anne felt overcome by uncertainty and a threat of imminent disaster. The external trigger was the arrest of the man who had supplied vegetables to the secret annex and had harbored two Jews in his own home. Anne wrote of feeling "so utterly broken" and of how difficult it was to be brave. She extrapolated from the vegetable man's case to their own: "The police forced the door there, so they could do it to us too! If one day we too should . . . . . no, I mustn't write it down, but I can't put the question out of my mind today."[50] Her yearning for air, space, and society—not the actual world beyond the walls and windows of the *Achterhuis* so much as the normality of peacetime—was replaced by a state of physical quivering: an accumulation of all the fear already faced, "in all its frightfulness." As she reported to Kitty, she was even reluctant to venture alone through the empty rooms downstairs to make her way to the lavatory while everyone else was upstairs listening to the radio. Yet, with a pen in her hand, she recovered to think in a balanced way about their situation. They were all anxious about the risks their helpers ran every day in taking care of them. In this context Anne's next sentence proposed the thesis that they would be better

[49] 3 May 1944, "a" text, p. 628.
[50] 26 May 1944, "a" text, pp. 660–61, her suspension points.

off dead; yet her second considered the antithesis, that hope is human; and her third sentence dealt with the resolution of these tensions in a knowable action.

> Again and again I ask myself, would it not have been better for us if we had not gone into hiding, and if we were dead now and not going through all this misery, especially as we should be sparing the others. But we all shrink away from that too, for we still love life; we haven't yet forgotten the voice of nature, we still hope, hope about everything.
>
> I hope something will happen soon now, shooting if need be—nothing can crush us *more* than this restlessness, let the end come, even if it is hard; then at least we shall know whether we are finally going to win through or go under. Yours, Anne M. Frank (Friday, 26 May 1944, "a" text, pp. 661–62)

That Anne herself, the youngest inhabitant of the secret annex did not "go under," but was capable of describing and rationalizing the experiences of the group, is testimony not merely to the resilience of youth but to the qualities of her imagination and personal courage.

## REWRITING RESISTANCE

While highly imaginative people may suffer acutely from the anticipation of fear, which can be either protective or debilitating, such sensibilities often also have the power to generate fantasy, fiction, and dreams which may be consoling. Anne Frank's pleasure and total engagement in writing led her to recreate stories and scenes from life in different literary forms. Like Roland, she had a good ear for speech and constructed dialogues among her companions in the annex that purport to transcribe real conversations within the diary's letters. Some of the events and voices that populate her diary were also rewritten as short stories. This new kind of fictional writing allowed her to be distracted from her surroundings and escape confinement into a parallel or alternative imaginary world. She became positively absorbed by something other than the boredom and fearfulness of actual daily life that she was committed to recording in her letters to Kitty and for future readers of her planned book. Yet the world of her stories was not merely an escape from reality; it also overlapped with actual experience and provided opportunities for some of these problems to be reassessed or transformed, and controlled.

The unfinished novella "Cady's Life" relates the experiences of a young girl in hospital after the traumatic violence of a road accident that necessitated a long period away from her family. Anne's assessment of her writing

was that "quite a lot of 'Cady's Life' is good ... but, on the whole, it's nothing." This is the entry, addressed to "Dearest Kitty," that explains her sense of
vocation as a writer: "For a long time I haven't had any idea of what I was
working for any more, the end of the war is so terribly far away, so unreal,
like a beautiful fairy tale."[51] The idea of a normal future is linked to the end
of the war, but even this seems a pretty fiction. The novella evokes themes
that dominate the diary, including the loneliness of an adolescent girl cut off
from a normal social life and forced into reliance on a life of the mind. There
are misunderstandings between Cady and her mother, which mirror incidents reported in the diary when Anne Frank rejected her mother in preference to her father. The narrator of the story sympathizes with Cady's attitude, which is endorsed by a senior nurse figure who decides that the
patient's mother should not "stay very long, because she wore Cady out with
her incessant nervous chatter, and it was plain ... that [Cady] was much
more eager to see her father than her mother."[52] The narrator also explains
Cady's thoughts: "There was no one she'd rather have chatted with than Sister Ank, who was calm and always spoke gently.... As she now began to
realize, it was this motherly tenderness that she had always felt the lack of"
(Tales, p. 72). But the creation of an independent voice for this motherly
nurse also allowed a dialogue to develop that includes criticism of Cady and
explores the background for her disappointment in her mother. Although
Cady is clearly another thinly disguised alter ego, she is also, significantly,
only one voice in the story. (While she is in hospital, Cady's father "brought
her a diary; now she often sat writing her thoughts and feelings. Cady had
never known that writing could give her so much pleasure. Life in the hospital was very monotonous.")[53] This multiplicity of voices offered wider opportunities for analysis and commentary on the problems that dominate
Anne Frank's diary.

When Cady is moved to a sanatorium in the country, she meets a young
man, and they soon become friends and confidants. The boy in the story,
Hans Donkert, is invested with many of the qualities Anne found lacking in
her first boyfriend, the van Pels's shy son, Peter. Hans is mature and sensitive
with deeper intellectual capacities than Anne's companion in the secret
annex. The pair "spoke of many things but they never went very deep and
Cady, who thought Hans was terribly nice, soon began to feel sorry that

[51] 5 April 1944, "a" text, pp. 586, 587.
[52] Anne Frank's Tales from the Secret Annexe, tr. Ralph Manheim and Michel Mok (London:
Penguin Books, 1988), p. 71; all quotations here from this edition. The Tales were originally published in Dutch, in 1949.
[53] Ibid., p. 74. Cf. "Cady had got so used to writing everything that happened around her in her
diary that soon she could describe her thoughts and feelings better there than anywhere else, except
to Hans" (p. 83).

their conversation never touched on anything but the most everyday sub-jects" (p. 80). The fantasy of wish-fulfillment takes over most obviously as the young couple sit alone in the woods, not only aware of their feelings for each other but also fully able to articulate them. Cady probes different per-sonal needs by asking her friend whether he believed in God. She was wor-ried that her prayers were ineffectual because, when life was good, she never really thought about what she was saying; prayer "was a habit like brushing [one's] teeth," but since her "accident," she has had "plenty of time to think about these things," and has become anxious: "Seeing that I never gave God a thought when I had good [fortune], why should He help me now in my hour of need? That question has stayed with me, because I know it would be only right and just for God not to think of me now" (pp. 81–82). Hans ar-ticulates what he imagines is a comforting reply: that since Cady in her "pain and fear" is now "really trying" to be sincere, he's "sure God won't leave [her] in the lurch. Trust Him, Cady. He has helped so many people." However, this cannot help the young woman who doesn't know if God ex-ists: "Who and what is God; no one has ever seen Him, after all; sometimes I have the feeling that praying to Him is praying to the air." Hans tells Cady to look around her at nature because "God is men's name for this great mir-acle"; this definition does not satisfy her, although she says it coincides with ideas she has had herself. Cady is not satisfied because she cannot distin-guish between a benevolent God, to whom she assumes she owes her recov-ery of health, and Fate, which was how she thought of God when she "was in great pain" (p. 82). This discussion is nowhere near approaching the ques-tion "Where was God in Auschwitz?" that was already engaging profes-sional theologians and philosophers as well as ordinary people of faith, and agnostics. Nevertheless, the conversation between Anne Frank's young peo-ple, confronting personal suffering, and discovering the comfort and confi-dence of loving human relationships beyond the family for the first time, is impressive. Hans and Cady resolve their discussion by settling for an idea of God within, a reference to human conscience and trust, which is essentially ethical, humanist, and pragmatic.

> "I often ask God for advice, so to speak, and when I do, I'm sure I get the one right answer. But, Hans, shouldn't that answer somehow come out of myself?"
>
> "As I've told you, Cady, God created people and all living things just as they are. Our soul and our sense of justice come from Him. The answer you get to your questions comes from yourself, but also from God, be-cause He made you as you are."
>
> "So you think God speaks to me through myself?"

"Yes, I do. And in speaking of these things, Cady, we have shown great confidence. Give me your hand as sign that we shall always trust each other, and when one of us is in difficulty and would like to talk to someone about it, then both of us will know where to turn."

Cady gave him her hand, and so they sat for a long while, hand in hand, and a wonderful feeling of peace grew up inside them. (p. 83)

This dialogue represents the thought processes of Anne Frank that surface in different places within her diary.[54] However, the dialogue within the story represents her ideas in a succinct and simplified, refined form presupposing a position in which such questions have already been resolved, perhaps through similar conversations with adults in the annex (although there is no mention of such discussions in the diary). Not unlike Boethius in his prison writing, but at her own very different level of intellectual competence and knowledge, Anne Frank projected a persona in her writing who found some consolation from philosophy within the context of a secure and comforting relationship with an imaginary interlocutor of the opposite sex.

## NARRATIVE SUBSTITUTIONS FOR THE SELF

In "Cady's Life" the voice of Hans takes the initiative within a conversation Anne Frank's diary reveals she initiated with Peter van Pels. The evocation of the couple's "wonderful feeling of peace" suggests her search for comfort and fulfillment in human love and the few precious moments reflected in the diary when she thought she had attained these goals with Peter. In writing this part of her story in this way the author seems to compensate herself for her recognition that Peter van Pels could never be a soulmate: she would have to create one for herself (possibly modeled on her father). The identities of Cady and Hans in the story, and of Anne and Peter in the diary are all literary constructs. Traces of a third set of relationships, and a third persona, present in Anne Frank's diary also surface in "Cady's Life." War breaks out while Cady is recuperating at the sanatorium; and when she is discharged, she visits a Jewish friend. Cady, whose full name is given as Caroline Dorothea van Altenhoven is emphatically not Jewish, indicative perhaps of yet another tactic whereby Anne escaped from her everyday identity and historical situation through writing: "I'm a Christian girl of respectable parents," she manages to say to a threatening German soldier, producing her identity card to support this statement (p. 88). The omniscient narrator explains:

[54] Cf. Wednesday, 23 February 1944, also Thursday, 15 June 1944 (*Diary*, pp. 497 and 676–77).

It was a hard time for the Jews. The fate of many would be decided in 1942. In July they began to round up boys and girls and deport them. Luckily Cady's girl friend Mary seemed to have been forgotten. Later it wasn't just the young people, no one was spared . . . Cady went through terrible experiences. Night after night she heard cars driving down the street, she heard children screaming and doors being slammed. Mr and Mrs van Altenhoven looked at each other and Cady in the lamplight, and in their eyes the question could be read: Whom will they take tomorrow? (pp. 86–87)

When Cady goes to visit Mary she has to ring the bell three times and call out her own name to reassure the occupants of the house before she can get any response. Inside she finds the whole family sitting tensely in silence with pale faces and packs on their backs, waiting. "The sight of all these pale, frightened faces was terrible. Every time a door slammed outside, a shock went through the people sitting there. Those slamming doors seemed to symbolize the slamming of the door of life" (p. 87). In Anne Frank's real life, the door to the secret annex, hidden behind the sliding bookcase, was all that stood between life and discovery (or death) for its occupants. A week later Cady finds Mary's family home sealed up; she is seized with despair at the thought of the fate of its deported occupants, and the narrative reports an impassioned series of questions that circle round and round in Cady's mind.

Why did Mary have to go away when she, Cady, could stay here? Why did Mary have to suffer her terrible fate when *she* was left to enjoy herself? What difference was there between them? Was she better than Mary in any way? Weren't they exactly the same? What crime had Mary committed? Oh this could only be a terrible injustice.

In the next sentence a nightmare image of the deportee haunts Cady's thoughts and reproaches her sadly.

And suddenly she saw Mary's little figure before her, shut up in a cell, dressed in rags, with a sunken, emaciated face. Her eyes were very big, and she looked at Cady so sadly and reproachfully.

Cady dissolves into convulsive crying, reproaching herself for being unable to help her friend.

Over and over again she saw Mary's eyes begging for help, help that Cady knew she couldn't give her.
    "Mary, forgive me, come back . . ."

Cady no longer knew what to say or to think. For this misery that she saw so clearly before her eyes there were no words. Doors slammed in her ears, she heard children crying and in front of her she saw a troop of armed brutes . . . and in among them, helpless and alone, Mary, Mary who was the same as she was. (pp. 88–89)

At this point the story stops and was left unfinished. Anne Frank had identified with Cady who identified herself with the little Jewish deportee, who are both "the same as she was." It is difficult for the modern reader with hindsight not to think of Anne Frank anticipating her own end in her empathy for Mary: "dressed in rags, with a sunken, emaciated face," and features associated with malnutrition and disease.[55]

Yet Anne Frank was instead reliving feelings of irrational guilt and shame at being a survivor; in particular, this story's inconclusive ending seems to be directly related to a series of vivid daydreams she had written about in the diary, concerning her school friend Hannah Goslar.[56] "Yesterday evening, before I fell asleep, who should suddenly appear before my eyes but Hanneli!" she wrote to Kitty, on Saturday, 27 November 1943.

I saw her in front of me, clothed in rags, her face thin and worn. Her eyes were very big and she looked so sadly and reproachfully at me, that I could read in her eyes: "Oh, Anne, why have you deserted me? Help, oh help me, rescue me from this hell!"

And I cannot help her, I can only look on how others suffer and die, and must therefore sit idly by and can only pray to God to send her back to us. (*Diary*, "b" text, p. 422)

Anne was troubled by her memory of a misunderstanding between them in the past. She was tormented by her inability to explain or comprehend the differences between their fates and to act in any way that would help her friend:

Oh, God, that I should have all I could wish for and that she should be seized by such a terrible fate. I am not more virtuous than she; she, too, wanted to do what was right, why should I be chosen to live and she probably to die? What was the difference between us? Why are we so far from each other now? (ibid.)

---

[55] Anne died in March 1945, a few days after her sister, Margot, both from typhus in the concentration camp at Bergen Belsen that was liberated by British troops on 15 April.

[56] Lies Goosens was the pseudonym Anne chose for her, which is how she is named in Otto Frank's "c" text edition of the *Diary*. For the relationship between the Frank and Goslar families, see Carol Ann Lee, *Roses from the Earth: The Biography of Anne Frank* (London: Penguin Books, 2000).

Toward the end of her letter Anne tells herself she must not go on thinking about this "because I don't get any further" but writes that she is still haunted by the girl's "pale face and imploring eyes" and "cannot free" herself from them. While Anne Frank wrote to Kitty, she talked to an alter ego through the medium of the imaginary correspondence; this was extended to include an address to the real girl on her conscience: "Hannelie, Hannelie, if only I could take you away, if only I could let you share all the things I enjoy" ("b" text, p. 423). A month later the diarist returned to thoughts about this friend, whom she had previously forgotten for many months but with whom she now identified: "And Hanneli, is she alive? What is she doing? Oh, God, protect her and bring her back to us. Hanneli I see in you all the time what my lot might have been, I keep seeing myself in your place."[57] In the diary Anne Frank attributed these dreams and fears to her own lack of a strong enough faith in God, which was also related to the theme of "Cady's Life." She resolved, in the diary, that she should count her blessings, not be selfish, and pray harder for a miracle to save her friends and fellow human beings. She was aware that she had made little Hannah into "a symbol . . . of the sufferings of all my friends and all Jews," and that when she prayed for her, she prayed "for all Jews and all those in need."[58] Through her diary Anne Frank herself later became this symbol for so many readers.

Within the diary the pitiful image of Hanneli is associated with an image of Anne Frank's late maternal grandmother as a guardian angel. This figure also recurs in the stories, in contexts of suffering and despair. "The Guardian Angel" (dated 22 February 1944) concerns an old lady and her granddaughter, who is the same age as Anne, living happily together at the edge of a large forest. One day the grandmother dies; the girl, who "knew hardly anyone and did not want to call in strangers . . . dug a grave under an old tree in the woods, and there laid her grandma to rest" (*Tales,* p. 42). She mourns continuously for four weeks; then her life and attitude are changed by the words of her grandmother, who announces in a dream vision that she has become the girl's guardian angel and will remain with her "just as before." The girl wakes, joyful at remembering her dream, to resume normal life and live happily ever after. This traditional idea of restorative consolation mediated through dream visions recurs at the end of another story, "The Fairy," written for Otto Frank's birthday, by 9 May 1944 (*Diary,* p. 639). In this

---

[57]   Wed. 29 December 1943, "a" text, p. 436. Hannah Goslar had already survived more than a year in Bergen-Belsen; she was later able to speak briefly to Anne Frank through a fence and threw over a bundle of food and clothing; see Hannah E. Pick-Goslar, "Her Last Days," tr. from Dutch by A. Meersschaert in *Anne Frank Reflections,* ed. Enzer and Solotaroff-Enzer, pp. 47–51.

[58]   6 January 1944, "b" text, p. 447.

version of the displaced grandmother scenario, an aged fairy dies and is mourned by everyone, yet her spirit lingers on among them: "When people slept, she returned to give them blissful dreams; even in their slumber they received the gift of wise counsel" (*Tales*, p. 65). The narrator of this story, a very young fairy, advises an older woman who is distressed.

> "Dear Lady," she said, "I don't know about such things from experience, and I know even less how to help you. But, just the same, I'd like to give you some advice, which I, myself, always follow when I feel lonely and sad."

The dream-revenant figure's "wise counsel" from beyond the grave, to commune with nature when one is distressed, is mediated by this survivor-storyteller doubling as another persona for Anne. She explains that a walk in the countryside will bring feelings of calm, a better sense of proportion, and the restoration of religious faith:

> "Only look at the blue sky and the trees, and you will gradually feel peaceful inside and realize that nothing is so hopelessly bad that something can't be done to improve it—even a little. . . . Alone with nature, all worries leave one. You grow first quiet, and then glad, and feel that God has not deserted you." (p. 64)

The repetition of this theme in the dialogic form of the diary as well as in several stories suggests its importance to the impressionable writer developing her similar thoughts in response to a specific situation.

In "The Flower Girl," a life of hardship and drudgery for the heroine, Krista—another patently non-Jewish figure—is transformed by brief periods of rest at twilight when she "lies down in the grass, her hands folded under her head, and looks up into the sky":

> In the field, amid the flowers, beneath the darkening sky, Krista is content. Gone is fatigue, gone is the market, gone are the people. The little girl dreams and thinks only of the bliss of having, each day, this short while alone with God and nature. (*Tales*, p. 41, 20 February 1944)

This motif was repeated a month later in yet another story, dated 25 March 1944—a first-person narrative entitled "Fear"—in which the writer is stricken with panic by wartime bombing and runs away during a particularly heavy evening raid when "the street was alight with a fearsome red glow."

> I couldn't possibly say how long I ran on with the image of the burning houses, the desperate people and their distorted faces before me. Then I

sensed that it had got quieter. I looked around and, as if waking up from a nightmare, I saw that there was nothing or no one behind me, No fire, no bombs, no people. I looked a little more closely and found that I stood in a meadow. Above me the stars glistened and the moon shone; it was brilliant weather, crisp but not cold. (*Tales*, p. 45)

Exhausted, the runaway lies down, and, looking up into the sky, realizes that she "felt very peaceful inside" and was no longer afraid.

A variation on this theme, as it was more often depicted in Anne Frank's representation of her actual experience in the diary and in the writing of other prisoners, is also found in the brief self-portrait of a young woman called "Jackie" who has rushed to the open window of her room in despair.[59] The narrator appreciates how "fresh air feels good on her tear-stained face"; Jackie raises her eyes higher and higher until she is staring at the moon and the stars. After an hour, she finds that she has recovered her composure and no longer feels trapped by her own misery. The wind has liberated her essential self:

as gust after gust of wind blows through the trees outside the house, as the sky darkens and the stars hide behind big, thick clouds, which look like bundles of blotting paper in the cloudy light and take on every conceivable shape. (p. 68)

Jackie's posture mirrors Anne Frank's descriptions of herself in the diary. The best view of the skyline from the secret annex was from Peter van Pels's room in the attic, where Anne went "to blow the stuffy air out of [her] lungs":

From my favorite spot, on the floor, I look up at the blue sky, the bare chestnut tree on whose branches the little raindrops shone, and at the seagulls and other birds gliding on the wind and looking like silver.... I looked out of the open window too, out over a large area of Amsterdam, over all the roofs and on to the horizon which was such a pale blue that it was hard to see the line.

"As long as this exists," I thought. "and I may live to see it, this sunshine, the cloudless skies, while this lasts, I cannot be unhappy." (*Diary*, "b" text, pp. 497–98)

[59] It is possible that this name was suggested by Anne's memory of her school friend Jacqueline van Maarsen, with whom she shared a love of Cissy van Marxveldt's stories about Joop ter Heul, which are set in Amsterdam. Joop's fictional best friend is Kit Franken. The suggestive collocation of these names is further enhanced by those of generic forms as Joop turns in the stories from letter writing to a diary; see Berteke Waaldijk, "Reading Anne Frank as a Woman," in *Anne Frank Reflections*, pp. 110–20, at 117.

Anne wrote these lines to Kitty on 23 February 1944 about her own experience and then immediately extrapolated from this to offer a general comment on the basis of the particular authority of her experience.

> The best remedy for those who are afraid, lonely or unhappy is to go outside, somewhere where they can be quiet alone with the heavens, nature, and God. Because only then does one feel that all is as it should be and that God wishes to see people happy, amidst the simple beauty of Nature. (p. 498)

The frustrations of confinement had been painfully evident only two months earlier when she wrote to Kitty about efforts to maintain her equanimity, which were not hers alone: "Believe me, if you have been shut up for 1½ years, it can get too much for you some days. In spite of all justice and thankfulness, you can't get rid of your feelings."[60] She was tormented by sensations of the wind in one's clothes and the cold on one's face when any of their helpers came in "from outside" smelling of "fresh air." On a beautiful day in February, invigorated by the spring and her newly awakened feelings for Peter van Pels, her longings—"to talk, for freedom, for friends, to be alone"—and claustrophobia, sent her from room to room looking for a spot to sniff the fresh air and "breathe through the crack of a closed window" ("b" text, p. 483). It was only in her imagination that Anne Frank, writer and prisoner, escaped into the fresh air, walked in the countryside, and lay on the grass starring into the sky that she glimpsed from the attic window. Yet she communed with the natural world in the personae of the lonely, sensitive young women she created in the fantasy world of her stories that reflected mirror images of the less amenable world of the secret annex already portrayed in her diary.

In her imagination Madame Roland also relived her past in her prison writing, creating a personal image of how she wished her friends (and history) to remember her. She intended that these literary memorials should represent her in her absence; she hoped to live on, as she and Anne Frank have done, by finding "some enduring place in the minds of future generations" in her various kinds of memoirs.[61] While both writers remain historic witnesses to momentous political events that reflect cruelty, hatred, and inhumanity, each of them also created the vehicle for her vivid literary afterlife that enables cultural memories of her as an individual writer-in-captivity to

---

[60] *Diary*, "b" text, p. 431, 24 December 1943.

[61] "...je ne voulais que la paix des justes; et moi aussi j'aurai quelque existence dans la génération future" (*Mémoires*, ed. De Roux [2004], p. 424; cf. English, Shuckburgh, p. 192). Cf. "I want to go on living even after my death! And therefore I am grateful to God for giving me this gift, this possibility of developing myself and of writing, of expressing all that is in me!" (*Diary*, "a" text, p. 569.)

persist as a symbol of her resistance and fortitude. This is why these works are uplifting despite their authors' persecution and horrific deaths. While Roland might have regretted Anne Frank's professed indifference to politics, she would have valued the younger woman's defiant engagement with larger philosophical issues that were grounded in personal observation and were also intrinsically political. What each of them said about the practice of writing, including the importance of some protected space in which to write about their lives, and the paradoxical pleasures and sense of freedom it brought them in confinement and in danger of death, is striking and insistent; it testifies to the consoling tactics and strategic value of writing in confinement that was both a means and an end to self-impression and self-preservation. Roland and Frank were each deeply attached to the material reality of their manuscript texts. The value each writer attached to her writing signifies its functions as an enduring substitute for her endangered life and identity.

A mental link to the natural world and images of the free skies recurs in many prisoners' writing;[62] like Anne Frank, Roland had imagined a retreat to the countryside, specifically the English countryside that she had visited with her husband in 1784. Poetry, specifically Thomson's *Seasons,* which she had kept by her in prison, was an important stimulus to her imagination and its freedoms. The next chapter shows how two twentieth-century prisoners—both poets—sustained themselves in captivity using their own and others' poetry to create images of the outside world and celebrate the consolations of friendship, memory, and imagination that helped them resist and survive as individual writers in prison.

---

[62] The roofscape, clouds and tree are familiar tropes of prison literature: cf. "Le ciel est par-dessus le toit / Si bleu, si calme. / Un arbre par-dessus le toit / Berce sa palme," Paul Verlaine (1873); cf. Wilde's "a wistful eye" that looks "Upon that little tent of blue / which prisoners call the sky" and variants repeated in his "The Ballad of Reading Gaol" (1898).

# CHAPTER 5

# The Consolations of Imagination and Lyric Poetry

This chapter explores the personal and the political tactics of two remarkable, yet little-known, twentieth-century poets who survived their imprisonments in life-threatening conditions and emerged from confinement to find that their prison poetry had been published and circulated widely, carrying political messages that went beyond their authors' initial situations and declared purposes of resistance and self-preservation.

Jean Cassou's thirty-three sonnets are signs of a private inner world that enabled him to resist the psychological pressures of his imprisonment during the winter of 1941–42. The memories and impressionistic dream world that had sustained Cassou in an intense and disciplined life of the mind were appropriated by others, to counteract a sense of shame at defeat and collaboration, yet also to inspire hope in readers who were encouraged to see these poems as affirming a national cultural resistance to German occupation and French fascism. By contrast, Irina Ratushinskaya set out to speak for a group of women political prisoners in the last years of the Soviet Union. She used her poetry to sustain the group's morale and willpower to resist the lies and cruelty of their oppressors who controlled the prison camp in which they were interned for various kinds of political dissent. It is clear that poetry was regarded by both sides in this ideological conflict as a political weapon, and hostile censorship affected her writing conditions. She was not permitted to read or write poetry openly, and handwritten copies of earlier Russian poets' works were also confiscated from her. However, the authorities could not eradicate the lyrics that she had committed to memory and recited to other prisoners to promote their consolation and solidarity. Ratushinskaya's poems had several personal and public functions; her themes reflected the experiences of these women prisoners and celebrated a communal identity as Russian dissidents. She used compressed lyric forms and emotive imagery drawn from Russian literary culture (as well as everyday life) to speak on behalf of the oppressed and to publicize their plight. Her poems testify to conditions in the prison camp, including illegal punishments and other infringements of civil rights, and were smuggled to the West for publication which helped to save her life.

Jean Cassou, *Trente-trois sonnets composés au secret / 33 Sonnets of the Resistance* (1943): Preserving the Liberty of a Poet

The memorable qualities of lyric forms were frequently important in the preservation of prisoners' poems but were especially crucial in the survival of the sonnets composed during World War II by the writer, critic, and art historian, Jean Cassou (1897–1986), during his imprisonment in a French military prison at Toulouse. After the German occupation of northern France, Cassou had escaped from Paris to lead a resistance group in Toulouse. He associated mainly with communist, antifascist intellectuals, including the surrealist poet, Louis Aragon. Cassou was arrested by Vichy French police in mid-December 1941 and released provisionally in February 1942. He was subsequently tried by a French military tribunal and served a formal sentence of one further year before rejoining the Resistance. According to his testimony in an introduction to the second edition of his *33 Sonnets composés au secret* (1962), during his pre-trial period of imprisonment in January and February, 1942, Cassou composed half a sonnet every night "as a way of passing the time."[1] (He slept very little on account of the cold.) It appears that he was unable to write them down until just before his provisional release, when his lawyer was allowed to provide pencil and paper, with a few books. For two months therefore, in a cell shared by one other—initially an informer—but in conditions of acute deprivation (without exercise, visits, letters, or reading matter), and fearing summary execution, Cassou composed his poetry lying in the dark, and kept reciting and revising it in his head. He explained subsequently that he chose the sonnet as the best form for "composition which involved pure brainwork and memory."[2] The written sonnets were passed to an underground publisher, Editions de Minuit, and printed in 1944 as a clandestine work of cultural resistance under the authorial pseudonym, Jean Noir. Publication in secret, at "midnight," and the "John Black" pseudonym were expedited by Louis Aragon who wrote an introduction for this first edition, setting Cassou's sonnets in the context of free-French nationalism and a French history of left-wing, intellectual, and political resistance. Aragon himself used the pseudonym François La Colère, punning on his patriotic righteous anger at the fate of the French prison poet and (conve-

---

[1] Jean Cassou, *33 Sonnets of the Resistance and Other Poems* [a parallel text edition], tr. Timothy Adès (Todmorden: Arc, 2004), p. 15. Other pastimes included singing, reciting poetry from memory, and Arabic lessons from his cell mate. See further Cassou's autobiography: *Une Vie pour la liberté* (Paris: Editions Robert Laffont, 1981), pp. 153–55.

[2] Cassou, *Une Vie pour la liberté*. See also *Jean Cassou (1897–1986): un musée imaginé* [exhibition catalog], ed. Florence de Lussy (Paris: Bibliothèque nationale de France / Centre Georges Pompidou, 1995), p. 162, item 266.

niently) ignoring the fact that Cassou was imprisoned by French fascist collaborators.[3]

It seems clear that Cassou's poetry meant something rather different to him as a prisoner. In his 1962 edition he acknowledged the pleasurable, consolatory work of creation as a general and paradoxical consequence of imprisonment:

> In the famous phrase, all poetry is poetry of circumstances. Those in which I composed my sonnets are certainly the best possible for providing a poet with a pure and complete experience of poetic creation. All we imprisoned poets agree that we have enjoyed a rare privilege; except that some have done so only during the experience itself, and without having, as I had, the additional good fortune of seeing the results in public later on.[4]

On this evidence, Cassou's creative efforts—the mental stimulation and imaginative freedom he claimed for himself—were their own reward at the time. This is also ironic since the prevailing mood of the poetic persona that he created for himself, night after night, was aptly described by his later pseudonym: dark, negative, introspective, subtly conflicted, or agonized. There is no consideration for any designated potential reader, even though the speaker sometimes addresses a second person as a dream vision or memory of another person. He wrote for himself gathering memories and aspects of his life, which may explain why he chose not to elucidate the symbolic resonances of these poems when they were reprinted after the war, although he had provided a commentary on his earlier wartime poetry, *La Rose et le Vin*, which he dedicated to three friends, to commemorate the experiences they had shared in the French Resistance during the winter of 1940–41.[5]

Aragon's adoption of Cassou's poetry, as signs of individual bravery and a French national spirit of liberty and fraternity, is best explained by reference to the poet's feat of composition rather than the sonnets' suggestive meanings or purpose. "He had no writing materials, this prisoner, save only time and his mental faculties. . . . He had to hold the poem up, as one might hold up a child out of the water."[6] Knowledge of the circumstances of their composition created their political significance or public meaning in the emo-

---

[3] Cf. "L'écourtement de la mémoire, c'est la mort. L'homme ou le peuple à mémoire courte, et qui vit, vit dans la mort, ce qui est pire que de mourir." J. Cassou, *La Mémoire courte* (Paris: Editions de Minuit, 1953), pp. 7–8, in *Un Musée imaginé*, pp. 144, 146. His thirty-three sonnets were reprinted by different presses in 1946, 1950, and 1962.

[4] Cassou, *33 Sonnets*, p. 16.

[5] Marcel Abraham, Claude Aveline, Georges Friedmann; see the standard French edition of Cassou's *Trente-trois sonnets composés au secret. La Rose et le Vin. La Folie d'Amadis*, ed. Florence de Lussy (Paris: Gallimard, 1995), p. 81.

[6] *33 Sonnets*, p. 17. Cf. this image in Bunyan's *Grace Abounding*.

tive simile of a child representing the future of French culture rescued from the flood. Aragon promoted the concept of a patriotic prisoner suffering for the cause of French freedom, an interpretation that was politically expedient in 1944. Cassou had been born in Deusto, near Bilbao, to Spanish-speaking parents who moved to France in 1901, and his antifascist resistance was only partly ideological—*communiste*—whereas it was always a more personal challenge, and necessity, for a man protecting his Jewish wife and family.[7] In 1944 the authorship of these sonnets was ostensibly unknown; they could not be acknowledged alongside Cassou's published works, which included novels, essays, and art history, because Cassou was still in a Vichy prison and would need to avoid publicity if he were to resume leadership of the regional Resistance.[8] Instead, Aragon suggested that Jean Noir's cell was representative of "that dismal cell in which our France finds herself imprisoned," and the sonnets were dedicated, in the pseudonymous poet's name, "à mes compagnons de prisons," signifying, in this context, all Frenchmen who resisted the German occupation and its Vichy proxies.[9] Aragon's introduction repeatedly invites readers to see the sonnet form as expressive of "freedom under constraint, the embodiment of thought in fetters," rather than as Cassou's consoling memories and intellectual distractions. The sonnets were published as representative signs of "man and his dreams"; their author was "a man entirely predestined to be here as the palpable echo of a deeper world." The human condition might be represented by "chains," literal and existential, but no man's imagination was bound by such confinement. Aragon offered Jean Noir's poems to contemporary readers as "poignant and inaccessible, and yet direct and uncontrived" embodiments of a "low murmur of ourselves" as human beings; he also offered them as "the lesson France gives the world . . . in her misfortune," in 1944. Their clandestine publication in wartime was an opportunity to demonstrate the paradox that these thirty-three sonnets were not merely "born in fetters" but also the "negation of those fetters."[10]

Aragon warns readers not to expect "prison poetry" (signifying "the description of the life led there, even the cries that go up from dungeons of

---

[7] Cassou and his family, including, his Jewish wife's parents, left Paris the day after he heard himself comprehensively vilified on French radio as "le communiste juif rouge espagnol front populaire franc-maçon anarchiste Jean Cassou" (*Une Vie pour la liberté*, pp. 142–51, at 142).

[8] See Florence de Lussy's chronology of the life of Cassou and list of his publications in her edition of *Trente-trois sonnets*, pp. 181–87. All quotations from the French texts are from this edition, which includes Aragon's introduction, pp. 19–40, and Cassou's preface to the second edition of his sonnets (1962), pp. 41–43. For fuller listings, see *Un Musée imaginé*, pp. 24–29 and 242–48. I am indebted to the invaluable translations by Harry Guest and his notes in *From a Condemned Cell: 33 Sonnets by Jean Cassou*, tr. H. Guest (Buckfastleigh: Itinerant Press, 2008).

[9] *33 Sonnets*, p. 16.

[10] Ibid., pp. 17–18, 24.

stone"), because the "prisoner enveloped in darkness is far from content to bear witness to hunger, thirst, cold, the pain of indignity and humiliation." Aragon denied that the sonnets had any restorative ideological or ethical content since readers who hoped "to find words in praise of these values for which this man was deprived of his freedom" would be disappointed. Instead, he asserted, "the poem is his great act of defiance of the contempt that he suffers. The poem is his superhuman effort to continue as a human being, to reach those regions of mind and heart which everything around him denies and debases."[11] Yet the poem as a mental construct is also an end in itself, and lyric in the double sense of subjective and vocal harmony. It was composed from sounds (in rhythm and rhymes), concatenated memories of an individual communing with himself, and the semantic associations of visual and literary imagery. Cassou later explained the importance of rhythm and harmony in his approach to composition:

> Si je sens un poème, un conte ou un roman se former en moi, je le vois d'abord dans le langage de la musique, je sens son tempo, qui peut être un allegro ou un andante. Une structure poétique est souvent, pour moi, une image, certes, mais plutôt ce que j'appelle une harmonie.[12]

The lasting appeal of these lyrics is their puzzling obscurity and suggestive evocations of a writer's inner world that can be felt and shared in sometimes vague yet often vivid, memorable language. The recording sensibility—if one assumes there is merely one—seems distinctive rather than typical, but the voice of a prisoner may just be detected in the retreat from an explicit dark reality into dreams and allegories, as well as the obsessive interiority also seen in prison writing by Charles d'Orléans, John Bunyan, Oscar Wilde, or Jean Genet.[13] The writer's image of himself as a poet and the night settings of his monologues often hint at his pain in meditating on a sensory reality that he is separated from by a place that is also a state of mind: "C'est ici la chambre des anges morts."[14] As Boethius had demonstrated, this infe-

---

[11] Ibid., pp. 18, 19.

[12] From a series of twelve radio broadcasts in 1964 published as *Jean Cassou Entretiens avec Jean Rousselot* (Paris: Editions Albin Michel, 1965), p. 45. Cassou's wife, Ida Jankélévitch, was a pianist who introduced him to Darius Milhaud, a close friend since the early 1930s, who later set six of Cassou's sonnets to music; two sonnets were also set by Henri Dutilleux.

[13] See earlier discussion; and *Charles d'Orléans in England (1415–1440)*, ed. Mary-Jo Arn (Cambridge: D. S. Brewer, 2000); Robert Epstein, "Prisoners of Reflection: The Fifteenth-Century Poetry of Exile and Imprisonment," *Exemplaria*, 15 (2003), 159–98; Rivkah Zim, " 'La Nuit trouve enfin la clarté': Captivity and Life Writing in the Poetry of Charles d'Orléans and Théophile de Viau," *European Journal of Life Writing*, 2 (2013), 79–109, http://ejlw.eu; and on Genet as prison writer, Françoise d'Eaubonne, *Les Ecrivains en cage* (Paris: Editions André Balland, 1970), pp. 193–219; Jean-Marc Varaut, *Poètes en Prison* (Paris: Librairie Académique Perrin, 1989), pp. 245–65; Ioan Davies, *Writers in Prison* (Oxford: Blackwell, 1990), pp. 224–30.

[14] Cassou, Sonnet 17, line 9, ed. De Lussy, p. 61.

rior, actual state of imprisonment may be evaded or modified at will through imagination, dreams, and a suggestive way with words that transcend reality to create a superior mental construct.

The variety of Cassou's mental world is reflected in his *sonnets composés au secret*, in the actual darkness where the poet created a paradoxical sense of privilege and satisfaction that protected his integrity and projected a subjective cultural identity. He could not know that he would survive nor that he would be able to write and thus liberate his verses in communicable forms, and yet, like Boethius, More, and Gramsci, he used the rhetoric of contrast and opposition as a tactical embodiment of his specific resistance to oppression: "un refus d'y consentir."[15]

### "A RARE PRIVILEGE"

The paradox of gain by loss dominated this prisoner's liminal existence—between life and death, silence and expression, light and dark, stasis and involuntary movement—because it animated his imagination. In the first lines of the first sonnet, an impersonal narrator describes a mythic scene in which a body, laid out on a funeral ship—as long as a dream—wafts among the stars without a sail. This explorer seems to come to life as his inward gaze unfolds; his purchase on life is this capacity for vision, represented by a water lily: "et le regard du voyageur horizontal / s'étale, nénuphar, au fil de l'aventure" (lines 3–4). The poet suggests the fragility but also the flexibility of the lily that floats on the surface, like the body, but is attached to nutrients on the river bed by a slender "thread of chance." The lily is both the object of the explorer's gaze and the sign of his imaginative journey between different states of being: fixed yet also floating, alive yet transient, powered by unseen connections, but uncontrolled. The iconic traveler is on a journey of discovery. In the second quatrain, a subjective voice questions whether this is the night in which he will finally resurrect himself on the edge of the grave. As the shrouded body sits up, the darkness is energized—"l'opacité... frissonne"—and transmits an inner quivering to the body that shakes under its chains ("liens") or mortal bonds, as if humanity were restored: like the lily supported by the surface tension of the water, life is tenacious, flexible, and beautiful. The sestet focuses on the darkness that already quakes, as if the passing explorer were powerful enough to control a force of nature. The paradoxical layers of visual sensory suggestion, allusion, and sheer mystery give this poem its surreal quality, implying a private dream world of creative connections. Yet the component images are cultural commonplaces: a ship,

15 *Un Musée imaginé*, p. 112.

a flower, and a journey.[16] Here the sense of being dead to the world is reversed by will and "a silent cry," with a galvanizing frisson, into an imaginative life that presages a future of marvelous potential.

Images of light and dark in Cassou's sonnets are often held in tense opposition to each other. Night and shadow signify loss and death but also creativity and opportunity. This tension occupies the poet-speaker in the octave of the second sonnet as he pursues an analysis of his situation, emphasizing its negativity. The speaker is dead to all fortune, hope, and space, but not to time, which chases up its harvest ("sa moisson") as it increases his suffering ("ma passion") in this situation of utter destitution ("ce dénuement"), which literally signifies a state of nakedness.[17] He transposes his suffering into the dream world that effaces consciousness and to which night upon night hurry him. The shadows there eat up shadows, continuing the sequence of strong physical actions that allow him to raise his head, yet only to the extent that a wall of dream enigmatically drinks his footprint: "à mesure qu'un mur de songe boit ma trace" (line 8).[18] This suggests an image of walking on a wet beach where the pressure of corporeal weight outlines a footfall, which is then obliterated by the subterranean water that reclaims the depression in the sand. In the sestet, the poet defines his liminal state: this is neither life nor annihilation. The newly dead children of his vigil wander about in this limbo: "De ma veillée / les enfants nouveau-morts errent dans l'entre-deux." His amorphous dream-world progeny, dead but in motion, are described as transparent flashes ("clartés") that come and go. They are impulses without a future, and subjective memories without a cultural past behind them. Yet in the final line these flashes are identified with Psyche, who burns within them, wings outstretched. The mythic allusion to a winged soul reclaims the sense of the sestet in a new context: the spiritual insights of poetry that visit the poet in his dark nights.[19] A point of rest is achieved as Cassou appears to co-opt the Platonic imagery of spiritual flight that had appealed to prisoners since Socrates and Boethius. But paradoxically, this is just as Psyche's wings (often associated in poetry with the short-lived beauty of a butterfly) are extended for take off. The mystery of the

[16] On Cassou's resolve to remain totally passive in the hands of his captors "avec un sens de la fatalité complète . . . J'étais Osiris dans la barque" and a link to the funeral imagery of Sonnet 1, see Daniel Leuwers, "Jean Cassou ou les méandres de la pensées prisonnière' [from an interview in 1973] in "La Poésie et la Résistance," *Europe*, special issue (July–August 1974), pp. 92–97, at 93, quoted by Jennifer Ross, "Jean Cassou: Freedom to Compose in Captivity," in *Six Authors in Captivity: Literary Responses to the Occupation of France during World War II*, ed. Nicole Thatcher and Ethel Tolansky (Oxford: Peter Lang, 2006), pp. 27–58, at 43.

[17] Sonnet 2, ed. De Lussy, p. 46.

[18] Cf. "my tracks are drowned in mental masonry" (tr. Adès, p. 27).

[19] The mortal Psyche—Cupid's wife—was placed in a palace (instead of a prison) by Cupid, who only visited her at night in darkness (Apuleius, *Golden Ass*, V, 1–5).

metaphysical conceit developed over thirteen lines culminates in a hopeful image: the newly dead progeny are metamorphosed and about to fly. Finally, therefore, the poetic enterprise is taking shape.

## THE CONSOLATIONS OF LOVE AND POETRY: "LE BESOIN DU LANGAGE PROPREMENT POÉTIQUE ME REPRIT"

Cassou's prison poetry correlates three themes—love, freedom, and poetry. In Sonnet 7 the poet is addressed familiarly by spirit guides who offer him a cup of dark shadows that will bring sleep and remove his misery, taking it like a crown—perhaps with the religious connotation of a wreath or crown of thorns—to the underworld. Like the Sybil who addresses Aeneas, the modern poet, like "a shivering sleepwalker," is promised safe passage through "the gate where no one goes": to the gardens of death. He expects the brilliant luster of the golden bough of myrtle (sacred to Venus) and the blood-colored anemone that sprang from her dead lover Adonis will bring him to the brink of "pure fulfilment." In this state dreams are assured; they will meet him by the hopeful morning light of an eternal tomorrow; he will be restored, a healed soul, and will recognize his glorious sisters: Love, Liberty and Poetry:

> Par le bleu matinal d'un éternal demain
> ils viendront tous à ta rencontre, âme guérie,
> et tu reconnaîtras, se tenant par la main,
> tes grandes sœurs: Amour, Liberté, Poésie.
> (Sonnet 7, lines 11–14; p. 51)

These restorative visitations by the sleeper's sisters are inspiring and comforting. The poet passes—as a unique privilege—beyond worlds of life and death finding his power and a fulfilling vision in ideas or dreams. Yet the border between these worlds is controlled by a cup of shadows ("cette tasse de ténèbres") signifying pain and adversity. The paradoxical advantage of imprisonment was the opportunity it provided in solitude and deprivation to create poetic visions. If this deprivation was later seen as necessary for poetry—"Ma poésie est fille du dénuement"[20]—the discipline and order of verse was also necessary for his mundane salvation to be effective. This salvation signifies not only Cassou's sonnets but also his communion with other poets' works: his intertextual dialogues of shared language, ideas, and aesthetics with writers whose values and credit had sustained a life of the mind through artistic forms and humane traditions: "dans l'époque la plus dou-

---

[20] See Cassou's commentary attached to *La Rose et le Vin* lyric sequence, in which he explained why he wrote poetry during the war; ed. De Lussy, p. 142.

loureuse qu'ait connue la société humaine et que, par contrecoup, ait subi mon misérable destin emporté dans cet orage, le besoin du langage proprement poétique me reprit."[21] Boethius, whose poetry had also revived his prisoner persona and incorporated the best of his poetic antecedents, would have understood. For Cassou the subjectivity of dreams, memories, and poetry—all born and kept alive but also buried in his head—was a vital means to protect humanity from the storms of war and fascism. Surreal images and intertextual allusions developed his private fantasy into art, making connections with a solid yet lively heritage to rebalance and stabilize his world. Love, Liberty, and Poetry—the prisoner's sisters—were necessary to maintain humanity, defend civilization, and resist the effects of adversity; they were not an evasion of reality but a means to transform, and thus to survive, its horrors. Sonnet form was Cassou's enabling and protective golden bough.

In the octave of Sonnet 6 the poet speaker lists arbitrary reminders of life in liberty, yet these also point to misfortune and night where he found the sources of the poetic voices he addresses:

> quels génies autres que l'infortune et la nuit
> auraient su me conduire à l'abîme où vous êtes?
> Et je touche à tâtons vos visages amis.
>     (Sonnet 6, lines 6–8; p. 50)

He recognizes their friendly faces by fingertip touch like a blind man. Sensory deprivation heightens imaginative insight. The poet is lifted and liberated from the abyss, seeing different sources of light that yield insights: the transient beauty of flowers like clouds and underground stars ("astres de ma caverne," line 14). He can therefore bless the paradoxically genial spirits of misfortune. This poetry of imprisonment also provided themes for Sonnet 3, which begins in another surreal landscape where the speaker loses himself among snowy peaks concealed within the "l'azur noir de son labyrinthe": his brain. No other path is open to him: he is a "vagabond" sunk beneath the metaphysical vault of his own lament: "enfoncé sous la voûte de sa propre plainte" (lines 2–4). In the second quatrain the poet invokes the holy dreams generated by imprisonment ("saintes / rêveries de la captivité") as he wanders lost in this maze of the mind; his captive dreams make and unmake themselves in the impression of deep mirrors that reflect his situation:

> . . . Les prisons
> sont en moi mes prisonnières et dans l'empreinte
> de mes profonds miroirs se font et se défont.
>     (Sonnet 3, lines 6–8; p. 47)[22]

---

[21] Ibid.

[22] Pierre Georgel's selection of Cassou's writing notes a comparison with the poetry of Victor

The sestet returns to the situation of the speaker, lost in this mental land-scape and so high up, like a trailing scrap of sky ("comme un chiffon du ciel," line 10), that his muffled cry can hardly be heard. Who will listen? The speaker in Sonnet 5 imagined the poets of the future returning to the day-light of a normal world. One day, he affirms defiantly, poets will come back to earth, recognize their most beautiful verses and retire satisfied in the eve-ning: "Les poètes, un jour, reviendront... reverront... reconnaîtront, ... dans le soir, / ils s'en retourneront en bénissant" (Sonnet 5, lines 1–2, 8, 12–13; p. 49). These chiming main verbs cast their own spell of blessing and reiterate a defiant hope for the future.

The prisoner's salvation was also mediated by his hopes for his family not merely his art. In Sonnet 3 the speaker invoked the bright image of his daughter in the shepherdess Alice-Abeille who serves as his guide back to the blue morning light of the future.[23] If she should hear a quiet voice say-ing, "This is your father," she is to come to the mountaintop (he says) and take him by the hand. Like other prisoners' dreams and memories of a happy family life Cassou's are enduring and redemptive even though they signify situations of loss and absence. It might be argued that this poem loses focus and ends in confused bathos since it ranges from snow-capped peaks to bright meadows, and from morning light to dark mazes locked inside the speaker's head. Yet it develops earlier themes from the first sonnets in several interesting ways that help to gloss the poet's situation. This vagabond with no other route open to him resembles the drifting explorer of Sonnet 1; the bright dawn of the meadow in Sonnet 2 strikes a contrast with the unnamed dark country that the speaker carries within his head and that—in imagina-tion—consumes the night; similarly, the newly dead children (or poetic ideas) wandering in liminal spaces between life and annihilation find their radical opposite in the bright shepherdess who can move purposefully, at her father's word, and guide him back to safety. The amorphous nature of the prison poet's dreams—his mental captives—also resemble the flashes of light that appear and disappear in the second sonnet; and the muffled call from the mountaintop that is barely heard seems here to revise the function of the energized "silent cry" in Sonnet 1. In spite of its confusing range of reference therefore, this third sonnet establishes the positive dominant roles of love (and family relationships) that protect, preserve, and comfort the poet. As Cassou held his poems in his mind, he revised and revisited them

---

Hugo and Alfred de Musset who also blended "le crâne et le cachot" in introspective landscapes. *Jean Cassou... Choix de texts*, Poètes d'Aujourd'hui, 165 (Paris: Editions Pierre Seghers, 1967), pp. 29–30.

[23] Guest's note indicates a pun on Anne-Isabelle, the name of Cassou's daughter; *From a Con-demned Cell.* Isabelle was born to his second wife, Ida, in December 1930.

extending the process of composition until the day they were written down and released from the labyrinth of his formal ingenuity. Aragon's emotive image of the child held aloft from the flood is not the whole story: dreams of daughterly devotion and the feminine "other" (as Boethius, More, and Gramsci acknowledged) are restorative too.

The hint of a haunting personal memory at the end of Sonnet 3 recurs in the next poem where the speaker addresses a mysterious female (using a formal singular pronoun) whom he dreamed he had carried indoors to a dark room. She had seemed a sister of one of those dear creatures he adored, but he could not see her face properly:

> Vous sembliez une sœur des chères créatures
> que j'adore, mais je ne vous connaissais pas.
> (Sonnet 4, lines 3–4; p. 48)

It was a frosty night of tingling anticipation ("sonore d'aventures," line 6), and he felt her light physical presence as she trembled from cold in his arms. The situation seems built from a specific memory, but it is explicitly a dream vision projecting a longing for human warmth, love, and intimacy. The focus is clear and yet suggestive, potentially erotic, yet also unselfish and unsentimental. The idea that she might be a sister of one of his dear *créatures* suggests that her image represents a mental construct or creation. In the first tercet, the poet acknowledged her exotic value and her loss: "Then I lost you like so many other things, the pearl of secrets and the saffron [colour?] of roses," all precious things that "the dream, or the earth" (each the antithesis of the other) "offer" to his heart (line 11). Her image evaporates in a wonderfully surreal pun in line 10 where the mysterious "perle des secrets" and "le safran des roses" can be elided to conjure a third mimetic image of *perles des rosées* (beads of dew), without the use of new words. Her literary antecedents in ancient myth (Orpheus's Eurydice, perhaps) and medieval dream-vision poetry are usually signs of loss and bereavement. The poet's dream vision and all his enigmatic memories evaporate every morning as he is led to the ironic "masterpiece" of a strong and clear (or glowing) sorrow:

> Signes de ma mémoire, énigmes, tout me mène,
> avec chaque soleil formé à si grand-peine,
> au chef-d'œuvre d'un fort et lucide malheur.
> (Sonnet 4, lines 12–14)

The light of dawn returns the dreamer, the poet, to the great affliction of his earthly prison. Yet the pathos evoked for a lost love, and (likely) the failure to grasp a memory of poetry, also created this small masterpiece of poetry.

Significantly, Cassou did not write about his life in prison but rather of its psychological impact upon him, especially as he sought the freedom to escape from it in imagination. He later acknowledged that Sonnet 8 was based on a nightmarish delusion, worked up from impressions of his arrival at the prison gates, on a cold winter evening, as a descent into an underworld: the cell and its emotional correlatives. Nevertheless, he insisted that there was nothing in the poem dealing expressly with the circumstances of his imprisonment. Cassou was pleased that Jean Rousselot, a fellow poet and *résistant*, in the course of a series of radio interviews broadcast in 1965, had found nothing about the prison in this poem besides "certaines colorations froides, métalliques, sanglantes et sordides."[24] These impressions translated into an ambience of tone reminiscent of myth, and into a theatrical image of bacchanalian excess as the speaker described that "evening of iron" and his arrival at the frost-covered castle where he found torn-up tree trunks circled by drunken crows:

Il n'y avait que des troncs déchirés,
que couronnaient des vols de corbeaux ivres,
et le château était couvert de givre,
ce soir de fer où je m'y présentai.
    (Sonnet 8, lines 1–4; p. 52)

(The orgiastic theme begins imperceptibly here with the mention of tearing and drunkenness but is perceived only with hindsight: "La scène était prête pour des acteurs / fous et cruels à force de bonheur," lines 13–14.) In the second quatrain the speaker defined his state of deprivation. He has neither his books, nor his sinful soul (his constant companion), nor the little girl who had so longed for life when he encountered her on earth. The child is an alter ego, but perhaps literally another figure of his daughter who represented a personal future. The sestet has an even stronger surreal quality—Cassou later described his vision as hallucinatory—on account of its mixture of classical and Nordic or Germanic mythology: "White sphinx's milk ran down the walls; / red blood of Orpheus stained the flags; / at windows blind as wall-eyed trolls / crude hands had strung a screen of rags."[25] Since the poet Orpheus who failed to recover his lost love from the underworld was torn to pieces in a Dionysian blood bath, the scene here is set for violent death.

The unreality of this vivid scene-setting frustrates, yet intrigues readers' expectations. The significations of even this sonnet—based (exceptionally)

---

[24] *Entretiens*, p. 37.
[25] *33 Sonnets*, p. 33.

on impressions of the actual prison—remain, as Cassou later insisted, the story of his inner life.[26] Poetry, he considered, was always secret, perhaps in the sense of authorial meaning being generally elusive or indeterminable. (He had composed his poems "dans la clandestinité. Mais la poésie est toujours clandestine.") Nevertheless, he affirmed, there is also "confidence and communication" in poetry. Myths and allusions to poetic traditions are traces of what he called the "dialogue" of the poet with poetry. These traditions form bridges between his inner life and readers, regardless of any private allusions to memories or feelings that Cassou later acknowledged as latent in a specific sonnet. Yet he also insisted that his knowledge of his past life, as it was reflected in poetry, was coded and only he held the key to their enigmas:

> Ces sonnets peuvent-ils paraître quelque peu mystérieux. Mais moi j'ai leur clef. Je sais à quel souvenir d'enfance ou de jeunesse, à quel instant de ma vie sentimentale, à quelle fantaisie de ma vie affective tel sonnet, tel vers fait allusion, et cela pour moi seul.[27]

This prisoner created poetry to preserve himself. These images and allusions to his past life sustained his integrity in prison where he was conscious of being reduced to a subjective core of personal identity: "réduit a moi-même." Unable to read or write, composing poetry was a response to his situation, but this was not directly reflected in his poetry, except in senses that may represent public and political contexts. The dark cold nights of self-fulfilling intellectual discipline and reverie were opportunities to escape the cell and re-create fragments of an alternative life—a life of imagination, light, and warmth.[28] Cassou defended his humanity by remembering and responding to the higher values he placed on liberty, life, and love; and finally, it was art rather than experience that made his poetry shareable.

## "A LOW MURMUR OF OURSELVES"

Several poets provided Cassou with ideas and associations that enhanced his dialogic exchange with different literary models. Sonnet 13 has been read as an address to the enemy of France; however, the contrast here be-

---

[26] "En somme, je puis vous assurer que, à part deux ou trois allusions—et, bien sûr, beaucoup plus directes que celles-ci—à la cause de la circonstance, voire à la circonstance elle-même, il n'y a dans ces sonnets que des choses, des figures, des sentiments, des secrets de ma vie privée." *Entretiens*, p. 37.

[27] Ibid., p. 36.

[28] See further the sensitive and illuminating appraisal by the philosopher (and poet's brother-in-law), Vladimir Jankélévitch, in "Le diurne et le nocturne chez Jean Cassou," *Cahiers du Sud*, 382 (1965), 241–47 [from a 1958 conference paper]. Jankélévitch does not mention *33 Sonnets* in this paper.

tween the human subject (addressed in the familiar *tu* form) and his impact on the external landscape seems more closely related to the poet's dark state of mind.[29] The octave seems to evoke a strong visual memory of a lonely street scene, pale cobbles and market squares where forsaken stalls and dusty kiosks shiver, and a passer-by (or pilgrim figure reminiscent of the explorer and vagabond personae), whose footsteps disturb the silence of the surrounding desolation: "C'est l'écho de tes pas qui forme un tel silence" (line 11). It is unclear whether these are the effects of war or merely a pathetic fallacy as human despondency is projected on to the scene by a figure who makes his view of the world in his own image. Human emotional reactions are apparent in inanimate objects rather than in the solitary passing pilgrim—a traditional metaphor for human life.

> Quelle stupeur se peint où tu portes les yeux,
> dans l'immobile cri des affiches, les glaces
> figées des magasins naufragés et la face
> de toutes ces maisons en attente du feu!
> (Sonnet 13, lines 5–8; p. 57)

(What amazement registers where you turn your eyes, / in the static cry of billboards, the concealed plate-glass / windows of wrecked shops and the front / of all those houses waiting for fire!)

Whatever he signifies, this pilgrim figure is an anti-life force—a loser—and in the sestet the speaker addresses him familiarly in the final expectation that, once he leaves (as bidden), life and laughter may return. If it is only his presence and the weight of his deathly influence that prevents the resurgence of the laughter, which should shake the roofs and windows, as his presence has made the dusty stalls in the square shiver in dread, then the final rhyme—"rire / surgir"—is affirmative, but also ironic, since the final phrase is negative action:

> Mais que vitres et toits enfin vibrent de rire,
> et les jardins des rois que ta seule présence,
> sous le poids de sa cendre, empêche de surgir!
> (lines 9–14)

In Sonnet 10, another image of an existential torment with universal applications, in the shape (revealed in the final line) of a savage beast, shadows a pair of lovers. The octave of this sonnet was based on memories of a local

---

[29] By contrast, Harry Guest sees the ending of this poem as looking forward optimistically to the liberation of France. Cf. *From a Condemned Cell*. See also in this vein Ross, "Freedom to Compose," p. 49.

festival in Andalusia seen by Cassou and his wife from a balcony.[30] The
poem evokes the sights and sounds of that evening's excitement shared with
the speaker and his beloved; he recalls a song—"*Rose d'Alexandrie*"—and
fireworks on the beach that studded and streaked the light–spangled sky. In
a spirit of childish anticipation and joy, the couple had rushed to watch the
village dancing:

> *Rose d'Alexandrie*. . . C'était une chanson
> qu'étoilaient et striaient les fusées de la plage.
> Et la nuit éclatait de partout . . .

The speaker's address to his *bien-aimée* marks the midpoint of the middle
line of the sonnet, and introduces a pivotal change of mood:

> Et pourtant, bien-aimée, que d'ombres sous ton front,
> et que nos mains tremblaient en tournant cette page!
> (Sonnet 10, lines 7–8; p. 54)

These shadows on her brow and the image of turning over a new leaf herald
the inevitability of change, and a new note of caution, as they recognize that
life must move on. Yet mingled emotions of joy and foreboding have per-
vaded the sonnet from its first line through allusions in the song to beauty
and death. The *Rose* signifies St. Catherine of Alexandria, martyred on a
wheel and transplanted to gardens of eternity as a bride of Christ. In the
sestet of his sonnet, Cassou's speaker refers to a rough-clawed beast that had
stalked the couple on the balcony as demented hope ("l'éspoir dément!").
This never-sated beast was always a force to be reckoned with, prowling
alongside them throughout life, in the difficult terrain of a forest where
their footsteps were more labored:

> Il était là!—Il est peut-être là toujours.
> Car nous sentons rôder le long de notre vie,
> à travers la fôret où nos pas sont plus lourds,
> une bête farouche et jamais assouvie.
> (lines 11–14)

The image is metaphysical, even traditional in fairy stories, but also surprising in this context as it turns a moment of celebration and sparkling light
into a darker, existential threat. And yet the beast is hope. This contrast between wild joyful dancers at the village celebration and the couple's heavier
steps through the forest reveals the human condition. Only human beings
acknowledge an inevitable death and yet maintain the paradoxical hope

---

[30] *From a Condemned Cell*, translator's note.

that prevents self-destruction. Foreboding is human.[31] This bittersweet but unsentimental poem suggests that we are all prisoners of our hopes, as well as fears, and liable to feel that claw ("la griffe") swoop down upon our shoulders. Perhaps it was the opening evocation of song that first attracted the attention of Darius Milhaud, who chose this Sonnet 10 as one of six by Cassou that he set to music after the war. Their appeal for other creative artists suggests that knowledge of the poet's imprisonment and experience of war enhanced these sonnets' authority or credit as existential commentary. Melody further expanded their expressiveness. As ever in Cassou's prison lyrics, emotive contrasts between light and darkness inform their intellectual and imaginative themes. When the speaker in Sonnet 15 imagines himself caught up in the folds of his beloved's dress and the "furtive kisses of her eyes," he anticipates the discovery that these traditional windows into the soul are like two guiding points of lost, and relit, stars; the lovers are literally inspired.

> Oh! Ce sera une récompense inattendue
> que de découvrir, comme deux points d'astres perdus
> et rallumés, le souffle de nos âmes légères.
> (lines 12–14; p. 59)

This discovery will spiritually reanimate the speaker, providing an unexpected consolation, for all that has been lost in darkness, yet may be rekindled by the new light of memory and imagination. He knows he will be infused with feelings of love, delicacy, yearning, hesitation: "je boiterai un peu, mais je connaîtrai l'amour" bringing dreams for the future: "an unexpected recompense," celebrated in the act of its (displaced) reception.

## THE CONSOLATIONS OF MEMORY: "CE SEUL PLAISIR NOURRIT MES HEURES SOLITAIRES"

The consolations of poetry, sensory pleasure, and an inner life of memories are also explicit in the opening lines of Sonnet 28: "Ce seul plaisir nourrit mes heures solitaires, / de redire à mon cœur que je sais se qui fut." The poet also tells his heart that his memory of song and color is a source not only of

---

[31] In his commentary to *La Rose et le Vin,* Cassou wrote of "true death ... that which integrates fully in life, that is accepted and beyond which hope continues to exist": ("c'est la mort véritable ... celle qui s'intègre à la vie, celle qui est acceptée et au-delà de quoi l'espérance subsiste"). Ed. De Lussy, p. 156. Cf. "L'homme meurt et l'homme aspire à mourir, et cette vie que je veux connaître, est une vie de mort. Il semble que les poètes se soient spécialement faits les complices de cette complaisance envers la mort, qui dort aux profondeurs de chacun de nous et nous fait fuir les obligations de la vie pour le rêve...." Jean Cassou, *Trois poètes: Rilke, Milosz, Machado* (Paris: Librairie Plon, 1954), p. 4; the book was begun in 1939, set aside during the war, and completed in 1951.

pleasure but also of nourishment: his mental freedom provides strength for solitary hours and comforts his heart. Sights and sounds trigger memories of places as well as people or events. Sonnet 25 evokes memories of Paris as a place "loved for so long, so long ago" that the speaker can imagine her monuments, in the setting sun, when they appear draped in blood against a sky the color of an aircraft's wing. He remembered hearing a distant song reborn like sparks raised from embers—"j'entendais renaître un chant / lointain, pareil à une levée d'étincelles"—and saw himself (at liberty) again in a low-ceilinged room with honey-colored walls, mahogany furniture, and vivid green chestnut trees through the leaded window. Memory recreates the past in specific visual details of color, as the spirit of the city, like the disembodied image of a face—proud and meditative—is reflected in a mirror ("dans le gel / du miroir pâle"); yet the fuzziness of its image and pallor are ghostly and unstable, as in a dream. Cassou's best poems evoke mystery as well as a specific place and time. The distant song that used to revive like sparks in his head is finally absorbed (*retentissaient*) by the cobbles in the festive street that rumble eternally, like the sea: life goes on perpetually.

An easy mind game for the prisoner to play from memories of other poetry was parody, which also arises from a rhetoric of contrast and opposition as the poet defined and refined his ideas, worked out in close intertextual dialogue with earlier works.[32] Sonnet 19 combined biblical themes and characters with an allusion to Victor Hugo's *Les Contemplations* (1856),[33] in the epigraph "Je suis Jean (V.H.)." Behind this allusion lies the Revelation of St. John the Divine, traditionally associated with the apostle, St. John the Evangelist, who was imprisoned on Patmos by the Romans and wrote in a highly metaphoric style to comfort his defeated countrymen.[34] Cassou's prison poet persona, Jean Noir, was named and probably invented by Aragon on this analogy. Cassou's mission as a modern poet defines itself in this sonnet by parodic contrast with the work and experience of both St. John the Baptist (as forerunner of Jesus) and St. John the Evangelist (or disciple, and a companion in tribulation). However, this John's consoling message is nothing more than a dream.

[32] Sonnet 9 was published with a note to explain that Cassou discovered a German romantic lyric, by Hugo Hofmannsthal, that he had known before the war, printed in a fragment of a German newspaper that found its way fortuitously into his cell. He translated it into French during the course of one sleepless night. Sonnet 18 also engages with German poetry in citing Rilke's "The Departure of the Prodigal Son" (from *Neue Gedichte*, 1907) based on the biblical parable. Rilke's poetry was important to Cassou who later wrote about its influence on him (*Trois poètes*). Sonnet 24 is an angry parody of Verlaine's lyric idyll—"Walcourt" (1874) from *Paysages belges*—indicated by a cue to the poem in Cassou's epigraph, identified in Guest's note; and see further Ross, "Freedom to Compose," pp. 51–52.

[33] Bk. 6:4, line 1: "Ecoutez. Je suis Jean. J'ai vu des choses sombres" (source from Guest's note).

[34] "I John, who also am your brother, and companion in tribulation." Rev. 1:9.

Je suis Jean. Je ne viens chargé d'aucun message.
Je n'ai rien vu dans l'île où je fus confiné,
rien crié au désert. Je porte témoignage
seulement pour le songe d'une nuit d'été.

Pour le songe d'une jeunesse retrouvée
sous les chaudes constellations d'un autre âge,
et parce que je veux entendre le langage
brûlant et vif de ce firmament éclaté.
    (Sonnet 19, lines 1–8; p. 63)

In spite of the punning ambiguity of "éclaté" (as sparkling or shattered), this very simple and direct series of allusive statements is untypical of Cassou's style. Yet this sonnet also culminates in a more usual synthesis generated from opposed terms in imagery of a paradoxical revelation. The speaker's roles of precursor and disciple are abolished ("en toi s'aboliront") in a paradoxical night of white shadow and total reflection ("l'ombre blanche et du total reflet"; line 14): the abstruse clarity of another apocalypse, revealing gain by loss in a violent and changed universe. This sequence of images may be compared with the second quatrain of Sonnet 20, where meditation on a winter sky, with a constantly changing cloudscape, becomes a metaphor for the way a poet's language—the least breath of air ("le moindre souffle d'air") can change perceptions of the material world.

Au clair de l'incessant échange,
c'est toi, le moindre souffle d'air,
langue légère, qui déranges
le diamant des vents contraires
et construis des règnes étranges.
Vive aurore se fasse airain,
ou roc le vaporeux de destin.
    (Sonnet 20, lines 4–10; p. 64)

## POETRY, DEATH, AND LIBERTY

Cassou later wrote that he loved Machado's poetry more than any other; he considered Spanish the best language for poetry and felt an emotional attachment since it was also his mother's mother tongue.[35] In Sonnet 21, "Tombeau d'Antonio Machado," he paid tribute to the poet who had fled Franco's Spain and died in exile at Collioure, not far from Toulouse, in February 1939, a year before the triumph of fascism in France. In "Tombeau"

---

[35] *Trois poètes*, pp. 92–93.

the speaker addresses his dead hero's saintly soul whose remains are to be liberated from the French "scenes of infamy / your light cannot purify" for repatriation[36] (lines 3–4). He imagined the poet's ashes returned to his homeland by a flight of bright birds (line 7), leaving only an urn broken in anger at the foot of a heap of stones where prisoners rot away: "au pied des pierres / où pourrissent les prisonniers" (lines 12–14). Dishonor makes France a land of sand ("n'est plus que sable"): barren, shifting, and unstable (line 6). The dead poet will achieve liberty through the desecration of his grave, an ironic act of merciful love, "la Charité" (line 1), that suggests the speaker's vision of death as liberation from the prison of mortality. The meaning and significance of a poet's death were also exemplified in the Latin epigraph to Sonnet 16 from the work of another Spanish-born poet—Lucan—added by Cassou when he wrote down his poems: *Admoto occurrere fato.*[37] An anthology of Latin poetry that Cassou received shortly before his provisional release included an extract from Lucan's *Civil War* (*Pharsalia*)—an epic poem that had especially appealed to readers in times of war or revolution. Lucan, like his uncle Seneca, was a forceful leader of intellectual resistance to Nero's tyranny. Cassou's sonnet seems to endorse Lucan's resolution to choose death when life has nothing better to offer; yet the key phrases are enigmatic and ambiguous. The unspecified subject is death, which approaches the speaker and his familiar companion—perhaps his soul, or another person who casts a separate shadow (cf. line 6):

> Viens, nous le trouverons au détour du chagrin,
> au niveau de la nuit, à fleur de transparence.
> Nous n'avons jusqu'ici connu que sa semblance,
> mais à pas de voleur lui-même approche enfin.
>     (Sonnet 16, lines1–4; p. 60)

(Come we will find it at the turning of affliction, / at the level of night, on the surface of transparency. / We have only known, until now, its likeness, / but with a thief's footstep it approaches finally.)

> Il fait sombre. Il est tard. Mais que s'attarde encore
> le noir épais de toute cette vie de mort!

(It's dark. It's late. But let the thick blackness of all this life of death linger behind, again!)[38]

---

[36] *33 Sonnets*, p. 47.

[37] Cf. "No life is short that gives man time to slay himself; [nor does it lessen the glory of suicide to meet doom at close quarters]." Lucan, *Pharsalia*, IV, 480 (translated from the Loeb edition as quoted in Guest's note). Lucan committed suicide in 65 CE.

[38] Cf. "Why must this life in death drag on relentlessly?' (tr. Guest); "But let's not expedite this

The octave seems to conclude that one should await the imminent arrival of death. But the sestet seems to follow Lucan into recommending a bold suicide:

> Le reste ne fût-il qu'un fil de crépuscule,
> un horizon de sang dans le calice amer
> que devant notre soif l'ange en riant recule,
> nous terrasserons l'ange et nous boirons la mer.

(If the remainder [of this life of death] were only a grain of dusk, / a bloody horizon in the bitter cup / that the laughing angel withdraws before our thirst [for oblivion] / we'd floor the angel and we'd drink the sea.)

Even if this tormenting angel of death were to be overwhelmed there is nothing to wait for except a short twilight and bitterness. So if we drink down the sea, we die defiant by our own choice and action. This bitter cup suggests an inversion or rejection of the figurative chalice accepted by the suffering Jesus at Gethsemane, and a literal reminder of the hemlock drained by Socrates at his execution from which he had refused to flee. Yet an angel is a biblical messenger from God so perhaps that word complicates, or challenges, the moral clarity of Lucan's view of suicide as noble. If this sonnet reflects Cassou's debate with Lucan's pagan culture, then it seems that, like Madame Roland, he endorsed Lucan's action. Even though death may come slightly sooner rather than later, it is preferable to resist by violence and a bold excess.

By contrast, the last of Cassou's prison poems, Sonnet 33, endorsed a different form of resistance, one that acknowledged death and suffering, yet recommended steadfast integrity and, finally, promised a form of salvation. The formal dialogue within this sonnet also recalls seventeenth-century neo-Platonic dialogues between the soul and God, or an inner debate between body and mind. In Sonnet 33 the second voice, who names herself *Constance*, is commanding and authoritative, yet the first speaker uses the familiar *tu* pronoun, suggesting a form of dramatized, internal debate between aspects of one person's self-knowledge:

> Quel est ton nom?—Constance.—Où vas-tu?—Je m'en viens
> de toi-même et retourne à toi-même.

The second speaker's face is covered with a shroud ("ce linceul") but refuses to reveal herself because the time is not ripe: "Il n'est pas temps encore." The

---

lifetime of the dead, this thick black night!' (tr. Adès, 2004). Cf. also Cassou's *Trois poètes*, p. 4, quoted in my note 31.

first speaker's expectation that his constancy would resemble the sister of one of his dreams[39] is not confirmed, and she commands him to be silent:

... Silence! Apprends que je suis ta captive
et qu'à chacun des coups soufferts par ton destin
se forme un trait de plus à ma beauté furtive.

(... Hush now. [You must learn that] I am ... your captive / Every blow from fate you undergo / adds one more touch to my elusive loveliness.)[40]

These are the paradoxical advantages of adversity; the inner beauty of stead-fastness will develop under conditions of trial.

Lorsque sera parfait ce visage fidèle,
ton cœur y pourra lire, aux lueurs de ton ciel,
et tes choix accomplis et tes maux acceptés.

(When this faithful face is perfected / your heart will be able to read there, by the gleams of your sky [cf. by your heaven's light (Adès)] / your accomplished choices as well as your suffering accepted.)

All the features of this captive's constancy will be perfected and revealed in an act of reading. *Constance* concludes with words of consolation and en-couragement, even as she confirms that all blessings are short-lived: his loves are already dead, but they remain his, and, in any case, he carries his death with him always. "Persist and you will be saved."

Brèves sont tes amours. Comptées et déjà mortes.
Mais ce sont tes amours. Et ta mort, tu l'emportes
toute avec toi. Persiste, et tu seras sauvé.
        (Sonnet 33, lines 12–14; p. 77)

At the end of the sonnet sequence, the prisoner's outlook is still bleak but not hopeless. The divided self is offered a prospect of salvation in a perfected moral beauty that grows in proportion as the soul suffers, or as long as his actual and existential imprisonment continues.[41] The faithful heart will eventually recognize itself by its moral actions, choices, and attitude to suf-fering. Love and death are contrasted: love is brief, and death is ever present. Yet the last words offer redemption if the speaker persists in his current course. If his loves remain figures of his art that may one day survive in writ-ten form, then poetry will one day save him.[42]

---

[39] See Sonnet 3, quoted earlier; cf. adored sister image with woman held in his arms.
[40] Guest's translation, adapted.
[41] Cf. Matthew 10:22.
[42] Cf. the poet's address to his "belles amours"—the poetic images and figures that a succession

Years later, in his "Hymn to Death," the first chapter of his meditation on the three poets he had known and admired—Rilke, Milosz, Machado—Cassou described poets in general as especially prone to a death wish ("cette complaisance envers la mort") that sleeps in the depths of each of us, and makes us flee from the obligations of life toward dreams. Just as the pilgrim's footsteps had created awareness of the silence of the street scene in Sonnet 13, so we need the presence of death to experience fully joy and life:

> Nous n'éprouverions pas tant de joie et tant d'orgueil à connaître la vie et rien de la vie si nous ne portions aussi dans notre cœur la présence de notre mort et si nous ne partagions la passion des poètes pour qui tant de moments furent présences de la mort.[43]

## POLITICS AND THE POET'S "RAISON D'ÊTRE"

Cassou insisted, in conversation with Rousselot, that he loathed idealism and that optimism was for fools: "J'ai horreur de tout idéalisme, au sens philosophique du mot, c'est-à-dire au sens de transcendence et d'irréalité."[44] "J'ai horreur de l'optimisme. C'est une philosophie d'imbéciles."[45] He thought that there were circumstances where the verbs "to believe" and "to hope" were meaningless. Yet, that one always had to create one's own purpose or *raison d'être*, from within, in order to live, to will, and to love:

> Il me semble qu'en quelque circonstance que ce soit il n'y a rien à croire ni rien à espérer. Ces deux verbes sont deux mots vides de sens. Mais il y a à vivre, à vouloir et à aimer, c'est-à-dire qu'il y a toujours, continuellement à se créer a soi-même sa raison d'être. (*Entretiens*, p. 218.)

It is not surprising therefore that several of Cassou's prison poems testified to his recent political engagement and aspirations. Sonnet 22, for example, protests against the suffering of the proletariat: in all countries, and since forever, the workers die. Their blood bathes the streets, they cry out and fall

---

of harmonious sounds makes outlast all that endures—in a poignant farewell, stretched in a mimetic sequence almost longer than breath can last to give them voice. Yet they are equal to the pure eternities of visual art, anticipating Cassou's later professional concerns as an art historian, promoter of modern art, and gallery curator: "A peine si le cœur vous a considérées, / images et figures / que la succession des concerts fait durer / plus que tout ce qui dure, / ô mes belles amours, dont les pays dorés / reflètent la peinture, / et déjà les adieux qui vont nous séparer / s'égalent à vos pures / éternités." (Sonnet 26, lines 1–9) The final word, "éternités," breaks across the formal boundary between octave and sestet in a defiant and prominent expression of liberation.

[43] *Trois poètes*, p. 6.

[44] *Entretiens*, p. 71. Cassou broke with the Far Left on the signing of the Molotov-Ribbentrop Pact in 1939 and was bitterly condemned by former colleagues after the war, but he maintained that he could not turn aside from human suffering or forgive the cruelty of Stalin's tyranny over life, liberty, and ideology.

[45] Ibid., p. 218.

in the smoke. They are killed by fire, cold, hunger, iron, and the wheel that represents industry. In unequal societies, the angry poet exclaims, it is always the workers as a class ("les ouvriers") who suffer. This description is followed in the sestet by a series of questions and exclamations addressed to God that echo the tone of some biblical psalmists who rage against injustice (cf. Psalms 73 and 94) in response to a moral and ethical fervor implanted within man.

> O Dieu de justice qui régnez, non aux cieux,
> mais dans le cœur de l'homme, au cœur de sa colère,
> ne vous répandrez-vous donc jamais sur la terre?
> Seigneur des forts et de la force, ouvrez les yeux!
> (Sonnet 22, lines 9–12; p. 66)

> (Oh God of justice who reigns, not in the heavens, / but in the heart of man, at the heart of his anger, / will you never, then, spread yourself over earth? Lord of the strong and of power, open your eyes!)

The deity that had (apparently) served the Establishment throughout history is urged to reconsider the status quo, and to act (through human consciences) to provide justice in the world, and equality for the dumb, downtrodden, and enslaved; even so, the poet is not hopeful. Habit and self-interest are restraints: "Les bouches sont muettes, les poings sont liés, / et la chaîne est très longue" (lines 13–14). This is not Cassou's most complex or profound poetry (the speaker's righteous anger can seem stilted and predictable), but it is socially and politically engaged. Figures of repetition and refrain-like phrases mimic the themes of remorseless exploitation and universality, in time, place, and conditions, by sound play on vowels and consonants:

> En tous pays, depuis toujours, les ouvriers ... dans la fumée. Le feu, le froid, la faim, le fer et la roue tuent les ouvriers. En tous pays de pierres nues, d'arbres pourris, de grilles ... rouillées, depuis toujours, ... le troupeau des journées saignées et abattues ...

This concern for the conditions of others' lives suggests that one of the paradoxical benefits of individual suffering may be a greater empathy with those who endure injustice. This empathy, in turn, may provoke political engagement.[46]

In Sonnet 23 (one of Cassou's best-known poems), the speaker defines his political stance through historical and literary allusions to the 1871 Paris

---

[46] "A ses yeux, le communisme est avant tout un humanisme" (Nicole Racine, in *Un Musée imaginé*, headnote to ch. 3, p. 109).

Commune. The first line alludes to a song by J.-B. Clément—*Le Temps des cerises*—which had become "a rallying cry for social justice" as revolutionary communards and anarchists took over Paris.[47] Clément's lyric had emphasized the brevity of the cherry season and the dream state that represented human life, in which the fruits that fall like drops of blood are picked. Cassou's sonnet echoes the last stanza of this song—"C'est de ce temps-là que je garde au Cœur / Une plaie ouverte! (*open wound*)"—in his opening lines, which thus became a cue for the revolutionary context, as well as a form of intertextual dialogue with the earlier poet:

La plaie que, depuis le temps des cerises,
je garde en mon cœur s'ouvre chaque jour.
(Sonnet 23, lines 1–2; p. 67)

The final lines greet the sudden dawn of a new armed struggle, as if it were a holiday: "Ah! jaillisse enfin le matin de fête / où sur les fusils s'abattront les poings!" The main verb—*jaillisse*—carries overtones of the blood that spurts, or gushes, from the open wound in the speaker's heart and from the "land which bleeds incessantly"—both signs of suffering that anticipate the bloodshed of violent insurrection. The sestet also alluded to Victor Hugo's pathetic female victims, Fantine and Cosette from *Les Misérables* (1862), who represent popular images of the Parisian underclass. Cassou's speaker asks France to explain why his life should be taken up with the rusty sobs of her old ways of doing things: why in this land of "blue roofs and grey songs," is action continually deferred? The poet was a prisoner of France and of its historic past.

By contrast, in Sonnet 17 the poet seems to address contemporary German occupiers, commanding them, directly and energetically, to leave and, this time, to stay away. The collective identity of the speaker's plural voice—we—epitomized a national spirit of resistance. France and Germany are not mentioned specifically, yet the political context that implies a clash of cultures, and "our" humiliation by a foreign power, suggests a cathartic wish fulfillment, and pity for the vanquished or oppressed. Elsewhere the speaker prays that his dark, oppressed lyric ("cette lyre obscure, / consternée sous la croix brouillée des galeries")[48] may recover in a flash ("un éclair"), insisting that it is time for action as well as wakefulness. There is no doubt that these

---

[47] Information from Guest's note. Cf. significance and historic parallel of the Commune in the wake of the siege and capture of Paris by German troops, in 1870, and the humiliation of the restored French government following the Franco-Prussian War.

[48] Sonnet 31, lines 1–2: "Grant that this lyre in its obscurity, / stunned by the addled cross of galleries..." (*33 Sonnets*, p. 57); Guest notes that the image of a twisted murky cross may suggest the swastika emblem of the Nazi occupiers.

sonnets envisaged both violence and the active revival of a poetic voice that would champion the oppressed.

In the aftermath of an apocalypse that may signify war, or the intrinsic violence of imprisonment, a personified force of nature (in Sonnet 32) is contrasted with the condition of a speaker (from line 7) who addresses his heart, which is close to breaking.

> L'univers insulté peut tenir sa vengeance,
> les jours renaître au jour et les soirs consolés
> répandre leur rosée de sang et d'innocence
> et s'ouvrir à la nuit comme des mains lavées.
> Revanche dans le ciel, totale et sans clémence!
> Oui, le tonnerre peut soulager la forêt.
>     (Sonnet 32, lines 1–6; p. 76)

(The outraged universe stores up redress; / days are reborn at daybreak; dusk's half-light, / consoled, distils their dew of blood and gentleness, / and opens like washed hands towards the night. / Vengeance in heaven: total, no remorse! / Yes, thunder can soothe the forest . . .)[49]

Yet there is no natural cycle that can renew human life once it is extinguished.

> Mais toi, tu n'obtiendras pour toi que le silence
> qui suit l'effacement de la chose jugée:
> Le blanc silence aux ailes de neige éperdues,
> dont le cri forcené mesure l'étendue
>     de l'assouvissement suprême.
>     (lines 7–11)

(But you, you will only get for yourself the silence—the white silence of distracted, snowy wings—that follows the obliteration of the condemned / whose frantic cry matches the extent of the last supreme satisfaction.)[50]

This existential anxiety was resolved in a new paradox at a critical "point" in history when fascism had exploited human weakness and created hatred:

> Au point où le mépris toute digue a rompue,
> cœur près de se briser, il ne te reste plus
>     qu'à mépriser le mépris même.

---

[49] *33 Sonnets,* p. 59; tr. Adès (adapted).

[50] Cf. "when you are judged, that silence shall be yours, / . . . white silence, snowy wings, abandonment, / whose frenzied cry marks out the true extent / of the supreme excessiveness" (tr. Adès). "That silence, white on wild snow-mantled wings, / by yielding one frenetic cry will gauge / the true extent of armistice" (tr. Guest).

(When hate has broken down every barrier / heart close to breaking, there remains nothing more for you / than to despise that same hate.)

Harry Guest remarks that, as, "night after night, Cassou lay awake forming these . . . sonnets which would seemingly die with him . . . he displayed . . . a private faith that civilised culture must—somehow—go on."[51] In addition, I believe, the hope that he might expose the betrayal of that culture's surrender to fascism may have invigorated the prisoner's poetic purpose.

When asked about the political and philosophical significance of hope in motivating French Resistance activities during the war, Cassou insisted that he distrusted hope: "Je me méfie de l'espérance." "La Résistance, ce n'était pas un pari [i.e., *bet, wager*]. C'est un choix moral, cela se situait sur le plan moral. Et sur le plan de l'action, c'était une résolution,"[52] by which he meant both a determination and also a solution to the moral problem the Resistance faced: fascist tyranny and hatred. Whereas, in his case, escaping Occupation to join the Resistance had been an ideological commitment and, above all, a practical necessity for his Jewish family, yet, as an intellectual, he had also relished an affinity for German romanticism in poetry and the visual arts. (He later speculated that this affinity had been an attraction of opposites: "Peut-être y a-t-il là un phénomène d'affinité des contraires.")[53] Resistance requires confrontation and opposition whether by conflict or contrast. Cassou expressed his constant concern with real life and the need, in his own art of poetry, to harness dreams, music, otherness, and allusive transformations to serve in the praise of the real world's riches and plenty:

> Je suis dans l'immanence, nous sommes au monde et notre poésie est au monde et est du monde. C'est-à-dire que ce qui en elle [i.e., *poetry*] est rêve, musique, étrangeté, métamorphose, tout cela demeure impliqué dans la réalité de la vie et ne prétend pas y échapper, à la plénitude et à l'exaltation de cette réalité de la vie et à renforcer notre conscience d'être.[54]

Poetry, like politics and ethics, was about life, rather than ideology. He carried his principles into art, and later explained to his interviewer why he admired Whitman, Goethe, and Rimbaud—"trois voix souveraines." Their poetry was innovative ("elle annonce des terres nouvelles"), but, above all, it was morally and politically engaged with the world, and humane: "c'est de la poésie engagée, parce qu'elle est humaine."[55] Although Cassou was a friend and admirer of surrealists and symbolists, and in later life did much to for-

---

[51] *From a Condemned Cell*, p. 2.
[52] *Entretiens*, p. 218.
[53] Ibid., p. 63.
[54] Ibid., pp. 71–72.
[55] Ibid., p. 62.

mulate public taste as a founder of public, modern art collections, he never abandoned a preference for figurative art, and for aesthetic ideas based on the moral artist's responsibilities as a maker.[56]

In Louis Aragon's emotive simile for the humanity he found in Cassou's sonnets, the prisoner (without writing materials) had saved each poem as if he were holding a child's head above water. Yet there is nothing childlike or innocently direct about these poems. As Harry Guest also remarked, comparing Cassou to the metaphysical poets of early modern France, he was "a supremely inventive lyricist, a brilliant coaxer of language into unfamiliar patterns which dazzle, astound, perplex, puzzle and, eventually, delight."[57] Delayed gratification in art is a mature pleasure. The survival of the unwritten poems depended on the physical survival of the poet and his will to resist oppression; this was fostered by his memories of Latin and vernacular poetic traditions, a philosophical heritage, including Platonic, Judeo-Christian, and Stoic ideas, and the mental and emotional guidance they provided. His mind was well stocked. These ideas expressed in memorable images and language had sustained earlier generations of cultured readers in many forms of distress and had helped to comfort and console them. Cassou would have been aware of a national heritage of humanist political poetry by French prisoners, including Charles d'Orléans, François Villon, Théophile de Viau, and André Chénier among others.[58] Such shareable literary resources also help readers to enjoy new poetry created in a continuous cycle of imitation and reaction. But many of Cassou's lyrics remain, by his choice, essentially enigmatic and personal because he created them for himself in a particular situation. Nevertheless, the prison poet Jean Noir was also recognized as a type of everyman who registered our darkness and existential pain in mythic contexts appropriate to his period culture and politics. To that extent, we also hear, as Aragon recognized, a "low murmur of ourselves."

Cassou's prison poems convey his figurative sense of being dead, cut off from normal life, and diminished, yet also forced into mental self-reliance by fear of death, in conditions of deprivation and a liminal state of existence. In these situations, poets resort to evocative memories and dreams, in order to cultivate (and maintain) vitality, order, form, and personal integrity in

---

[56] For Cassou, surrealism in art was exciting because it valued openness in form and concept, but he became critical of what he called "ce prodigieux mouvement" because he thought that "dogma" had drained its vitality and become limiting (ibid., pp. 77–78). After his wartime experiences, Cassou seems to have become suspicious of organized "movements."

[57] *From a Condemned Cell*, p. 3. Cf. Georgel on Cassou as "cet héritier des baroques espagnols"; *Jean Cassou. Choix de textes*, p. 42 (and p. 49).

[58] See Zim, " 'La Nuit trouve enfin la clarté': Captivity and Life Writing in the Poetry of Charles d'Orléans and Théophile de Viau"; and references cited.

their writing. The darkness that permeated Cassou's *vie intime* may have been literal too, during long winter nights, but there are always spots of color—blue roofs and eyes in peacocks' tails, honey walls, red anemones and blood stains, cherries and rusty iron—in the sonnets. The logic of contrast and opposition, dialogue and dialectic, characterized the oppressed poet's mental processes in his culturally conditioned responses to captivity. The brevity of sonnet form was appropriate because his imagination was lyrical and responsive to structures defined by sound, rather than merely pithy and epigrammatic. Cassou also used expectations of the coincidence of style and form to provide him with opportunities for various approaches to a single theme or idea. Just as the brooding introspection of many dark sonnets is offset by flashes of light energy—"le langage brûlant et vif de ce firmament éclaté,"[59] so the imagery drawn from subjective experience and dreams can reveal a passion for political engagement and artistic and cathartic defiance. The sonnet has been used for personal responses to public contexts, as the works of Petrarch, Milton, and many others demonstrate. Making art, or realizing values and ideas in disciplined, meaningful, and repeatable forms of expression, in the face of fear and oppression, is always an act of human defiance with personal and political consequences. Form matters. The making process—creativity—occupies the highest faculties of imagination and intellect, while the time and effort involved not only *take* time (in different ways) but also make it pass in surprising ways that paradoxically *give* time and satisfaction or relief. The making and the effect often distort and seem to transcend the ordinary experience of time, as the prisoner Bonhoeffer also found to his surprise and gratification. Writing was therefore self-sustaining and consoling for the prison poets who could abstract their life of the mind from terror by ranging freely—as the English early modern defender of poetic art insisted—within the zodiac of their own wit and will.[60] The allusive and elusive qualities of poetry need not obey the logic of argument in order to communicate with others and stimulate changes in their perceptions and understanding by offering associative leaps and combinations of metaphor, simile, and sound play. Boethius's paradigmatic work had mingled both verse and prose for different purposes and effects in each form. Just as making poetry could protect and preserve the poet's self, so it might inspire others to resist the debasing effects of fear and thus to protect themselves.

By contrast with Cassou's subjectivity, Irina Ratushinskaya wrote more openly for others recognizing the social and political role of the poet, espe-

---

[59] Sonnet 19, lines 7–8.
[60] Cf. Philip Sidney, *The Defence of Poesie* (c. 1581–83).

cially the Russian dissident poet. Her poems provided fellow prisoners with much needed respite and renewed self-confidence; they also channeled her intellectual efforts to continue resistance, yet also promoted reflection that eventually led her to consider death as her only way to freedom.

## Irina Ratushinskaya, *Pencil Letter* and *No, I'm Not Afraid* (1982–86): Preserving the Life of a Poet

That, which is the most important, comes later, and in the meantime, it's as though I'm in training for it, testing myself in different situations. And I have no values other than to tell no lies, and to endure whatever I must.[61]

Poetry was both the pretext for imprisonment and the salvation of the science teacher and human rights campaigner from Odessa, Irina Ratushinskaya (b.1954). In August 1981 she and her husband were threatened by the KGB secret police; they were told they would be arrested if they continued to support international demonstrations of solidarity with political dissidents in the USSR and to circulate news of human rights abuses in clandestine publications. In December 1981 they were arrested at a demonstration by dissidents in Moscow, and each served a ten-day sentence in prison. This was Ratushinskaya's first experience of imprisonment; worse was to follow.[62]

### "IN TRAINING"

Her poetry from the late 1970s was inspired by the Russian "Silver Age" poets, including Anna Akhmatova and Marina Tsvetayeva, whose works had circulated unofficially in the USSR and the West. A fellow student, Ilyusha Nisanovich, had introduced her to the works of the "quartet" or four great poets while she was at university in Odessa.[63] Thereafter Ratushinskaya's poetry reflected her political and humanitarian concerns in a culture she recognized as corrupted by official lies, where fear inhibited free expression in art. An early lyric written in September 1978 had envisaged her "first es-

---

[61] Irina Ratushinskaya, *Grey Is the Colour of Hope*, tr. Alyona Kojevnikov (London: Hodder & Stoughton, 1988), p. 206.

[62] See her husband Igor Gerashchenko's "About the Arrest of Irina Ratushinskaya," in *No, I'm Not Afraid*, tr. David McDuff (Newcastle upon Tyne: Bloodaxe Books, 1986, rpt. 1987), pp. 17–22; for background information, see the preliminary matter in this edition of selected poems in English, pp. 9–71. For an autobiography, intercalated with her biography of her husband, see Irina Ratushinskaya, *In the Beginning*, tr. Alyona Kojevnikov (London: Hodder & Stoughton, 1990).

[63] See *In the Beginning*, p. 105: "In one week I was buried under an avalanche of all that, which had been carefully concealed from our generation." Cf. her "My Motherland" [1982], in *No, I'm Not Afraid*, p. 71; see also Joseph Brodsky, introduction to *No, I'm Not Afraid*, p. 14; Osip Mandelstam and Boris Pasternak complete the "quartet."

cape" from guilt, fear, and apathy in separating herself from the indifference of the "majority." The poet promised never to forget the freedom of her youthful innocence; thus her conscience would (she hoped) remain clear, and she should have nothing to reproach herself with in years to come. She would neither remain silent nor turn away from those who suffered injustice and felt "the imprint of betrayal."[64] She later explained that writing "poetry in prison was my essential need, maintaining silence under interrogation was no more than elemental decency, and refraining from shameful, cowardly recantations—the only way to preserve my self-respect."[65]

Ratushinskaya's conscientious stand was strengthened by her Christian faith and ethics. Deploying a rhetoric of negation to register her resistance, she identified herself with a Russian tradition of dissident poets who were proud not "to bend the knee" like serfs and sought no protection or "armour in verses":

> Only save from corruption
> What to us—alone—is law and honour,
> That we may grow by our breathing
> And say our verses out loud
> Though we dare not say our names.[66]

Russia's poets were seen as guardians of justice and humanity whose "breathing," or expression, might liberate a people who were "all convicts" in a prison state, watched, controlled, and unable to communicate freely: "Our coffee / Smells of burnt letters, / And a smell of opened mail fills / The post offices."[67] Here the dialogue of interpersonal correspondence is compromised by suspicion, and the smell indicates corruption. Writing is a sign of freedom that needs protection and has its martyrs.

Among the poems written before her own arrest are several that refer to the death or execution of poets. In the "Ballad of the Wall," the poet's persona dreamed of her "canonisation among those saints / Who have not finished singing / To the heavens"; as the singer approaches "the burnt-out masonry / Against which the shoulder-blades must press to their uttermost," in facing death by firing squad, she sees "The imprint / Of two wings."[68] Political anxiety and historical imagination led the poet to empathize with this

---

[64] "Not for me twenty years on," in *No, I'm Not Afraid*, p. 75, lines 8–9.
[65] *In the Beginning*, p. 245.
[66] "No, don't save, don't preserve," Kiev 1980, in *No, I'm Not Afraid*, p. 78.
[67] "But we shall remain," in *No, I'm Not Afraid*, p. 83.
[68] Ibid., p. 84. Cf. "I don't know how they'll kill me: / Whether they'll shoot me down at the start of the turmoil—/ And I will press my confused hands / Against the hole where my heart was." 15 June 1983, in *Dance with a Shadow*, tr. D. McDuff (Newcastle upon Tyne: Bloodaxe Books, 1992), p. 47, lines 1–4.

prisoner in his "uttermost" state before the fatal shot liberates his soul from its existential prison of the body. This image of the victim of Stalinist oppression literally becomes an impression: death by a wall and the image of the poet's soul leaving its "imprint" in signs of winged escape by flight recurs in Ratushinskaya's prison poetry. Cassou's "le blanc silence aux ailes de neige éperdues" had reworked the same trope.[69] This image of the soul in flight also symbolized the transmission of her ideas in writing—secretly, in Russian, and openly in English translations by David McDuff, among others: how "these lines will soar." The emblem of resistance was not merely symbolic; she knew that the Soviet Union had an old habit of silencing writers. "It's a family trait of Russian poets / To be shot at, like banners. / And it's done by roster": it's not personal but it's inevitable.[70]

Several poems about the general conditions of life under a repressive regime reflect the tensions that were inevitable in the build-up to the first arrest in December 1981: "Why / Do half our escapes take place in dreams?" asked the dissident poet. The reality of a hunt by merciless figures "who direct fate with cold fingers," and strain at the leash like tracker dogs, to entrap people, oppressed those with no prospect of salvation:

Out of the trap of the mirrors,
Which, like oysters, have half opened
Their avid valves—run!
. . .
Across the desert of the asphalt,
Across the dry land—
Leaving
A trail that never grows cold,
Losing our way
Unable to ask for protection—
We leave, run, pant . . .
Before us
No Moses.[71]

The paradoxical ambiguity in the English translation of "Leaving" suggests entrapment, as it first connotes exile, yet, secondly, the opposite sense of re-

---

[69] Sonnet 32, line 9, quoted earlier.

[70] "We're untranslatable," 1982, in *No, I'm Not Afraid*, p. 108. Cf. "I shall write. / Then burn what I have written" (p. 82); she had been warned on 15 August 1981 that her poems undermined the Soviet regime and were a threat to the security of the Soviet Union; ibid, p. 20. Cf. "the Russian poet is not fated / to die an untroubled death . . . ," Anna Akhmatova, *Selected Poems*, tr. Richard McKane (Newcastle upon Tyne: Bloodaxe Books, 1989), p. 115, "One can leave this life so simply," lines 3–4.

[71] "Why," in *No, I'm not Afraid*, p. 87.

maining. This nightmare of pursuit recurs in history. Redemption in life seemed unlikely; there was no Moses to part this red sea to lead a nation of slaves pursued by tyrannical masters, yet unlike Bonhoeffer's use of this trope, Ratushinskaya did not see herself in a moral leadership role. The KGB had ordered her to stop writing poetry, and she knew that Russian dissidents did not live long or peaceful lives; some committed suicide.

> Don't ask yourself: "Am I a poet?"
> They won't take long to make you one of their poets.
> All the means—from the bullet to the rope—
> Are available to you from birth.[72]

The poet's calling or vocation was uncomfortable, but silence was not an option for a moral being.[73] Yet, on the eve of her second arrest, which led to a sentence of seven years hard labor in a "strict regime" prison camp with an additional five years in internal exile, Ratushinskaya questioned whether "in the midst of silence" from others it would be "possible to take this disfavoured call / For the absolution / Of guilt" committed by indifferent people.[74] She was charged and convicted on 5 March 1983 of anti-Soviet agitation in that she had "prepared and disseminated" certain poems. The literary traditions that she had promoted and reinterpreted for her contemporaries were founded on religious and philosophical ideals that placed her in conflict with the Soviet regime solely by challenging its restrictions on freedom of conscience and free speech.

She continued to compose poetry in the camp at Barashevo in Mordovia, three hundred miles to the southeast of Moscow. From time to time she endured extreme deprivation in prison punishment cells when she infringed regulations by defending the legal and human rights of a group of up to twelve women prisoners of conscience who lived together in a segregated "Small Zone" (within the main camp), comprising a dormitory and workshop for glove making behind three rings of barbed wire and high fencing.[75] Her new poems, written on small strips of paper that could be rolled up like cigarettes, were smuggled out of the camp and published in the West by supporters including members of International PEN and church groups.[76] Po-

---

[72] "Don't ask yourself . . . ," Kiev 1981, in ibid., p. 89. (Marina Tsvetayeva had committed suicide.)

[73] Cf. "A true poet cannot lie. To be silent, or to be reluctant to see the world in which one lives in its true colours—that is also a lie!" anonymous comment on the poet's arrest in *No, I'm Not Afraid*, p. 27.

[74] "From an unfamiliar window," 16 September 1982, night, in ibid., p. 114.

[75] For conditions in the Small Zone, see the report by Amnesty International (July 1985) reprinted in *No, I'm Not Afraid*, pp. 31–36.

[76] For facsimiles (actual size), see her *Pencil Letter* [collection of poems, translated by different hands] (Newcastle upon Tyne: Bloodaxe Books, 1988), pp. 91–96.

litical efforts to secure her release built up in May 1986, following publication of the first English edition of her poems, *No, I'm Not Afraid*, in 1984. The former British foreign secretary, David Owen, on a diplomatic visit to Moscow in 1985, presented a copy of her poems in English translations to the Soviet president, Mikhail Gorbachev. Ronald Reagan, the U.S. president also received a copy and on the eve of the summit meeting in Reykjavik, in October 1986, Ratushinskaya was released. Publicity surrounding this double presentation of her poems had made her release symbolic of a new era in international politics: glasnost.

Poetry had caused her persecution and imprisonment, yet it also protected the moral and ethical integrity of the poet and her companions in prison; later on, in English translation her prison poetry was also directly instrumental in securing her release, which saved her life. After four years in the "strict regime" (penal servitude) camp, it was clear that she would have been unlikely to survive the full term of her sentence. The main focus of this chapter is on the poems that preserved the writer's self-image in memorable forms of lyric memoir that also came to represent others. Her poetry stimulated resistance and provided evidence of her companions' suffering and courage, in clear, affective expression that eventually helped to hasten reform and mitigate the effects of illegal punishments.

## "TESTING MYSELF IN DIFFERENT SITUATIONS"

Ratushinskaya composed poetry in the midst of personal suffering, which reflects events, thoughts, and feelings as they occurred. The external evidence for the situation of the writer is provided by the circumstances surrounding the transmission of the smuggled texts and the prose memoir she wrote soon after her release.[77] Short lyric forms were easily portable in clandestine copies and, like Cassou's sonnets, were easily memorized before they could be written down. She composed in her head, reciting the new poems to her companions in the Small Zone and the punishment cells, only writing them down in secret when opportunities arose to send them out to supporters. Many of these lyrics are dated, and the place of composition is noted, as if they were journal entries that relate the texts to specific contexts, such as punishment cells and solitary confinement. The occasional nature of these poems not only aided their wider political functions as evidence of persecution but also sustained relationships and ethical values among the prisoners of conscience in the Small Zone. Yet poetry was frequently also a personal reaction to the trauma, fears, and deprivations induced by impris-

---

[77] *Grey Is the Colour of Hope*. The prisoners wore gray uniforms.

onment. The tone and themes of many poems are therefore very dark, but there are flashes of irony and humor, which offered antidotes to hatred. Such poems were also tactical means of self-preservation and provide further testimony to the principles established in antiquity and Boethius's prison writing that one "cannot impose on a free mind, and . . . cannot move from its state of inner tranquillity a mind at peace with itself." Practical experience severely tested this principle.

In the spring of 1983, just before the court confirmed her sentence, Ratushinskaya wrote about herself—the convicted poet—in an unusually personal situation that she treated with ironic, self-mocking humor:

> That traitress and apostate,
> That mote in the government's eye,
> That especially dangerous criminal—
> What a joke!

The heavy-handed interpolation reminds readers of the distance between two opposite points of view. The reality is both bathetic and literally true: "—she's cutting a tooth. / It knocks like a chick in an egg, thrusts out, / Quite oblivious of everything," even the iron bars at the window:

> So what if the window's covered in iron?
> Everything's growing—that's what spring is for!

The poet reflects on how her resistance is emboldened by pain.

> My sentence is awaiting confirmation,
> The Supreme Court is in session . . .
> I ought to be whimpering for leniency—
> But my seditious tooth prevents me!

She transfers her ironic criminality to the painful new growth—a sign of "wisdom"—that erupts to escape, yet controls her thoughts and attitude:

> It stews its way out all morning,
> Like a starling gobbling my head . . .
> My good-for-nothing wisdom!
> You've chosen a fine place to assert your rights!

Her parody of the authorities' overreaction to what comes naturally reflects the bizarre situation in which a tooth can be seditious and a poet can be a dangerous criminal. Heavy irony emphasizes the discrepancy between a scale of values that sets a tooth against an iron bar and "regulations [that] forbid the possession / Of this sharp, cutting object" against the natural energy and impulses of the spring hatchling. In this way, Ratushinskaya faced the consequences of her arrest by speaking out in a passive-aggressive self-realization that impersonates and ridicules the powers of the authoritarian state which saw her as a threat: "What do you mean it just grew? That's impossible! / There's nothing about it in the rules!"[78] The confrontation and dialogue continued. Assertions of willpower to hold back what she called the "plague" of totalitarianism, and the paradoxical self-sacrifice that this resistance strategy entailed dominate many of her poems in different moods.[79]

One of her most moving poems—"I will live and survive"—was written in the prison hospital after she had been assaulted and concussed while resisting an illegal forced feeding in September 1983. As she looked back on the continuous past of the first year in prison, she also projected her mind beyond the present to create a dialogue with others. Even the prospect of such testimony was consoling. Imagining what her future testimony would be, in response to sympathetic questions after her release, had become another tactic of defiance.[80]

> And I will render homage to the dry September
> That became my second birth.
> And I'll be asked: "Doesn't it hurt you to remember?"
> . . .
> But the former names will detonate in my memory—
> Magnificent as old cannon.
> And I will tell of the best people in all the earth,
> The most tender, but also the most invincible,
> How they said farewell, how they went to be tortured,
> How they waited for letters from their loved ones.
> And I'll be asked: what helped us to live
> When there were neither letters nor any news—only walls,
> And the cold of the cell, and the blather of official lies,
> And the sickening promises made in exchange for betrayal.

The poem is this memorial testimony of resistance by and for a community, and of actions described in the later narrative memoir but here composed in the midst of events with no known conclusion: self-realization and preservation are anticipated as a form of prophetic wish-fulfillment, added to the consolation of writing. The enabling power of imagination is represented as

---

[78] "That traitress and apostate," in *No, I'm Not Afraid*, p. 125.

[79] "To My Unknown Friend," in *Pencil Letter*, p. 30: "There are feasts of plague without end / . . . a searchlight shines in our faces, / And effaces the touch of death / . . . And we stand in the midst of our fates, / Setting our shoulders against the plague. / We shall hold it back with ourselves, / We shall stride through the nightmare./ It will not get further than us . . . ," lines 6–8, 11–15, tr. D. McDuff; Small Zone, 26 February1984.

[80] "I will live and survive," 30 November 1983, in *No, I'm Not Afraid*, p. 132, lines 7ff.

a baptism of ice that takes place soon after her first experience of torture and is recognized by the prisoner as a "gift" that, like baptism, "can only be received once." This complex of icy translucent crystals conjured visions of escape beyond the terror of surveillance and control, for a group of outlaws and free spirits, imagined in a pattern of blue radiance:

> And I will tell of the first beauty
> I saw in captivity.
> A frost-covered window! No spyholes, nor walls,
> Nor cell-bars, nor the long-endured pain—

These prison objects are not worthy of remembrance. By contrast,

> Only a blue radiance on a tiny pane of glass,
> A cast pattern—none more beautiful could be dreamt!
> The more clearly you looked, the more powerfully blossomed
> Those brigand forests, campfires and birds!

The prisoner is inspired by images of freedom, space, warmth, and song.

> And how many times there was bitter cold weather
> And how many windows sparkled after that one—
> But never was it repeated,
> That upheaval of rainbow ice
> . . .
> Such a gift can only be received once,
> And perhaps is only needed once.

The application of this symbolic gift fired the poet's fight for survival in her writing as well as in person. She was motivated to "trudge with the convoy," for as long as might be necessary, by the ambition of every moral witness to "remember everything—/ By heart!—they won't be able to take it from me."[81] She promised that she would use her memories to testify to the free world, reject the "blather of official lies," and make her torturers acknowledge their abuses of human rights. Her purpose to describe "the eyes of human suffering" in affective poetry was considered audacious as well as seditious. As Boethius and Bonhoeffer (and generations of other prison poets) had found, the mind could, and did, transcend the cell and travel freely, in imagination. Poetry became portable testimony as the poet's gift, her gain by loss, transformed real situations of oppression, for her own and others' consolation, permeating the prison walls, literally and figuratively.

---

[81] "I will travel through the land (to Tanya and Vanya)," 12 November 1983, in *Pencil Letter*, p. 26, tr. McDuff.

Although many of Ratushinskaya's poems are reflective and subjective relating to her poetic vocation and spiritual experience, they also suggest moods and feelings that could be shared by their first audiences in the Small Zone and speak to later readers everywhere. "The Spider Mathematician" depicted the secret sharer of the cell as a "half-witted prison prophet," "crucified on coordinates," whose work might be relied upon to "count the days of my sentence, please."[82] The tone of "Some people's dreams pay all their bills" was similarly bittersweet as it represented a woman prisoner's "childish, flouted right / To beauty" that plagued her dreams in the form of a velvet dress, "Cherry-red and sumptuous as sin":

My day is like a donkey, bridled, laden,
My night deserted, like the prison light.
But in my soul—it's no good! I am guilty!—
I keep on sewing it, and in my mind I make
The thousandth stitch . . . [83]

This poem was passed into the wider camp outside the Small Zone and became a favorite with other women prisoners.[84] In "A clumsy saw," dedicated to Tanya Velikanova (another political prisoner), to commemorate her move into internal exile, the poet articulated her hopes for Tanya's future: "Freedom will be treading on your heels." The other women would only need to survive in order to follow their "quiet angel" in her flight from prison. Yet, at the end, the poet comments in her own singular voice, "I've no strength to say farewell."[85] The poem substitutes for that message and instantiates it.

The consoling, expressive, and supportive functions of poetry in the prison community were not restricted to these new occasional lyrics. Ratushinskaya's memory was a source of other poets' works, which were recited either in company or alone when the vitality of her intellectual efforts to escape through a life of the mind helped her to endure periods in solitary confinement. "I sit on the floor, leaning against the radiator—/ A southerner, no-gooder! / Long shadows stretch from the grating, following the lamp. / It's very cold." At this point the cold, sleepless prisoner notices a mouse behind the latrine pail and wonders: "What will warm us quicker—a firm ode of Derzhavin, / A disfigured greeting of Martial, / Or Homer's

---

[82] *No, I'm Not Afraid*, p. 122.

[83] Ibid., p. 124, April 1983.

[84] E.g., when in transit to the punishment cells she was often asked to recite it for them; see *Grey Is the Colour of Hope*, p. 29. At other times prisoners asked her for stories, and she told them about the prisoner's romance and revenge by Alexander Dumas's Count of Monte Cristo; *In the Beginning*, p. 251.

[85] "A clumsy saw," 1 September 1983 in *No, I'm Not Afraid*, p. 129.

bronze?"[86] She had attempted to bring manuscript copies of poems by Push-kin, Tyutchev, and others into the prison camp for her own consolation, but these had been confiscated on the assumption that they were her own compositions. Dialogue was necessary, and a one-way conversation with a personified mouse was better than none.

> I talk to the mice and the stars,
> I've watered the spring onions,
> I'll crumble a rusk on the sill for January,
> And he will cut a pattern for me on the casement window
> In transparent sugar—two wings.[87]

But, as Ratushinskaya noted, "no one's voice has yet / Winged its way to freedom, / Nor performed freedom, *svoboda*, / Even though it's a Russian word."[88] There is no simple equation of word and action.

Among her literary representations of the self-preserving conviction that she associated with young dissidents are two poems in which a speaker identifies with Jacob and Sisyphus as biblical and classical types of endurance or defiant courage beyond ordinary human limits. These poems reaffirm the attributes most necessary to a prisoner in Ratushinskaya's situation—audacity and tenacity. The biblical hero, Jacob, "the first soldier of solitude," who wrestled "In close combat with the Immortal . . . Giving back the strength he had won / From his God," personified daring and unvanquished self-respect. He was "Endowed with the highest valour" in an "ordeal as cruel as death," and the poet in her punishment cell (in August 1985) celebrated Jacob as "The first one called who answered, / The first one marked with this hand" of struggle, whose biblically inspired offspring (among whom she counted herself) bear "freedom . . . in their blood."[89] The poet in her punishment cell also cited Sisyphus "who rejects the taunts of Zeus" as one of several wily iconoclasts with whom she compared her own stubbornness in resisting totalitarianism and a power that merely threatened "Life long torment / For immortal souls":

> I am stubborn.
> If not I, then who?
> And again and again:

---

[86] "I sit on the floor," in ibid. p. 134, 16 December 1983. Cf. Bonhoeffer singing psalms in his cell.

[87] "I talk to the mice and the stars," in ibid, p. 136, January 1984. See *Grey Is the Colour of Hope*, p. 23 for confiscation of poetry in manuscript.

[88] "Like Mandelstam's swallow," in *No, I'm Not Afraid*, p. 139.

[89] "Jacob," in *Pencil Letter*, p. 56, tr. D. McDuff. Ratushinskaya's active Christian faith informs several poems and was understood by many other prisoners—within and beyond the Small Zone—as sufficient explanation for the ideas and ethical values that informed her everyday behavior.

No, the cold
Will not reach beyond consciousness—
Warm rivers flow there![90]

Only a few months earlier she had written that with the audacity of the young, who are "blessed . . . by no sense of limit," "Sedition and ambition see us through":[91] the ambition to resist and survive as oneself.

In the subzero conditions of a punishment cell in October 1985, Ratushinskaya watched her breath—her poetic voice—condensing and imagined how the clouds it might form would precipitate as snow, and thereby bear witness to an unnamed "woman's moans" before an open, human court of appeal:

There's no tampering with these stubborn witnesses,
No reaching them, no stuffing them into prisons.
The snow will fall thickly like evidence
Onto your roofs, umbrellas, mackintoshes.
The unsolicited truth stares you in the face,
It does not spare the clever or the stupid . . .
With white conscience they'll cover the streets
To make you shudder before you step on them.

Metonymically, "they" are the dissident prisoners trampled by the indifferent and complaisant whose consciences may be pricked by a poet's breath. Like Cassou's image of a poet's insubstantial "langue légère," the slightest breath of air (*le moindre souffle d'air*) can change perceptions of the material world, merely by changing the cloudscape.[92] The freedom of the skies transmits the truth of this poet's testimony:

The damp here makes voices hoarse
But they can still break through the slime of cement.

The clouds that "crowd together"—like a "regiment of horse" seen from the cell—"always incredibly high" above the Mordovian landscape are indifferent to the suffering they have witnessed and "will bear without flinching the convict's stare." Yet "sometimes breaking down they cry buckets over the field . . . / Taste the bread—it is a little bitter."[93] There is a long sequence of such snow-bearing clouds. Their metaphorical doubles fall lightly, with casual naturalness in exquisite forms of light-reflecting beauty; like human be-

[90] "Stubborn like Sisyphus," lines 11ff., dated September 1985, in *Pencil Letter*, p. 58, tr. Helen Szamuely with Richard McKane.
[91] "Crafty old man," Small Zone, April 1985, in ibid., p. 52; tr. Carol Rumens.
[92] Sonnet 20, lines 5–6, quoted earlier in text.
[93] "The damp here," in *Pencil Letter*, p. 62; tr. H. Szamuely with R. McKane.

ings each of their ingenious, crystalline forms is unique. In their vulnerable transience they are charged with an ironically potent lyric intensity. At such subjective moments of pain, anxiety, and loneliness, poetry gave the prisoner hope and self-confidence, while her insights gained affective political expression in language and forms that moved others.

Resistance to psychological manipulation by KGB tactics required total self-control in preserving one's composure and free will. Family visits were often canceled as punishments for trumped-up charges to destabilize the political prisoners' resolve to resist oppression. The women of the Small Zone held hunger strikes in protest at canceled rights to visits (and the withholding of correspondence) whenever one of them was targeted. Their actions in mutual support were accompanied by written protests at the violations of prison regulations, and on many such occasions a poem from Ratushinskaya helped to bolster group solidarity. While all the political prisoners in the Small Zone made sacrifices for their rights to justice, Ratushinskaya's youth and religious premises, that one is never alone in God's presence and the soul is immortal, seem to have inspired a disregard for personal welfare in feats of endurance and resistance that were considered as reckless as they were courageous. This is most evident in the poetry of the hunger strike.

## "TO ENDURE WHATEVER I MUST": POETRY OF THE HUNGER STRIKE

The lyrics Ratushinskaya composed and memorized in the unheated cells of the camp's internal prison where she endured solitary confinement and a regime of starvation rations, without warm clothing or bedding, are rooted in the specific situation and often reflect states of physical weakness, pain, and fear. Fasting, as many religious ascetics have long been aware, can induce acute sensory perceptions. In the memoir written after her release, she explained:

> Hunger strikes have the effect of sharpening your sense of smell and perception of colour, your eyesight becomes keener and the small details of your environment stand out in unusually bold relief. I remember standing once over our well, and studying a yellowed poplar leaf in its dark brown waters: and this leaf seemed so breathtakingly beautiful, that I deliberately delayed dipping my bucket into the water.[94]

In the most severe conditions of the punishment cells, Ratushinskaya also reported "incredibly vivid and beautiful dreams ... marvellous music" and

---

[94] *Grey Is the Colour of Hope*, p. 122.

"delicious aromas."[95] She reported that in nearly all of those dreams she had sensed that she could fly and never experienced such dreams anywhere except in the extreme sensory deprivation of this regime (known by the acronym SHIZO):

And I flew in my dreams and shuddered
When I thought my time would come soon.
But the voice had spoken: "If not I, then who?"
It had spoken so long ago—
I had no choice in the matter.[96]

Her resistance was strengthened by its expression. She felt obliged and inspired to continue the resistance she had practiced when starting out on her "predestined road" as a dissident poet.[97] As the shivering prisoner covered her shoulders in rags, she asked herself "how many such evenings to live through," and reaffirmed her decision to trust that she need "not fear to grow wings since" she was "destined for life after all!" and, if not in this world, then hereafter. If she were to find "a paper boat bearing a blessing" on the river of forgetfulness—"You must die"—that would have to be accepted: "Is that so distressing? / You just feel slightly sick, / As you enter the stain on the wall."[98] Ratushinskaya later reported that when she had become delirious in SHIZO, she had felt that she "was being drawn into the shapeless stain on one of the walls, and clutched at the [water]pipe to avoid being sucked into that dark patch" identified with oblivion.[99] On that occasion she saw herself literally and figuratively holding on. Yet, even "as the heart is giving out, and the hands grow weaker," she wrote that she would go on flying in her dreams.[100] She had put her faith in God, and afterward she rationalized her suffering by articulating her belief that it was "no great sorrow to lose one's life":

That, which is the most important, comes later, and in the meantime, it's as though I'm in training for it, testing myself in different situations. And I have no values other than to tell no lies, and to endure whatever I must.[101]

Other political prisoners had explained that the regime's "perpetual lies" were worse than physical torture. This was why the best strategy for resis-

[95] Ibid., p. 166.
[96] "It's not that I'm scared," lines 13ff., dated SHIZO, June 1985, in *Pencil Letter*, p. 55; tr. R. McKane with H. Szamuely. Cf. *Pencil Letter*, p. 58, for repetition of the self question: "If not I, then who?" in a poem dated September 1985.
[97] *Pencil Letter*, p. 18; tr. R. McKane with H. Szamuely.
[98] Ibid., p. 37, dated from SHIZO November 1984; tr. Alan Myers.
[99] *Grey Is the Colour of Hope*, pp. 243–44.
[100] "It's not that I'm scared," in *Pencil Letter*, p. 55.
[101] *Grey Is the Colour of Hope*, p. 206.

tance was telling the truth and facing it. This principle, essential for any moral poet, helped Ratushinskaya to understand that prison was less to be feared than other people. Self-regard, dignity, and honesty would enable the women in the Small Zone to "remain free" to be themselves so long as they remained free from fear.[102]

The hunger strike was a dangerous yet politically effective tactic to express the prisoners' freedom from fear. Gambling with their lives in this way reinforced a sense of moral superiority and strength of will among those who appeared weakest or most disadvantaged. Like her defiance in continuing to write poetry to tell the truth, the strike was seen as a form of self-defense. The reckless courage of these political prisoners' protests made them feared and admired throughout the camp. In a devotional poem dated from SHIZO, December 1984—"Isn't it time to return?"—the poet spoke on behalf of fellow prisoners for whom life had been reduced to a pointless cycle of suffering. In these circumstances, she argued, they had earned the right to die. The form of the poem implies a debate with God on the analogy (but in different contexts) of several biblical psalms that also ask "How long, O Lord?"[103]

> Isn't it time, O Father
> To return home from distant shores?
> . . .
> How often must we die before You say "yes"?

We, she argues, have "overstayed our welcome" and "paid our debts in full":

> For ourselves and also for others.
> A hundred times betrayed, all is fulfilled—what more?
> Which avalanche must we stop with our shoulders?
> Into what struggle must we hurl
> Ourselves between two enemies?
> And which sky must we hold up?

These are the impossible tasks of epic myth. "On every path" and in all societies, prisoners are identified by the look in their eyes; they are shot against every wall "without trial."

> Our horses are waiting, Father,
> Our pastures are bare!

and there is nothing left to support life.

---

[102] Ibid., pp. 129; 39; and cf. pp. 132–33.
[103] Cf. Psalm 13; see also psalm singing by other prisoners in SHIZO, ibid., p. 247.

Look—we have gone down all the appointed roads,

and, specifically, also left monumental words of testimony:

> And have carved here on stone
> All the words that need to be said
> For the right to go
> Without a backward look.[104]

Like Roland the poet argues her case for a tactical withdrawal from the battle of life, yet her words also testify to her literary strategy of resistance and the consoling thought that she has written.

Another poem, dated the previous month from the Small Zone, had voiced one side of a personal dialogue with her "uncompromising reason" urging her intellectual self not to weaken at the thought of all that must yet be endured. (There is no evidence that she had direct knowledge of Boethius's work.) She insisted that reason, truth, and argument must prevail and might yet "preserve" her as they guided her life's journey.

> Preserve me, my uncompromising reason,
> Don't let the reins go now, only half-way.
>
> A long time yet we must fight off together
> The suffocating nights, the prison airs,
> The prison dreams—hallucinations, almost,
> ...
> Not knowing how long the term, and not possessing
> The right yet to declare our strength is done.[105]

This appeal to "reason" concludes: "Keep me from harm—and I'll watch over you." This is the bargain of a rational prisoner with hope. A year later, however, Ratushinskaya was weaker physically, and she became convinced that personal integrity and mental self-control ("the reins" that had enabled Boethius and every other thinker in prison to maintain or argue for "freedom from fear") might not suffice. She came to believe that the KGB officers were no longer just trying to break her will. After the traditional one-day hunger strike to mark Political Prisoners' day in October 1985, Ratushinskaya was committed alone to the icy punishment cell and realized that she was unlikely to survive the physical torment of this regime, designed to break psychological resistance. The previous "game" of cat and mouse between the authorities and the political prisoners had depended on a fine

---

[104] "Isn't it time to return?," in *Pencil Letter*, p. 39; tr. H. Szamuely with R. McKane.
[105] "But only not to think," in *Pencil Letter*, p. 38, Small Zone, November 1984; tr. D. McDuff.

balance between the authorities' fear of bad publicity (if anything untoward should happen to a known political prisoner defending her rights under the Soviet penal code) and that prisoner's willingness to risk her health and life. By October 1985 she was exhausted, and it seemed that the KGB was indifferent to international reactions to her plight. She concluded that the authorities had decided to let her die from cold and hunger.

> No, I decided, I won't let that happen. I have had enough of your punishment cells and your intrusive hands. You want to finish me off? Then the sooner, the better! I am leaving your walls—I'm free of you! Do you really think that I shall try to hang on to a life which you have turned into torture.[106]

Like Bunyan and Roland, she had calculated the political advantage of her own death as a statement about her life and values, and later elaborated in dramatic tones on her reasoning with herself, and the conversations she had had with her tormentors:

> I said no word to him, of course, but these were my thoughts. The warder escorting me sighs solicitously: "Oh, Irina! Do you really intend to die?"
> "That depends on the will of God. But this is the last time they'll torture anyone.... This time they've overreached themselves. I'll be their last victim."[107]

She survived, and after her release recorded the suicide of another prisoner, Galya, whom she saw as a displaced projection of her own story and for whom she would testify upon her own restoration to life as a writer:

> Right until the evening I hear the next door cell being swabbed out. There must have been a lot of blood. Nobody will be held responsible for this death, and it will not be reported by the world press: it will pass unnoticed, nobody will know. She'll be written off with a convincing diagnosis, the records will be clean, and another nameless, numbered grave will be dug in Mordovian soil, to be powdered with grey snow from a grey sky. A few years later it will be bulldozed, to make room for more.[108]

Ratushinskaya implies that Galya's death was an act of despair, yet being prepared to sacrifice one's own life in such a situation was also a paradoxical

---

[106] *Grey Is the Colour of Hope*, p. 280.

[107] Ibid., p. 281.

[108] Ibid., p. 282. According to her memoir, Ratushinskaya survived, after drifting in and out of consciousness for two weeks, because a new camp commandant convinced her that he would not have sanctioned this illegal torture and begged her not to make him responsible for her death. Subsequently, conditions in the Small Zone improved, the prisoners were no longer subject to solitary confinement in the punishment cells, and they ended their hunger strike protests.

tactic to preserve the integrity of the self, and make a final statement of independence to confound the oppressor. As Gramsci had realized in his cannibals story, there were physical limits to mental freedom after all.[109]

## PARTING—"AND THE RAILS LIKE TWO KNIVES / SLICE THE WHITE DISTANCE"

The cosmic scale of innumerable personal losses is nevertheless felt in the
yearning tones of "The stars have flown" where vast expanses of "the snows
of all Russias" are set against the significance of the fall of a single snowflake
upon the poet's shoulder. The speaker notes that the opportunity to wish
upon a melting snowflake might foretell a miracle. So when another flake
"rebelled and broke from the flock / And settled like a bird awkwardly on
[her] shoulder," she imagined, "It waits for the ineffable word, is slow to
melt" and lets her "whisper hastily, stumblingly—/ You know just what."
This stumbling movement and ineffable word create a moment of possibility and hope. The prisoner's monologue continues to address an absent intimate friend and concludes with ironic observations that acknowledge the
idealism and neediness of the "eternally young."

> Over us December bursts its banks.
> It is brave as a Hussar, its generosity is without reproach.
> . . .
> But we are so eternally young
> That the snows of all Russias are not enough for our wishes.[110]

The landscape beyond the prison and Russian folk traditions also fostered links with the outside world and feature in two other lyrics composed
in the camp prison during January 1986. In the "Song of Long Ago," the
speaker asks forgiveness from her little sister and brother for going alone to
a place unknown—"Beyond the Charred Forest"—to gather cranberries.
Counting the berries makes her oblivious to sorrow. "The first berry—/
Blood-drop from a bird" signified the "Preordained parting" of a pair of
swans; the second berry—"A girl's crimson blood"—meant that "Riding
Tartars" had loosed their arrows. But the third berry related to the future:

> Tomorrow, my intended
> Begins his journey,

---

[109] See chapter 2. The imprisoned lawyer Hans Litten sang an early nineteenth-century political
protest song—"Die Gedanken sind frei"—when forced to contribute to the prison's celebrations for
Hitler's forty-sixth birthday. Litten committed suicide in Dachau concentration camp in 1938 after
being tortured. See further Benjamin Carter Hett, *Crossing Hitler: The Man Who Put the Nazis on
the Witness Stand* (Oxford: Oxford University Press, 2008).

[110] *Pencil Letter*, p. 73, January 1986; tr. R. McKane with H. Szamuely.

To return or not—
If God's will be done.[111]

The speaker refuses to go near this berry for fear of dreaming about its disastrous potential by analogy with the deadly significations of the other berries. However, in the last poem from this period of internal imprisonment, the folkloric associations and symbolism of an unknown forest that reached into the skies were transformed. In a new spirit of optimism, the speaker evoked an image of the heavens as a place of "echoing expanses of high ceilings" "where thoughts are arched, / Voices are unfamiliar" but "solemn vaults solicitously / Take us, like children, by the chin / And make us raise our eyes." This is a "conservatorium, refuge of windy strings," a place of safety and harmony, where—in spite of the poet's invisible suffering—imagination rekindles faith, and a "mystery hides behind the wall": the sky and the forest merge into a vast natural cathedral to which the speaker will go, in life or death, for relief:

I'll come to you with a weary heart,
. . .
As into a dark-blue forest of half-remembered tales,
Where everything has always ended well.[112]

Recourse to subjects from the natural world—imagined or remembered—provided relief for many prisoners and symbolic links to transcendent forces. In the "Song of the Wave," the inevitability of suffering and death in time—past, present, and future—is represented by the voice of the wave that addresses a bereft figure standing on the shore. The occasion for the poem seems specific, but the message of the song of the sea is universal, indifferent, and inevitably turbulent:

He has left you behind and come to me—
So how then am I to blame?
Yes, stand all you like at Whitestone Lee—
The ending is still the same.

Don't torture your eyes with the salt sea-spray,
Don't walk by the water's hem.
For of course as I'm breaking, your tracks I'll erase
Like all traces left there by men.

This perpetual eradicating motion of the sea conflates the effects of death and time, but there is some consolation for the bereaved. "You never will see

---

[111] "Song of Long Ago," January 1986, in *Pencil Letter*, p. 74; tr. Lyn Coffin with Sergei Shishkoff.
[112] "The echoing expanses . . . ," January 1986, in *Pencil Letter*, p. 75; tr. Daniel Weissbort.

him, but till you are grey, / Till the final pain in your breast." The wave will make the dead fisherman comfortable, by working "silken cushions of sea-grass" and pressing kisses on his mouth, but will "never call him to wake."[113] Only death will reunite parted lovers.

This was one of the last poems written in the Small Zone. In the KGB prison at Kiev in August and September 1986, Ratushinskaya remained hopeful of release on account of the new outlook and tone of the Gorbachev government but uncertain whether this would be a false or genuine release since she still had eight years of her sentence left to serve. Because she was badgered to make an appeal for clemency, which she refused, she feared that at her reunion with her husband "the way [would] be barred / By the gate of our new separation"—perhaps the final journey. In which case, readiness is all:

> Start clashing, keys: our souls won't be crushed
> By a return ticket's stamp or two.
> The time will come—for five minutes, bitter, hushed,
> How much credit, in centuries, will we be due?[114]

Several poems had expressed a yearning for life yet also figured death in the sadness that had followed all her fellow prisoners' farewells to their families as the visitors' train departed: "And the rails like two knives / Slice the white distance."[115] In her penultimate prison poem the dissident poet addressed the "Motherland" that was "growing into [her] ribcage," as if she were already dead, buried, and decomposed. The prospect of release seemed absurd. Yet again the prisoner contemplated counting out time: in breaths, groans, nights, and years, while bending over poems that had to be hidden from warders who controlled symbolic and literal keys. It was "so difficult to be alive" that she could more easily contemplate the grasses closing in over her body and the spirit being wafted beyond the clouds, except that, once more, she asked for time to write "the most important line" of verse, which is constantly deferred and one of the consolations (and frustrations) of writing:

> Wait, don't sound the all-clear
> I've yet to write the most
> Important line.[116]

---

[113] "Song of the Wave," Small Zone, June 1986, in *Pencil Letter*, p. 76; tr. Alan Myers.

[114] "Rendezvous," KGB Prison, Kiev, 13 August 1986, ibid., p. 79; tr. Lyn Coffin with Sergei Shishkoff.

[115] "We have learnt to say goodbye (for Valery Senderov)," dated from SHIZO, November 1985, ibid., p. 65; tr. H. Szamuely with R. McKane.

[116] "Motherland, you're growing," in *Pencil Letter*, p. 80, KGB Prison, Kiev, September 1986; tr. H. Szamuely with R. McKane.

## THE PROVOCATION AND THE CONSOLATION
## OF POETRY: "TO TELL NO LIES"

Ratushinskaya's lyric verses are rooted in the situations she experienced and direct responses to them, both at a personal level—as a poet in Russian, condemned for writing poetry as "anti-Soviet agitation"—and as the representative voice of a group of dissidents in the Small Zone of a labor camp. The poet articulated their fears and hopes and recorded the dangers and oppression as well as the warmth and humanity of their enforced communal life. She had testified to her own and others' suffering and endurance, their battles against lies, hypocrisy, cynicism, and sadism. She wrote to console herself and others, evoking memories and cultural traditions by drawing the normal world of ordinary human endeavor and personal responsibility into the amoral ambit of the labor camp, its internal prison, and punishment cells. She had lingered over language that evoked ways to count time, configure symbols of flight and release, or images of beauty and unique structures in nature, such as snowflakes and cloudscapes that connected her to immense outdoor spaces, and that she forged into links between her experience of the prison and the free world beyond. Poetry was a reaction to oppression before and after her arrest. But that is also partly why she wrote as a Russian poet within a tradition established early in the twentieth century by the "quartet" of Mandelstam, Akhmatova, Tsvetayeva, and Pasternak. One of Mandelstam's translators into English explained how even by standing "in defiance of the currents of his time," including the literary tastes promoted in Stalin's Soviet Union, a poet gained "political status and impact." Mandelstam had remarked to his wife that there was no other regime that killed people for writing poetry: "Only in our country is poetry respected."[117] In a poem addressed to the spirit of O. M. [Osip Mandelstam], "Who left neither son nor home, / Lifted into the blizzard in the midst of a line," Ratushinskaya's poet-speaker recognizes that because he had "blessed" her, through his poetry, "for this frozen journey" she was not afraid to look death, the "driver of the black horses in the eye-sockets"—neither was she frightened by "the circling and trembling of strange birds / Nor the rumbling of the last cloudy limit" in her own premonitions of mortality. She envisaged that like some classical shade from the Elysian fields, Mandelstam, her favorite poet, would guide and protect her as he came out "to the riverbank to greet" her. It was comforting to think that he was waiting "by the edge of the murky water" and that as she approached death he would "walk on the firmament" giving her his hand, "so that oblivion / Does not splash up to my knees."[118]

---

[117] Osip Mandelstam, *50 Poems*, tr. Bernard Meares (New York: Persea Books, 1977), p. 20.
[118] "O.M.," August 1983, in *Dance with a Shadow*, p. 50.

The poetic tradition of resistance was upholding her and her art. As Joseph Brodsky noted in his introduction to Ratushinskaya's lyrics in 1984: "Any art, and especially poetic art, which has to do with language, is always simultaneously older and longer-lasting than the state.... Hence the state's fear and hatred of a genuine poet, its jealousy and hatred for that which will outlive it."[119]

On 9 October 1986, Ratushinskaya was finally released from prison and driven home by the KGB. On that day she wrote her last prison poem; it depicted a natural image of delicate trepidation and questioned the miracle of human identity, yearning for life and inspiration. The prevailing water imagery—"A ray of forgotten light / Gingerly tests the water"—reflects the amorphous, shifting, essential wholeness of nature and creation:

> The heron walks in the marsh,
> Its legs like a pair of compasses.
> The cold, like a greenish shadow,
> Lies upon the forest.
> The air, dense and grey,
> Itself lies down under its wing.
> Above is the twilit sky,
> . . .
>
> A ray of forgotten light
> Gingerly tests the water.
> Now our endless evening
> Has gone off on its circular course.
> Beasts, people and birds,
> And voices, and specks of light—
> We pass through all like ripples,
> And each one disappears.
> Which of us will recur?
> Who will flow into whom?
> What do we need in this world
> To quench our thirst?[120]

The awkwardness of the heron's gait and the indeterminate status of the marsh (neither dry land nor water), the paradoxical substantiality of the dense, gray air that lies down like an animal beneath the heron's wing, and the twilight setting (neither day nor night), all symbolize the poet's liminal state. The circular motions of the earth, its diurnal course, and the ripples of

---

[119] *No, I'm Not Afraid*, p. 14.
[120] "The heron walks in the marsh," in *Pencil Letter*, p. 81, Kiev, 9 October 1986; tr. Daniel Weissbort.

light and water connect the present "now" with existential mysteries that haunt us especially after a crisis.

Like Boethius and her Russian predecessors, Ratushinskaya believed it was the poet's duty to tell the truth and that freedom and imprisonment were also states of mind.

> Like Mandelstam's swallow
> Parting falls towards the heart,
> Pasternak sends the rain,
> And Tsvetayeva—the wind.
> So that the Universe's turning may be achieved
> Without a false note,
> The word is needed—and poets alone
> Are answerable for this.[121]

For writing poetry, she had been persecuted by a regime that maintained power by lies, fear, injustice, and violence. She promised Russia

> In the accursedness of your victories,
> In the anguish of your impotence,
> In the nausea of your hangover—

to "still come and stand before you / and look into your eyes."[122] As an active Christian (aligned with Polish Roman Catholicism) and a freethinking physics graduate, she had challenged the norms of state institutions and power but sought to maintain justice and human rights within the letter of the political constitution and legal system. Ratushinskaya's fellow prisoners in the Small Zone issued an appeal to the world in 1984 to draw attention to her mistreatment, describing her as a "woman of clear and incisive intellect, a courageous and active defender of human rights" whose "poems have flown to every corner of the country like swallows of freedom."[123] Before long, they were translated and distributed throughout the English-speaking world. Her poetry was both a provocation and a consolation. It caused her persecution and then became the sign of her resistance, providing a means to strengthen endurance and engage with worlds, past and present, beyond the control of the state. Finally, it also redeemed her from fear, and from imprisonment. Yet it was not necessary to be a poet to be consoled and uplifted by poetry. She knew as a reader of poetry that literary strategies of resistance were not confined to writers. She therefore recited different kinds of poetry (not only her own) to prisoners in neighboring cells and on the

---

[121] *No, I'm Not Afraid*, p. 139, 25 April [1984?]; tr. David McDuff.
[122] "For the cry from the well," [5 July 1984], ibid., p. 141.
[123] For text of appeal and signatories, see ibid., pp. 65–66.

prison transport train. She thereby provided comfort and pleasure, as well as a new voice and outlook to those who identified with and repeated the ideas and feelings expressed in both vigorous and reflective lyrics.[124] In these actions she was consciously responding not only to a Russian tradition of lyric poetry but also to ancient traditions of the functions of art with moral precepts for delightful and prophetic teaching. Poetry in prison sustained her integrity and extended her humanity.

The *communard* French Resistance leader and the Russian dissident responded to their different conditions in captivity by writing lyric verses for similar strategic reasons. They sought and claimed to find, in the order and stability of verse forms, the resources that enabled them to survive and represent themselves. Lyric poetry has always been seen as a sign of humane values and personally expressed human experience. (The affective, expressive powers of lyric may transcend time and place because they are appealing and easily transmitted in memorable short forms, even in translations that do not retain the sonorities of the original language but may retain cross-cultural memories of readers' native or acquired languages.) These prison poets combined intellectual pursuits with aesthetic pleasure that confirmed their values, and gave solace, by concocting new worlds and subjective identities from memories, dreams, and shareable cultural experiences, including other literature. They wrote to reconfigure and control reactions to the actual world of fear, pain, and uncertainty.[125] Cassou's lyric poetry created an alternative reality in vivid, often surreal imagery drawn from his dreams and memories of life and art. The sights and sonorities that preoccupied his life of the mind enabled him to withdraw from his cell into another ingenious space within. Yet poetry was not merely a retreat from the world of the prison but also a means of escaping its horrors. He only wrote down his sonnets after the work of composition had done its work in him. By contrast, Ratushinskaya's salvation by poetry was deferred until her work was published in the West, and her life was saved by the adroit political manipulation of her poems in English translations. In both cases, publication by others was instrumental in circulating news of the poets' resistance in captivity as well as preserving their lyric self-impression.

[124] She was aware that Mandelstam had read Pushkin's poetry to the three guards who escorted him and his wife into internal exile, calling them "the scholars of Pushkin" and a "tribe of young lovers of gleaming-toothed verse" (*50 Poems*, pp. 87 and 110, Voronezh, June 1935); cf. *Grey Is the Colour of Hope*, p. 29, and *In the Beginning*, pp. 133, 303–4. On the train transporting different kinds of prisoners, mostly ordinary criminals, she was invited by some to recite a poem and chose one that she had dedicated to Andrei Sakharov: "Don't attempt to coerce" (*Grey Is the Colour of Hope*, p. 18). Cf. *No, I'm Not Afraid*, p. 66.

[125] Cf. "Moments of memory of the unsurvived summer / Came to me and stood outside the door, / Simple and solemn as children," and "What do you remember of us, my sad one, / As you send me weightless dreams?," in *Dance with a Shadow*, pp. 41, 53.

Cassou deflected opportunities in later life to gloss his prison poems and experiences, yet, like Ratushinskaya, he had composed poetry in the midst of personal suffering that was known to reflect (directly and indirectly) contemporary events, thoughts, and feelings; readers understand that for both poets the pressures of the moment during captivity became creative sparks and therefore that whatever emerged from these conditions has a special claim for attention and human interest. After her release, Ratushinskaya wrote two memoirs, and the writing that came later, with hindsight and in safety, was different. The poet and her readers knew the crisis of oppression and confinement was over; yet readers were also stimulated to thoughtful and sympathetic engagement with her insights to which they granted the authority of experience. Writing against the grain of a repressive ideology and resisting persecution from a subjective viewpoint in lyric or prose narrative can be an objective contribution to the ethics and politics of prison writing. The final section of this book examines the strategies of one former prisoner whose name became a byword for the authority of experience as he struggled for forty years to interpret his and other prisoners' experiences of the Holocaust in different kinds of writing and analysis.

# PART III

# Testimony for Mankind

CHAPTER 6

# With Hindsight and Beyond Resistance

Primo Levi, *If This Is a Man* (1947) and *Ad ora incerta*
(1947–86): Resisting the Demolition of a Man

Primo Levi's revisions of his experiences in Auschwitz stand alone. He wrote
with hindsight because during his thirteen months in Auschwitz he was unable to write: normal life was brutally suspended, and he poured all his
physical energies and intellect into the struggle to survive. Traumatic memories are especially persistent and Levi's various forms of memoir and reaction to his experiences have come to represent the most developed and sear-
ing Holocaust testimony that since the later 1940s has evolved in many
different forms.[1] Levi's writing epitomizes the ethical incentives of prison
writing as testimony for mankind that not only engages new readers but also
challenges them, going well beyond testimony as an end in itself. His own
life had been saved so he wrote not to defend or preserve any image of himself. The "millennial hatred" that had given rise to the so-called Final Solution had not been defeated at the end of the war and remained an existential
threat to humanity. Many people preferred not to examine either the reasons behind the policy or the practical means whereby a "civilized" society
had colluded in implementing a systematic campaign for the mass extermination of their fellow citizens. As time passed Levi's relationship with his

---

[1] The best guides to Primo Levi's works remain his own writings since he revisited the implications of his experiences at Auschwitz all the rest of his life. Besides Levi himself, Robert S. C. Gordon's *Primo Levi's Ordinary Virtues from Testimony to Ethics* (Oxford: Oxford University Press,
2001, rpt. 2003) has been an inspiration. For a variety of other valuable approaches, see further, Dan
Michman, *Holocaust Historiography: A Jewish Perspective; Conceptualizations, Terminology, Approaches and Fundamental Issues* (London: Vallentine Mitchell, 2003); Zoë Waxman, *Writing the
Holocaust: Identity, Testimony, Representation* (Oxford: Oxford University Press, 2006); and *Gray
Zones: Ambiguity and Compromise in the Holocaust and Its Aftermath*, ed. Jonathan Petropoulos
and John K. Roth (New York: Berghahn Books, 2005), in which Levi's works provide the substance
of the editorial narrative linking different sections. A standard biography is Ian Thomson, *Primo
Levi: A Life* (London: Hutchinson, 2002); I have also used the English translation of Myriam Anissimov's *Primo Levi: Tragedy of an Optimist* (London: Aurum Press, 1999); and there are many useful thematic approaches to Levi's writing in *The Cambridge Companion to Primo Levi*, ed. Robert S.
C. Gordon (Cambridge: Cambridge University Press, 2007).

readers and his capacity to recall his experiences changed. He tried different approaches to the same strategies as public knowledge of the atrocities became more widespread and attitudes to his subject matter gradually evolved. While it was vital to confront what had happened, it was even more urgent to understand and analyze how it had occurred for the sake of ensuring that it could never happen again. For forty years, Levi's unflinching moral integrity provided testimonies based on the evidence of his own experience, written in simple and accessible, but never sentimental, language.[2] He began, significantly, with lyric poetry in the first months after his epic journey home to Turin; he was searching for a way into a narrative that he had long feared would be rejected. Lyric was emotionally liberating and powerfully suggestive. He went on to address different audiences, writing personal memoir, short stories, essays, and several kinds of educational journalism; and he remained an occasional poet. Levi, an industrial chemist, became a writer specifically in order to tell the terrible story that dominated his life and that he insisted had momentous significance for everyone. He reframed and analyzed these themes for the rest of his life in different literary forms and contexts because his sense of justice, duty to history, and hopes and fears for the future of humanity—his resistance to the distortions and apathy that had created Nazi persecution—never weakened. For all the calm clarity of the scientist's prose, Levi also wrestled with his understanding of a poet's moral duty to make a difference in the world. There were no precedents for his historic situation, even in the arbitrary tyranny of Stalin's USSR, and very few parallels possible with the experiences of other prisoners discussed so far here. Nevertheless, the cultural traditions Levi invoked to help him share his story with a worldwide readership included the Bible and the epic poetry of Dante, thereby exploiting a circle of influence in which representation of the experience of prisoners at the margins of life and death can draw from and feed back into established literary traditions and conventions.

At the end of Canto 26 in Dante's *Inferno,* the poet's master, Virgil, conjures the spirits of dead heroes to speak from the flames of their funeral pyre. Ulysses tells the ancient and medieval Italian poets about his last voyage: how the ship was overwhelmed by huge seas whipped up by a whirlwind

[2] Elie Wiesel's testimony from Auschwitz is often compared with Levi's, but their religious and cultural sensibilities were very different from each other's. The contrast may be considered analogous to that between popular conceptions of classical and romantic sensibilities. Levi had no contact with Wiesel's northern European Yiddish-Ashkenazi culture until he entered the camp and little sympathy with the remnants of Hasidic mysticism as reactions to the Enlightenment that had flourished, especially in the villages of many central and eastern parts of European Jewry. He remained suspicious of all forms of religious enthusiasm and cultivated an ethical, rationalist approach to Judaism often associated with the medieval scholar and scientist Moses Maimonides.

that blew off an alien shore far beyond the company's normal range of navigation. When the whirlwind struck, their ship went down "in a roaring smother / With all the waters . . . as pleased Another, / And over our heads the hollow seas closed up." Ulysses had made this journey to "rummage through the world exploring it" in order to prove (or test and provide evidence of) "all human worth and wickedness." He claimed to have been driven by a restless itch that no family ties or feelings could overcome.[3] In chapter 11 of Primo Levi's *If This Is a Man,* the author describes the moment this canto came to mind, "who knows how or why," in Auschwitz, during a brief respite from hard labor when his workmate had said that he wanted to learn Italian.[4] When Levi returned home to his family in Italy, after the war, he found that the need to tell the story of his camp experiences, to make other people "participate in it," had taken on "the character of an immediate and violent impulse"—a compulsion beyond Ulysses' "restless itch—that competed," as he said, with "other elementary needs." As he began to resume normal life he found himself talking about the whirlwind that had struck his life to anyone who would listen, including strangers on the train as he commuted to and from work.[5] Like the epic stories of antiquity, this oral tradition of his narrative gradually took on a fixed form, and in periods snatched from breaks at work and in evenings at home, Levi wrote down the story of his metaphorical shipwreck in the depths of that alien world located far beyond any normal means of moral navigation: Auschwitz. Many writers have used the sea as a symbol for restless exploration, for dangers in life through uncharted waters and (like Boethius and several other prison writers) for exploration of the human condition. Like Dante's Ulysses, Levi explored the unique and alien world of his experience—the Nazi concentration camp (or the Lager, as he persisted in designating it)—to provide evidence, tested upon himself, of the human condition. Like Dante's Virgil he conjured the spirits of the dead whose funeral pyres had lit up the skies above Monowitz-Buna and Birkenau, in Upper Silesia, to testify

[3] *The Comedy of Dante Alighieri: Hell (L'Inferno),* tr. Dorothy L. Sayers (Penguin Books, 1949), pp. 235–37. See further Judith Kelly, *Primo Levi: Recording and Reconstruction in the Testimonial Literature* (Market Harborough: Troubador Publishing, 2000), pp. 65–69; Risa B. Sodi, *A Dante of Our Time: Primo Levi and Auschwitz* (New York: Peter Lang, 1990), pp. 50–51, 60–79.

[4] *If This Is a Man* and *The Truce,* tr. Stuart Woolf (London: Sphere Books, 1987), pp. 118–21. All further references incorporated in the text are from this edition. The standard title in editions published in the United States is *Survival in Auschwitz.* For full bibliographical details about the publication of Levi's works, see Roger Eliot Stoddard, "Primo Levi," *Book Collector,* 55 (2006), 525–54, a reference I owe to Hugh Adlington; and *Cambridge Companion to Primo Levi,* pp. 189–99.

[5] See Levi's note to a stage version of *If This Is a Man* (Turin: Einaudi, 1966), pp. 5–8, translated by Sharon Wood and reprinted in Primo Levi, *The Black Hole of Auschwitz,* ed. Marco Belpoliti (Cambridge: Polity Press, 2005), pp. 23–27 at 24. He also elaborated on this description in an interview with Anthony Rudolf in 1986; see Primo Levi, *The Voice of Memory: Interviews 1961–87,* ed. Marco Belpoliti and Robert Gordon (Cambridge: Polity Press, 2001), pp. 23–33, at 27.

to readers beyond his personal reach in "a speaking tongue vibrant to frame language" that might adequately express this "abomination" (p. 118). Levi returned to this task in several different forms with different emphases in each of three major works of testimony between 1947 and 1986.

*If This Is a Man*, first published in 1947 but not widely disseminated until a second edition in 1958, was self-consciously framed as a survivor's memoir, and the earliest parts to be written—he began at the end, with the last ten days in the camp infirmary prior to liberation by the Soviet Red Army in January 1945—take the form of dated journal entries from those momentous days. As the book grew, it became more than the sum of its parts, engaging readers in consideration of specific moral issues, and enlarging on the strict narrative—which remained the core of the book—with the author's retrospective commentary. His wife helped him to organize the episodic chapters into a coherent whole. As a professional scientist and fully aware of the importance of the credibility of the witness in any form of testimony, Levi tried to write about people and events he knew from firsthand experience. He was aware that exaggeration and hearsay could undermine his primary function: "to furnish documentation for a quiet study of certain aspects of the human mind."[6] Levi's voice in this book is that of a thoughtful writer: compassionate, not dispassionate; mostly calm and slow to anger, but not unemotional.[7] The literary qualities of his book make it more than a memoir but no less of a historical document. As he indicated in 1986, his memories of books had made it possible for him "to re-establish a link with the past, saving it from oblivion and reinforcing [his] identity."[8] Recurrent imagery of shipwreck, the precision and vitality of other well-placed similes and literary allusions, the juxtaposition of details, careful control of verb tenses, the representation of direct and reported speech, and the pace of narrative development all indicate Levi's broad literary culture and rhetorical prowess. The deployment of these resources is unobtrusive and discreet and fulfills his purpose not merely to "tell our story" but also to make readers share and "participate" in it. Although Levi was careful to restrict this first narrative to his own testimony, the clarity of his prose and its spare eloquence impart a compelling, universal quality to his story. The symbolism of the prisoner's unconscious choice of Dante's Ulysses canto as an appro-

---

[6] *If This Is a Man*, preface, p. 15. For a succinct yet detailed account of the personal, political, and literary contexts, see Ian Thomson, "Writing *If This Is a Man*," in *Primo Levi The Austere Humanist*, ed. Joseph Farrell (Oxford: Peter Lang, 2004), pp. 141–60.

[7] See, e.g., his persona's response to Kuhn's prayer prior to the last selections for the gas in October 1944, *If This Is a Man*, pp. 135–36.

[8] On Levi's appreciation of the uses of "culture," especially his own application of the Ulysses canto, and the value of his memories of books in preserving his sense of personal identity in Auschwitz, see *The Drowned and The Saved*, tr. Raymond Rosenthal (London: Sphere Books, 1989), p. 112.

priate text for demonstrating the best use of the Italian language was a revelation to him in his real inferno. Subsequently, it also stands in symbolic relationship to Levi's ethical concerns as a Holocaust survivor and writer.[9]

## "HERE, LISTEN . . . OPEN YOUR EARS AND
## YOUR MIND, YOU HAVE TO UNDERSTAND"

Levi and contemporary Italian readers would have studied this canto from
the *Inferno* at school, and despite the frustration he felt at the "hole" in his
memory, which prevented his total recovery of the text, Primo (as I shall call
his narrative's prisoner persona) was apparently able to recall and recite
many lines that he translated into French for his companion as they walked
to fetch their unit's soup ration. "So on the open sea I set forth." Primo comments on the subtlety of Dante's verb as connoting "strong and audacious"
action: "It is a chain which has been broken, it is throwing oneself on the
other side of a barrier" (p. 118). In the context of their situation ("we know
the impulse well") Primo becomes anxious and excited as familiar words
that had furnished his mind since childhood, take on new meaning. Addressing his companion (who may also stand for Levi's later reader), Primo
urges: "Here, listen . . . open your ears and your mind, you have to understand, for my sake":

> Think of your breed; for brutish ignorance
> Your mettle was not made; you were made men
> To follow after knowledge and excellence. (p. 119)

This is both an indictment of the Nazi persecutors who had brutalized
themselves by treating fellow beings as less than human (*Untermenschen*),
and, as Dante's Ulysses intends, encouragement to men adrift beyond the
navigational limits of the known moral and physical world.

Primo says that he was overwhelmed by his new understanding of this
passage, which he seemed to be "hearing" for the first time: "like the blast of
a trumpet, like the voice of God. For a moment I forget who I am and where
I am." Such similitudes and this elevated tone, rare in *If This Is a Man*, sug-

---

[9] The theological implications of "holocaust" are unfortunate, but the word has become widely
used and understood in its special application in this context; for a convenient summary of the historiography, see my note 1 (Michman, *Holocaust Historiography*). Cf. the unintended consequences
of Dante's medieval Christian vision of Hell in a series of graduated punishments for sinners. Levi
did not infer any guilt as attaching to the victims of the Nazi extermination camps from the logic of
his allusion to Dante's epic. Risa Sodi points out that these allusions are "a heuristic device intended
to initiate the reader into the *univers concentrationnaire* and not an overarching metaphor" intended
to define Levi's experience: "The Rhetoric of the *Univers Concentrationnaire*," in *Memory and Mastery: Primo Levi as Writer and Witness*, ed. Roberta S. Kremer (Albany: State University of New
York Press, 2001), p. 41. See also Gordon, *Primo Levi's Ordinary Virtues* (2003), pp. 68–70.

gest intuitions that transcend the gap between the normality of the free writer's world and the horror of the enslaved prisoners' liminal existence in Auschwitz. When his companion had asked him to repeat the verses, Primo thought that he might just be humoring him, yet perhaps it could mean more:

> Despite the wan translation and the pedestrian, rushed commentary, he has received the message, he has felt that it has to do with him, that it has to do with all men who toil, and with us in particular; and that it has to do with us two, who dare to reason of these things with the poles for the soup [kettle] on our shoulders. (p. 120)

The Jewish agnostic, like the Christian-humanist poet, had designs on his readers: here Primo's impulse to share his insight with his companion; later, Levi's insistence on testifying to readers in shared cultural codes—including epic poetry and similes for the voice of a deity he could not believe in—that bear witness to the highest ethical values.[10] Such overt didacticism is rare in this book, but in the author's preface (and elsewhere) there are asides that explain why he was writing. Primo had detained his companion because there was something more important than soup, even in Auschwitz.

> It is vitally necessary and urgent that he listen, that he understand . . . before it is too late; tomorrow he or I might be dead, or we might never see each other again. I must tell him, I must explain to him about the Middle Ages, about the . . . unexpected anachronism, but still more, something gigantic that I myself have only just seen, in a flash of intuition, perhaps the reason for our fate, for our being here today. (p. 121)

The specific intuition here refers to the medieval poet's concept of the will of God in the pagan Ulysses' anachronistic description of their ship tossed about so "that the prow went down, as pleased Another."[11] However, throughout the book, as will be seen, there are more subtle and repeated emphases on the difficulties of understanding and communication between individual human beings.

In the preface, Auschwitz is defined as the logical conclusion of a commonly held conviction that "every stranger is an enemy," which "lies deep down like some latent infection" and normally "betrays itself only in random, disconnected acts, and does not lie at the base of a system of reason."

---

[10] Cf. "Sunset at Fossoli" the last three lines are quoted from Catullus: death is unending night; Levi, *Collected Poems*, tr. Ruth Feldman and Brian Swann (London: Faber and Faber, 1988), p. 15, 7 February 1946; cf. *Ad ora incerta* (Milan: Garzanti Editore, 1984; 2nd ed., 1988), p. 21.

[11] Cf. Lina N. Insana, *Arduous Tasks: Primo Levi, Translation, and the Transmission of Holocaust Testimony* (Toronto: University of Toronto Press, 2009), pp. 110–22, esp. 114–15 and 262–63, n. 31, on Levi's insight into Jewish history and Nazi anti-Semitism through this part of Dante's text.

But when—as happened in Nazi Germany—this "latent infection" is carried rigorously to its philosophical end, then "there is the Lager": the extermination camp.[12] Levi's fear, as witness, survivor, and ethical writer, was that "so long as the conception subsists, the conclusion remains to threaten us"—all of us. This sustained the urgency of his concern that "the story of the death camps should be understood by everyone as a sinister alarm-signal," to rouse all of humanity (p. 15). Levi emphasized here that "everyone" should understand—it is a personal responsibility—because (as he well knew) any unthinking surrender to collective prejudice leads to inhumanity, and in the unprecedented case of the Nazi regime's organized corruption of language and reason—twin signs of human beings—to ruthless and systematic genocide.[13] In later life, Levi identified his "vitally necessary and urgent" impulse to understand and repeat this story with the action of Coleridge's obsessive Ancient Mariner, who represents another traumatized survivor. The title and epigraph of his second volume of poetry, *Ad ora incerta*, translate the words of Coleridge's mariner, who is tormented by feelings of guilt at having survived his shipmates.[14]

In this first extended work, the significance of human recognition, understanding, and communication, combined with Dante's "hollow seas" imagery, provides recurrent themes for Levi's story. He distinguished between the drowned and the saved among all the prisoners whom he had classified from their first entry into the camp as having "reached the bottom."[15] As the feet of newly arrived prisoners first touch the bottom, there is a moment of revelation when dressed identically in "unrecognizable rags," with "broken-down boots" and shaved heads, they see themselves metonymically as broken down and unrecognizable: "we do not dare lift our eyes to look at one another." They had passed from being individu-

---

[12] The functions of the Monowitz-Buna complex were supposed to be industrial production by I. G. Farben using slave labor, but the chimneys of the crematoria at Birkenau were dedicated, like those at other extermination camps, e.g., Treblinka and Sobibor, to mass murder.

[13] Levi attributed his survival to his "good fortune" in having been deported as late as February 1944 when the regime had greater need of slave labor in Monowitz-Buna and so conceded "noticeable improvements in the camp routine" in order "to lengthen the average life-span of the prisoners destined for elimination" (*If This Is a Man*, p. 15 "Author's Preface").

[14] Cf. guilt in "The Survivor" poem haunted by the submerged people: "No one died in my place." In the interview with Anthony Rudolf (see my note 5), Levi said that he read Coleridge's poem after the war and was upset to recognize himself in the figure of the Ancient Mariner. See further Insana, *Arduous Tasks*, pp. 56–92.

[15] Ch. 2 of *If This Is a Man* is entitled "On the Bottom"; cf. ch. 9, "The Drowned and the Saved." Cf. "If the drowned have no story, and single and broad is the path to perdition, the paths to salvation are many, difficult and improbable" (p. 96); this Christian imagery with its theological resonance represents Levi's convenient literary shorthand in addressing the majority of his readers. The civilian prisoners who regarded the Jews as "untouchables" thought that since they had been reduced to such conditions in the camp they "must be tainted by some mysterious, grave sin" (pp. 126–27).

als to a miserable mass; and their shame was greater than when they had been naked. Only "free" men look each other in the eye. Yet each finds his image "reflected in a hundred livid faces, in a hundred miserable and sordid puppets. We are transformed."

> Then for the first time we became aware that our language lacks words to express this offence, the demolition of a man. In a moment, with almost prophetic intuition, the reality was revealed to us: we had reached the bottom. (p. 32)

All of Levi's writing resists this demolition process. He built his testimony by searching for words to express what normal language could not represent because, ultimately, this "offense" remained incomprehensible. Even those who had previously suffered persecution and violence had never known its like.[16] Everything had been taken from them, even their hair. The next step in the demolition process was to deny the prisoners access to language: "If we speak, they will not listen to us, and if they listen, they will not understand" because "they" do not recognize the "strangers" or acknowledge their humanity. During the camp induction process Primo and others anticipate the survivors' torment: they fear that their story is too crazy to be believed in the normal world. A prisoner who had studied in Italy and claimed to have "a little heart" comes to speak to the new arrivals. It is clear that the man spoke enough Italian to be understood literally, but that what he said was incomprehensible in any language. In this context the parameters for ordinary human judgment are also destroyed; this situation is beyond comparisons. Levi borrowed the language of humanist epic in attempting the ethical process of making new meaning from metaphor in intertextual dialogue. Levi's account is sensitive to ordinary assumptions about the impossibility of what happened in the camps.

The prisoners' "prophetic intuition" that the offense against humanity perpetrated in the camp would be considered incredible outside it explains the theme, form, and allusions in one of Levi's earliest postwar poems, dated 10 January 1946, composed a few days before the first anniversary of the liberation of Auschwitz. This poem, "Shema" (the Hebrew imperative means "hear" or "listen"), incorporates a parodic adaptation of biblical verses comprising the beginning of the prayer at the core of all Jewish liturgies and personal devotions, and thus carries extraordinary resonance.[17] Levi

---

[16] Cf. p. 129: "free words" by contrast with "a new, harsh language."

[17] The *Shema* is the first prayer learned by children for twice daily repetition, and its opening words are prescribed for repetition by the dying since they express the fundamental tenet of Judaism: "Hear ô Israel, the Lord our God, the Lord is one." See further [*The Order of Prayers for the whole year*] *The Authorised Daily Prayer Book: Hebrew Text English Translation with Commentary*

professed no personal religious faith but had been brought up in contact with the rites and culture of Italian Judaism.

> You who live secure
> In your warm houses,
> Who return at evening to find
> Hot food and friendly faces:
>
> Consider whether this is a man (*Considerate se questo è un uomo*),
> Who labors in the mud
> Who knows no peace
> Who fights for a crust of bread
> Who dies at a yes or a no.
> Consider whether this is a woman,
> Without hair or name
> With no more strength to remember (*ricordare*)
> Eyes empty and womb cold
> As a frog in winter.
>
> Consider that this has been (*Meditate che questo è stato*):
> I commend these words to you.
> Engrave them on your hearts (*Scolpitele . . .* )
> When you are in your house, when you walk on your way,
> When you go to bed, when you rise.
> Repeat them to your children . . . [18]

In traditional Judaism such repetition and recreation of the history of God's dealings with his children are religious imperatives. In commending his own words to his readers who lived safe and comfortable lives, and in commanding them to "Carve" or "Engrave" those words on their hearts, so that they might be remembered in all places, at all times, as living memorials rather than written ones, Levi spoke alongside the God of Moses: "And these words, which I command thee this day, shall be upon thy heart; and thou shalt teach them diligently unto thy children, and shalt talk of them when thou sittest in thy house, and when thou walkest by the way, and when thou liest down, and when thou risest up."[19] His poem also ends with curses that

---

*and Notes*, ed. J. H. Hertz, rev. ed. (London: Soncino Press, 1976), pp. 116–27 (text) and 263–69 (note on meaning and history).

[18] Cf. *Collected Poems*, p. 9, 10 January 1946; *Ad ora incerta*, p. 15.

[19] Deuteronomy 6: 6 and 7. Levi omitted the first two verses of the *Shema*, which proclaim the unity and unconditional love of God, concepts beyond Levi's comprehension, before and after Auschwitz; cf. Deut. 6:4–5. Thomson, in *Primo Levi: Austere Humanist*, p. 146, notes the background of the Nuremberg trials in the genesis of this poem. Cf. the Moses figure in Bonhoeffer's and in Ratushinskaya's poems.

echo those found at the conclusion of several biblical psalms that insist on individual responsibility for righting injustices in the world:

> Or may your house crumble,
> Disease render you powerless (*impedisca*),
> Your offspring avert their faces from you.

This last climactic line may be read as a sad premonition: for many years Levi's two children refused to read and discuss *If This Is a Man*. In the beginning, the new prisoners did not comprehend even their Italian-speaking informant. Then they dreamed anxiously that, if they survived, no one would believe their testimony. The need to find a language in which to communicate and then to persuade others to act on their new knowledge of his experience drove Levi's career as a writer with hindsight. The principles behind his work were testimony for mankind and a defense of civilization.

## "GIVING VENT TO A MILLENNIAL ANGER": DIALOGUE AND DIALECTIC FRUSTRATED

While *If This Is a Man* testifies to man's inhumanity to man, which Levi denoted in the problems of communication and understanding in the camp, his book also demonstrates the antidote to these problems. The contrasts between humane and inhumane attitudes, and their consequences for life or death, are subtly revealed by a series of simple but eloquent cross-references made within adjacent, or nearly adjacent, passages of text. During the prisoners' induction into the camp, Levi set their expectations of normal communication against its frustration. When the train doors opened at Auschwitz, the Italian prisoners were assailed by "that curt, barbaric barking of Germans in command which seems to give vent to a millennial anger" assimilated from centuries of European Christian anti-Semitism (p. 25). Even after a German Jew became their translator, no meeting of minds was possible. The presiding officer looked through the translator "as if he were transparent, as if no one had spoken" (p. 29). There is no communication without mutual recognition. The strangeness of the experience might be madness or even a joke. The German's "manner of laughing" involved cruel deception and sarcasm that betrayed the corruption of a relatively cultivated mind. The translator is hesitant "because he knows that it is useless"; there can be no meaningful dialogue. " 'The officer says you must be quiet, because this is not a rabbinical school.' One sees the words which are not his, the bad words, twist his mouth as they come out, as if he was spitting out a foul taste" (p. 30). Levi's simile reminds readers of the actual, foul-tasting water from the tap that had tantalized the newly disembarked prisoners. Surely,

Primo had reasoned then, it seems obvious that (*Wassertrinken Verboten*) is a "joke" (p. 28). In equating "bad words" with foul water in the context of another "joke," Levi also hints at the deadly "millennial anger" that animated the officer's anti-intellectual derision. (The contrast with a rabbinical seminary evokes a hubbub from lively minds paired in dialogue with each other—the traditional method—to search out the significances of biblical texts and their commentaries.) Yet once they had overcome their initial shock, the prisoners were able to communicate simply by looking "at each other without a word," so that, although what was happening "was all incomprehensible and mad," they had indeed understood what awaited them (pp. 26–27). Furthermore, even their ordinary guard could communicate, in "pidgin language," when it suited him. This guard is cruel but tactically courteous when pursuing his private enterprise in asking for the prisoners' money or watches since they would have no further use for them. At this, Primo reports a different kind of "anger and laughter" among the prisoners, who have understood the guard all too well, yet also find their emotional reaction "brings relief." Any understanding is better than none, but the direct communication of unprecedented horror, as the prisoners learn, is more difficult. The author's attempt at dialogue with his readers will be similarly problematic.

The new prisoners discover that "no one here speaks willingly" (p. 35). In the camp the truth was partly hidden by euphemism and indirection so that its full horror was displaced by the mental effort of deciphering an unfamiliar puzzle: "The only exit is by way of the Chimney." Jokes and madness combined in unsettling paradoxes. But there were new codes and signifiers in the numbers each prisoner carried in an indelible tattoo on his left forearm: "The funereal science of the numbers of Auschwitz, which epitomize the stages of [the] destruction of European Judaism" (p. 34). Levi's strange but precise circumlocution—"funereal science"—contrasts with the starker but therefore more comprehensible statement of what these numbers meant for European Jewry—the earliest, low-numbered deportees were long dead (cf. p. 58).

Arbitrary violence, malice, and obfuscation that had shocked and bewildered the new prisoners are epitomized when Primo, still desperately thirsty, breaks off "a fine icicle" that is "brutally" snatched away by a "prowling" guard (p. 35). "'*Warum?*' I asked him . . . '*Hier ist kein warum,*'" came the stark reply. There is no reasoning "why," or possible dialogue, and the consolations sought by Boethius and other prisoners are not available. Brutality opposes reason. Levi, the survivor, comments impersonally: "If one wants to live one must learn this quickly and well." It is a real question whether one wants to live in this situation; is it reasonable to want to live? Levi's bitterness is revealed in lines borrowed from Dante's *Inferno* again (canto 21, lines 48–49), where he quotes the direct speech of the devils who sarcastically torment new arrivals in hell, being plunged up and down in a stream of boiling pitch: the fiendish antithesis of a bathing party in the river near Lucca: "No Sacred Face will help thee here! It's not / A Serchio bathing party" (p. 35). If the Lager is another inferno, these prisoners are beyond divine help; there is no reason for a "prowling" animal's brutality. The prisoners have become numbered items on a loading schedule, "*Stücke*," not men, in the eyes of their persecutors, therefore their fate is decided "lightly," "with no sense of human affinity," in a system based entirely on "utility" and hate (p. 33). "We know that we will have difficulty in being understood, and this is as it should be." In a direct address to readers, Levi urged recourse to a human faculty beyond mere reason: "Imagine now a man who is deprived of everyone he loves," and at the same time everything he knows of his normal life and all his possessions. This appeal to readers' imaginations and empathy was essential to Levi's ethical purpose as a writer. The result of such deprivation—in any circumstances, Levi's language suggests—"will be a hollow man, reduced to suffering and needs, forgetful of dignity and restraint, for he who loses all often easily loses himself" (p. 33). His consciousness that the camp system produced many hollow men, lacking individuality and self-affirmation, prompted his insistence that the best men died and the survivors, including himself, were neither saints nor martyrs. Only in the relative calm of the camp sick bay did anyone with "some seeds of conscience" begin "to consider what they have made us become, how much they have taken away from us, what this life is." In that place apart, with time to think, Primo recognized that there was a greater threat than death: "We have learnt that our personality is fragile, that it is much more in danger than our life; and the old wise ones, instead of warning us 'remember that you must die,' would have done much better to remind us of this great danger that threatens us" (p. 61). Significance is synthesized by contrastive oppositions.

The antidote to the fiendish system of the camps is repeatedly presented as "human affinity." At the end of the book, Levi affirmed his premise that "part of our existence lies in the feelings of those near to us" (p. 178), as he acknowledged his gratitude to those companions who had helped each other to maintain that vital human affinity, by which he means an abstract, ideal quality, not merely contact or a standard of decency. Alongside the German guard's refusal to explain about the icicle, Levi placed a contrasting exchange with the young ironsmith, Schlome. As new arrivals searched "for a voice, a friendly face or a guide" to this infernal region, Schlome caught Primo's eye; although there were language barriers, this did not prevent their communicating with warmth, and for a serious purpose, by trial and error, mime, gestures, and word by simple word. The boy nodded encouragingly when Primo told him he was a chemist: *"Chemiker gut"* (p. 37), yet also confirmed that he shouldn't drink the water. Schlome's message is conveyed in part by words—many not understood by Primo—but most emphatically by his look of concern and serious manner. Primo asks, *"Warum?"* echoing his attempted dialogue with the German guard. It takes effort (and mutual respect) to communicate, but Schlome made his companion understand, then introduced himself by name, asked Primo's name, and his own important question: "Where your mother?" Gradually Schlome *"understands"* that Jews live in Italy; finally he *"approaches. . . and timidly embraces"* his new acquaintance; this sequence of verbs (my emphasis) describes the processes of human affinity and, as here, its radical attachment to the idea of a mother figure. The prisoner was "filled with a serene sadness that is almost joy." The survivor and narrator with hindsight, commented: "I have not forgotten his serious and gentle face of a child, which welcomed me on the threshold of the house of the dead."

Another person whose understanding and empathy proved unforgettable was Alberto, who perished on the forced march with retreating German forces during the night of 18 January 1945. Levi credited Alberto's remarkable survival in Auschwitz, "unscathed and uncorrupted," to his "intelligence and intuition" which, even at the age of twenty-two, had Machiavellian qualities: "He understood before any of us that this life is war; he permitted himself no indulgences, he lost no time complaining and commiserating with himself and with others, but entered the battle from the beginning" (p. 63). Alberto's chief tactical advantages in battle were his intuitive sensitivity to others, lack of arrogance, and tenacity:

> He reasons correctly, often he does not even reason but is equally right. He understands everything at once: he knows a little French but understands whatever the Germans and Poles tell him. He replies in Italian and with gestures, he makes himself understood and at once wins sympathy. He fights for his life but still remains everybody's friend. He "knows" whom to corrupt, whom to avoid, whose compassion to arouse, whom to resist. (p. 63)

Loyal teamwork between the two young, naturally curious and adaptable individuals sharing with the other all the small benefits they gained from stealth, ingenuity, and barter in the murky "grey" zones of camp existence, extended their chances of survival. Levi's tribute to his friend distinguished his humanity as well as his rarity: "He himself did not become corrupt. I always saw, and still see in him, the rare figure of the strong yet peace-loving man against whom the weapons of night are blunted" (p. 63). Levi's narrative depicted one further variation on this paradigm of the prisoner as hero, which is all the more extraordinary because of its entirely selfless generosity. Levi doubted whether his relationship with Lorenzo, a non-Jewish, Italian civilian worker, could "be understood except in the manner in which we nowadays understand events of legends or the remotest history," an analogy that also explains Levi's allusive intertextuality in his literary method (p. 125). Lorenzo was a myth in his own time. Levi acknowledged that many of the contacts between civilian workers and his own enslaved companions were different in that, "even for the most pagan consciences," they remained questionable: "on the margins of the permissible and the honest." Yet Lorenzo's humane actions in bringing him "a piece of bread and the remainder of his ration every day for six months" protected Primo's physical existence and his humanity. Lorenzo also wrote a postcard to Levi's mother and brought him the reply. "For all this he neither asked nor accepted any reward, because he was good and simple and did not think that one did good for a reward" (p. 125). This definition extends the sense of the proposition—if this is a Man. Lorenzo's "humanity was pure and uncontaminated, he was outside this world of negation," and Levi credited Lorenzo with inspiring him not to forget that he too was a "man" (p. 128).[20] Levi's rhetorical trope contrasts Lorenzo's innate goodness and simplicity with Alberto's intelligence and intuition, and compares both with Schlome's childlike seriousness and spontaneous affection, but he credited them all with the capacity to uphold and inspire essential values for humanity in any situation. These individuals whose characters are sketched, however briefly, in *If This Is a Man*, resisted "negation" in their different ways, and withstood "the black hole of Auschwitz."[21] He preserved the memory of their names and actions in writing because they became part of his personal history and were instrumental in conveying more widely *what* had happened, and *how*, in Auschwitz. While their individuality was crucial, their representations were also indebted to the commonplaces of Levi's cultural heritage.

## HEALING PROPERTIES: "STORIES OF A NEW BIBLE"

Levi's narrative demonstrates what distinguishes and upholds the righteousness of individuals with reference to universal models of pagan and Judeo-Christian epic. In Levi's use of the Hebrew Bible, especially the story of the Children of Israel's liberation from slavery in the book of Exodus, personal histories partake of communal memories, and vice versa. He knew that

---

[20] See also my later comments on Lorenzo.
[21] See title, in my note 5.

nothing was impossible, and no horror was too incredible. The writer's testimony recollected memories to be shared with readers because without memory there is no moral life. Epic stories helped to maintain memories and moral life.

Storytelling was a popular pastime; during moments of reprieve and long winter evenings the necessity of dialogue prevailed, and prisoners talked to each other. The stories of their past lives were all their stories: "They take place in Norway, Italy, Algeria, the Ukraine, and are simple and incomprehensible like the stories in the Bible. But are they not themselves stories of a new Bible?" (p. 72). The authority of experience substitutes for the old cultural authority of "holy writ." Levi associated these stories heard in the camp with the Bible because to him they were emblematic, moral histories, and yet timeless. The prophet-poet of Auschwitz who voiced the lamentations of prisoners, recorded their miseries, and (perhaps) relieved their ever-present sufferings in controlled, artistic forms of expression, has no personal name in Levi's narrative. He is simply "the storyteller" who showed them verbal images of themselves, as Levi was to do later in his writing addressed to the wider world. On dark winter evenings, "the storyteller" crept in, "secretly" and soon gathered an attentive crowd.

> He chants an interminable Yiddish rhapsody, always the same one, in rhymed quatrains, of a resigned and penetrating melancholy (but perhaps I only remember it so because of the time and the place that I heard it?); from the few words that I understand, it must be a song that he composed himself, in which he has enclosed all the life of the Lager in minute detail. (p. 64)

Wachsmann, the storyteller's host, was another kind of being; he had an intense inner life of great spiritual power. Primo's comrades tell him that Wachsmann is a rabbi, "in fact a *Melamed*, a person learned in the Torah, and even more, in his own village in Galicia, was famed as a healer and a thaumaturge" (p. 74). Levi's portrait of him was complicated by his own lack of sympathy with the man, yet they both recognized the healing properties of stories (*consolatio* is a form of healing). Wachsmann's small build and physical weakness had caused him to be relegated to the duty of *Scheissbegleiter*; he was therefore responsible for escorting his companions to the latrine which was "an oasis of peace," yet he was also concerned with the life of the mind. Levi, the agnostic commentator and urban sophisticate, acknowledges with grudging irony that he was impressed by the village rabbi's talents and mentality, since he had "managed to work for two years without falling ill and without dying, but on the contrary is lit up by an amazing vitality in actions and words and spends long evenings discussing Talmudic questions incomprehensibly in Yiddish and Hebrew with Mendi, who is a modernist rabbi" (p. 74).[22] There are few descriptions of the role of religion or the life of the scholarly mind in Levi's account, but here he credits Wachsmann's love for Torah (denoting God's law in the first five books of the Hebrew Bible) and for his neighbor with a life force. Levi claimed he found the whole topic "incomprehensible"; yet there is a trace of envy tinged with warmth, in this paradoxical sketch of the lowly *Scheissbegleiter* whose mind moved beyond sordid physicality into esoteric dialogue with his "modernist" debating partner, and who drew in the storyteller for everyone's solace. In a similar vein, Levi also evoked the sustaining cultural memories of the Sephardi Jews from Salonika who supported each other by communal singing. These are the kinds of cultural expression that affirmed human affinities and solidarity—singing, storytelling, scholarly debate—helping individual prisoners to resist the pressure of the Lager, its remorseless "negation of beauty" and life, and its ultimate incomprehensibility.

One fine spring day Primo's neighbor had announced: "*Das Schlimmste ist vorüber*... the worst is over"; the new height of the sun had increased an irrepressible human impulse to hope. (Any pagan could concur.) Nearby, "those admirable and terrible Jews of Salonica, tenacious, thieving, wise, ferocious and united, so determined to live, such pitiless opponents in the struggle for life," were standing in a circle, shoulder to shoulder (literally and metaphorically) to "sing one of their interminable chants" (p. 77). Primo knew one of their number, Felicio, who shouted, "L'année prochaine à la maison," adding, "à la maison par la Cheminée!" The ironically named Felicio (literally, fortunate) had been at Birkenau and survived. As he and his fellows "sing and beat their feet in time and grow drunk on songs" (p. 78), they are liberated from their inhibitions by the rhythms of historic time. Felicio's greeting is an ironic parody of the concluding prayer of the Passover *seder*: the annual ritual telling (and exposition) of the story of the liberation from Egyptian slavery that every Jewish father is obliged to tell his children, as if it were his personal experience. The narrative and dialogue at the dinner table is completed (after four obligatory cups of wine) with the wish that next year the company should celebrate in their spiritual home, Jerusalem. Felicio's paradox reiterated the camp commonplace that the only escape from his generation's slavery was in the smoke released from burning bodies at the Auschwitz-Birkenau crematoria. One way, or another, Passover celebrates the time of "our freedom" from slavery and persecution, and the *seder*

---

[22] Cf. "Wachsmann," a man of "wax" if a generic rather than proper name, is symbolically radiant or "lit up" (like a candle in the dark) and protected by his inner life. Cf. subsequent comments on "Felicio."

ends with communal singing of folkloric songs that enable the company to refamiliarize themselves with contemporary realities, including the inevitable power of the angel of death, killed by the Almighty, in the last verse of the last song. The final focus thus returns to life and the power of God's love to defeat death. Levi nowhere explicitly tells his readers that these Greek Jews are celebrating Passover, but the spring setting and the reiteration of this theme elsewhere in his work suggests that its understated significance here was important to him in explaining the human condition.

Levi's description of his deportation from Italy and last night in the holding camp at Fossoli also reframes "exodus" as an inversion of the biblical "time of our freedom" in its parodic treatment of the theme. On the night before the Jewish prisoners boarded the trains to death or slavery, he witnessed the rituals of mourning being enacted by a group of Jews from Tripoli, alongside the mothers' nightlong preparations for their families' departure. Levi's narrative voice also insists that "many things were then said and done among us; but of these it is better that there remain no memory" (p. 22). In thus closing down options to witness and remember, he reversed the old biblical and rabbinic injunction to remember the Israelites' redemption in this world in the exodus from Egypt (cf. Exodus 12:42). In a late poem, "Pesach" (dated 9 April 1982), Levi repeats the words, events, and symbolic resonances of the *seder*'s ritual telling whereby "time reverses its course,"

> Today flowing back into yesterday,
> Like a river enclosed at its mouth.
> Each of us has been a slave in Egypt,
> Soaked straw and clay with sweat,
> And crossed the sea dry-footed.
> You too, stranger.
> This year in fear and shame (*in paura e vergogna*),
> Next year in virtue and in justice.[23]

Empathy as a function of the historic imagination provided the ethical framework for a better way of life: for "us" and the "stranger." The best way to improve the world, according to Levi, storyteller and prophet of a new exile in the post-Holocaust world, is to remember kindness to strangers, those different from ourselves. Without that "kindness" we are not human beings. We recognize our human affinity with others by communication with them. Traditional receptions of biblical history teach an ethical im-

---

[23] "Passover," *Collected Poems*, pp. 51–52; cf. *Ad ora incerta*, pp. 56–57.

perative: "And a stranger shalt thou not oppress; for ye know the heart of a stranger, seeing ye were strangers in the land of Egypt."[24]

Whereas there may be no moral life for a community without memory (and history), pain and conscience are always individual. Levi's narrative contrasts the collective unconscious of the prisoners (who dreamed the same dreams of home and food) with the painful return to subjective consciousness that occurred in "moments of reprieve" from physical hardship and on waking from sleep. With respite, thoughts and feelings associated with normality would return briefly; shame, guilt, and fear that no one would believe their stories would also torment individual prisoners alike. Levi's fear that his testimony would be disbelieved had informed his allusions to literary authorities and traditions shared with his readers. The ultimate impossibility of sharing the experiences of the camp with anyone who was not there was a paradox faced by many writers of Holocaust testimony, who nevertheless wrote in the hope and expectation of achieving some effective communication with their readers. Levi was aware that after the war some camp survivors committed suicide. They died for their own unknowable reasons as individuals, but also, as Levi himself acknowledged in some of his early poetry, as members of a group that had experienced feelings of guilt and shame simply because they were survivors. Levi wrote with hindsight of his fellow prisoners as either the "drowned" or the "saved," but it was clear to him that no personal merit could be attributed to the survivors who might, in some superficial sense, seem to be "saved." (Similarly, the "drowned" were not sinners as his analogy with the characters of Dante's *Inferno* might have implied if taken to its logical conclusion.) Unlike Boethius, More, and Gramsci such binary distinctions did not formulate his ethical thinking even if they were convenient in characterizing and representing his ideas for readers. Survival could be problematic.

Self-love may be the base-line criterion for operation of the Golden Rule, but in the camps—among the slaves—the stark consequences of the need to love oneself often conflicted with the interests of neighbors and strangers alike. In the second-century Talmudic collection commonly known as the *Ethics of the Fathers,* Levi found the words of Rabbi Hillel (fl. 30 BCE–10 CE), used for the title of his novel *If Not Now, When?* (1982) and for the refrain of the song he composed for the novel's Jewish partisan heroes: "If I am not for myself, what am I? / And if I am only for myself, what am I? /

---

[24] Exodus 23:9; cf. 22:20 and Leviticus 19:34 "The stranger that sojourneth with you shall be unto you as the home-born among you, and thou shalt love him as thyself; for ye were strangers in the land of Egypt: I am the Lord your God." Cf. the Golden Rule: "Thou shalt love thy neighbour as thyself," Leviticus 19:18, *The Pentateuch*, ed. J. H. Hertz, 2nd ed. (London: Soncino Press, 1975), pp. 563–64.

And if not now, when?"[25] In Auschwitz, the prisoners felt the pressure inherent in Hillel's first line; but later, many survivors seem to have regretted the implications of the second line. Levi's writing was part of his answer to Hillel's challenging questions, which emphasized the ethical responsibility of individuals for themselves in the specific context of Jewish wisdom literature and rabbinic traditions.

The strength of the ethical paradigms represented by Levi's pen portraits (including those of Alberto and Lorenzo) was founded on their subjects' individuality. Yet he also showed how "fear is supremely contagious" and how the herd instinct (combined with other factors) had corrupted humane impulses upon which depend recognition of oneself in the other, and communication with others. As liberation by the Red Army drew closer, Primo had tried unsuccessfully to dissuade two Hungarian boys from joining the mass evacuation in their weak physical state and without strong shoes: "I tried to explain, but they looked at me without replying. Their eyes were like those of terrified cattle" (p. 160). These boys had a choice but, infected by fear, they followed the herd. In the simile for their eyes, traditionally windows on the soul, Levi indicates that their humanity was compromised. He remembered seeing them, like "shapeless bundles, lurching into the night," and drawing upon the testimony of others, added that, unable to keep up, they were killed by German guards. Fear had diminished their capacities to make individual judgments, as free men with free will, even where self-interest was at stake. However, a few pages later Levi described the effects of the hard but rational decision he and fellow patients (we) had made to defend their own interests at the expense of others (they) when a bombing raid set fire to the hospital.

> Dozens of patients arrived, naked and wretched, from a hut threatened by fire: they asked for shelter. It was impossible to take them in. They insisted, begging and threatening in many languages. We had to barricade the door. They dragged themselves elsewhere, lit up by the flames, barefoot in the melting snow.

With hindsight the writer's sympathy is with the rejected ones who retreat trailing "behind them streaming bandages" (p. 163). The whole scene, like one from Dante's *Inferno*, is backlit by fire. These men are "patients," neither prisoners nor cattle. The implied dialogue between both sets of desperate men was rational—"they asked ... it was impossible"—yet those who barricaded the door had to choose whether some survived and some were

---

[25] See "Author's Note," *If Not Now, When?*, tr. William Weaver (1985) (London: Sphere Books, 1988), pp. 279–80; see also *Daily Prayer*, ed. Hertz, pp. 624–25, text and note on *Ethics of the Fathers* 1:14.

turned away to an unknown fate, or all were overwhelmed. Levi's impersonal form of language, "it was impossible," distances himself from the shame of his share in this tragic dilemma.

The rebirth of human affinity and generosity toward strangers occurred only after the evacuation and the bombing. Primo, with two French civilian prisoners, had succeeded in finding basic necessities: a stove and potatoes. Levi recalled that "when the broken window was repaired and the stove began to spread its heat, something seemed to relax in everyone" (p. 165). The Lager was losing its grip on them. One of the others then proposed that "each of them offer a slice of bread to us three who had been working. And so it was agreed."

> Only a day before a similar event would have been inconceivable. The law of the Lager said: "eat your own bread, and if you can, that of your neighbour," and left no room for gratitude. (p. 166)

They had recognized the justice and longer-term self-interest implicit in ensuring that the strongest among them could continue to forage and protect the weaker ones. The sharing of bread was a symbolic action in which those "who had not died slowly changed from *Häftlinge* [prisoners] to men again," able and willing to cooperate freely and trust others: "It was the first human gesture that occurred among us." The restored men were still in danger from disease, fire, starvation, and violent death, but on this first evening in freedom, Levi remembered, "we felt at peace with ourselves and with the world. We were broken by tiredness, but we seemed to have finally accomplished something useful—perhaps like God after the first day of creation" (pp. 166–67).[26] They had separated their continuous night from a new day and thus laid their foundations for a new world order; yet these first steps had been possible only by excluding others who could not be accommodated.

## SUBMERGED PEOPLE AND FACELESS PRESENCES

Shame began to oppress the prisoners at the execution of one of the rebels who had blown up a crematorium at Birkenau. Levi reported the death of this hero as traumatic for the witnesses; as Ultimo, the Last Man's bold affirmation, "*Kamaraden, ich bin der Letz*," "pierced through the old thick barriers of inertia and submissiveness, it struck the living core of man in each of us" (p. 155). The officer presiding at the hanging of the rebel had asked an undifferentiated mass of degraded slaves if they had understood what was happening. The question Levi considered has a different signifi-

---

[26] Cf. Genesis 1:1–5.

cance. "Who answered '*Jawohl*'? Everybody and nobody: it was as if our cursed resignation took body by itself, as if it turned into a collective voice above our heads." By contrast, everyone had understood the meaning of the Last Man's last message and had felt diminished by the contrast between him, a whole man whose being was suffused by a free human spirit, and themselves. His words may have "struck the living core of man" within each, but they remained "an abject flock . . . standing, bent and grey" with drooped heads. Significantly, Levi also particularized the response, indicating that Alberto and Primo were "oppressed by shame" and unable to "look each other in the face."

> To destroy a man is difficult, almost as difficult as to create one; it has not been easy, nor quick, but you Germans have succeeded. (p. 156)

Here, "you Germans" addresses not only the Nazi perpetrators of this demolition of a man but also the book's contemporary German readers whom he wished to engage in discussion. It reminds all readers of the nature of the offense committed against humanity. The "Final Solution" was primarily an industrial killing process but even before the genocide took place, its victims were to be systematically degraded, reduced, and broken. The system had created a mass of dazed "men in decay" with whom it was (apparently) not worth attempting to communicate. Their shock and lethargy were considered threatening to others for whom their rejection was thus a form of unconscious self-preservation. Writing with hindsight, the survivor Levi acknowledged his own shame at Primo's scorn and impatience with the suffering masses who did not adapt to their slavery or "disentangle the infernal knot of laws and prohibitions until their body [was] already in decay, and nothing [could] save them from selections or from death by exhaustion" (p. 96). Among the other prisoners and slave laborers these were known as the *Muselmänner*. Levi's narrative rhetoric also denies these men-in-decay their humanity by denying them their individuality: they are unable to hold their heads up above the flood.

> All the musselmans who finished in the gas chambers have the same story, or more exactly, have no story; they followed the slope down to the bottom, like streams that run down to the sea. . . . Their life is short, but their number is endless; they, the *Muselmänner*, the drowned, form the backbone of the camp, an anonymous mass, continually renewed and always identical, of non-men who march and labour in silence, the divine spark dead within them, already too empty to really suffer. (p. 96)

The sea image, like that of the "flock" at Ultimo's hanging, merges their identities; their silence symbolizes their spiritual emptiness as the language of this description inverts the biblical creation of man in the image of God, on the sixth day of creation. The impersonal narrative voice of the survivor colludes in their decay (they are "too empty to really suffer"): "One hesitates to call them living: one hesitates to call their death death, in the face of which they have no fear, as they are too tired to understand" (p. 96). In this most terrible sentence in the book, the signs of human life are reduced to fear of death.

The effects of such trauma in others, Levi's rhetoric suggests, compromised the humanity of the observer and raised ethical questions for writer and reader. Is this rejection of the mass of suffering others different in kind, or merely degree, from several different episodes where individuals had failed to recognize their human affinity with others? Mostly these were occasions when Primo was personally humiliated, or ignored.[27] The crucial difference is that readers know how Primo felt because the writer Levi tells us, and the anonymous masses who decayed before Primo's eyes and "finished in the gas chambers" have "no story" besides the impact they had on the writer haunted with hindsight: "They crowd my memory with their faceless presences" (p. 96). In the Lager "where man is alone and where the struggle for life is reduced to its primordial mechanism," self-interest meant that no one bothered to consider these "men in decay" who disappeared "without leaving a trace in anyone's memory" (pp. 94–95). Ground down, they dragged themselves along "in an opaque intimate solitude" until they died in this existential solitude, even though the majority of them died as naked victims of mass extermination, crammed into gas chambers as numbered items in a factory producing corpses. Levi offered their collective image to readers as testimony to the atrocity of the historic event, to warn mankind about its potential (when faced by some "ferocious law" of a primordial jungle) to abandon justice and compassion to persons who are different or unknown. Yet he also acknowledged his need to expiate his consciousness of having been so compromised by his own suffering and fight for survival that he had rejected (as defeatist) and ignored (as powerless) "the drowned" whom he remembered only as faceless automata, lacking the vital signs of a rational, divine spark:

> They crowd my memory with their faceless presences, and if I could enclose all the evil of our time in one image, I would choose this image which is familiar to me: an emaciated man, with head dropped and

---

[27] E.g., by the Poles on the threshold of Ka-Be (p. 55), and in the reactions of the German civilian workers in the chemistry laboratory, especially the man who wiped his dirty hands on Primo treating him like a rag (pp. 113–14, 149).

shoulders curved, on whose face and in whose eyes not a trace of a thought is to be seen. (p. 96)

In "Buna," his first poem written after the war, the poet imagined himself back in the Lager, as the "whistles terrible at dawn" call "the multitudes with dead faces" to another "day of suffering": "A day like every other day awaits us."[28] Yet now the "musselman," respected as an unknown individual whom the poet sees in his "heart," is addressed as the "tired companion." The poem articulates sympathy, understanding, and, inevitably, regret as the speaker revises and corrects his past scorn in the grammar of historic present tenses.

> I read your eyes, sad friend (*compagno dolente*),
> In your breast you carry cold, hunger, nothing.
> You have broken what's left of the courage within you (*Hai rotto dentro
>   l'ultimo valore*).
> Colorless one, you were a strong man,
> A woman walked at your side.
> Empty companion who no longer has a name,
> Forsaken man who can no longer weep,
> So poor you no longer grieve,
> So tired you no longer fear.
> Spent once-strong man (*Uomo spento che fosti un uomo forte*).

The speaker's consciousness of the ordinary human past of this "once-strong" man rounds out the representation of his "companion," imagining a woman at his side, and giving him a history. The blank memory of "multitudes with dead faces" is revised with a single, ethical focus. The theme of recognition—human affinity—and understanding that developed in *If This Is a Man* seems to begin here as the poet reads his companion's eyes and, having done so, speculates anxiously about a future meeting in freedom: the poet's present.

> If we were to meet again
> Up there in the world, sweet beneath the sun,
> With what kind of face would we confront each other (*Con quale viso ci
>   staremmo a fronte*)?

If, after the execution of Ultimo, Primo and his companion were unable "to look each other in the face" because of their shame, this later retrospective

---

[28] *Collected Poems*, p. 5, 28 December 1945; cf. *Ad ora incerta*, p. 11. See further Giovanni Tesio, "*At an Uncertain Hour*: Preliminary Observations on the Poetry of Primo Levi," in *Primo Levi: Austere Humanist*, pp. 161–70.

anxiety suggests the speaker's feelings of guilt for the implied accusations read in his companion's eyes.

Nearly forty years later the survivor remained haunted by memories of the Lager and returned to the situation of Coleridge's obsessive survivor, the Ancient Mariner, whom he quoted in an extended epigraph to his poem, "The Survivor."

> *Dopo di allora, ad ora incerta,*
> Since then, at an uncertain hour,
> That agony returns:
> And till my ghastly tale is told,
> This heart within me burns.
>
> Once more he sees his companions' faces
> Livid in the first . . . light,
> Gray with cement dust,
> Nebulous in the mist,
> Tinged with death in their uneasy sleep.
> At night, under the heavy burden
> Of their dreams, their jaws move,
> Chewing a non-existent turnip.[29]

The collective unconscious represented by the starving prisoners' dreams menaces the tormented survivor whose former companions do not rest in death; the narrative voice frames that of a speaker who imagines the dead are angry; he is provoked to speak to them directly in the first person:

> "Stand back, leave me alone, submerged people,
> Go away. I haven't dispossessed anyone (*Non ho soppiantato nessuno*),
> Haven't usurped anyone's bread.
> No one died in my place. No one.
> Go back into your mist.
> It's not my fault if I live and breathe (*Non è mia colpa. . .*),
> Eat, drink, sleep and put on clothes."

The shift from third to first person is not merely a rhetorical device to increase the dramatic quality of this outburst. The change of person particularizes the agony of the survivor. Unlike the Ancient Mariner, this storyteller finds no relief. As Levi recalled (in his description of the prisoners' dreams), as soon as one crisis was relieved, another came into view and so on, ad infinitum: "For human nature is such that grief and pain—even simultaneously suffered—do not add up as a whole in our consciousness, but

[29] *Collected Poems*, p. 64, 4 February 1984; cf. *Ad ora incerta*, p. 70.

hide, the lesser behind the greater, according to a definite law of perspective" (p. 79). If the survivors' memories had obeyed this law of perspective, they should have diminished with the distance traveled (in time) from the focal point. However, time did not always help these survivors who in their later years often found that as more immediate concerns receded (after retirement or as shorter-term memories were lost), their new more numerous moments of reprieve provided more time to consider the distant past. Levi revisited his past in Auschwitz in *If This Is a Man*, in *Moments of Reprieve* (*Lilit e altri racconti*, 1981)—discrete, short stories drawing on his own and other survivors' memories—and in essay form in *The Drowned and the Saved* (1986). The last line of his poem "The Survivor" alluded to another significant context in Dante's *Inferno* where the poet claims that Ser Branca d'Oria "has by no means died; / He wears his clothes and sleeps and drinks and eats" only to be told that this is an illusion.[30] D'Oria's whole life was a fiendish mirage; he is identified by Dante as one of those sinners whose soul is already in hell even though, in "the upper world," "his body walks and seems a living man." Levi returned to the upper world from the depths of the Lager, determined that his agony of the uncertain hour, in which had recurred involuntary memories and a haunted moral consciousness, should be made useful; and he shared his survivor's testimony, that could not be forgotten, lest it should be repeated in ignorance by future generations.

## Primo Levi, *Moments of Reprieve* (1981): In Defense of Civilization

Thirty-five years after his return to Italy, Levi published a collection of short stories, *Lilit e altri racconti,* playfully described as "paralipomena," signifying matters either omitted from or added to the "first two 'Books of Chronicles'" in his "new Bible": *If This Is a Man* and an account of his journey home—*The Truce*. These new stories revisit earlier themes and characters but with a different emphasis. Over the intervening years, more Holocaust testimonies and a range of historical studies had been published, modifying his readers' attitudes to these terrible events. If the larger picture of what had happened in the camps and elsewhere throughout Occupied Europe was becoming clearer, some of Levi's ideas and impressions had also settled into different patterns, as his own studies broadened the context of his personal experience. For example, he professed a greater understanding

---

[30] Canto 33, lines 123, 140–41 (*Inferno*, tr. Sayers, p. 282). Cf. Charlotte Delbo, asked whether she still lived "with Auschwitz" (as a survivor) is reported to have replied, no, "I live beside it" (Lawrence Langer, *Holocaust Testimonies: The Ruins of Memory* [New Haven: Yale University Press, 1991], p. 5).

of the religion and culture of Ashkenazi Jewry, which had been virtually wiped out in Central and Eastern Europe. With the passing of time, he was also more ready to acknowledge positive actions by some of the ordinary Germans he had encountered; and he felt that more could be revealed after a person's death. In addition, Levi was able to incorporate other survivors' testimony, to supplement his own, since he no longer needed to defend his status as a witness by drawing solely on personal experience. His voice as storyteller is calmer and more detached than in his first books. But his authority and judgment were still based on his own identity as a camp survivor. Through his writings Levi had become a world figure, regarded by many as a modern prophet with important messages for humanity, because he had seen the Lager, and had "outlived the ordeal" to tell his tale and appraise those of others, in accessible, clear, short forms of writing.[31] The apparent simplicity of his pared-down style appealed to a wide readership in many languages, and Levi kept a close eye on the styles and semantic choices (and their nuances) of his works' translators. Levi's voice remained that of a trusted guide through the "infernal" regions of the visible world. Like his master Dante, rather than Dante's Virgil, he cast his own shadow as a human being over these regions and their significance for post-Holocaust times.[32]

Whereas his first testimony—of "things that imperiously demanded to be told"—about the demolition of a man was haunted by the faceless shadows of the "drowned," in the preface to *Lilit e altri racconti* (1981) he insisted on telling stories about real " 'men' beyond all doubt."[33] The scenarios "are hardly ever tragic," and they are often positive. He called them "bizarre, marginal moments of reprieve" (p. 10) that revealed someone's distinctive human identity. Other people acknowledge the "reality" of distinctive human identities when they can be persuaded to recognize elements of themselves in the writer's subjects. Levi's new subjects are "the different": those in whom he had recognized "the will and capacity to react, and hence a rudiment of virtue ... even if the virtue that allows them to survive and makes them unique is not always one approved of by common morality." The ambiguities of "virtue" signifying both strength and morality, which Boethius and others had played upon, reflect the ethical problems that in-

---

[31] Cf. Lawrence Langer's view of survivors as those "who outlived the ordeal"; "Legacy in Gray," in *Memory and Mastery*, p. 205.

[32] Cf. "analogies can be useful, but must not be misused. For Levi, the Holocaust and the death camps are ultimately unique. We abuse our analogies if we allow them to convey more horror to another experience than the experience merits in its own grounds." Frederic D. Homer, *Primo Levi and the Politics of Survival* (Columbia: University of Missouri Press, 2001), p. 15.

[33] Published in English as *Moments of Reprieve*, tr. Ruth Feldman (London: Sphere Books, 1987), p. 9.

here in all human choices but were especially difficult in the camps where life was always at risk and expectations derived from normal experience were redundant.

## "MARGINAL MOMENTS OF REPRIEVE"

These new stories not only took greater risks with readers' perceptions of human reactions and potential during the Holocaust. They were also shaped and interpreted in fuller knowledge of the problems inherent in writing and testimony.[34] In the preface he admitted that, while he had not forgotten "a single thing" from the Lager, when it was "as if... my mind had gone through a period of exalted receptivity, during which not a detail was lost," the passage of time had nevertheless "accentuated the tendency to round out the facts or heighten the colors: this tendency, or temptation, is an integral part of writing, without it one does not write stories but rather accounts" (p. 11). These terms, "story," "account," have to be understood in relation both to each other and to time. In returning to these "facts" after more than three decades, the relatively stricter form of "account" or chronicle representation of one detail after another had become impossible. His vivid traumatic memories persisted, but he realized that the inevitable slippage between life and art (the partial viewpoint of the original recording consciousness and the overlay of a mediating narrator) was exacerbated by the passage of time. Levi also reported his difficulty in separating his memories from his accounts of his memories. In relating the story of Joel König, "Tired of Imposture," Levi warns:

> Anyone who has the opportunity to compare the true image of a writer with what can be deduced from his writings knows how frequently they do not coincide.... But how pleasant and cheering is the opposite case: the man who remains true to himself in what he writes.... The mask is the face. (p. 127)

Levi's satisfaction on reading König's autobiographical account was enhanced by his comparing the literary mask with the impression of his personal acquaintance. König, a young Jewish scientist and Levi's German counterpart, had evaded capture ("as if by a miracle") to become "a Chaplinesque hero, at once naïve and shrewd, open to imaginative improvisation, never desperate, fundamentally incapable of hatred or violence, in love with life, adventure, and joy" (p. 131). König's account of his experiences was

---

[34] On the general problems in this context cf. Franca Molino Signorini, "The Duty and Risk of Testimony: Primo Levi as Keeper of Memory," in *Memory and Mastery*, pp. 173–96, esp. 188–89 on memory as admonition.

truncated, because, although he had expanded it in an oral narration at Levi's prompting, he was, as Levi described him, "tired, tired of deception and disguises," even of the honest "deception" in writing about his own life (p. 135).[35] Levi's judgment as a survivor and a more experienced writer thus stands between the subject and the reader; it was his ambition as a writer to affirm "the mask is the face." Effective testimony for others depends on the credibility of this affirmation. Finally, that assessment is a matter of trust and literary experience. There were more bizarre elements to relate, reveal, and study in exploring the human condition. He collated his memories with those of other survivors' testimonies, yet remained acutely aware that neo-Nazi apologists were trying to distort their truth of lived experience as prisoners. Levi, the storyteller, says he came to know "The Story of Avrom" by chance, "like a saga transmitted from mouth to mouth, with the risk that it will become distorted or embellished and that it may be mistaken for a fictional invention" (p. 117). These were the writer's and historian's fears, rather than his subject's. Ironically, Avrom, "a polyglot," no longer had a language that was truly his; yet he had set down "his memories" as best he could, "without the ambitions of the literary man or historian," in the newly acquired Hebrew language of his final home "so that a record of the things he saw and lived [would] be preserved." In the interim Avrom's memories had been fixed "in the form of bare and unpretentious notes, veiled by the distance of time and space" as they waited for restoration "to the full breath of life that is inherently in them" (p. 123). Levi's comment on the practices of life writing—his own, as well as others'—is embodied literally in this image of resuscitation. Hindsight offers a view of a completed action, but the distance from that action also subtly changes significance. Paradoxically, Levi acknowledged that it was easier to write about the dead.

At the beginning of "Lorenzo's Return," Levi discussed with his new readers the problems encountered in writing about a living person: even with the best of motives "such a task . . . verges on the violation of privacy and is never painless for the subject" (p. 149). If truth is an ideal, and if the mask does match the face, it still remains a problem to determine whose truth-to-life takes priority.

> Each of us, knowing or not, creates an image of himself, but inevitably it is different from that, or, rather, from those (which again are different from one another) that are created by whoever comes into contact with us. (p. 149)

---

[35] Massimo Lollini explores Levi's related ideas of autobiography and testimony in "Primo Levi and the Idea of Autobiography," in *Primo Levi: Austere Humanist*, pp. 67–89.

Finding our image in someone else's writing "with features that are not those we attribute to ourselves is traumatic." The feeling behind this comment was less likely to be attributable to the semi-literate Lorenzo than to the self-conscious writer of testimony. Levi's reticence had prevented him from telling Lorenzo's story more fully in *If This Is a Man* in 1947. Many years after Lorenzo's death, Levi returned to the image of this man whom he had ensured would be ever present to him since he had named both his children in memory of this remarkable benefactor. "Lorenzo's Return" is a tribute by the writer who felt that he owed its subject a "duty" to "recreate the image" that he had kept of him (p. 150). Yet this image is necessarily the writer's image. In spite of his recognition of the problems of writing memory, Levi acknowledged his need to continue re-creating the "host of details [that] continued to surface," so many years later, from the depths of his own memory (p. 9). He had found that the "experience of Auschwitz was far from exhausted," leading to the return of his agony "at an uncertain hour"; yet, he was also distressed that these memories would fade away if not recorded.

> A great number of human figures especially stood out against that tragic background . . . begging me one after another to help them survive and enjoy the ambiguous perennial existence of literary characters. (p. 10)

The paradoxical experience of tragic catharsis allowed the memories of the storyteller to "survive" and permitted him to "enjoy" his own life: the writer's art lets him live a better life in reality and promote it for others.

The English title "Moments of Reprieve" signifies acts or events that imply someone's experience in relieving the literal and figurative sentence of death under which the prisoners existed; yet this edition is framed by the most ethically challenging of its subjects, first, "Rappoport's Testament," and finally, "Story of a Coin," which explores a view of the controversial leader of the Lodz ghetto, Chaim Rumskowski. This structure emphasizes the moral ambiguities of metaphorical gray areas in forced compromises by victims of Nazism. Yet Levi's representation of his narrative self as sentient and thoughtful provides an ethical counterpart to his description of the hedonistic Leon Rappoport who, according to Levi,

> lived in the Camp like a tiger in the jungle, striking down and practicing extortion on the weak, and avoiding those who were stronger; ready to corrupt, steal, fight, pull in his belt, lie, or play up to you, depending on the circumstances. He was therefore an enemy, but not despicable or repugnant. (pp. 19–20)

The terms of this judgment are pragmatic. Rappoport was a highly educated man, but Levi, assuming an intimacy that he could never prove, indicated that "it had been easy for him to leave behind, at one fell swoop, whatever civilian education [or 'culture'] he found superfluous." This "tiger" had resorted to the law of the jungle not merely without compunction but also with intellectual pride. Sandwiched between these stories are more uplifting subjects that exemplify moments of relief amid the moral murkiness of the "gray zone." By contrast, these offer bright spots of joy, energy, tenderness, hope, and humor depicted in the lives of principled, self-aware men who remained exceptional and distinct from the mass of "submerged people." In these subjects Levi went beyond historic testimony to illustrate and gloss his own defense of civilization in human beings who may not have survived but resisted the figurative forces of darkness and gray areas.

## BRIGHT SPOTS—"HOLDING EVIL IN OPPROBRIUM"

The original keynote story, "Lilith," indicates Levi's reappraisal and defense of the lost civilization of prewar eastern European Jewry. The story is based on the vivid characterization of a second storyteller, Tischler (his name is generic, signifying a joiner or cabinetmaker) who resembles the narrator's alter ego as a maker and an "unbeliever." "His step was brisk . . . his speech was careful and precise, and he had an alert face, laughing and sad" (p. 39). Tischler relates midrashic and cabbalistic variants on the story of Lilith, Adam's first wife according to some versions of her story, a she-devil, and God's mistress according to others: "an unimaginable scandal" that is in one way "the cause of the evil that occurs on earth; in another way, it is its effect" (p. 44). The Tischler's embedded storytelling within Levi's text mirrors the writer's actions and includes commentary on the genesis of all stories in the creative pleasure of the telling.

> "Of course [says Tischler] I don't believe this, but I like to tell these stories. I liked it when they were told to me, and it would be a shame if they were lost. In any case, I won't guarantee that I myself didn't add something, and perhaps all who tell them add something: and that's how stories are born." (p. 42)

That is also, he implies, how such stories embody and speak for lost generations whose culture would die without the accretions implicit in a new telling for new readers and audiences. The Tischler and Primo called themselves "twins" because they had discovered that they shared a birthday, the very day of their chance meeting while hiding from work in the Lager. In honor of their twenty-fifth birthdays, the Tischler had shared his special treat—half an apple—with Primo, enabling the later writer to evoke a parodic imitation of the fall of man. Eating the apple in full knowledge of good and evil, reverses their fallen state as slaves hiding in a sewer casing, and inaugurates a brief moment lived as freeborn men with leisure to share the good things of life, especially stories, and the mutual pleasures of companionship. (Judaism does not recognize a concept of Original Sin.) Tischler's character represents an expansion of the storyteller figure from *If This Is a Man* who had told "little anecdotes" and recited "long strings of verses" in Yiddish; Tischler had teased Primo as an ignorant Western Jew, an Epicurean, and an unbeliever, because he had had no previous contact with Yiddish culture. When he congratulated his "twin" on his birthday, wishing him *mazel tov*, or good fortune, in a half-ironic way since he considered that neither was likely to see another birthday, he also seems to speak to, and about, the vanishing cultural traditions he represents metonymically. The narrator comments: "Fortune has been good enough to me but not to Tischler," as he evokes the survivor's "unassuageable sadness" that became Levi's addition to the tale, passing on midrashic explanations for the origin of evil (p. 44). The narrator concludes: "It is inexplicable that fate has chosen an unbeliever to repeat this pious and impious tale, woven of poetry, ignorance, daring acumen, and the unassuageable sadness that grows on the ruins of lost civilizations" (p. 45). The material text embodies the mossy accretions that grow on these ruins. It also aligns Levi's pragmatic functions as a storyteller with Boethius (especially in the mythic poetry of the *Consolation of Philosophy*) and the other defenders of threatened civilizations: More, Gramsci, and Bonhoeffer.

In the fifth story, "Our Seal," Levi introduced his readers to a reserved, dignified man in his forties who had "lived on music" to resist "demolition" and sustain his inner life (p. 58). Wolf's art is a natural, constant state of his being: he "secreted music as our stomachs secreted hunger" and was always "mewling a musical theme." Eventually, he acquired a violin in the camp which he played for himself, in the spring sunshine, and "all those who came by stopped to listen with a greedy look, like bears catching the scent of honey, avid, timid, and perplexed" (p. 62). The honey they crave on waking from hibernation, a form of suspended animation, is food for the soul: music. One man who had previously tormented and teased the musician lay "almost spellbound. On his gladiator's face hovered that veil of contented stupor one sometimes sees on the faces of the dead, which makes one think they really had for an instant, on the threshold, the vision of a better world." Even in Auschwitz where every day was endured on this threshold, one man's music, played freely and naturally, had the power to transform a combative cynic. Wolf's music transcended the infernal reality of the Lager in lifting the veil to reveal an inner life of harmony and avid integrity that was an attraction and brief consolation to others. Levi represented Rappoport (the "tiger") who had studied medicine in Italy, and Wolf, the Berlin pharmacist, as antithetical types of life scientist, yet credited both with inner resources that had synthesized contrasting modes of resistance that were latent in each type of man but exploited by choice.

In "The Cantor and the Barracks Chief," Levi again compared and contrasted two representative human types but this time in extended formal dialogue with each other. The privileged German barracks chief, Otto, was a political prisoner; it was rumored that he had belonged to the "old-guard German Communist Party." He was "respected" for "his heavy fists" and quick reflexes (pp. 75–76), and Levi illustrates his character by describing how he imposed his authority on a dim-witted Polish peasant boy who never washed. Otto had tried to communicate "first in a nice way, that is to say with insults shouted in his [German] dialect, then with slaps and punches, but in vain" (p. 76). The storyteller explains that these had no effect because Vladek, who understood very little German, also seemed "unable to connect cause and effect, or perhaps didn't remember the blows from one day to the next." Levi does not attribute Vladek's resistance to authority as anything other than the habit of a boorish, brutal life that had become normal. Eventually the barracks chief, "frowning as if he were performing a task of great precision," resolves their conflict of wills by imposing his on the boy who was scrubbed until he was so clean he was unrecognizable (p. 77). The audience at this performance, including the storyteller, had laughed and concluded, by a negative comparison, that their chief "was not one of the worst": character is action.

Levi sets up this scene in preparation for a contrasting challenge, a few days later, by a more subtle, refined, and principled man who had served as a part-time cantor in a Lithuanian synagogue. Ezra was a quiet man, like many of Levi's heroes, who seldom spoke, never raised his voice, and had bright, lively eyes, denoting intelligence. He was tall and thin by contrast with the burly Otto. It was the eve of the holiest day in the Jewish calendar—Yom Kippur, "the Day of Atonement and of forgiveness," which is a fast day. Levi represents himself as a witness with perfect recall of Ezra's direct address to the barracks chief in which he explained how "for us today is a day of atonement and I cannot eat my soup. I respectfully ask you to save it for me until tomorrow evening" (p. 78). Although Otto was astounded that anyone in the camp should refuse food; instead of giving Ezra a slap—dialogue mitigates violence—he told him to come back later, because while Otto was a brutal man he was also naturally curious.[36] Ezra explains that al-

---

[36] At the beginning of "The Quiet City," Levi remarked: "It might be surprising that in the Camps one of the most frequent states of mind was curiosity. And yet, besides being frightened,

though he should not work on this holy day, the Jewish law [of *pikuach nefesh*] "allows disobedience of almost all precepts and prohibitions in order to save a life, one's own or another's"; therefore he will work because he knows that otherwise he will be denounced and killed. However, he had decided to "observe the prescribed fast . . . because he wasn't certain that this would lead to his death" (p. 79). The subtlety of this distinction in these circumstances arouses Otto's curiosity to know for what sins Ezra was atoning.

> Ezra answered that he knew about some but perhaps he had committed others unwittingly, and that moreover, in the opinion of some wise men, which he shared, atonement and fasting were not a strictly personal matter. Probably they contributed toward obtaining forgiveness from God for sins committed by others. (pp. 79–80)

Such topics discussed in tentative scholarly tones ("in the opinion of . . . Probably") characterized many theological and philosophical debates, and it is noticeable that Ezra's reasoning here is voiced in the third-person form of a reported speech. While Levi seldom explored the role of religion in the lives of his fellow prisoners and had shown little sympathy for those who had continued to pray in Auschwitz, over time he had come to reassess its significance for others who had resisted the Lager, as his interest in the spirituality of the Ashkenazi Jews in the camp developed.[37]

Levi's writing attaches high symbolic value to the man who lives by the craft skills of his hands. Ezra was a watchmaker whose precision in understanding tiny mechanisms comes to symbolize his creative engagement with the detail of religious law and its ethical applications in real time. As Ezra explained his interpretation of the Yom Kippur liturgy, which includes a reading of the book of Jonah ("yes, the one who'd been swallowed by the fish"), Otto was "torn by amazement, the desire to laugh, and still another feeling to which he no longer could give a name and which he believed had died in him, killed by the years of ambiguous, savage life in the Camps" (p. 80). As Ezra warms to his scholarly theme, explicating the story of the "stern prophet" who had argued against God's forgiveness of the "idolators" in Nineveh, who "could not distinguish their right hand from their left," Otto begins to think about its applications:

---

humiliated, and desperate, we were curious: hungry for bread and also to understand" (*Moments of Reprieve*, p. 99).

[37] In *If This Is a Man* he was adamant that if he were God, he "would spit at Kuhn's prayer," but even in the context of the selections for the gas chamber, he possibly also misunderstood the nature of this man's prescribed daily ritual of praise and prayer (pp. 135–36). For an overview of the broader topic, see Michman, " 'In Faithfulness Thou Hast Afflicted Me' (Psalms 119:75): Remarks on Trends in Religious Faith during the Holocaust," in *Holocaust Historiography*, pp. 285–99.

"What are you trying to tell me with this story of yours? That you're fasting for me too? And for everybody, even for—them? Or that I should fast too?"

Ezra answered that, unlike Jonah, he was not a prophet but a provincial cantor. But he must insist on asking Mister Barracks Chief for this favor: that his soup be saved until the following evening, and also next morning's bread. But not to keep the soup warm, that was not necessary. It was all right for Otto to let it get cold. (pp. 80–81)

Yet more intrigued Otto had demanded to know the reasoning behind this corollary. Levi's earlier characterization of him as "frowning as if he were performing a task of great precision" aligns the mentality of the two men as not incompatible after all. Dialogue enables communication and respect as their debate progressed in a civilized way. Otto, whose former "political militancy" had been "rigorous," rediscovers the "long lost pleasure" of the "heated polemics at his [Communist] party meetings." The dialectical materialist questioned whether since their soup was so very thin the topic was one of *eating* on Yom Kippur.

Ezra explained to him that the distinction was irrelevant. On fast days one neither eats nor drinks, not even water. However, one does not incur divine punishment if one swallows food with a total volume smaller than that of a date, or liquids of a volume smaller than that which can be held between cheek and teeth. In this accounting, food and drink are not added up.

Otto muttered an incomprehensible phrase in which the word *meshuge* was repeated. (The word means crazy in Yiddish, but all Germans understand). (p. 81)

The outcome of this exchange was not only increased understanding between the German and the Jew but also, as so often in Levi's work, a contingent act of human kindness: the ultimate proof of theory. Otto had taken the mess tin, filled it, stored it safely for the duration of Yom Kippur, and Ezra had considered his soup ration "particularly generous." Levi is careful to explain that he had heard the details of the interview from Ezra himself, soon after it took place. Many years later, writing as a free man defending an ethical concept of civilization, Levi was able to place this story in its long historical context.

Actually Ezra wasn't really *meshuge*. He was heir to an ancient, sorrowful, and strange tradition, whose core consists in holding evil in opprobrium and in "hedging about the law" so that evil may not flood through the gaps in the hedge and submerge the law itself. . . . many have behaved like

Ezra throughout migrations and slaughters without number. That is why the history of the Jewish people is so ancient, sorrowful, and strange. (p. 82)

This last explanation can be read as betraying an even sadder ambiguity that reflected upon Levi's response to his difficult relationship with the concept of faith. As a young man he had stood behind Ezra in the soup queue and had heard the full story from Ezra at that time. Yet he had not retold it until he could interpret the account in a meaningful context: his reappraisal of how that "core" of law and ethical practice had sustained men of justice and integrity who had scorned evil and neither "drowned" nor been "submerged," but resisted to defend their principles and cultivate a spiritual life for altruistic reasons.

# Conclusion: Beyond Testimony

In the preface to his last book, *The Drowned and the Saved*, Levi acknowledged, "the truth ... has come to light through a long road and a narrow door" because "the best historians of the Lagers emerged from among the very few who had the ability and luck to attain a privileged observatory."[1] This paradoxical "privilege" of higher ground above the flood—finding "a way, granted or conquered, astute or violent, licit or illicit, to lift oneself above the norm" (p. 26)—explained both the narrowness of the door and its restricted viewpoint. Although the metaphorical Drowned and Saved of this title hark back to the earlier horrific vision of shipwreck, Levi's distinctions between the submerged ones and the survivors are purposefully blurred. Paradoxically the dead may have preserved their own humanity while losing their lives, but many of the survivors were left with a sense of shame, and even guilt, at their compromises or neglect of others. In addition, it is clear that all were ashamed of what had been done *to* them.

After forty years, and at a different stage in the developed historiography of the Holocaust that he had helped to instantiate, his purpose shifted from both the simpler and more complex historic testimonies of his earlier books. Finally, he wrote to analyze and interpret various themes in the evidence that he had transmitted to readers throughout the world. He wrote as a philosopher on larger moral questions, and in dialogue with other commentators, including Jean Amery who committed suicide in 1978. Levi's last task was to consider, on the basis of his experience, and on behalf of all members of responsible societies, "how much of the unique camp world is dead and will not return?" In these discursive, analytical essays the author stands aside to speak of "they" when referring to all those who had suffered in the camps, to insist that "one is never in another's place," and none of us should assume we can know how our resources of humanity and culture would stand up in extreme situations (p. 43). No one returned from the gas chambers. Simple distinctions between "us" and "them," or good and evil, or victims and per-

---

[1] *I Sommersi e i salvati* (Turin: Giulio Einaudi, 1986); cf. *The Drowned and the Saved*, tr. Raymond Rosenthal (London: Sphere Books, 1989), p. 7.

secutors could not operate in this jungle where, except for special cases, solidarity among the oppressed was largely absent. Instead, other people were "a thousand sealed-off monads" engaged everywhere in "a desperate hidden and continuous struggle" (pp. 23–24). Even the jungle metaphor fails to describe the ordinary nightmare of human isolation. The Lager in its entirety was unique and must never be repeated; but, as Levi reminded his readers, within the camp an ironic, slang term for never was *morgen früh*. By the time he wrote *The Drowned and the Saved,* it was clear that genocide had recurred elsewhere in the world; therefore the microcosm of the Lagers would always need analysis and critical appraisal by and for new generations. Descriptive testimony of what had happened and commemoration of what had been lost would not suffice: one could never say never.

## NAVIGATING MEMORY IN STORIES FOR LIFE

In his essay, "The Memory of the Offence," Levi considered how many people "fabricate for themselves a convenient reality" when the present or the past is a burden (p. 14). The wishful thinking evident in rumors that had permeated the camp were "consolatory illusions" that people "fabricated for themselves, and reciprocally administered to each other" as if they were medicines (p. 19). Such protective mechanisms are not limited to the microcosm of the Lager. Levi's observation emphasized the operation of such rumors as consolations reinforced by and for a group, and out of consideration for each other as members of that group, when the truth, if faced alone, might be too painful, or extinguish hope. They were navigating uncharted seas; who was to say what could reasonably be expected in the bizarre world of the Lager. Levi, the survivor, knew that we need fictions in order to accommodate reality, not to negate it. Yet, one further consequence of the passage of time was the confidence he derived from his reputation as a witness and a writer. His testimony and analysis had proved to be in consonance with those of others, and he was more prepared to commit to publishing details of the less than admirable elements of his own and fellow prisoners' behavior. This explains both the moral theme in the second essay on the "grey zone of *protekcja* and collaboration" and one of the most devastating consequences of trauma and existence in the Lager, "Shame," the subject of the third essay. "Coming out of the darkness, one suffered because of the reacquired consciousness of having been diminished" (p. 56). Liberation brought the sorrow of "becoming men (that is responsible)" again (p. 52). This was why (he believed) there were more suicides among the survivors when they turned "to look back at the 'perilous water'" in which they had been submerged, rather than while they were struggling to stay alive (p. 57).

New arrivals were rarely received by other inmates as either friends or "companion[s] in misfortune"; the newcomer was typically mocked or tricked by fellow prisoners, envious "because he still seemed to have on him the smell of his home" (pp. 24–25). This poignant phrase evoked a range of associations from the homely comforts of ordinary life to the pangs experienced by prisoners who recognized how far they had departed from those norms of social life and human affinity. Levi broadened his calm statement of fact to reflect more generally on the macrocosm—the contemporary world of "our civilization"—that he shared with his readers and was determined to defend and refine:

> It is probable that the hostility towards the *Zugang* was in substance motivated like all other forms of intolerance: that is, it consisted in an unconscious attempt to consolidate the "we" at the expense of the "they," to create, in short, that solidarity among the oppressed whose absence was the source of additional suffering, even though not perceived openly. Vying for prestige also came into play, which in our civilisation seems to be an irrepressible need: the despised crowd of seniors was prone to recognise in the new arrival a target on which to vent its humiliation, to find compensation at his expense, to build for itself and at his expense a figure of a lower rank on whom to discharge the burden of the offences received from above. (p. 25)

Significantly, Levi's language here mirrors the conceptual frame he describes: the *Zugang* is a traumatized individual; but then "he" becomes a "target" for the impersonal "crowd" and "its" deflection of the "offence" imposed from higher up the system. Understanding this dynamic in the "grey zone" and the incomplete limits that separated victims from persecutors was necessary, if (as Levi argued) "we want to know the human species, if we want to know how to defend our souls when a similar test should once more loom before us, or even if we only want to understand what takes place in a big industrial factory" (p. 26). This is also why we read all prison writing.

The applications of these observations, based on the authority of his experience, embrace moral philosophy, ethics (with implications for theology), and "even" the politics of management and commerce. The moral writer, haunted witness, and retired industrial chemist had experience of all these. Levi's rhetoric shocks readers, jolted out of "our" complacency as we follow this progression from the magisterial overview of the species in the spiritual and poetic imperative to defend "our souls" (traditionally, those high-value, eternal signs of our unique selves), to mundane industrial relations. This descent from the abstract to the particular mechanized environment was deliberate and meaningful. Levi knew that the Lagers were not really infernal regions or a jungle, neither supernatural nor natural. They were created by "civilized" technocrats to be industrial factories exploiting slave labor, and as disposal units for millions of human beings exterminated by the *Grundlichkeit* of German military procedures. The struggle to survive in such conditions meant that many felt shame not merely at their failures to respond to others' needs (on the limited occasions when they might have done so), but also for when they might have "deliberately damaged, robbed or beaten a companion" in competition with themselves. Levi's own consciousness of shame was reflected in his assessment that "the worst survived ... the best all died" (p. 63). He also acknowledged an illogical supposition, one he shared with others, that in surviving they had somehow displaced others more "worthy" than themselves: "It is a supposition, but it gnaws at us; it has nestled deeply like a woodworm; it is not seen from the outside but it gnaws and rasps" (p. 62). Eventually such gnawing and rasping parasites destroy their human hosts who are reduced in this trope to wooden bodies.[2] Culture and intelligence did not defend the intellectual in Auschwitz, yet paradoxically they became a cornerstone of the literary edifice he constructed to strengthen the ethics of modern societies by advertising our weaknesses.[3]

While there could be no "complete witness" because no one person had seen it all, and thus general significance had to be extrapolated from the partial testimony of individuals, because of the shame induced by what had happened to them, many survivors—those who outlived the ordeal—were unable to turn away from their part of the larger whole:

> The just among us, neither more nor less numerous than in any other human group, felt remorse, shame and pain for the misdeeds that others ... had committed ... [W]hat had happened was irrevocable. It would never again be able to be cleansed; it would prove that man, the human species—we, in short—were potentially able to construct an infinite enormity of pain; and that pain is the only force that is created from nothing, without cost and without effort. It is enough not to see, not to listen, not to act. (p. 66)

Ethical action must be built upon individual responsibility to resist inhumanity, fear, and apathy. The image of writing as the record of individual

---

[2] Cf. "Anyone who has suffered torture never again will be able to be at ease in the world, the abomination of the annihilation is never extinguished" (Jean Amery tortured by the Gestapo before being deported to Auschwitz; quoted in *The Drowned and the Saved*, p. 12).

[3] "... culture could be useful even if only in some marginal cases and for brief periods. It could enhance an hour, establish a fleeting bond with a companion, keep the mind alive and healthy; it definitely was not useful in orienting oneself and understanding." "The Intellectual in Auschwitz," in *The Drowned and the Saved*, pp. 114–15.

memory, like the tattoo as the sign of the forces of history impressed by violence, must be indelible if writing about individual experiences that stand for "details of the larger picture" can become a remedy for useless violence (p. 85). The trauma of the tattoo was its symbolic meaning: "This is an indelible mark, you will never leave here; this is the mark with which slaves are branded and cattle sent to the slaughter, and that is what you have become." Levi's pronoun "you" includes the reader. "You no longer have a name; this is your new name" (p. 95). Later, this mark carved onto the body signified the prison writer's intention to inoculate the world against its atavistic tendencies by publishing not only testimony about the past but also analysis of it for the future. Levi refused to have his Auschwitz tattoo removed after the war because he would not deface the "necessary" memory of the offense it symbolized; there were so few left "in the world to bear this witness." Even after death this sign remains, inscribed, by his instruction, upon his memorial stone with his name and dates of birth and death.

## "THE AIMS OF LIFE ARE THE BEST DEFENCE"

All prison writing bears witness to someone's story and experience, with wider political significance if it offers testimony to resistance against tyranny or injustice and suffering, for a public moral purpose. Writing with hindsight, Levi believed that his intention, formed in the Lager, to testify to his experiences had sustained his will to survive. But what does it mean to survive? In *The Drowned and the Saved* he concluded that "the aims of life are the best defence against death: and not only in the Lager" (p. 120); he refused to dwell on the presence of death when the aims of life were so urgent. Afterward the aims of civil life compelled him to write to warn and protect others. Levi also admitted that in observing the struggle for life he had underestimated the value of strong cultural traditions, including religion, among those who had resisted despair to stand out above the submerged ones as "small jagged and coloured islands" against a "grey illimitable sea of the semi-alive who . . . no longer asked themselves any questions" (p. 119). Unable to read or write in the Lager and forced to defend his existence, Levi had nevertheless recognized the importance of his education that helped to keep his "mind alive and healthy" and not merely to climb above the mass of fellow prisoners by finding work as a chemist alongside German civilians. Nothing in his earlier life had made it possible to understand the reality of Auschwitz: "Reason, art, and poetry are no help in deciphering a place from which they are banned" (p. 115). However, his intellect and education (especially, he said, his scientific training), had helped him to observe, analyze, and assess people and situations as they were, and that had allowed him to extrapolate for the future. Ordinary experience of the world was less valuable than the conceptual tools for evidence-based evaluations.

Intellectual curiosity informed by the fruits of learning that went beyond personal experience had helped many writers in prison to sustain positive aims for life, which their writing, in turn, transmits to readers. These confined and persecuted writers usually sought to engage the attention of specific readers, but some also wrote to address readers in an unknowable future, aware that by attaching their work to a varied continuum of literary tradition that linked different generations, they could speak to and for others. New and bewildering experiences may be defined and analyzed in terms of familiar forms and commonplaces, which are later received by readers as both specific and representative. Resistance and consolation in literary terms require iteration and transformation of the prisoners' experiences. The literary models of the prevailing culture make them communicable. Readers are impressed by signs of struggle and resistance, and of imaginative and intellectual escape in response to defined situations. While there is no substitute for the authority of the prisoner's carceral experience, to be effective, as Levi and Boethius realized, the prison writer's testimony had to engage readers, to move both their understanding and their actions in order to approximate even a simple surrogacy through combinations of biographical fact with suggestive metaphors, intertextual allusions, and literary forms. The writing of all these prisoners maintains their urgent incentives to consider the aims of life. Their texts show that adversity could be useful not least because it was human and hopeful to make a virtue out of necessity rather than to surrender in silence. The creativity of these prisoners cannot compensate them for their suffering, which has no meaning or value of itself. Yet it is evident from this study that their recourse to writing in extremis meant something vitally important to each of them and that their creativity in so many different kinds reflects the life-enhancing qualities of rich literary traditions, and the consolations of imagination that remain the basis of hope. Levi was aware that "a single Anne Frank excites more emotion than the myriads who suffered as she did but whose image has remained in the shadows. Perhaps it is necessary that it can be so; if we had to and were able to suffer the sufferings of everyone, we could not live" (p. 39).

## CULTURE AND THE AIMS OF LIFE

This study has defined a pragmatic typology of writing by prisoners of conscience or persecuted minorities that connects literature and life. The politics of prison writing demonstrates the principles relating to a literary sphere inherently concerned with power and resistance, and the absolute priority of effective communication for safeguarding humane values in civilized societies. Yet the survival of these works that defend civilization, preserve the individual, and testify for humankind, the strength of their appeal to different sets of historic readers, and their impact in different contexts on the prisoners' reputations as writers and thinkers have always functioned as indicators of their authors' eloquence and rhetorical persuasiveness. We may be convinced yet remain the same because unmoved; only persuasion changes ideas and actions. Lyric and dialogic forms have predominated in prison writing as traditional forms for deriving and expressing complex arguments, and from the urgent, practical needs of prisoners as writers to communicate with others and not merely to express and console themselves or record their ideas. Such testimonies, as we have seen, can also give voice, respect, and honor to the experiences of those unable to testify for themselves.

Throughout this study it has also been apparent that there are real and necessary links between literary traditions representing actual or imaginary prisoners. Further exploration of this virtuous circle of influence in which representation of the experience of prisoners can feed back into other literary works and conventions would require another volume to consider prison tropes in other writers' works, from antiquity to the postmodern Holocaust novel. Conceptions of the human condition as a state of metaphorical imprisonment persist and have informed the ideas of Dante, Villon, Shakespeare, Dickens, Dostoyevsky, Kafka, and so many other writers of distinction and cultural influence. In every case discussed here of actual prisoners' writing produced in confinement, under extraordinary pressure, and with hindsight by Levi at various stages after release, the importance of having a well-stocked mind to draw upon personal memories and memories of books—especially the Bible—has been crucial. The memories of books helped in determining not only how the prisoner responded to captivity but also how the writer was able to share that response with readers using the figurative exchanges in allusion and intertextuality. Vicarious literary experiences of history and the otherness of the past also build cultural traditions that can foster and strengthen independent thought, pragmatic dialogue, and the ordinary altruistic virtues that flow from alert humane sympathies and good communication. We cannot live to our full potential without these bedrock cultural traditions.

Writing that lives on to critical acclaim keeps memory alive for different generations of readers, shoring up testimony that engages and defends us all. Thoughts may be free, yet ideas are never harmless. The potency of ideas of justice and tolerance, of personal integrity and humanity lived well in practice often exceeds and outlives their proponents in writing. Clearly readers make their own meanings over and above those intended by authors, and therefore the diachronic element of juxtaposition and typology in the structure of this book has recognized that all these prisoners are in some ways our contemporaries. We examine our own aims for life alongside the ideas and values they sifted by experience. Nevertheless, the synchronic setting of each prisoner's writing has also recognized the irreducible otherness of their historical situations and experiences. Ironically, as we have seen, the powerless vulnerability of the historic prisoner may be superseded by a greater and longer-lasting influence through the power and fame of his or her writing. The ghost of Boethius walked through prison walls and down long centuries of persecution to teach and console generations of new readers and writers throughout the Middle Ages and beyond; in our postmodern age, Primo Levi has similarly become an indispensable guide to the perplexed, in reasonable but never dispassionate writing. In the intermediate centuries, thoughtful writers in captivity have sought to understand and mitigate their darkest days by writing for themselves and us. The literary afterlife of a writer's fame, promoted by editors and publishers, is realized in the responses of readers. These prisoners' vital self-impressions and the urgent clarity of their analyses of cultural values may inspire readers to build new lives and aspirations: the aims of life are also the politics of prison writing in action. The consolations of their writing can touch and teach us all.

# SELECT BIBLIOGRAPHY

Akhmatova, Anna. *Selected Poems*, tr. Richard McKane (Newcastle upon Tyne: Bloodaxe Books, 1989).

Anissimov, Myriam. *Primo Levi: Tragedy of an Optimist*, tr. Steve Coxe (London: Aurum Press, 1999).

Beckstrand, Lisa. *Deviant Women of the French Revolution and the Rise of Feminism* (Madison: Fairleigh Dickinson University Press, 2009).

Bethge, Eberhard. *Dietrich Bonhoeffer: Theologian, Christian, Contemporary*, tr. Eric Mosbacher, Peter and Betty Ross, Frank Clarke, and William Glen-Doepel, ed. Edwin Robertson (London: William Collins, 1970, rpt. 1977). First published in German, 1967.

Blanc, Olivier, ed. *Last Letters: Prisons and Prisoners of the French Revolution, 1793–1794*, tr. Alan Sheridan (New York: Farrar, Straus & Giroux; London: André Deutsch, 1987). First published in French, 1984.

Boethius, Anicius Manlius Severinus. *The Consolation of Philosophy*, tr. David R. Slavitt (Cambridge, MA: Harvard University Press, 2008).

———. *The Consolation of Philosophy*, tr. V. E. Watts (Harmondsworth: Penguin Books, 1969, rpt. 1986).

———. *The Theological Tractates* and *The Consolation of Philosophy*, Loeb Classical Library, ed. and tr. H. F. Stewart, E. K. Rand, and S. J. Tester (Cambridge, MA: Harvard University Press, 1973, rpt. 1990).

Bonhoeffer, Dietrich. *Fiction from Prison: Gathering Up the Past*, ed. Renate and Eberhard Bethge with C. Green, tr. U. Hoffmann (Philadelphia: Fortress Press, 1981).

———. *Letters and Papers from Prison*, ed. John W. de Gruchy, tr. I. Best, L. E. Dahill, R. Krauss, and N. Lukens, in *Dietrich Bonhoeffer Works*, 8 (Minneapolis: Fortress Press, 2010).

———. *Letters and Papers from Prison, the Enlarged Edition*, ed. Eberhard Bethge, tr. Reginald Fuller, Frank Clarke, and John Bowden (London: SCM Press, 1971, rpt. 1986). First published in German, 1970.

———. *Voices in the Night: The Prison Poems of Dietrich Bonhoeffer*, ed. and tr. Edwin Robertson (Grand Rapids, MI: Zondervan Publishing, 1999).

———. *Von Guten Mächten: Gebete und Gedichte*, ed. Johann Christoph Hampe (Munich: C. Kaiser, 1976).

———. *Widerstand und Ergebung*, ed. C. Gremmels, E. Bethge, R. Bethge with I. Tödt, in *Dietrich Bonhoeffer Werke*, 8 (Gütersloh: C. Kaiser, 1998).

Bonhoeffer, Dietrich, and Maria von Wedemeyer. *Love Letters from Cell 92*, ed. Ruth-Alice von Bismarck and Ulrich Kabitz, tr. John Brownjohn (London: Harper-Collins, 1994). First published in German, 1992.

Brenner, Rachel Feldhay. "Writing Herself against History: Anne Frank's Self-Portrait as a Young Artist," *Modern Judaism*, 16 (1996), 105–34.

Brombert, Victor. *The Romantic Prison: The French Tradition* (Princeton: Princeton University Press, 1979).

Bunyan, John. *Grace Abounding with Other Spiritual Autobiographies*, ed. John Stachniewski with Anita Pacheco (Oxford: Oxford University Press, 1998, rpt. 2008).

———. *The Pilgrim's Progress*, ed. Roger Sharrock (Harmondsworth: Penguin Books, 1968).

———. *The Poems*, ed. Graham Midgley (Oxford: Clarendon Press, 1980).

Cammett, John M. *Antonio Gramsci and the Origins of Italian Communism* (Stanford: Stanford University Press, 1969).

Carnochan, W. B. "The Literature of Confinement," in *The Oxford History of the Prison: The Practice of Punishment in Western Society*, ed. Norval Morris and David J. Rothman (Oxford: Oxford University Press, 1995), pp. 427–55.

Cassou, Jean. *Entretiens avec Jean Rousselot* (Paris: Editions Albin Michel, 1965).

———. *From a Condemned Cell: 33 Sonnets by Jean Cassou*, tr. Harry Guest (Buckfastleigh: Itinerant Press, 2008).

———. *33 Sonnets of the Resistance and Other Poems* [a parallel text edition], tr. Timothy Adès (Todmorden: Arc, 2004).

———. *Trente-trois sonnets composés au secret. La Rose et le Vin. La Folie d'Amadis*, ed. Florence de Lussy (Paris: Gallimard, 1995).

———. *Trois poètes: Rilke, Milosz, Machado* (Paris: Librairie Plon, 1954).

———. *Une Vie pour la liberté* (Paris: Editions Robert Laffont, 1981).

Chadwick, Henry. *Boethius: The Consolations of Music, Logic, Theology and Philosophy* (Oxford: Clarendon Press, 1981).

Davies, Ioan. *Writers in Prison* (Oxford: Blackwell, 1990).

d'Eaubonne, Françoise. *Les Ecrivains en cage: essai* (Paris: Editions André Balland, 1970).

Dunan-Page, Anne, ed. *The Cambridge Companion to Bunyan* (Cambridge: Cambridge University Press, 2010).

Ellmann, Richard. *Oscar Wilde* (London: Hamish Hamilton, 1987).

Enzer, Hyman Aaron, and Sandra Solotaroff-Enzer, eds. *Anne Frank: Reflections on Her Life and Legacy* (Urbana: University of Illinois Press, 2000).

Fiori, Giuseppi. *Antonio Gramsci: Life of a Revolutionary*, tr. Tom Nairn (London: NLB, 1970). First published in Italian, Bari, 1965.

Fleishman, Avrom. *Figures of Autobiography: the Language of Self-Writing in Victorian and Modern England* (Berkeley: University of California Press, 1983).

Foucault, Michel. *Surveiller et punir: naissance de la prison* (Paris: Editions Gallimard, 1975). Translated by Alan Sheridan as *Discipline and Punish: The Birth of the Prison* (London: Allen Lane, 1977; rpt. Penguin Books, 1979).

Frank, Anne. *Anne Frank's Tales from the Secret Annexe*, tr. Ralph Manheim and Michel Mok (London: Penguin Books, 1988). First published in Dutch, 1949.

———. *The Diary of Anne Frank: The Critical Edition, Prepared by the Netherlands State Institute for War Documentation*, ed. David Barnouw and Gerrold van der Stroom, tr. Arnold J. Pomerans and B. M. Mooyaart-Doubleday (London: Viking, Penguin Group, 1989).

Franklin, H. Bruce. *The Victim as Criminal and Artist: Literature from the American Prison* (New York: Oxford University Press, 1978). Expanded and revised, with a new introduction, as *Prison Literature in America* (1989).

Gelfand, Elissa. *Imagination in Confinement: Women's Writings from French Prisons* (Ithaca: Cornell University Press, 1983).

Gibson, Margaret, ed. *Boethius: His Life, Thought and Influence* (Oxford: Blackwell, 1981).

Georgel, Pierre. *Jean Cassou. Choix de textes. Bibliographie, portraits, fac-similés*, Poètes d'Aujourd'hui, 165 (Paris: Editions Pierre Seghers, 1967).

Godsey, J. D., and Geffrey B. Kelly, eds. *Ethical Responsibility: Bonhoeffer's Legacy to the Churches* (New York: Edwin Mellen Press, 1981).

Gordon, Robert S. C., ed. *The Cambridge Companion to Primo Levi* (Cambridge: Cambridge University Press, 2007).

———. *Primo Levi's Ordinary Virtues: From Testimony to Ethics* (Oxford: Oxford University Press, 2001, rpt. 2003).

Gramsci, Antonio. *Gramsci's Prison Letters:* Lettere dal Carcere, *a Selection*, tr. and ed. Hamish Henderson (London and Edinburgh: Zwan and the *Edinburgh Review*, 1988).

———. *Letters from Prison*, 2 vols. ed. Frank Rosengarten, tr. Raymond Rosenthal (New York: Columbia University Press, 1994).

———. *Prison Notebooks*, vols. 1 and 2, ed. Joseph A. Buttigieg, tr. J. A. Buttigieg and A. Callari (New York: Columbia University Press, 1992).

———. *Selections from the Prison Notebooks,* ed. and tr. Q. Hoare and G. N. Smith (London: Lawrence and Wishart, 1971, rpt. 1986).

Greaves, Richard L. "Conscience, Liberty, and the Spirit: Bunyan and Nonconformity," in *John Bunyan and English Nonconformity* (London: Hambledon Press, 1992), pp. 51–70.

———. *Glimpses of Glory: John Bunyan and English Dissent* (Stanford: Stanford University Press, 2002).

———. "John Bunyan," in *The Oxford Dictionary of National Biography* (Oxford: Oxford University Press, 2004; online revisions, http://www.oxforddnb.com/view/article/3949).

Gruchy, John W. de, ed. *The Cambridge Companion to Dietrich Bonhoeffer* (Cambridge: Cambridge University Press, 1999, rpt. 2008).

Harding, Christopher, Bill Hines, Richard Ireland, and Philip Rawlings. *Imprisonment in England and Wales: A Concise History* (London: Croom Helm, 1985).

Harlow, Barbara. *Barred: Women, Writing, and Political Detention* (Hanover: Wesleyan University Press, 1992).

Haslam, Jason. *Fitting Sentences: Identity in Nineteenth- and Twentieth-Century Prison Narratives* (Toronto: University of Toronto Press, 2005).

Hawkins, A. H. "John Bunyan, the Conflictive Paradigm," in *Archetypes of Conversion: The Autobiographies of Augustine, Bunyan and Merton* (Lewisburg: Bucknell University Press, 1985), pp. 73–99.

Homer, Frederic D. *Primo Levi and the Politics of Survival* (Columbia: University of Missouri Press, 2001).

House, Seymour Baker. "Thomas More," in *The Oxford Dictionary of National Biography* (Oxford University Press, 2004; online revisions, http://www.oxforddnb.com/view/article/19191).

Hyde, H. Montgomery. *The Trials of Oscar Wilde* (New York: Dover Publications, 1973).

Insana, Lina N. *Arduous Tasks: Primo Levi, Translation, and the Transmission of Holocaust Testimony* (Toronto: University of Toronto Press, 2009).

Iskander, Sylvia Patterson. "Anne Frank's Reading: A Retrospective," in *Anne Frank Reflections on Her Life and Legacy*, ed. Hyman A. Enzer and Sandra Solotaroff-Enzer (Urbana: University of Illinois Press, 2000), pp. 100–109. Revised from *Children's Literature Association Quarterly*, 13 (1988), 137–41.

Jankélévitch, Vladimir. "Le diurne et le nocturne chez Jean Cassou," *Cahiers du Sud*, 382 (1965), 241–47.

Joll, James. *Gramsci*, Fontana Modern Masters series, ed. F. Kermode (Glasgow: Fontana/Collins, 1977).

Kelly, Judith. *Primo Levi: Recording and Reconstruction in the Testimonial Literature*, Hull Italian Texts (Market Harborough: Troubador Publishing, 2000).

Langer, Lawrence. *Holocaust Testimonies: The Ruins of Memory* (New Haven: Yale University Press, 1991).

———. "Legacy in Gray," in *Memory and Mastery: Primo Levi as Writer and Witness*, ed. Roberta S. Kremer (Albany: State University of New York Press, 2001), pp. 197–216.

Larson, Doran. "Toward a Prison Poetics," *College Literature*, 37 (2010), 143–66.

Lee, Carol Ann. *Roses from the Earth: The Biography of Anne Frank* (London: Penguin Books, 2000).

Lerer, Seth. *Boethius and Dialogue: Literary Method in* The Consolation of Philosophy (Princeton: Princeton University Press, 1985).

Levi, Primo. *Ad ora incerta* (Milan: Garzanti Editore, 1984; 2nd ed. 1988).

———. *The Black Hole of Auschwitz*, ed. Marco Belpoliti, tr. Sharon Wood (Cambridge: Polity Press, 2005).

———. *Collected Poems*, tr. Ruth Feldman and Brian Swann (London: Faber and Faber, 1988).

———. *The Drowned and the Saved*, tr. Raymond Rosenthal (London: Sphere Books, 1989).

———. *If This Is a Man* and *The Truce*, tr. Stuart Woolf (London: Sphere Books, 1987).

———. *Moments of Reprieve*, tr. Ruth Feldman (London: Sphere Books, 1987).

———. *The Voice of Memory: Interviews, 1961–87*, ed. Marco Belpoliti and Robert Gordon, tr. Robert Gordon (Cambridge: Polity Press, 2001).

Lollini, Massimo. "Primo Levi and the Idea of Autobiography," in *Primo Levi: The Austere Humanist*, ed. Joseph Farrell (Oxford: Peter Lang, 2004), pp. 67–89.

Lussy, Florence de, ed. *Jean Cassou (1897–1986): un musée imaginé* [exhibition catalogue] (Paris: Bibliothèque nationale de France / Centre Georges Pompidou, 1995).

Lynch, Beth. *John Bunyan and the Language of Conviction* (Cambridge: D. S. Brewer, 2004).

Lynch, Kathleen. "Into Jail and into Print: John Bunyan Writes the Godly Self," in *Prison Writings in Early Modern England*, ed. William H. Sherman and William J. Sheils, *Huntington Library Quarterly*, 72 (2009), 273–90.

Mandelstam, Osip. *50 Poems*, tr. Bernard Meares (New York: Persea Books, 1977).

Marenbon, John, ed. *The Cambridge Companion to Boethius* (Cambridge: Cambridge University Press, 2009).

Martz, Louis L. *Thomas More: The Search for the Inner Man* (New Haven: Yale University Press, 1990).

Martz, Louis L., and Richard S. Sylvester, eds. *Thomas More's Prayer Book: A Facsimile Reproduction of the Annotated Pages* (New Haven: Yale University Press, 1969, rpt. 1976).

McNally, Mark, and John Schwarzmantel, eds. *Gramsci and Global Politics: Hegemony and Resistance* (London: Routledge, 2009).

Michman, Dan. *Holocaust Historiography: A Jewish Perspective: Conceptualizations, Terminology, Approaches and Fundamental Issues* (London: Vallentine Mitchell, 2003).

Moorhead, John, *Theodoric in Italy* (Oxford: Oxford University Press, 1992).

More, Thomas. *Correspondence of Sir Thomas More*, ed. Elizabeth Frances Rogers (Princeton: Princeton University Press, 1947).

———. *De Tristitia Christi,* in *The Yale Edition of the Complete Works*, 14, ed. Clarence H. Miller (New Haven: Yale University Press, 1976).

———. *A Dialogue of Comfort against Tribulation*, Everyman's Library, 461 (London: J. M. Dent, 1910, rpt. 1946).

———. *A Dialogue of Comfort against Tribulation,* in *The Yale Edition of the Complete Works*, 12, ed. Louis L. Martz and Frank E. Manley (New Haven: Yale University Press, 1976).

———. *Selected Letters*, ed. Elizabeth Frances Rogers (New Haven: Yale University Press, 1961, rpt. 1967).

———. *A Treatise on the Passion*, in *The Yale Edition of the Complete Works*, 13, ed. G. E. Haupt (New Haven: Yale University Press, 1976).

Newey, Vincent. "'With the eyes of my understanding': Bunyan, Experience, and Acts of Interpretation," in *John Bunyan Conventicle and Parnassus: Tercentenary Essays*, ed. N. H. Keeble (Oxford: Clarendon Press, 1988), pp. 189–216.

O'Daly, Gerard. *The Poetry of Boethius* (London: Duckworth, 1991).

Parker, Harold T. *The Cult of Antiquity and the French Revolutionaries* (Durham, NC: Duke University Press, 1965).

Petropoulos, Jonathan, and John K. Roth, eds. *Gray Zones: Ambiguity and Compromise in the Holocaust and Its Aftermath* (New York: Berghahn Books, 2005).

Prescott, Anne Lake. "The Ambivalent Heart: Thomas More's Merry Tales," *Criticism*, 45 (2003), 417–33.

Priestley, Philip. *Victorian Prison Lives: English Prison Biography, 1830–1914* (London: Methuen, 1985).

Questier, Michael. "Catholicism, Kinship and the Public Memory of Sir Thomas More," *Journal of Ecclesiastical History*, 53 (2002), 476–509.

Ratushinskaya, Irina. *Dance with a Shadow*, tr. David McDuff (Newcastle upon Tyne: Bloodaxe Books, 1992).

———. *Grey Is the Colour of Hope*, tr. Alyona Kojevnikov (London: Hodder & Stoughton, 1988).

———. *In the Beginning,* tr. Alyona Kojevnikov (London: Hodder & Stoughton, 1990).

———. *No, I'm Not Afraid*, tr. David McDuff (Newcastle upon Tyne: Bloodaxe Books, 1986, rpt. 1987).

———. *Pencil Letter* [collection of poems, translated by different hands] (Newcastle upon Tyne: Bloodaxe Books 1988).

Reventlow, Henning Graf. *The Authority of the Bible and the Rise of the Modern World*, tr. John Bowden (London: SCM Press, 1984). First published in German, Göttingen, 1980.

Roland, Marie-Jeanne. *Lettres de Madame Roland*, ed. Claude Perroud, 4 vols. (Paris: Imprimerie nationale, 1902–15).

———. *Mémoires de Madame Roland*, ed. Paul de Roux (Paris: Mercure de France, 2004). First published 1966, rpt. 1986.

———. *The Memoirs of Madame Roland*, tr. and ed. Evelyn Shuckburgh (London: Barrie & Jenkins, 1989).

Roper, William. *The Life of Sir Thomas More*, in *Two Early Tudor Lives*, ed. Richard S. Sylvester and Davis P. Harding (New Haven: Yale University Press, 1962).

Ross, Jennifer. "Jean Cassou: Freedom to Compose in Captivity," in *Six Authors in Captivity: Literary Responses to the Occupation of France during World War II*, ed. Nicole Thatcher and Ethel Tolansky, Modern French Identities, 54 (Oxford: Peter Lang, 2006), pp. 27–58.

Saunders, Max. *Self Impression: Life-Writing, Autobiografiction, and the Forms of Modern Literature* (Oxford: Oxford University Press, 2010).

Schlingensiepen, Ferdinand. "Dietrich Bonhoeffer: Der Gefangene von Tegel und die heilende Kraft der Erinnerung," in *Gottesfreundschaft: christliche Mystik im Zeitgespräch*, ed. D. Langner, M. A. Sorace, and P. Zimmerling (Fribourg: Academic Press, 2008), pp. 277–90.

Signorini, Franca Molino. "The Duty and Risk of Testimony: Primo Levi as Keeper of Memory," in *Memory and Mastery: Primo Levi as Writer and Witness*, ed. Roberta S. Kremer (Albany: State University of New York Press, 2001), pp. 173–96.

Sodi, Risa B. *A Dante of Our Time: Primo Levi and Auschwitz* (New York: Peter Lang, 1990).

———. "The Rhetoric of the *Univers Concentrationnaire*," in *Memory and Mastery: Primo Levi as Writer and Witness*, ed. Roberta S. Kremer (Albany: State University of New York Press, 2001), pp. 35–55.

Spargo, Tamsin. "'I being taken from you in presence': *Grace Abounding to the Chief of Sinners* and Claims to Authority," in Spargo, *The Writing of John Bunyan* (Aldershot: Ashgate, 1997), pp. 43–67.

Stoddard, Roger Eliot. "Primo Levi," *Book Collector*, 55 (2006), 525–54.

Sturrock, John. *The Language of Autobiography* (Cambridge: Cambridge University Press, 1993).

Summers, Joanna. *Late-Medieval Prison Writing and the Politics of Autobiography* (Oxford: Clarendon Press, 2004).

Tesio, Giovanni. "*At an Uncertain Hour*: Preliminary Observations on the Poetry of Primo Levi," in *Primo Levi: The Austere Humanist*, ed. Joseph Farrell (Oxford: Peter Lang, 2004), pp. 161–70.

Thomson, Ian. *Primo Levi: A Life* (London: Hutchinson, 2002).

———. "Writing *If This Is a Man*," in *Primo Levi: The Austere Humanist*, ed. Joseph Farrell (Oxford: Peter Lang, 2004), pp. 141–60.

Trapp, J. B., and Hubertus Schulte Herbrüggen, eds. *"The King's Good Servant": Sir Thomas More, 1477/8–1535* (London: National Portrait Gallery, 1977).

Trouille, Mary. "The Circe of the Republic: Mme Roland, Rousseau, and Revolutionary Politics," in *Literate Women and the French Revolution of 1789*, ed. Catherine R. Montfort (Birmingham, AL: Summa Publications, 1994), pp. 81–109.

Varaut, Jean-Marc. *Poètes en prison. De Charles d'Orléans à Jean Genet* (Paris: Librairie Académique Perrin, 1989).

Waxman, Zoë Vania. *Writing the Holocaust: Identity, Testimony, Representation* (Oxford: Oxford University Press, 2006).

Wilde, Oscar. *The Complete Letters of Oscar Wilde*, ed. Merlin Holland and Rupert Hart-Davis (London: Fourth Estate, 2000).

———. *The Complete Works of Oscar Wilde*: vol. 2, *De Profundis, "Epistola: in carcere et vinculis,"* ed. Ian Small (Oxford: Oxford University Press, 2005).

Wright, Thomas. *Oscar's Books* (London: Chatto & Windus, 2008).

Zerner, Ruth. "German Protestant Responses to Nazi Persecution of the Jews," in *Perspectives on the Holocaust*, ed. Randolph L. Braham (Boston: Kluwer-Nijhoff, 1983), pp. 57–68.

Zim, Rivkah. *English Metrical Psalms: Poetry as Praise and Prayer, 1535–1601* (Cambridge: Cambridge University Press, 1987, rpt. 2011).

———. "'La Nuit trouve enfin la clarté': Captivity and Life Writing in the Poetry of Charles d'Orléans and Théophile de Viau," *European Journal of Life Writing*, 2 (2013), pp. 79–109. http://ejlw.eu.

———. "The Reformation: The Trial of God's Word," in *Reading the Text: Biblical Criticism and Literary Theory*, ed. Stephen Prickett (Oxford: Blackwell, 1991), pp. 64–135.

———. "Writing behind Bars: Literary Contexts and the Authority of Carceral Experience," in *Prison Writings in Early Modern England*, ed. William H. Sherman and William J. Sheils, *Huntington Library Quarterly*, 72 (2009), 291–311.

# INDEX

Adorno, Theodor, 15
Aeschylus, 12
Akhmatova, Anna, 241, 243n70, 260
Alington, Alice, 99–101
Amery, Jean, 302, 305n2
Aragon, Louis, 214–17, 223, 229, 239; and child
   in flood trope, 215–16
authority of experience, 4, 7, 13–14, 18, 32, 44, 68,
   97–98, 116, 123, 128, 129–30, 173, 264, 281,
   304
autobiography. *See* life writing

Bell, George, bishop of Chichester, 52
Bethge, Eberhard, 48, 50, 52, 54, 55n49, 55n50,
   56, 57, 58, 60, 62–63, 65, 66, 68, 69, 70, 75, 76,
   78. *See also* Bonhoeffer, Dietrich
Bible, 6, 14n22, 51, 52, 56, 59, 68–70, 75–77, 86,
   88, 92–93, 95–96, 123, 127, 130–31, 132–34,
   136, 138, 140, 144–45, 152, 153, 158–59, 161,
   229, 235, 268, 275n19, 280–84, 308. *See also*
   Jeremiah; Jesus of Nazareth; Jonah; Moses;
   Psalms, Book of; St. Paul; St. Peter
Boethius, Anicius Manlius Severinus (*Of the
   Consolation of Philosophy*), 9–10, 12, 15, 16,
   21–47, 49, 55, 56, 57, 60, 63, 64, 67, 78, 85, 89,
   94, 103, 107, 108, 172, 205, 217–18, 219, 240,
   246, 255, 292, 297, 307, 309; captivity trope in,
   28, 33, 35, 41; dialogue and dialectic in, 27–28,
   31–32, 35–37, 42; and family, 22, 34, 37, 42,
   44; on free will, 27, 30, 43, 93; God in, 29–31,
   33, 35, 42, 93; and lyric poetry, 26, 37–39, 42,
   43–44; and memory, 27, 34–35; Orpheus
   myth in, 37–38; paradox (gain by loss) in, 28,
   33, 45–46; Philosophia persona (feminine
   "other") of, 24–26, 34, 36, 39–42, 46, 63, 84;
   Prisoner persona of, 23–27, 29–30, 34, 36,
   39–42, 43, 46; readers and reception of, 28, 31,
   35–36, 37, 40–42, 43–47, 85; suffering in,
   28–29, 46 (*see also* ethics)
Bonhoeffer, Dietrich, 16, 47–78, 83, 95, 103–4,
   125, 172, 200n4, 240, 297; conditions of
   imprisonment of, 6, 48–49, 54–55, 58; "The
   Death of Moses," 75–76; on dialogue (in
   letters), 62; on dialogue with the past, 49,

63–64; on effects of fear, 66; and ethics, 47–49,
58, 65, 67, 68–69; on freedom in death, 75; on
freedom in thought, 65–66; "The Friend," 60,
62–63; friends and family of, 50–51, 55 (*see
also* Dohnanyi, Hans von; Bethge, Eberhard;
Hase, Paul von; Wedemeyer, Maria von); and
Jews, 48, 51–52, 69; "Jonah," 75, 76–77;
"Lance Corporal Berg : A Narrative," 55; and
music, 49, 50–51, 55, 65; "Night Voices in
Tegel," 71–75; "The Past," 60–62; "By Powers
of Good," 77–78; "Sorrow and Joy," 63;
"Stations on the Road to Freedom," 75; on
suffering, 53–54; theology in prison of, 54, 57,
58–59, 68–75 (*see also* Bible; Jesus of
Nazareth; Psalms, Book of); "Who am I?," 50,
66–68
Bosc, L-A-G., 186, 189
Brodsky, Joseph, 261
Bunyan, John, 17, 121–42, 149, 217, 256; and the
Bible, 126, 127, 128–29, 130–31, 132–33,
139, 140–41; and challenger trope (Satan, the
Tempter), 129, 131, 135; confinement tropes
of, 126–27, 139–40; context and conditions of
imprisonment, 124–25; and family, 122, 125;
on God, 122, 127, 129, 134, 138, 139, 141;
*Grace Abounding*, 122, 124, 126, 127–42,
147, 150; and memory, 17, 130–34; and
paradox of gain by loss (suffering as privilege),
123, 134, 136; *Pilgrim's Progress*, 126–27,
139, 144, 150, 159n50; *Prison Meditations*,
126, 136, 144; *A Relation of the Imprisonment*, 124–25; and sea, flood trope, 126; and
women of Bedford, 140–41; on writing, 131

Carnochan, W. B., 15
Caron, Antoine, 101–102
Cassou, Jean, 17–18, 213, 214–40, 251, 263–64;
conditions of imprisonment, 214; on death,
215n3, 218–19, 228n, 231–34; and family,
216, 222, 224, 227; and feminine "other" trope,
223, 224; and imprisonment tropes, 216, 221,
233; and memory, 214, 215, 223, 225, 228–29,
245; and music, 217, 228; and myth and poetic
tradition, 219, 220, 223, 224, 225, 227, 229,

CPSIA information can be obtained
at www.ICGtesting.com
Printed in the USA
LVHW091738170121
676730LV00035B/665